Y0-ARH-030

Harvard Business School

Research Colloquium

CONTRIBUTORS

Robert L. Ashenhurst

Izak Benbasat

J. Daniel Couger

Albert B. Crawford, Jr.

Gordon B. Davis

Edward E. Lawler III

F. Warren McFarlan

James L. McKenney

Richard O. Mason

Allan M. Mohrman, Jr.

Richard L. Nolan

Carl H. Reynolds

John F. Rockart

Everett M. Rogers

Michael S. Scott Morton

Karl E. Weick

The Information Systems Research Challenge

. . . PROCEEDINGS . . .

Edited by F. Warren McFarlan

Harvard Business School Press
Boston, Massachusetts

The statements of fact, opinions, and conclusions expressed in this volume are those of the authors. Neither the Harvard Business School, it Faculty as a whole, nor the President and Fellows of Harvard College reach conclusions or make recommendations as results of Faculty research.

Harvard Business School Press, Boston 02163

Printed in the United States of America.

ISBN 0-87584-161-9

This volume is dedicated to Professors Emeriti Robert N. Anthony and Walter Frese, who provided the leadership that started the Harvard Business School's teaching and research programs in information systems.

TABLE OF CONTENTS

PART III / MANAGEMENT OF THE INFORMATION SYSTEMS RESOURCE

PART IV / INFORMATION SYSTEMS TECHNOLOGY AND CORPORATE STRATEGY

PART V / BUSINESS SCHOOL RESEARCH STRATEGIES

APPENDIX

FOREWORD

Founded in 1908, the Harvard University Graduate School of Business Administration celebrated its seventy-fifth anniversary in the academic year 1983-84. We chose to take this opportunity to involve our faculty in thinking seriously about the challenges and opportunities ahead in important fields of management research and teaching.

Field-based empirical research, within and across organizations, has always been fundamental to Harvard Business School's ability to meet its objectives of educating business managers and helping to improve the practice of management. In some respects, we are creating a distinctive model of research. We have often broken through the bounds of traditional disciplines and methodologies to borrow whatever tools and concepts were needed for a particular inquiry. In addition, we have been less concerned with testing existing theory than with generating new insights. And while we often find ourselves drawn to problems that are broad in scope, we strive for results that are operationally significant to managers.

Because Harvard Business School faculty members are committed to pursuing research on the way business actually does function, as well as theoretical explorations of how it perhaps should function, they can give students and practitioners a vital perspective on the real world of professional practice. Their continuing close contact with operating businesses keeps Harvard Business School faculty at the frontiers of management practice. Research conducted by the faculty often yields insights that are of considerable practical benefit to managers in both day-to-day operations and longer-range planning.

In sponsoring the colloquium series of 1983-84, we hoped to set the course for research development over the next decade, and in particular to encourage greater emphasis on multiperson, multiyear studies of major issues. The complexity of many issues confronting business today almost requires that academicians find more effective forms of collaboration in doing our research. The problems we study are often beyond the capacity of any individual researcher.

In addition to encouraging a reshaping of researchers' work habits, the conferences promised to help strengthen the ties between Harvard Business School and the outside academic and business leadership communities. The series comprised sixteen conferences held at the Harvard Business School campus, each lasting two to five days. Papers were presented by eighty members of the HBS faculty and an approximately equal number of practitioners and academics from other institutions. Altogether, some 450 academics and practitioners were involved as discussants and participants.

Some of these colloquia focused on current research topics, such as U.S. competitiveness in the world economy, productivity and technology, global competition, and world food policy. Others concentrated on establishing agendas for the coming decade's research and course development in a particular field. Clearly, these were not tasks to be attempted in isolation. Rather we wanted to work jointly with others in business, government, and the academic world who could contribute and would themselves gain from the undertaking. The papers presented in this volume have all benefited from the thoughtful discussion they received at the colloquium.

Beyond exploring research findings in particular areas, we hoped that these colloquia would sustain and enliven the continuing dialogue between students and practitioners of management. From that melding of perspectives, we have found, insights emerge that can revitalize the education of future managers and refine current professional practice. In that spirit of cooperative endeavor, I am proud to introduce this collection of essays.

John H. McArthur
Dean of the Faculty
Harvard Business School

ACKNOWLEDGMENTS

We are grateful to Dean John H. McArthur of the Harvard Business School and Professor E. Raymond Corey, director of the school's Division of Research, for their encouragement and financial support of this endeavor. We owe a debt to Associate Professor James Cash and Assistant Professors Gregory Parsons, Leslie Porter, and Michael Vitale for their efforts in helping to structure and execute the colloquium. Special thanks are due to Susan M. S. Brown for editing all the material in this volume and minimizing dissonance among the many writing styles of the authors who contributed to it. Finally, our gratitude goes to our office staff--Lillian Braudis, Maureen Donovan, and Alys Reid--who spent many hours ensuring that both the colloquium and this manuscript came to a successful conclusion.

GLOSSARY OF ABBREVIATIONS

CAD/CAM	Computer-aided design and manufacturing
CSF	Critical success factor(s)
DP	Data processing
DSS	Decision support system(s)
ESS	Executive support system(s)
IR	Information resource(s)
IS	Information system(s)
IT	Information technology
MIS	Management information system(s)
MS	Management science
MSS	Management support system(s)
SAST	Strategic assumption surfacing and testing

The Information Systems Research Challenge

INTRODUCTION

F. Warren McFarlan

Information systems (IS) is a very young field in the context of general management. Although many years could be considered its start, perhaps the best is 1952, the year large-scale computers were introduced into the private sector in the United States. Since that time sustained dramatic decreases in cost and changes in the diverse technologies of computing, telecommunications, and remote office support devices have created a continuous explosion of applications opportunities on the one hand and a kaleidoscope of management implementation issues on the other. The technology already developed assures that this dynamism will continue unabated for at least another decade.

Recent applications of IS have shifted significantly, partly because of increased applications know-how, but more fundamentally because of the technology's vastly extended capability. Many functions and tasks previously built into software are now being built into hardware, changing the entire concept of applications development. New applications targets have emerged, and many former theories about good management practice have shifted sharply as software-based management tools are developed and expert systems, artificial intelligence, and interorganizational systems command greater attention. Under these circumstances, it is difficult to find enduring insights on where to apply or how to manage the assimilation of IS technology.

The IS field requires applied multidisciplinary research. On the one hand, deep understanding of changing hardware and software issues and data base structures (the specialty of IS researchers) is needed. Another approach to the field considers how technology can influence an organization; it includes research on change management and relies heavily on the efforts of organization theorists. Viewed from a more managerial perspective, another paradigm is to think of IS as being "a business within a business." This paradigm draws on concepts from fields as diverse as marketing, operations management, management of technological innovation, and organization theory. Already each of these areas has produced valuable insights on how IS technology can be better managed. Finally, the use of IS technology to affect channels of distribution, product cost structures, and the nature of products offered has driven this field close to corporate strategy and marketing and brought it face to face with the ideas of competitive strategy and value added. The problem of effectively combining these disciplines is knotty.

The difficulty of research on IS is increased by the extremely limited number of qualified scholars currently available. And many IS researchers, although they possess strong technology skills, lack the tools and perspectives necessary for cross-disciplinary work. Further, even if they have such skills, IS scholars are often not intellectually inclined to undertake these complex studies. Unfortunately, scholars in other disciplines already have such rich agendas that they must be strenuously coaxed to look at IS issues. Scholar renewal poses another significant problem. Researchers in IS who rely on the insights of two years ago find themselves out of the mainstream far more quickly than their colleagues in other fields.

Also complicating the problem is the limited number of high-quality refereed journals (such as MIS Quarterly) that report on IS research findings. Further, the inevitable lead times for manuscript preparation and review mean that an extended, in-depth study, carefully crafted and appropriately reviewed, may be largely obsolete by the time it is published.

Finally, the financial temptations to join the world of practitioners exert relentless pressure on both academics and doctoral students to direct their careers away from research. This has both reduced the intake into the field and increased the outflow of productive midcareer talent.

Given all these issues, it is not surprising that the IS field is still struggling to define, clearly articulate, and execute a meaningful research tradition. Consequently, IS research is all too often viewed with unease in business schools. Neither deans nor other faculty members are comfortable determining quality output or even what criteria should be brought to bear in this dynamic field. A limited number of useful paradigms have been developed, but even many of these, like Richard Nolan's stages theory, have been largely overtaken by the passage of time. It is not surprising that different institutions hold widely varying notions about a suitable IS research strategy, and there is a significant lack of consensus within the field about what direction research should take in the next decade. Clearly, IS is a turbulent and complex area in which new insights on future research directions and methodological approaches are gratefully received.

Objectives

In this context, the information systems colloquium and this book were sparked by multiple objectives. The first goal was to try to highlight the research needs of the field in a way that might influence both the overall amount and the direction of research on IS in business schools and other settings.

The second objective was to facilitate sharing of the focuses of work in process at the many small, often isolated, research centers in the field. Although business schools strongly advocate planning in general, they have been much slower to apply this discipline to themselves. To the best of our knowledge, before this colloquium none of the schools represented had an explicit written strategy for IS research. Thus, a crucial ingredient for analyzing the overall direction of research in the field was missing.

A third important objective was to surface debate and insight on appropriate research methodologies for such a turbulent area. The colloquium could provide an opportunity to explore the possibility that rather crude seismographic forecasting tools offer better insights than elegant research methods, which build small structures in a landscape of continuous violent earthquakes.

A fourth objective was to encourage IS researchers to explore different tools and research traditions and urge researchers in other disciplines to include IS in their investigations through highlighting the interfaces between issues in IS and those in other fields. By pinpointing the areas of greatest uncertainty and identifying fields and institutions in which research potentially relevant to management problems is being done, the colloquium could also help professional managers administer their operations and allocate their scarce financial resources more effectively.

Finally, the book emerging from this colloquium would be a vehicle for communicating to deans, other administrative officers, and faculty members in other disciplines what the dominant IS research themes and efforts should be. This could lead to larger and more focused financial investments in the field as well as encouragement of more cross-disciplinary research projects. Further, the book could help IS doctoral students identify the major areas of opportunity for research.

Colloquium Program

To tackle this ambitious agenda we brought together a group of the best academicians and practitioners for three days. The program was structured to encourage continuous interactions in formal discussions and informal meetings.

A series of papers by academicians and practitioners illuminating key aspects of the field was commissioned. To facilitate the exchange of views, each paper was discussed for 90 minutes by a representative subsection of the colloquium participants under the leadership of a moderator. Recording secretaries noted the highlights of each discussion, and all the sessions were tape-recorded. (The tape recordings could be carefully analyzed later to uncover subsidiary, but potentially important points that might have been overlooked in the heat of exchange.) Following discussions of the individual papers in each research area, the group reassembled and each paper's moderator and recording secretary briefly summarized the essence of their sessions. Then the plenary session discussed the broader aspects of the area for 90 minutes.

Because of the colloquium's strong business-school research orientation, each school represented was invited to prepare a brief statement of its research strategy. Three hours were set aside at the end of the program to examine the strategies as a totality. These concluding discussions permitted forthright consideration of how effectively the academic community is dealing with the crucial issues in IS. In retrospect, we consider this one of the most useful aspects of the colloquium. It forced participants to make explicit some critical but largely undocumented notions.

Definition of Research Areas

Under the leadership of Harvard Professors Warren McFarlan and James McKenney, a steering committee of leading academicians was formed to plan the content and structure of the IS Colloquium. The members were Professor Robert Ashenhurst from the University of Chicago's Graduate School of Business, Professor Gordon Davis from the University of Minnesota's School of Management, Professor Richard Mason from the University of Arizona's College of Business and Public Administration, and Professor John Rockart from the Sloan School of Management at the Massachusetts Institute of Technology.

Recognizing that the structure of the colloquium and the types of papers commissioned would influence the direction of the discussions and the nature of their conclusions, the steering committee labored to subdivide the field in the most useful way possible. They developed a four-part structure, which is outlined below.

Management Support Systems

The proliferation of cheap hardware, the development of large commercial data bases, and the sharp reduction of costs of remote devices, graphics, and telecommunications equipment have brought affordable customized computer-based tools to the fingertips of managers and their support staffs. Staff and management are much more able to use microcomputers actively for a variety of decision support purposes. The steering committee felt that customizing and structuring data bases and evaluating their ability to assist individual decision-making activities were a major research area for the 1980s. Research on executive decision support systems must draw on the disciplines of technology, psychology, artificial intelligence, and business policy. Business school strategies reveal that this is seen as the most intriguing research area in IS today; it has captured the largest number of scholars. Yet the disturbing question is, Are they the right researchers going at the right question, or are they computer technicians researching a problem of which computer technology is the least important part?

Information Systems Technology and Organization

The anticipated impact of IS technology on how firms are organized and the extent to which the technology permits and encourages quite different organizational forms have been of long-standing concern. These issues were first raised by Harold Leavitt and Thomas Whisler in their landmark 1958 Harvard Business Review article. Many of their dreams have not yet appeared or have emerged in different forms, yet the steering committee believed that we are now much closer to realizing these ideas. The microprocessor has already revolutionized delivery of a great variety of services. The full impact of these past and future services on the organization, however, is exceedingly complex and needs research. Researchers broadly schooled in the behavioral and organizational sciences must be involved in this work. A partnership needs to be established between academicians with these backgrounds and the specialists in touch with IS technical reality. In terms of Alfred Chandler's classic "Strategy and Structure," the new technology offers the possibility of quite different structures, which can then facilitate different strategies. Whether that possibility could and should be converted to reality, however, is another issue.

Management of the Information Systems Resource

A massive portfolio of systems applications is currently in place, but it is being made obsolete by changing business needs and new technologies. Managers of IS resources must rebuild their portfolios and effectively manage their complex data center operations and large staffs. Questions of project management, operations management, staffing, and new development methodology all pose considerable difficulties for practitioners and represent important opportunities for IS researchers. Security, privacy, and related issues are also relevant. This is one of the oldest streams of research in IS, but the committee felt that a major agenda of work in the area remains.

Information Systems Technology and Corporate Strategy

The fields of business policy and IS have politely coexisted in most academic institutions with scarcely any impact on each other for the past two decades. Business policy researchers have seen IS as an important, but clearly support function in a firm executing broad strategies defined without IS input. Researchers in IS, from the business policy perspective, have been so interested in technology and implementation that they have not encompassed the broader aspects of corporate strategy. The steering committee believed that this gap in communication has become increasingly serious and unacceptable. Information technology is being used more and more to develop new channels of distribution to customers, to provide the bases of new products, and to afford the opportunity for major changes in operations. Further, little research has been done on the increasing use of information technology to enable innovative differentiation strategies. The technology clearly has a dimension beyond incremental improvement of decisions and automation of transaction systems. The committee felt that it is becoming an important element in overall strategy.

The remainder of this book is built on the structure described in the previous section. Each of the four major parts begins with an introduction by a member of the steering committee, outlining his understanding of the area, explaining in more depth why it was defined as it was, and describing the rationale behind the selection of each paper. The papers are then presented, each followed by a short summary of additional issues and perspectives raised in its colloquium discussion. Finally, at the end of each part, a summary of the plenary discussion on the area is presented. This focuses particularly on ideas for future research. Not surprisingly, no consensus on research agendas was reached, and none was imposed in the summaries. The steering committee hoped that these summaries in conjunction with the other material in each part, would capture the complexity of the area and stimulate readers to reevaluate their own research agendas.

Part V contains a collection of business schools' research strategy statements and a summary of the colloquium discussions on them. This part highlights current research directions and permits readers to compare what is being done in business schools with the issues raised in the rest of the book--what should be done. The imbalance and mismatch between these two sets is perhaps the most disturbing and most stimulating aspect of this book.

PART I

MANAGEMENT SUPPORT SYSTEMS

INTRODUCTION TO PART I

John F. Rockart

The academic world first awoke to the field of computer-based support of managers barely a decade ago. Ralph Sprague and Eric Carlson, in their well-received 1982 book on decision support systems, noted that "the concepts involved in DSS were first articulated in the early 1970's by Michael S. Scott Morton under the term 'management decision systems.' A few firms and a few scholars began to develop and research DSS, which became characterized as _interactive_ computer-based systems that _help_ decision makers utilize _data_ and _models_ to solve _unstructured problems_."

The firms and scholars to which Sprague and Carlson referred were reacting, either explicitly or implicitly, to the challenge Scott Morton had laid down in his seminal 1971 book, _Management Information Systems_. He wrote, "Computer technology has advanced at a rapid rate but thus far has had little, if any direct impact on managerial action. This new technology offers the possibility of coupling the manager, at any level, and in any environment, with information and decision-making support from the computer. These technological advances, then, call for a shift in thinking by managers and systems designers at least as radical as that required when computers were first introduced at the functional level in the late 1950's."

A decade later that shift in thinking is still in progress. But whether it is called _management decision systems_, _decision support systems_ (as it has been called through most of the decade), or _management support systems_ (which appears to be the more appropriate term), the field which has resulted from that shift in thinking is no longer the sole property of a "few firms and a few scholars." The term _decision support systems_, as is painfully obvious, is now in vogue. It is applied to anything and everything that might possibly lure a manager into purchasing hardware, software, a system, a concept, or printed matter.

The colloquium sessions on management support systems (MSS) were focused on understanding the maze of diverse efforts and slogans that are now vying for the opportunity to support managers with computer power. In particular, we hoped to understand the nature of the field, its current research profile, and the most fruitful directions for future research. This part was titled "management support" rather than "decision support" because, as Peter Keen and others have made clear, not all the observable systems support decisions, but they do all support the management process in one way or another. We strove to indicate the breadth of the field in the part title.

It was taken as a "given" that this field is important. The evidence is abundant. In leading companies today nearly 50% (in some cases more) computer use is by end users. Products of all types are flooding this market. (Not the least of these is the personal computer, which is bringing inexpensive computer power to all segments of organizational life.) And a significant number of researchers in management schools are devoted to work in this field.

It is certainly appropriate that the first paper in this part is by Michael Scott Morton. He centers his attention on two issues--the nature of the field and the current state of research. To do this, he presents a review of some 300 articles published in the field in the past three years. Scott Morton defines MSS broadly as "the use of information technologies to support management." He emphasizes the word support, because, in his words, it "differentiates MSS from many other applications of information technology." He reaches several interesting conclusions about research in the field. There is a disproportionately large amount of work in development of methodologies and frameworks. This is coupled with a lack of empirical testing of these methods and concepts, and, in Scott Morton's opinion, far too little work on the impacts of MSS. In many other areas little or no work is being done, or at least reported, leaving MSS--and especially executive support and data support--a badly underresearched field.

Izak Benbasat, in his paper, centers on methodologies for conducting research in MSS. In contrast to Scott Morton, he confines his attention to three major research areas within the field: implementation; the managerial interface with the hardware, software, and analytical tools that make up the support system; and the decision-making process. He discusses a representative sample of studies in each area and groups the studies by the research vehicles they used. Finally, Benbasat assesses the appropriateness of various research methods for MSS studies.

Although he recognizes others, Benbasat focuses on four research methods: case studies, field studies, sample surveys, and laboratory experiments. He argues that sample surveys appear to have little value. In contrast, case studies were exceedingly useful during the pioneering years of the field. They yielded significant insights into development and implementation. Today, however, field studies and laboratory experiments to test past insights and provide a more explicit understanding of particular aspects of MSS appear increasingly necessary.

Albert Crawford writes from the standpoint of a practicing information systems executive. Concerned with the implementation of a "strategic computing vision" developed at Digital Equipment Corporation, he stresses the significant changes in the information systems field. These include a dramatic shift in focus from developing operational systems to supporting end user computing, expansion of the field to cover all aspects of information (including mailrooms and printing plants), and the increasing importance of networks. In contrast to Scott Morton and Benbasat, Crawford concentrates on areas of needed research, especially aspects of the "infrastructure" that allow MSS to be supported effectively and accessed by all.

Crawford suggests six areas for research: information architecture (including computers, telecommunications, and data), data resource management, network management, artificial intelligence, project life cycle concepts, and cost-value analysis. In all these areas pragmatic work is necessary to develop concepts, tools, and processes that can be implemented. Crawford expresses little interest in research on the fine points of decision making, cognitive style, and the like. He is greatly concerned, however, with several large "messy" problems with which few MSS researchers have dealt. Crawford suggests that without solutions to these problems, the proper technological infrastructure and corporate guidelines to facilitate effective use of MSS will be lacking.

A reading of these three papers provides several significant impressions. The first and inescapable fact is that the field is exceedingly broad. Research on effective delivery of MSS relates to a wide spectrum of disciplines, from the "hard" to the "soft" sciences. Further, there is much to be done. Questions ranging from the complex and open ended to those requiring rigorous thought and method cry out for answers. Finally, all authors--each with a note of hope and expectation--indicate a need to focus further on expert systems as the next frontier.

THE STATE OF THE ART OF RESEARCH

Michael S. Scott Morton

Background

This is a time of broad technological change; unprecedented "information power," in the form of the ubiquitous personal computer as well as the more traditional time-sharing system, is becoming available to users. Organizations are trying to cope quickly with a proliferation of varied computers by networking them internally and linking their systems to others outside. And the information systems field itself is undergoing rapid change. Systems professionals, in either the corporation or the university, are now clearly in the minority as innovators and implementors of information technology. They are surrounded and outnumbered by "end users," all of whom are increasingly armed with computer capacity and powerful software tools that they can apply directly.

The spread of information power to users is transforming management support systems (MSS) from an interesting but somewhat isolated use by a small core of creative individuals to a central management tool. One increasingly finds MSS woven into the very fabric of management. This evaluation has just begun; the enormity of its impact has not yet been felt.

The goal of this paper is to identify some patterns in the ongoing research on MSS. The patterns have been drawn from a search through some 300 articles published over the last three years in the journals in the reference list. We selected 80 articles as representative of the best research work in the field. The final articles we chose focus most on the MSS dimension and are probably representative of the kind of work going on at this

---

This paper could not have been written without the able help of my assistant, Andrea Hatch, and the work of John Poole and Marc Gordon, who did a great deal of the early literature search. Diane Gherson provided some much needed assistance, particularly in the development of the positioning framework. I have benefited from the input of all my colleagues and am particularly grateful for the substantive help given by Michael Treacy.

time. These publications are primarily American, but we did attempt to scan the relevant European journals.

Definition

The term management support systems is open to a great many interpretations. For the purposes of this paper we define it as "the use of information technologies to support management." Rapid changes in technology make it necessary to include in MSS several forms of information technology that go beyond and are quite different from the computer used in traditional data processing--for example, teleconferencing, electronic data bases, and graphics work stations. And our understanding of systems continues to evolve as new information technologies redefine the frontier of possibilities. This is why our definition of MSS is not restricted to computer technologies. However, the term support provides the foundation for our definition and differentiates MSS from many other applications of information technology. We have emphasized support in our review of the literature and excluded research whose primary goal is to replace rather than support managers.

Many writers in the past two years have begun to redefine our concept of management systems to delineate more clearly the importance of information and related technologies. The information era will require new and sophisticated forms of management (see Rockart and Scott Morton, 1983). Naisbitt, in his book Megatrends (1982), is perhaps the most visible author to highlight the shift to an information era. In his first chapter, on the transition from an industrial society to an information society, he provides some provocative illustrations of how far America has moved in this direction. He further outlines the implications of this evolution for organizations and their managers in his chapter on networking, where he quotes Intel's vice chairman, Robert Noyce: "What we've tried to do is to put people together in ways so that they make contributions to a wider range of decisions and do things that would be thwarted by a structured, line organization." Elsewhere Naisbitt gives examples of information technology providing the tools to do this.

Technologies

Technologies related to management support systems can be divided into four major categories: hardware, software, communications, and methodological tools.

Hardware

There is no reason to suppose that one form of computer hardware and related components is more relevant to management than any other. Therefore, MSS hardware includes the full spectrum of computers (micros to mainframes) and the full spectrum of ways they are made available to management (remote access from a central location or fully distributed access in one's local site or office).

Software

Software for management support takes many forms, including tailor-made special-purpose applications, general-purpose modeling packages, and information bases. At the core of each is a language that defines the software's capabilities.

Communications

Management support systems can now use communications via both narrow-band and broad-band paths that extend both inside and outside the organization. This allows applications, such as videoconferencing, that have not traditionally been considered part of the computer-based MSS domain. However, these uses are part of information support for management.

Methodological Tools

The continuing progress in behavioral science, management science, and the study of management decision making has made it apparent that a class of methodological tools exists which should be classified as "technologies." These include many of the techniques in decision analysis that have been exercised by the operations research community. Other methodological tools are oriented toward helping the MSS builder. These include techniques for determining information requirements and planning implementation strategies.

Types of MSS

We will discuss three broad categories of MSS: data support, decision support, and executive support systems.

Data Support Systems

The traditional data processing use of technology is assumed to be largely confined to transaction processing and low-level (clerical) operational use--both outside the domain of this paper. However, to the extent that these systems produce information as a by-product, they fall in the purview of MSS. Thus, the data bases that traditional data processing generates are a potential element of management support. Indeed, the whole area of building, maintaining, and providing access to information is directly relevant to MSS.

Research in this segment of the field has resulted in data base management systems that can be and are being used as part of MSS. We will call these data support systems. These systems provide information regardless of use or user; examples are the Disclosure TM Service, The Source (belonging to Reader's

Digest), the numerous information bases of the New York Times, and the data bases of firms like Data Resource Inc. The literature does not discuss data support system use, but faculty in the field are aware of dozens of applications.

Decision Support Systems

The second class of MSS are decision support systems (DSS). For the purposes of this paper DSS are considered a subset of management support systems focused on a specific decision or class of decisions. As many authors have pointed out, a general broadening (and consequent debasing) of the term DSS has caused it to lose most of its specific meaning. In particular, there has been a lack of differentiation between the system (of human decision maker and related computer-based support) and the tools with which the computer in the system is created. Thus, for example, Interactive Financial Planning System (IFPS) is a language--and by all reports an effective one--but for the purposes of this paper it is not a DSS. It is a tool for building a DSS.

One of the best broad discussions of the evolution of the concept of DSS is in Sprague and Carlson's Building Effective Decision Support Systems (1982). Their focus is on what DSS are and how to build them, not on their organizational impacts and implications. If those who used the term DSS would first read this book, we could better focus on a common definition. For our purpose, a system must apply to a particular class of decision to be considered a DSS. From examples in the literature it is possible to identify four distinct classes of decisions and estimate their incidence (see Figure 1).

Figure 1. *Classes of Decisions and Their Incidence*

	Decision Made by Individual	Decision Made by Group
Ad Hoc Decision	SOME	VERY FEW
Institutionalized System (Ongoing Decision)	MANY	VERY FEW

The DSS reported in the literature are not necessarily representative of all that have been built. However, those covered in the reference list of this paper fall into the cells in

Figure 1. It is instructive to compare four excellent papers by Bonczek, Holsapple, and Whinston (1979a, 1979b, 1980a, and 1980b) with Sprague and Carlson's book. Taken together, these sources highlight the inevitable conflict between our desire for generality and the demands imposed by specific problems. Bonczek, Holsapple, and Whinston are more optimistic about moving toward the general, although many of their ideas await confirmation in practice.

Bonczek, Holsapple, and Whinston (1980b) and Luconi and Scott Morton (1983) define the next generation of DSS, namely intelligent support systems. Intelligent support systems are a form of DSS in which the human decision maker combines heuristics and a knowledge base to produce answers for a certain class of unstructured problem. They are not presented in this paper as separate from DSS because they merely use different tools and therefore support a different class of decisions. They remain focused on a specific problem or class of problems. The intelligent support systems that are beginning to surface are outgrowths of the work in artificial intelligence and expert systems. It is interesting to note here that much of the work in expert systems is primarily aimed at replacing managers, not supporting them.

Three articles in our literature search in the general area of artificial intelligence apply to MSS. The most specific is by Ben-Bassat (1981), who looked at a military application that has useful implications for business. A more generic discussion is given in Bonczek, Holsapple, and Whinston (1980b). They provide some succinct descriptions of work in the expert systems field. None of their examples can really be described as MSS, but they do offer good samples of the current state of the art in artificial intelligence. Luconi and Scott Morton (1983) provide a framework that tries to position intelligent support systems as a logical outgrowth of DSS. Drawing on experience in building a prototype and testing it in use, they identify the opportunities and pitfalls that can be expected as intelligent support systems applications evolve. In this paper we have classified as support systems the one or two expert systems and related applications that have begun to be developed for supporting managers.

Executive Support Systems

Executive support systems (ESS) are focused on a manager's or group of managers' information needs across a range of areas. Rather than being limited to a single recurring type of decision, ESS incorporate in one system the data and analytic tools to provide information support for many managerial processes and problems. Thus, ESS encompass a broader concept than DSS. Executive support systems also differ in another important respect from DSS. The majority of ESS are data retrieval oriented, whereas most DSS are modeling oriented (see Figure 2).

Figure 2

	Decision Support Systems (DSS)	Executive Support Systems (ESS)
Data Retrieval Oriented	FEW	MANY
Modeling Oriented	MANY	FEW

Decision support systems tend to have as their foundation a model of some aspect of a particular type of problem. The model provides a structure for the relationships among relevant data and allows the decision maker to perform complex analysis with relative ease. In contrast, the broader focus of ESS cannot usually be accommodated by a model or series of models.

Methods and Tools

In looking at the literature on MSS it also proved useful to examine the tools and methods being applied. The literature shows six categories of tools, which we will identify on a continuum that roughly represents their portability--that is, the ease with which someone other than the original inventor or designer can use them. Starting with the least portable--methodologies and frameworks--the spectrum progresses to the most portable--hardware, including the physical computer, the network, and the color graphics terminal.

Methodologies

The methodologies proposed in the literature are predominantly concerned with how to build a DSS. As such, they would perhaps be better described as prescriptive processes, the results of which will yield a "good" system. Alter (1982) is of this type. The author sets out to identify the conditions under which a DSS can or should be developed and used without professional help. However, the methodologies described in such articles are difficult for others to adopt because they lack specific implementation directions. This is true even of some extensive methodological developments, such as the one Sprague and Carlson describe in Chapter 4 of their book (1982).

If these methodologies were capable of adoption, it would be possible to move to a level of research as yet largely unexplored and compare and contrast methodologies. The lone example of a comparison that surfaced in our literature search was Alavi and Henderson (1981). They make specific recommendations after comparing two different methodologies.

It is a measure of Herbert Simon's enormous contribution that all methodologies in the DSS arena, to the extent that they are grounded in theory at all, use his basic view of decision making. None of the material we found was based on anything more fundamental or recent than Simon's work--an impressive testimony to his insights.

In the emerging area of ESS, the most visible methodology is Rockart's critical success factors, based on work by Robert Anthony and Ronald Daniels. This methodology has been used successfully by others and thus can be said to meet the test of portability. However, it seems to be the only one that has been widely used, so if we are to take the absence of instances in the literature as a guide, methodologies are not easily transferable.

Data Base Technologies

Data base technologies are a classic area of computer science that are very useful for MSS. However, the absence in the literature of illustrations of data base technology application and use for MSS suggests that these technologies are still in the early phase of their life cycle. The popular literature offers evidence that they are being applied to the office; for example, *Fortune* magazine has run an extensive series of advertisements by International Data Corporation that focus on commercial applications. Experience in office support might lead to progress in applying data base technology to real MSS.

An excellent overview of data base technologies is given by Manola (1980). On the basis of Blanning's 1979 discussion of DSS functions, Manola identifies the software- and data-oriented requirements of a DSS and describes how data base technology might contribute to satisfying them. In particular, he identifies six areas of data base technologies:

1. Data models and data base system architecture
2. Data transmission and mapping
3. Data base access languages
4. Active data base management systems
5. Distributed data base systems
6. Data base hardware

This list provides a sense of the enormous power builders of MSS can draw on once tools are available. Manola illustrates the considerable progress in areas 1 and 2, where commercial products have recently been released. In area 3 he points out that data base access work has shifted to providing powerful query-based capability for the casual user. This has involved considerably sophisticated system architecture to prevent the hardware requirements from becoming excessive. Progress, as Manola points out in his references, has been considerable. Areas 4, 5, and 6 are the focuses of intensive research and are beginning to yield results that are usable as parts of MSS, both decision and executive support systems.

Manola's article, and some of the references he mentions, implies that a crucial piece of technology is becoming available to those who wish to build and install MSS. The large body of literature coming from basic technology research by computer vendors and universities indicates that increasingly powerful data base tools applicable to MSS will continue to become available.

Languages and Packages

Management support systems are fundamentally dependent on the power of the tools available for their development. The literature has a number of surveys of such languages; some of the more interesting are included in the reference list. One of the best is a survey of 237 firms by Brightman, Harris, and Thompson (1981). As they point out, there are two basic forms of language--general-purpose languages, such as FORTRAN and APL, and commercial modeling languages, such as IFPS, SIMPLAN, and CUFFS. There are well over 50 commercial modeling languages available. The study focuses on financial modeling languages, which are particularly useful for model building, one component of certain kinds of MSS. The results show that 53% of the firms surveyed used financial modeling systems. Of these, 44% were using a general language and 56% had a commercial language.

The survey was designed to investigate the impact of commercial modeling languages on the adoption and design of financial modeling systems. The authors establish that these languages do indeed simplify the model-building process and make it possible for decision makers or related staff to build their own systems without the aid of a "data processing" system person. They go on to document the advantages users found in support systems of this type. As one would hope in the use of an MSS, advantages include the ability to do more analysis and ask "what if" questions. However, other advantages include perceptible improvements in the decision process and better decisions. This study stands out as one of very few that actually takes the trouble to sample users and assess the state of current practice and user reactions. The authors also identify further issues on which to follow up, including the question of industry differences in patterns of use.

One very suggestive issue Brightman, Harris, and Thompson raise is barriers to use, in an organization, of financial modeling systems and, by analogy, of MSS in general. They find that the lack of a person to champion a model and the cost of the system are the biggest barriers. This suggests that we are still in an evolutionary stage of MSS (or at least DSS, which constitute all their examples) that might be described as "technology first." A "champion" is necessary for a model primarily if the model is being sold, rather than a solution to a business problem. The literature on languages spends almost no time on a "business need first" perspective. As tools become more user friendly, the use of DSS comes to be a more readily accepted way of doing business. Languages become just one more tool to build a DSS for supporting the solution of a business problem. Fortunately, the costs of building DSS with these languages and using them on the job are going down rapidly, so we can expect these two barriers to fall.

Models

Models are one of the tools often used as a basis for MSS. As represented by operations research, they are one of the oldest disciplines available to those interested in MSS. It is interesting that much of the literature on models in MSS, certainly in the journals we surveyed, deals with sophisticated, often optimization, models. However, no recent literature of which I am aware suggests when such models are appropriate.

The concept of simple models that provide insight to the manager was not represented in any of the literature in this survey. Nor does there seem to have been any published work on types of models since Alter's 1976 analysis of 56 case studies of DSS. In this study Alter identifies four categories of models used as part of DSS:

1. Accounting relationships--used for estimating the consequences of a decision
2. Representational models, normally simulation models
3. Optimization models
4. Suggestion models

Judging from the literature, the vast preponderance of model use is in the financial area and is of the accounting relationship form. There are some interesting exploratory efforts to develop a language, using predicate calculus, to formalize "stating modeling knowledge" (see Bonczek, Holsapple, and Whinston, 1981). If this project is successful, application-specific modeling knowledge will not need to be embedded in the computer program. However, this whole area requires extensive further research before implementation will be possible.

It is interesting to contrast the decision sciences view of models and their development in the context of MSS with views from a different discipline. For example, John Morecroft, of the Systems Dynamics Group at MIT, describes working with a group of senior marketing executives in a major U.S. manufacturing firm (1982). He discusses the concept of "support" and then particularizes this to "strategy support" and concludes that for highly unstructured strategy questions this means providing insight into the consequences of pursuing strategic initiatives once they have been formulated. Modeling is fit into a framework where mental models and formal computer models (in this case systems dynamics models) result in debate and discussion followed by reformulation and, finally, consensus on a strategy. Morecroft argues from his experience that a formal model in this context must

Be a vehicle for extending argument and debate
Be a generator of opinions not answers
Deal in concepts with which management is familiar

Morecroft finds that the key for effective model-based strategic support is to use the model in a dialectical fashion, to challenge prevailing management opinion. He shows a very different view of the role of models--as vehicles for debate rather than providers of answers. Morecroft's paper is the only one in the current literature that follows a model through its use in practice.

Interface Technologies

One set of technologies that can significantly affect the growth and acceptability of MSS are those that address the interface between the human and the system. They include new hardware, such as joysticks and mice, and the software necessary to provide color graphics, windows, and other features.

Closer to the more obvious MSS needs is the work necessary to translate Bonczek, Holsapple, and Whinston's "language system" (1980b) into a general-purpose reality. This language system is defined as "the sum total of all linguistic facilities made available to the decision maker by the DSS." The authors point out that the system is characterized by the syntax that it furnishes to the decision maker and by "the statement commands or expressions that it allows the user to make." Thus, to them the language system is one of three components of DSS, the other two being the knowledge system and the problem processing system. This most useful generic description of a DSS allows the authors to make some interesting points about the role of artificial intelligence in the DSS of the future. They do not, however, expand on their view of the likely evolution of the language system.

Researchers do not appear to regard the interface question for MSS as worthy of much work; no serious articles on the subject surfaced in the recent journals. Occasionally, though, a theoretical piece raises some interesting ideas. One example is Studer's 1983 article on an adaptable user interface for DSS.

The heart of his approach is twofold: first, system users should be provided with an "application model" through three types of graph structures:

The application structure graph
The operator structure graph
The operator data graph

Second, a dialogue should be provided that allows end users to select components and execute the existing model using facilities to "navigate" through the graph structures. Studer's description is extensive, but he gives no hint of experience with use, either in a laboratory or an organization.

In short, there is a real dearth of practical experimentation in user interface work, and new ideas seem to move unusually slowly into testing. To the extent that the interface technologies are important, it appears that the widespread use of MSS will be held back by the absence of developmental work in this area.

Hardware and Networks

Much of the impetus in MSS appears to come from the relentless drop in cost of hardware and to be augmented by the changes in communications technology. An excellent article by Benjamin (1982) makes the point that in the future we can expect continued drop in cost and increase in functionality. This is represented by the migration of some MSS tools, such as languages, over to micros. Thus, a number of language vendors, such as IFPS, are making their languages, or subsets, available on personal computers. Down-loading of central files from the mainframe to the personal computer also appears to be occurring. However, these and other hardware and communications changes are happening so rapidly that no research on them has yet appeared. One can merely pick up anecdotal illustrations from *Business Week* or *Fortune*. This suggests that much more research will be needed just to capture the implications of recent hardware developments.

One of the few articles published in this area is Keen (1983). He develops persuasive arguments for and against microcomputer-based DSS. The key points of his resulting policy statement are

1. The role of the organization is to encourage use, not to control use
2. Full authority is to be given to end users
3. A coordinator role should exist to provide education, user support, and recommendations on software, hardware, and other issues

However, Keen does not go on to elaborate the implications of these technological developments for computing in the organization. It seems obvious that MSS in an organization with such a sensible policy will become all-pervasive. Hardware changes will begin to blur the lines between what we see as a distinctive category, existing MSS, and the rest of the things managers do. In short, MSS will become part of the fabric of the management job.

Research Typology

There are possibly as many ways of laying out a typology of research categories in MSS as there are professors active in the field. The criteria for judging a typology are vague, but surely one is that it be found useful. However, all researchers who develop their own typologies are likely to find them useful! With considerable trepidation, therefore, we submit the following nine categories as one possible typology: build a prototype, construct a methodology, develop a theory, formulate a concept, perform empirical tests (both laboratory and real world), conduct a survey, describe a case, and declare a "truth."

Each of these categories will be described briefly and an example of MSS research for each will be given. Of course, many research efforts fall in more than one category, for example, a prototype DSS that is tested in a laboratory setting.

Prototype

The prototype is basically an engineering concept of research, which, fortunately, has its proponents in the MSS field. An example, found in Moskowitz's "DSS/F" (1982), is a PASCAL-based DSS for financial applications with a number of innovative uses of virtual memory that permit an unusually interesting collection of features.

Methodology

A methodology is constructed whenever researchers take the trouble to base their procedure on theory or on the deductive process gained by trial and error over time in the field. An example would be Sprague and Carlson's (1982) work with ROMC (representations, operations, memory aids, and control mechanisms), their methodology for building a DSS.

Theory

To develop a theory is possibly the toughest research task of all. It requires not only extraordinary insight, but also extensive work with existing theories. We have found no new theories relevant to the MSS field in the recent literature. Of course, Simon's work on decision making remains as powerful as ever, as do many behavior theories, such as the Lewin-Schein model (see Schein, 1969).

Concept

The term concept here is meant to suggest a framework that is found useful in organizing ideas and suggesting actions. Concepts can in time lead to a theory. A recent example of a concept would be Rockart's work on critical success factors. This concept has gained credibility and usefulness through its testing by many people in actual empirical situations.

Empirical Laboratory Test

Empirical lab testing attempts to simulate real-world behavior in an artificial setting using students or managers. The literature search for this paper uncovered only a few experiments; one of the most interesting was Alavi and Henderson (1981). They tested two alternative strategies--one traditional and one evolutionary. The process-oriented evolutionary strategy proved more effective. Such controlled lab experiments can be most valuable; their infrequent use is hard to understand.

Empirical Real-World Test

Empirical real-world tests should eventually be used to evaluate the effectiveness of any new concept, methodology, or system. Such tests can be of two types--focused or general. Rockart (1979) used the focused type to assess his critical success factors methodology. The general test is exemplified by Fuerst and Cheney (1982). They tested the factors affecting DSS usage of eight systems and 64 subjects. Their hypotheses were derived from prior studies, and the outcome of their study verifies the importance of the DSS's relevance and the quality of user training. The few real-world tests found in the literature indicate that they are performed, or at least reported, infrequently.

Survey

This category of research represents projects that survey a particular population (users, builders, or others) in organizations to determine the existence or absence of something. Surveys may be used to establish whether a particular class of language is used, or whether a user is satisfied with the quality of service received. Surveys differ from general empirical tests in that surveys do not attempt to establish causal relationships based on theory or deductive work from prior studies. The work by Rockart and Treacy (1982) represents a fine example of this genre; they found five common characteristics among 16 users of ESS.

Case

Describing a case often provides a rich sense of the context and nuances of an application. This seems to be particularly true in MSS work, which has so many dimensions and facets. One example would be Ben-Bassat's fascinating artificial intelligence-based DSS (1981).

"Truth"

Periodically workers in the field of MSS are moved to declare a "truth." Ideally, a declaration is made by a wise person whose experience has led to a genuine insight. When this occurs, the idea immediately strikes one as "right," even without the corroboration of theory, implementation, or use. The difficulty is that what strikes one reader as insightful may strike another as foolish. Only time can reveal the truth. Keen's "Policy Statement for Managing Microcomputers" (1983) is an example of this research style.

Summary of Research Status

We can use a three-dimensional matrix to look at the state of the art in research in MSS (see Figure 3).

Figure 3. *Categories of Research*

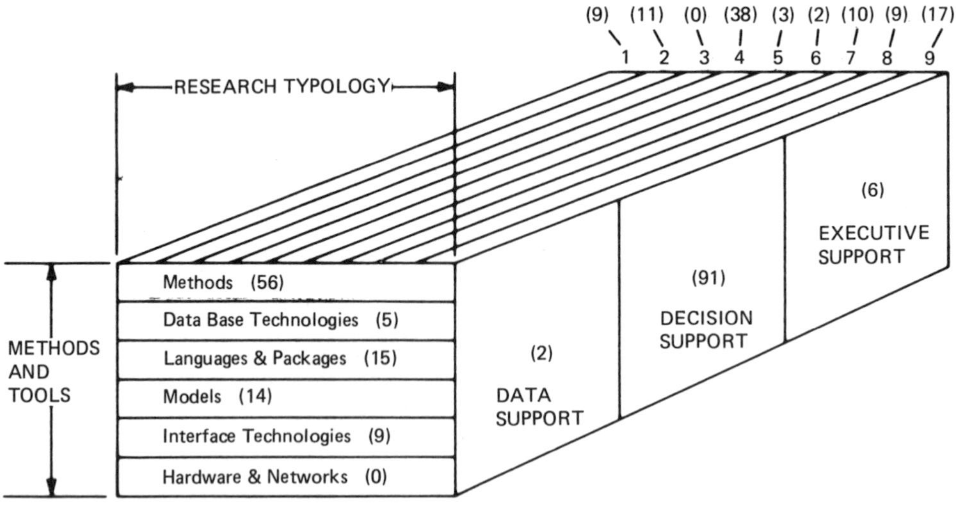

(Numbers in parentheses represent pieces of research, in each category, found in the literature search)

We have suggested that three types of management support are adequate for our purposes: data support, decision support, and executive support. It should be no surprise to discover that, by far, the largest number of articles culled from the literature are in the decision support category. This testifies to the life cycle stage of the concept, if nothing else. However, if we now take each slice in turn to produce a two-dimensional grid, the patterns in Figures 4-7 emerge.

Figure 4. *Research on Data Support System*

	← Research Typology →								
	1	*2*	*3*	*4*	*5*	*6*	*7*	*8*	*9*
					Empirical Tests				
Methods & Tools	*Proto-type*	*Method*	*Theory*	*Concept*	*Lab*	*Real*	*Survey*	*Case*	*"Truth"*
Methods				X					
Data Base Technol-ogies									
Languages & Packages									
Models				X					
Interface Technol-ogies									
Hardware & Networks									

Figure 5. *Research on Decision Support Systems*

← Research Typology →

Methods & Tools	*Proto-type*	*Method*	*Theory*	*Concept*	*Empirical Tests*		*Survey*	*Case*	*"Truth"*
					Lab	*Real*			
Methods	XX	XXXX XXXX		XXX XXXX XXXX XXXX XXX	XX X	X	XXXX	XXXX X	XXXX XXXX XXXX
Data Base Technologies	X			XX				X	
Languages & Packages	XX			XXXX			XXX		XXXX
Models	XX	XXX		XXX XXXX				X	
Interface Technologies	X			XXXX		X		XX	X
Hardware & Networks									

Figure 6. *Research on Executive Support Systems*

	←——— *Research Typology* ———→								
					Empirical Tests				
Methods & Tools	*Proto-type*	*Method*	*Theory*	*Concept*	*Lab*	*Real*	*Survey*	*Case*	*"Truth"*
Methods ologies				X			XX		
Data Base Technol-ogies		X							
Languages & Packages	X						X		
Models									
Interface Technol-ogies									
Hardware & Networks									

Figure 7. *Research on Management Support Systems*

	1	*2*	*3*	*4*	*5*	*6*	*7*	*8*	*9*	
	←---- *Research Typology* ----→									
					Empirical Tests					
Methods & Tools	*Proto-type*	*Method*	*Theory*	*Concept*	*Lab*	*Real*	*Survey*	*Case*	*"Truth"*	
Methods	XX	XXXX XXX		XXXX XXXX XXXX XXXX XXXX	XX X	X	XXXX XX	XXXX X	XXXX XXXX XXXX	56
Data Base Technologies	X	X		XX				X		5
Languages & Packages	XXX			XXXX			XXXX		XXXX	15
Models	XX	XXX		XXXX XXXX				X		14
Interface Technologies	X					X		XX	X	5
Hardware & Networks										0
	9	11	0	34	3	2	10	9	17	

Conclusions

The patterns of research work, or lack of it, revealed in Figures 3-7 bring us to four specific conclusions and an overall observation.

1. We still appear to be in the very early phases of research in MSS. So far almost all the work has been with DSS; only around early 1982 did we begin to see published results on data and executive support systems. It will be interesting to see if the development of these "product" types will be accompanied by appropriate empirical testing and observation.

2. There appears to be a disproportionally large amount of work in methodologies and frameworks. This is not in itself bad, but it is unfortunate that almost no work falls into the area of empirical testing of the methodologies or frameworks. Insights gained from testing, or at least reporting on use, could greatly improve the methodologies. A similar assessment can be made of the research on languages. The lack of testing or surveying experience in the field removes a major source of insights that could lead to important changes in a new generation of languages and in the practice of management.

3. The surprising failure to find published research on hardware and communications networks may well be the result of a faulty search process. It does not seem reasonable that hardware, at least, is not currently a primary research focus in MSS. However, our search, which included the Association for Computing Machinery publication Computing Reviews, did not produce any articles. It may also be that the business schools have, thus far, done most of the research and publishing in the MSS field. This community may not be drawn to focus on hardware. However, the increasing availability of low-cost MSS hardware tools may lead to more research in this area.

4. There is another surprising vacuum--the lack of work on the "impacts of MSS." Much work has been done on the impacts of traditional management information systems, but virtually nothing on the impacts of MSS. If this lack is real, and not simply an error of our literature search, it is a sad commentary on the state of the field. A careful examination of the impacts of MSS is needed if we are to improve the effectiveness of their use. This literature survey indicates that those in the field make declarative statements and build interesting new tools which are never tested by practical use, comparative evaluation, or user opinion.

Overall, we have to conclude that there is an unfortunately large number of unexplored areas. A further dimension of this fact was revealed by the bibliographies of the 93 items referenced here. We counted the sources referenced in these bibliographies and how many times each was cited (see Table 1). In the vast majority of cases a source was cited by only one author. In short, those in the MSS field do not build on collective experience; research efforts appear to be individualistic and fragmented.

Table 1. *Count of Sources Cited in Bibliographies of Ninety Three Selected MSS Articles*

Sources	*Times Cited*
259	1
40	2
27	3
10	4
1	5
3	6
0	7
1	8
2	9
2	10+

The heavily cited sources were

	Times Cited
Keen and Scott Morton (1978)	20
Sprague (1980)	10
Alter (1980)	9
Bonczek Holsapple, and Whinston (1980)	9
Gorry and Scott Morton (1971)	8

Our four conclusions on the state of research in MSS are reflected in the many issues raised at the 1981 Conference on Decision Support Systems held by the American Institute for Decision Sciences. The discussions at this conference are summarized in Dickson (1980), Hackathorn (1980), Methlie (1980), and Wagner (1980). A major concern was the lack of research on the support needs of groups and committees. Participants in the conference felt that organizational MSS may represent many problems not found in single-user or single-decision MSS. Research into these issues may address our concern about a lack of research on executive and data support systems.

Other issues were raised at that conference regarding the tools of MSS: software languages and design, implementation, and evaluation methods. Particular concern was expressed about the lack of substantive results addressing the evaluation and justification of MSS. The discussants' concerns mirror our concern for more research on the impact of support systems on the organization. The value of an MSS is in its impacts. If we can study these in greater depth, understand and catalog them, then we move a step closer to understanding where best to apply

MSS to improve the effectiveness with which organizations operate.

If the research we found is a measure of the maturity of the MSS field, then it has much growing to do. We hope that future research will begin to fill in the many blank areas in Figures 4-7.

One prospective area of study that may fill in some of these gaps is artificial intelligence. This topic has been worked on by some of the best researchers in the country for over 20 years. Its recent leap into the limelight (see Alexander, 1982, and "Artificial Intelligence," 1982) is partly the result of the availability of inexpensive and powerful programming tools for "heuristic" work. This is important because of the insatiable hardware appetite of any realistic application. There are years of work ahead (see Bonczek, Holsapple, and Whinston, 1980b). Research is needed in all the following areas: natural language; knowledge engineering (the ability to extract and encode the knowledge in a human's mind); tools and techniques to build domain-specific knowledge; and tools, techniques, and models to construct the general-purpose "inference engines" that will work on domain-specific knowledge.

In the meantime, for those interested in MSS there is the attraction of addressing a whole new class of management problems (see Luconi and Scott Morton, 1983). Their support will be particularly useful where precise rules cannot be made explicit in a computable form, but where heuristics can genuinely be helpful. Intelligent support systems may be one of the most fruitful areas of MSS research in the decade ahead.

This look at the future from a detail level can be instructive. However, it is also useful to look at the driving forces in the field from a macro perspective. This can be done in terms of both supply push and demand pull.

On the supply side we have, as always, the hardware vendors. However, with software becoming a major part of their sales, they are likely to keep flooding the market with tools that can be built into MSS. The resources of the hardware vendors are being mightily leveraged by the host of software firms and users who are launching new products.

The other supply push is the information coming from the 20 years of building internal transaction processing and other data processing systems, which in many firms are supplying the information. When we add to this information what is coming from external data base purveyors, it is clear that there is an abundance of information, which causes an inevitable supply-side push in MSS.

The same pattern can be seen on the demand-pull side, where a multitude of forces converge on management. In response, a general MSS, such as we have defined in this paper, can be of real use. The widespread needs caused by the global economy, the necessity to increase productivity, and other forces all suggest that management at all levels must think "smarter."

This has always been necessary, but it will be more so in the 1980s and 1990s. The ability to harness the burgeoning supply of new technology to meet business demands will prove invaluable. If MSS can reach their potential to help achieve this, they will become an integral part of business. Like the telephone, we will take them for granted.

Our literature survey suggests that we are far from being at such a point. But the trend is in the right direction. Certainly the new technologies are driving us ever forward.

Bibliography

Akoka, Jacob. "A Framework for Decision Support Systems Evaluation," Information and Management (Netherlands), July 1981.

Alavi, Maryam. "An Assessment of DSS as Viewed by Senior Executives," MIS Quarterly, December 1982.

Alavi, Maryam; and Henderson, John C. "An Evolutionary Strategy for Implementing a Decision Support System," Management Science, November 1981.

Alexander, Tom. "Thinking Machines" (series of two articles), Fortune, May 17, 1982, and June 14, 1982.

Alter, Steven L. "Computer-aided Decision Making in Organizations: A DSS Typology," Massachusetts Institute of Technology, Center for Information Systems Research (CISR) Working Paper 11, May 1976.

______. Decision Support Systems: Current Practice and Continuing Challenges (Reading, Mass.: Addison-Wesley, 1980).

______. "What Do You Need to Know to Develop Your Own DSS?" DSS-82 Transactions, June 1982.

"Artificial Intelligence: The Second Computer Age Begins," Business Week, March 8, 1982.

Bariff, Martin; and Ginzberg, Michael. "MIS and the Behavioral Sciences: Research Patterns and Prescriptions," in Proceedings of the Third International Conference on Information Systems (Ann Arbor, Mich., 1982).

Ben-Bassat, Moshe. "Research into an Intelligent DSS for Military Situation Assessment," DSS-81 Transactions, June 1981.

Bendifallah, S. "Knowledge-based Decision Support Systems: Social Significance," in Proceedings of the Twenty-sixth Annual Meeting of the Society for General Systems Research of the American Association for the Advancement of Science, Vol. 1 (Washington, D.C., 1982).

Benjamin, Robert I. "Information Technology in the 1990s: A Long-Range Planning Scenario," MIS Quarterly, Vol. 6, No. 2, June 1982.

Blanning, Robert W. "A Relational Framework for Model Management in DSS," DSS-82 Transactions, June 1982.

Bonczek, Robert H.; Holsapple, Clyde W.; and Whinston, Andrew B. "Computer-based Support of Organizational Decision Making," Decision Sciences, April 1979a.

_______. "The Integration of Data Base Management and Problem Resolution," Information Systems, Vol. 4, No. 2, 1979b.

_______. "The Evolving Roles of Models in DSS," Decision Sciences, Vol. 11, 1980a.

_______. "Future Directions for Developing DSS," Decision Sciences, Vol. 11, 1980b.

_______. "Generalized DSS Using Predicate Calculus and Network Data Base Management," Operations Research, Vol. 29, No. 2, March-April 1981.

Brightman, Harvey J.; Harris, Sydney C.; and Thompson, William J. "Empirical Study of Computer-based Financial Modeling Systems: Implications for Decision Support Systems," DSS-81 Transactions, June 1981.

Briggs, Warren G. "An Evaluation of DSS Packages," Computerworld, March 1982.

Chung, Chen-Hua. "Implementation Issues in Problem Processing of DSS," in Proceedings of the Sixteenth Annual Hawaii International Conference on System Sciences, June 1983.

De, Prabudda; and Sen, Arun. "Logical Data Base Design in DSS," Journal of Systems Management, Vol. 32, No. 5, May 1981.

DeSanctis, Gerardine. "An Examination of an Expectancy Theory Model of DSS Use," in Proceedings of the Third International Conference on Information Systems (Ann Arbor, Mich., 1982).

Dhar, Vasant; and Daniels, Ronald. "A Process Model of Information Requirements Analysis for Strategic Decision Support," in the American Institute for Decision Sciences, Thirteenth Proceedings, 1981.

Dickson, Gary. "Issues for the Future in DSS" (Report of Discussion Group 1), DSS: Issues and Challenges, Proceedings of the International Institute for Applied Systems Analysis (IIASA), June 1980.

Disclosure Online News, November 1981 (5161 River Road, Bethesda, Md., 20816).

Findler, Nicholas V. "An Expert Subsystem Based on Generalized Production Rules," in Proceedings of the Sixteenth Annual Hawaii International Conference on System Sciences, June 1983.

Fuerst, William; and Cheney, Paul. "Factors Affecting the Perceived Utilization of Computer-based DSS in the Oil Industry," Decision Sciences, Vol. 13, No. 4, 1982.

Ginzberg, Michael J. "DSS Success: Measurement and Facilitation," New York University, Center for Research on Information Systems Working Paper 20, 1981.

Gorry, Andrew; and Scott Morton, Michael S. "A Framework for Management Information Systems," Sloan Management Review, Vol. 13, No. 1, Fall 1971.

Gulden, Gary. "A Framework for Decisions," Computerworld, December 1982.

Gulden, Gary; and Arkush, E. S. "Developing a Strategy Profile for DSS," DSS-82 Transactions, June 1982.

Hackathorn, Richard D. "Issues for the Future in DSS" (Report of Discussion Group 4), in DSS: Issues and Challenges, Proceedings of the IIASA, June 1980.

Hackathorn, Richard D.; and Keen, Peter G. W. "Organizational Strategies for Personal Computing in Decision Support Systems," MIS Quarterly, September 1981.

Hamilton, Scott; Ives, Blake; and Davis, Gordon B. "MIS Doctoral Dissertations: 1973-1980," MIS Quarterly, September 1981.

Huber, George. "Organizational Science Contributions to the Design of DSS," in DSS: Issues and Challenges, Proceedings of the IIASA, June 1980.

_______. "The Design of Group DSS," in Proceedings of the Sixteenth Annual Hawaii International Conference on System Sciences, June 1983.

Ives, Blake. "Graphical User Interfaces for Business Information Systems," MIS Quarterly, Special Issue 1982.

Jacob, J. P.; and Sprague, Ralph H., Jr. "Graphical Problem Solving in DSS," in Proceedings of the Thirteenth Annual Hawaii International Conference on System Sciences, Data Base (USA), Vol. 12, No. 1-2, Fall 1980.

Keen, Peter G. W. "DSS and Managerial Productivity Analysis," Massachusetts Institute of Technology, CISR Working Paper 60, October 1980a.

_______. "DSS: Translating Analytic Technology into Useful Tools," Sloan Management Review, Vol. 21, No. 3, Spring 1980b.

_______. "DSS: Lessons for the 80s," Massachusetts Institute of Technology, CISR Working Paper 70, June 1981a.

_______. "Value Analysis: Justifying DSS," MIS Quarterly, Vol. 5, No. 1, 1981b.

_______. "Adaptive Design for DSS," Data Base, Vol. 12, No. 1-2, Fall 1982.

_______. "A Policy Statement for Managing Microcomputers," Computerworld, May 16, 1983.

Keen, Peter G. W.; and Scott Morton, Michael S. Decision Support Systems: An Organizational Perspective (Reading, Mass.: Addison-Wesley, 1978).

Kingston, Paul. "Generic DSS," Managerial Planning, Vol. 29, No. 5, March 1981.

Larreche, Jean Claude; and Srinivasan, Paul. "Strataport: A DSS for Strategic Planning," Journal of Marketing, Vol. 45, Fall 1981.

Lindgren, Richard. "Justifying a Decision Support System," Data Management, Vol. 19, May 1981.

Lucas, Henry C., Jr. "An Experimental Investigation of the Use of Computer-based Graphics in Decision Making," Management Science, Vol. 27, No. 7, July 1981.

Luconi, Fred; and Scott Morton, Michael S. "Artificial Intelligence: The Next Challenge for Management," Massachusetts Institute of Technology, CISR Draft Working Paper, October 1983.

Manola, Frank. "Database Technology in DSS: An Overview," in DSS: Issues and Challenges, Proceedings of the IIASA, June 1980.

Martin, Merle P. "Determining Information Requirements for DSS," Journal of Systems Management, Vol. 33, No. 12, December 1982.

Methlie, Leif. "Issues for the Future of DSS" (Report of Discussion Group 2), in DSS: Issues and Challenges, Proceedings of the IIASA, June 1980.

Monypenny, Richard. "Person/Role Conflict in the DSS-Corporate Interface," DSS-82 Transactions, June 1982.

Moore, J. H., and Chang, M. G. "Design of DSS," in Proceedings of the Thirteenth Annual Hawaii International Conference on System Sciences, Data Base (USA), Vol. 12, No. 1-2, Fall 1980.

Morecroft, John. "Strategy Support Models," Massachusetts Institute of Technology, Draft Article, July 1982.

Moscowitz, Robert. "DSS/F: Paving the Way for Sophisticated Software," Interface Age, June 1982.

Naisbitt, John. Megatrends (New York: Warner Books, 1982).

Neumann, Seev; and Hadass, Michael. "DSS and Strategic Decisions," California Management Review, Vol. 22, No. 2, Spring 1980.

Paul, Louis. "DSS: An Idea in Search of an Identity," Computerworld, Vol. 16, No. 44, November 1982.

Pitt, Joel. "DSS/F: A Financial-Modeling and Reporting Package," Info World, May 17, 1982.

Rockart, John F. "Chief Executives Define Their Own Data Needs," Harvard Business Review, March-April 1979.

Rockart, John F.; and Scott Morton, Michael S. "Implications of Changes in Information Technology for Corporate Strategy," Massachusetts Institute of Technology, CISR Working Paper 98, January 1983.

Rockart, John F.; and Treacy, Michael. "The CEO Goes On-Line," Harvard Business Review, January-February 1982.

Sagalowicz, Daniel. "Using Personal Data Bases for Decision Support," in DSS: Issues and Challenges, Proceedings of the IIASA, June 1980.

Sage, A. P., and Lagomasino, A. "Knowledge Representation and Interpretation in Decision Support Systems," in the Proceedings of the 1982 IEEE International Conference on Cybernetics and Society (New York: Institute of Electrical and Electronics Engineers, 1982).

Sanders, G. Larry. "A DSS for Identifying Critical Success Factors," in the American Institute for Decision Sciences, Thirteenth Proceedings, 1981.

Schein, Edgar. Process Consultation: Its Role in Organization Development (Reading, Mass.: Addison-Wesley, 1969).

Scher, James M. "Distributed DSS for Management and Organizations," DSS-81 Transactions, June 1981.

Seils, Harold L. "Do DSS Really Support?" Computerworld, Vol. 16, No. 26, June 1982.

Sheinin, Roman L. "The Structure of Decision Support Systems," in DSS: Issues and Challenges, Proceedings of the IIASA, June 1980.

Shrivastava, P. "DSS for Strategic Ill-structured Problems," Proceedings of the Third International Conference on Information Systems (Ann Arbor, Mich., 1982).

Sprague, Ralph H., Jr. "A Framework for Research on DSS," in Ralph H. Sprague, Jr., and Goran Fick, eds., Decision Support Systems: Issues and Challenges (Elmsford, N.Y.: Pergamon Press, 1980a).

_______. "A Framework for the Development of a DSS," MIS Quarterly, Vol. 4, No. 4, December 1980b.

_______. "DSS: A Tutorial," DSS-81 Transactions, June 1981.

Sprague, Ralph H., Jr.; and Carlson, Eric. Building Effective Decision Support Systems (Englewood Cliffs, N.J.: Prentice-Hall, 1982).

Sprague, Ralph H., Jr.; and Panko, Raymond. "Criteria for a DSS Generator," in the American Institute for Decision Sciences, Thirteenth Proceedings, 1981.

Studer, R. "An Adaptable User Interface for DSS," in Proceedings of the Sixteenth Annual Hawaii International Conference on System Sciences, June 1983.

Suyderhoud, Jack P. "The Role of Risk Assessment in the DSS Evaluation Process," in Proceedings of the Sixteenth Annual Hawaii International Conference on System Sciences, June 1983.

Thierauf, Robert. DSS for Effective Planning and Control: A Case Study Approach. (Englewood Cliffs, N.J.: Prentice-Hall, 1982).

Treacy, Michael. "Where DSS Technology Is Going," from a discussion, April 1983.

Tucker, J. H. "Implementation of Decision Support Systems," in Proceedings of the 1981 IEEE International Conference on Cybernetics and Society (New York: Institute of Electrical and Electronic Engineers, 1981).

Vierck, _____. "DSS: An MIS Manager's Perspective," DSS-81 Transactions, June 1981.

Wagner, G. R. "Issues for the Future in DSS" (Report of Discussion Group 3), in DSS: Issues and Challenges, Proceedings of the IIASA, June 1980.

_______. "Beyond Theory Z with DSS," DSS-81 Transactions, June 1981a.

_______. "Computerized Mind Support for Executive Problems," Managerial Planning, Vol. 30, No. 2, October 1981b.

_______. "DSS: The Real Substance," Interfaces, Vol. 11, No. 2, 1981c.

_______. "DSS: Dealing with Executive Assumptions in the Office of the Future," Managerial Planning, Vol. 30, No. 5, March-April 1982.

Wang, Michael S. Y. "Bridging the Gap between Modeling and Data Handling in a DSS Generator," in American Institute for Decision Sciences, Thirteenth Proceedings, 1981.

Wang, Michael S. Y., and Yu, Keh-Chiang. "A Hierarchical View of Decision Support Software," in Proceedings of the Sixteenth Annual Hawaii International Conference on System Sciences, June 1983.

Watkins, Paul R. "Perceived Information Structure: Implications for Decision Support Design," Decision Sciences, Vol. 13, 1982.

Welsch, Gemma. "Successful Implementation of DSS: The Role of the Information Transfer Specialist," in the American Institute for Decision Sciences, Thirteenth Proceedings, 1981.

DISCUSSION: SCOTT MORTON PAPER

In the discussion of Michael Scott Morton's paper, it rapidly became clear that the dimension of most interest was the types of management support systems (MSS). Just what are the subcategories of MSS? Does it make a difference what they are? What is the most useful nomenclature for the various types? The discussion opened on this topic and returned to it time and time again.

There was general agreement on the decision support system subcategory. These are systems that "focus on a decision," which put "a broad range of computer software at the user's disposal." Data support systems, a category new to the community, received almost no discussion. The discussion centered primarily on executive support systems.

It was clear that the term executive support caused some misgivings. "I'm concerned about the word executive by itself, as one which is very value laden," one researcher said. Another, noting that executive support connoted, for him, systems focusing on analytical capabilities, felt that the executive support category "runs into trouble when you go ahead and talk about electronic message systems." Others felt that to concentrate on executive support would be to "squint down the wrong end of a telescope." They pointed out that the greatest growth in business populations has been in the professional groups, and that these are the people on whom research efforts should be focused. "Senior management, whether we like it or not, often does have all kinds of support. Let's work on supporting professionals, engineers, accountants, systems analysts."

Most participants, however, clearly believed that there was at least one category of MSS in addition to decision support systems. They noted that the "class of decisions that executives and some others make are not really amenable to most of the activities seen in decision support systems, and so we need a new categorization scheme." Some termed this area organizational support. One participant felt that the focus should be on managerial personnel as "boundary spanners"--a role in which most executives fit.

Whether we are dealing with an "executive," a "monitoring and planning role," or a "boundary spanner," it does appear that there is an important new category of personnel who need support different from traditional "decision support." "Decision support systems two, three, four years ago were totally unstructured, just like executive support systems are today. Now we know how to do a few things with decision support systems. And now there is another class of undefined problem [and resulting system] that we have to have help with," said one participant.

This new categorization also seems important from a research perspective. As one researcher noted, "The ways you build them, test them, and evaluate them are different for the two classes." Another pointed out that the concept of decision support provided focus for a great deal of research effort. It resulted in the field beginning "to do a lot of research on decision making, using behavioral decision theory, integrating these concepts into our notions of design, integrating the basic world of psychologists and social scientists in all aspects of the work." He felt that as we move into this new type of support the basic theories and models used and the type of research performed would change significantly. "Some really different theoretical bases to build our research on and to look at issues and design methodology" might be developed.

Although there would undoubtedly have been no general agreement on a taxonomy of MSS, two participants did attempt it. One suggested the field be divided by a traditional, well-understood classification: "professional support systems, clerical support systems, and executive support systems." Another participant divided the systems along the spectrum of "user friendliness." "The first systems we built were for clerks . . . an internal population whom you could beat to use them. And basically, you did. They were enormously unfriendly, but . . . it really didn't matter. . . . The next set of systems we built was for a professional population, who were occasional users. . . . These systems had to be somewhat friendlier, . . . and response time had to be somewhat better, because the [users] might complain to somebody upstairs or they might use an outside time-sharing service, but again they were an internal population. The systems that are being built today, that I see in the industrial world . . . are for customers. And they require a totally different type of commitment. You need different response times; you need different kinds of reliability." It was unclear where this speaker put executive support, but she seemed to consider it part of the final category.

Although there was heavy emphasis on attempting to understand the types of MSS, the discussion often turned to "research directions." Much time was spent noting that there is considerable MSS research in the real world. Some felt that the universities were basically in a "lag" position. Academics are developing a significant number of methods, but relatively few researchers are testing others' methodologies. This was explained by one researcher, who noted that "this particular world, it seems to me, is moving very fast. And by the time you do your careful scientific study and get it published, the problem is no longer relevant."

The discussion turned to the need to monitor and better understand the many experiments going on in the real world. There was a general feeling that not enough of this is being done. One researcher noted that "I'm as guilty as anybody else.

I should be doing more empirical research, really monitoring what's happening, and tracking it."

But there was far from total clarity on the proper role of academics in the field. One industrial participant suggested quite explicitly that academics should be making useful generalizations from what is going on in industry. "I think that in American industry today our companies present one of the largest research and development playpens in the world for information technologies. We're trying to solve some problems, and we don't have the time or the inclination to go back and generalize and develop the proof. . . . A tremendous amount of generalization" is needed to draw the appropriate wisdom and understanding from what is going on and provide guidance for both future researchers and industry itself.

Much time was spent attempting to address all the "white space" in the four matrices of Scott Morton's literature review. There appeared to be general agreement that current work was disproportionately weighted in favor of constructing methodologies and declaring "truths." This was accompanied by a distinct lack of empirical testing. Comments were also made on the quality and usefulness of much of what is written. One participant felt that many researchers tend to "rush into print" without careful substantiation of their "general truths."

Finally, the need for additional behavioral input into MSS research was strongly noted. But the difficulty of obtaining this was also recognized. Participants felt that the technical world and the behavioral world within academia are sharply divided. As one researcher remarked, "I've been firmly rooted in both camps and it's an impossible task. It's like being on the dock and the boat. The dock is the behavioral psychology literature in which we have a well-developed tradition. The boat, which is going farther and farther away, is the fast-moving technology, and you're split. Frankly, I've had to jump in the boat." The people who stayed on the dock, he noted, "were very socio, but not very techy."

Others, however, wondered aloud whether "one can have a sensible management information systems department without having a significant percentage of researchers there with a behavioral background." Even recognizing that the dialogue and friction that come from putting the two worlds together is great, this speaker felt a strong need for the combination. One industry manager stated that this need was being realized in the corporate world also. Both agreed that, as we have moved from paperwork processing systems to support systems, the field has come to require different types of research.

A similar "two-culture" problem exists between data processing and end users. There is a need for those two worlds to come together, and this area offers untold opportunities for university-based research.

The session was summed up by those who noted that the MSS area does not have an "established theory." Rather, as one participant said, the field is in a "pretheoretical" state. Therefore, we need to develop theory. But significant empirical work is necessary to provide the basis for useful theory.

AN ANALYSIS OF RESEARCH METHODOLOGIES

Izak Benbasat

The objective of this paper is to illustrate alternative strategies and methodologies for conducting empirical research in management support systems (MSS). Although some of the pioneering studies in management (including decision and executive) support systems were conducted in the early 1970s (for instance, Scott Morton, 1971), only within the last five years has this field received increased attention. Recent works by Keen and Scott Morton (1978), Sprague and Carlson (1982), and Bennett (1983) have discussed the historical evolution of the field and presented the rationale for developing MSS.

I will use the following working definition of an MSS adapted from these authors:

> A conversational, interactive computer-based system used by managers as an aid to decision making in semistructured decision tasks.[1] The system supports rather than replaces decision makers. It focuses on the effectiveness of decision making by extending the range and capability of managers' decision processes. It applies to decision tasks that have sufficient structure to allow computer support but for which human judgment is essential.

I would like to thank Tony Bailette, Marty Bariff, Mike Ginzberg, Bob Goldstein, Jack Rockart, and Bob Zmud for their helpful comments on the various drafts of this manuscript.

[1] Stabell (1979) defined structure as follows: "A task is unstructured when (1) the objectives are ambiguous and nonoperational, or objectives are relatively operational but numerous and conflicting, (2) it is difficult to determine the cause (ex post) or changes in outcomes and to predict (ex ante) the effects on outcomes of actions taken, (3) it is uncertain what actions might affect outcomes" (pp. 1-2).

In its simplest terms the MSS can be described as the decision maker (manager) with a problem to solve, a computer and analytical tools, and the interface between the manager and the computer. This paper excludes research that focuses primarily on computer science methods for building hardware and software or on operations research methods for developing analytical tools. Because the selection of research methods depends on the questions being investigated, I have identified three major research areas on the basis of my definition of an MSS and the topics that have been emphasized to date. The first research area is the implementation of MSS--issues concerning their use and acceptance. The manager's interface with the hardware, software, and analytical tools that make up the support system is the second area of research discussed. The third area deals with describing and understanding the decision activities a system will support.

This paper expands on the three major research areas identified; outlines and compares strategies for conducting research; and finally provides examples of empirical studies in each of the three research areas, discusses the research strategies and methodologies used, and offers some suggestions on their comparative advantages for investigating specific issues in MSS.

Major Research Issues

Implementation

Various definitions of implementation have appeared in the management information systems (MIS), operations research, and decision support systems literature. Schultz and Slevin (1975) described implementation from a number of viewpoints, including selling the product, obtaining user involvement, developing mutual understanding between the designer and the manager, and focusing on the organizational change processes necessary for model or system acceptance. Alter (1980) defined implementation as the way the system was conceived, developed, and installed. According to Churchman (1975), the implementation process takes place when the managers of the organization are influenced by the experts' (designers') recommendations and put those recommendations into action. The process also includes retrospective evaluation.

The key distinction between the implementation of MSS and the traditional data processing "system development life cycle" is the relatively unstructured nature of the decision tasks being supported. This makes it difficult to determine the specifications of the "final" MSS product. Various means--such as prototyping, the middle-out approach, and the evolutionary approach--have been proposed to manage this iterative design process. Evaluation of these is a researchable area. A number of studies have examined the fit between decision maker characteristics and the type of support system used. Another area of research interest has been managing a successful implementation process.

The Manager-Computer Interface

According to Carlson (1983),

> DSS [decision support systems] users are discretionary users. Their use may be frequent or infrequent, routine or ad hoc, interactive or batch mode, "hands-on" or via an assistant. Whatever the form of use, there is an interface between the user and the DSS. Even if a DSS provides extremely powerful functions, it may not be used if the interface is unacceptable. Even when a decision maker uses a DSS via an assistant, the interface must provide a meaningful framework within which information is presented and inputs are given (p. 65).

This quotation identifies the following research question: Under what conditions is the direct or indirect (intermediary-assisted) use of the MSS most appropriate?

Bennett (1983) distinguished the presentation language, through which the system communicates with the user, from the action language, through which the user instructs the system. The presentation language includes alternatives such as charts, graphics, tabular formats, and colors, and the types of helps, prompts, and error messages the computer system gives the user. Alternatives for the action language include the type of language (command versus natural languages, menu interfaces, linear versus two-dimensional positional languages) and data entry options such as keyboard, light pen, and audio input. The comparative benefits of these alternatives and the contexts in which they are appropriate are researchable issues.

Decision Processes

Because the MSS supports and extends the manager's decision-making capabilities, a description of current decision processes is required before a system can be designed. According to Stabell (1983):

> The diagnosis of current decision making and the specification of changes in the decision processes are the activities that provide the key inputs to the design of the decision support system. Diagnosis is the identification of problems in current decision behavior; it involves determining how decisions are currently made, specifying how decisions should be made, and understanding why decisions are not made as they should be. Specification of changes in the decision processes involves choosing what specific improvements in decision behavior are to be achieved and thus

> defining the objectives of a computer-based decision support system (p. 233).

Libby (1981), a researcher in accounting and human information processing, argued along the same lines, stating,

> Some would argue that there is no need to understand how information is being used, but only the optimal way different sets of information can be processed and the best combination of information and processing methods. However, before one can decide that a change is necessary, a baseline is needed to measure the incremental benefits of the change. This calls for an understanding of how decisions are currently being made and a measure of current decision performance. Perhaps more important is that knowledge of how decisions are being made highlights flaws and inconsistencies in the process, which are clues to specific methods of improving decisions (pp. 3-4).

The methodologies for describing decision activities could serve two purposes:

1. "Information requirements analysis" is a tool by which the designer at the predesign stage can understand how decisions are presently made, what information sources are available to the manager, and what type of models the manager uses.

2. Research in human information processing investigates the strengths and weaknesses in human decision making: the heuristics used, the observed biases in judgment, and the types of decision aids available to the decision maker.

Empirical Research Strategies

Research on MSS can be carried out in a wide range of settings and by a variety of strategies. These strategies, and their comparative strengths and weaknesses, have been examined in depth in the behavioral science literature.[2] Van Horn (1973) and Hamilton and Ives (1982) discussed their use in information systems research. This section presents brief background on these strategies.

---

[2]See Runkel and McGrath (1972) and Stone (1978) for a general discussion of research strategies. See Swieringa and Weick (1982) for a discussion of laboratory experiments.

Studies in Natural Behavior Settings

Case studies, field studies, and field experiments study the phenomenon of interest in the setting where it occurs naturally. These three strategies differ in their degrees of experimental design and experimental controls.

Case studies examine a single organization, group, or person in detail. Data are usually collected through multiple means, such as interviews, observations, and documentary materials. Case studies do not involve experimental designs or controls. Investigators usually intend to generate hypotheses rather than test them.

Field studies involve experimental design but not experimental controls. The independent variables are not manipulated by the investigators; their values are generally obtained through questionnaires or interviews. Investigators attempt to relate the dependent variable or variables to various explanatory (independent) variables by correlational or cross-sectional analyses. However, the lack of control over the independent variables and the fact that all variables that might influence the dependent variables cannot be measured make causal inferences from field studies highly tenuous. The purpose of a field study could be to test hypotheses, describe the workings of a system, or develop hypotheses.

In field experiments investigators manipulate one or more independent variables of interest and try to control other variables that might confound the experimental findings. Investigators often select the persons, groups, or organizations to receive the experimental treatments and either assign the subjects to the treatments randomly or match the treatment groups on some key variables. Field experiments, therefore, are more likely to disrupt the naturalness of the phenomenon being examined than are case and field studies. The focus in field experiments is on testing hypotheses.

Studies in Contrived and Created Settings

Laboratory experiments take place in settings constructed by researchers for given research studies; the settings have no prior existence independent of the investigators' purposes. In laboratory experiments investigators assign subjects to control and treatment groups. The investigators manipulate one or more independent variables to measure their effect on the dependent variables. Virtually all other independent variables that might confound the results are tightly controlled. The independent and dependent variables are defined precisely. Laboratory experiments have the advantage of replicability. Their major focus is hypothesis testing.

One way to categorize laboratory experiments is to distinguish between person-computer experiments (experimental simulators) and judgment tasks. In a person-computer experiment the managers or subjects model themselves and a computer program (such as a business game) is used to model the rest of the organization and its environment (Van Horn, 1973). The judgment task strategy captures a subject's information utilization and decision-making approaches through techniques such as protocol analysis or regression formulations. Figuratively, in person-computer experiments the subjects come to the laboratory, whereas in judgment task strategies the investigators take the laboratory to the subjects. Subjects perform their normal tasks but are observed by investigators, who use a structured data collection approach (Swieringa and Weick, 1982).

Setting-Independent Studies

In sample surveys investigators elicit the opinions, attitudes, or beliefs of a certain group (for example, managers) regarding some issue of interest. The data are collected through interviews and/or questionnaires. Respondents are contacted in their offices or homes or through the mail. In this strategy the behaviors analyzed are assumed not to be influenced by the setting in which they are elicited; the subject group is the important factor. There is no experimental manipulation of the independent variables, and the extraneous variables are controlled statistically. The focus could be exploration of variables or hypothesis testing.

Discussion

How does a researcher decide which strategy is most appropriate for investigating MSS? There are three possible ways to answer this question; all assume that there is no best overall strategy.

The first approach is to assess research methodologies independently, without reference to the subject area in question (such as implementation research). The general advantages and disadvantages of the different research strategies are outlined in Table 1. As Stone stated (1978), selection of a particular strategy is mainly a question of trade-offs:

> It should also be noted that no single strategy has "favorable" ratings on all dimensions. The implication of this latter point is that in deciding to use one research strategy as opposed to others, the researcher always makes trade-offs: the selection of a strategy that maximizes naturalness of the research setting entails a loss of control over independent and confounding variables; the selection of a strategy that allows for rigorous control over confounding variables entails a concomitant loss in the generality of a study's findings, etc. The choice of one strategy as opposed to another at any given stage in the study of some phenomenon (formulation of hypotheses, testing of hypotheses, establishing the external validity of a detected relationship, etc.) should be guided by the purpose of the

research, [and/or] the resources available to the research (p. 115).

Table 1. *Comparison of Empirical Research Strategies*

Rated Dimension	*Case Study*	*Field Study*	*Field Experiment*	*Laboratory Experiment*	*Sample Survey*
COST:					
Initial "Setup"	L-H	M-H	M-H	M	H
Marginal Cost per Subject	L-H	M	M	L	L-M
VARIABLES:					
Strength of Independent Variables	H	H	M	L	H
Range of Variables	L-H	H	M	L	H
Potential for Manipulating Independent Variables	N	N	M	H	N
CONTROL:					
Potential for Testing Causal Hypotheses	N	L	M	H	L
Potential for Study to Change Researcher	H	M	M	L	L
Potential for Controlling Confounding Variables	N	L	L-M	H	L
SETTING:					
Naturalness of Setting	H	H	H	L	H
Degree to Which Behavior Is Setting Dependent	H	H	H	H	L
GENERALIZABILITY:					
Applicability of Study's Results to Different Populations	N	L	L	L-H	H

N: None L: Low M: Moderate H: High

Source: Adapted from Stone (1978, p. 116).

The second approach is to study each area in MSS with a number of research strategies to compensate for the limitations of each. I will discuss the use of multiple strategies where appropriate.

The third recommendation is to select a strategy on the basis of the purpose of the research and the nature of the research area. For example, action research approaches are more appropriate if the researcher seeks to understand the dynamics of change during implementation of a new system.[3] For each research area, this paper discusses why some strategies are more suitable for particular issues.

Application of Methodologies to Research Areas

Implementation

There are two major approaches to the study of implementation. One attempts to identify and measure the influence of the factors, such as top management support or user participation in design, that are instrumental in achieving success or causing failure. This is identified as factors study. The second approach views implementation as a process of organizational change. It emphasizes studying the dynamics of implementation, that is, understanding the behavior of the different parties in the implementation process. This approach is called change process research (Schultz and Henry, 1981). Case studies, field studies, laboratory experiments, and sample surveys have been used in each of these approaches. The empirical studies on implementation that are discussed or referenced in this section can be arranged in the matrix shown in Table 2.

Table 2. *Implementation Studies Research Strategies*

RESEARCH EMPHASIS		*Case Studies*	*Field Studies*	*Sample Surveys*	*Laboratory Experiments*
	Factors Approach	Alter (1979)	Lucas (1978) Chowdhury (1983)	Chowdhury (1983)	Huysmans (1970) Lusk (1973) Benbasat and Dexter (1979) Dos Santos (1982)
	Change Process	Gerrity (1971) [A] Hurst et al. (1983) [A] Keen and Gambino (1983) [A]	Ginzberg (1979) [M] Robey and Farrow (1982) [M]		Botkin (1974) [P] Alavi and Henderson (1981) [M] King and Rodriguez (1981) [M]

A: Action Research M: Guided by Change Models P: Protocol Analysis

[3] For a detailed treatment of the action research approach, see Susman and Evered (1978).

These studies can be categorized in more detail by the methods they use--action research, protocol analysis, or models of the change process from organizational behavior literature (such as the Lewin-Schein model [Lewin, 1952; Schein, 1961]).

Case Studies (Factors Approach). A good example of the use of the case study (and the factors study) approach to implementation research is the work by Alter (1979) concerning implementation risk analysis. His conclusions were based on structured histories of 56 decision support systems. Interviews were conducted to investigate what situational factors favored or opposed successful implementation; what actions were taken in response to these factors; and what determined whether these actions were successful.

The interview data were analyzed through a relatively ad hoc combination of quantitative and qualitative arguments, described in Alter (1975), to determine the impact of different risk factors, the relationships between risk factors and implementation strategies, and the problems encountered in applying various strategies.[4]

Field Studies (Factors Approach). Chowdhury (1983) extended Alter's work on implementation risk analysis by studying 21 user-developed decision support systems. The study sample consisted of practicing managers and professionals enrolled in an executive M.B.A. program. As part of a course requirement, they were asked to develop, using the Interactive Financial Planning System (IFPS) modeling language, an MSS that had some relevance to their organizations. Questionnaires were administered after system completion to determine the extent to

---

[4] Alter (1979) identified the following implementation risk factors: (1) Nonexistent or unwilling users, (2) Multiple users or implementors, (3) Turnover among all parties, (4) Inability to specify purpose or usage, (5) Inability to cushion impact on others, (6) Loss or lack of support, (7) Lack of experience, (8) Technical or cost effectiveness problems.

He suggested the following implementation strategies: (1) Divide the project into manageable pieces (use prototypes, use an evolutionary approach, develop a series of tools); (2) Keep the solution simple (be simple, hide complexity, avoid change); (3) Develop a satisfactory support base (obtain user participation, obtain user commitment, obtain management support, sell the system); (4) Meet user needs and institutionalize the system (provide training programs, provide ongoing assistance, insist on mandatory use, permit voluntary use, rely on diffusion and exposure, tailor systems to people's capabilities).

which problems associated with the factors Alter had identified influenced system development and to assess the applicability of the various strategies Alter had suggested to systems developed by end users.[5]

Chowdhury's study has the characteristics of a field study. It has a clearly defined experimental design; it is based on a model developed by another research study; it tests a number of hypotheses, such as the relationship between the use of implementation strategies and success, using analysis of variance tests. It is, of course, not a field study in the precise meaning of the term because the systems were not developed in a natural organizational setting. However, the methodology Chowdhury described could be used to replicate the study in the field.

Sample Surveys (Factors Approach). A second set of questions analyzed in Chowdhury's (1983) study concern the usage and acceptance of computer-based decision systems in organizations. These issues were analyzed under three scenarios: the present state, the desired state, and a third state, which assumes that an MSS is available for organizational use. The influence of an MSS in bridging the gap between the present and desired states was examined from the perspective of managers who had developed such a system.[6]

This part of Chowdhury's study is an example of a sample survey approach. The investigator attempts to elicit the opinions of managers who have developed their own support systems to determine how such systems could enhance the use of computer-based systems by management.

Laboratory Experiments (Factors Approach). Huysmans (1970) tested the hypothesis that implementation success can be enhanced by building a model that better matches the manager's

---

[5] Chowdhury (1983) reported that significant implementation problems were associated with the difficulties in using the computer terminal and using the IFPS modeling language. "Difficulty of model validation" emerged as an additional implementation risk factor in the manager-developed decision support systems. All implementation strategies except "use prototypes" and "develop a series of modelling tools" were employed in the study environment. However, no significant relationships were observed between levels of project success and the degrees to which these strategies were used.

[6] The results indicated that there are less than enthusiastic acceptance of computer-based systems in the respondents' organizations and significant gaps between the present and desired (should be) states. They also indicated that MSS would be instrumental in closing these gaps.

decision-making style. He conducted a laboratory experiment to measure the influence of a manager's cognitive style (analytic versus heuristic) on the acceptance of the management scientist's recommendations. The recommendations were generated by the "explicit understanding" or "general understanding" methods. The major difference was the inclusion of formulas to support the recommendations (a quantitative analysis approach) in the explicit understanding version. Huysmans found that heuristic subjects had a lower degree of acceptance when presented with recommendations generated by the explicit understanding method.

Lusk (1973) and Benbasat and Dexter (1979) conducted similar experiments. Their results show that a match between the style of the decision maker and the method used to present information leads to better implementation success. Dos Santos (1982) evaluated the influence of structured model use on the ability to find problems, prioritize them, and discover alternative courses of action. One group of subjects were not required to structure the use of the model and could vary its three controllable variables in any sequence they chose. The other subjects were asked to use the model by first manipulating one controllable variable at a time. Only after they had varied each variable could they manipulate pairs of variables, and finally all the variables, in a single run of the model. Results indicated that the "structured" treatment led to a superior problem-solving process.

These laboratory studies could be characterized as factors approaches to implementation research. The factors (independent variables) are the characteristics of the decision maker and the methods used to generate or present information. The dependent variables are acceptance of the outcomes, satisfaction with the system, and quality of decisions generated using the system.

Case Studies (Change Process Approach). Case studies can be used to understand the process of organizational change and capture the dynamics of the situation during implementation. Gibson (1975) provided an overview of this approach based on his experiences in implementing a planning model for a bank:

> My role and that of a research colleague working with me in these implementation projects might be described as participant observation or action research. As such our involvement had two purposes. On the one hand, we sought to observe, record, and interpret behavior and events longitudinally on a case-by-case, exploratory basis. Our aim here was to develop concepts and relationships and to test working hypotheses toward the building of a theory that would be closely grounded in the data and that would yield immediately useful findings for practitioners concerned with the implementation of models. On the other hand, we were committed to assisting and facilitating the implementations. In this respect we worked closely with and between the

> model builders and the users and undertook to exert influence on the parties as it seemed appropriate (p. 53).

Similar approaches to research on implementation are described by Gerrity (1971), Hurst et al. (1983), and Keen and Gambino (1983). Gibson's (1975) experience with the longitudinal, action-research approach revealed both advantages and problems with this methodology. A major disadvantage is the difficulty of replicating the results. The problem of generalizing findings was also raised by Keen and Gambino (1983). Gibson suggested using multiple case studies and tailoring the results from one sample to the working hypotheses and instruments for the next to aid theory building and testing. Another problem is the interference of researcher action with researcher observations. Gibson believes that the researcher's involvement, necessitated by unforeseen delays in model completion, clearly interfered with the longitudinal hypothesis-testing aspects of the research.

On the positive side, this methodology is helpful for observing processes over time. It reveals how unexpected events outside the scope of the implementation project and the interaction of the parties involved in it affect the processes. In summary,

> A longitudinal methodology which puts the implementation researcher in close touch with the users and builders and their total set of concerns is more appropriate for documenting these events and their effects on implementation. It is only when we have faced the fact that these events threaten to make messy our hoped-for clean models of the implementation process, and documented the events and their impacts, that we can build more valid models and provide more useful help to managers and OR/MS [operations research/management science] practitioners (Gibson, 1975, p. 72).

<u>Field Studies (Change Process Approach)</u>. Ginzberg (1979) utilized the Kolb-Frohman (1970) model of the consulting process to study implementation as a process of organizational change. This model contains seven stages. The scouting, entry, and diagnosis stages are concerned with preparing the client system for change. The planning and action stages involve the change itself. The evaluation and termination stages relate to institutionalizing the change within the organization. Ginzberg hypothesized that success in implementation would be positively correlated with the degree of resolution of the issues presented at the various stages of implementation. For example, an issue at the entry stage is to convince people in the organization that the project is necessary. Data collected from 29 projects in 11 organizations supported the hypothesis; users in successful

projects reported a significantly better resolution of the issues at each of the seven stages.[7]

Laboratory Experiments (Change Process Approach). Botkin (1974) studied the learning process of subjects facing a novel situation. One of his major research goals was to examine whether an "intuitive computer system" would improve the performance of subjects exhibiting an intuitive cognitive style. The intuitive computer system allowed the subjects to impose their own processes and not be constrained by a predetermined model of response.

Data were captured by tape-recorded protocols of the verbalized thoughts each subject was asked to contribute during the learning process. Subject inputs to the computer were also captured in a file. Botkin found that intuitive users made effective use of certain basic principles embodied in the intuitive system. For example, they exhibited an unordered and unpredictable search path, marked by radical jumps from levels of generality to levels of narrow detail. Botkin concluded that an intuitive computer system suits the adaptive needs of intuitive subjects, and that programs lacking such elements would be less usable by intuitive managers.

Alavi and Henderson (1981) investigated the influence on system use of two alternative strategies for implementing decision support systems--traditional and evolutionary. The major dependent variable of their study was utilization of the linear decision rule model as an aid for production scheduling decisions in a simulated factory environment.

The two implementation strategies used differed in the way the model was introduced to the subjects. In the traditional strategy the model was portrayed as providing a valuable tool that could be theoretically shown to help them solve their problems. The evolutionary strategy attempted to create a "felt need" for the decision aid by comparing the normative linear decision rule model with the descriptive model of a subject's decision-making behavior. Felt need is an important component of

---

[7] Ginzberg's (1979) field study also measured the perspectives of the different participants involved and the influence of the organizational variables on the change process. Users and designers characterized both the process and outcome of a number of projects differently. The organizational complexity of the system developed was also identified as a potentially important contingency in implementation.

the unfreezing stage, which according to the Lewin-Schein model is a critical element in the change process.[8]

The subjects were asked to make a series of decisions after which a linear regression approach was used to model each one's information utilization behavior. Comparisons of the terms and coefficients of the regression (descriptive) and linear decision rule (normative) models made the subjects aware of the cost implications of their decision behavior, their decision biases, and their inconsistencies in decision making. Subsequently, in the experimental session the subjects were told that use of the linear decision rule decision aid was optional. Data analysis indicated that usage of the model was highest when it had been implemented in an evolutionary fashion.

This study is an interesting application of the change process approach to researching implementation in the laboratory. In addition, it employs a judgment task approach through the use of linear regression modeling to capture the information utilization behavior of the subjects.

Discussion. In this section implementation studies were categorized by their focus (factors or change process studies) and the type of research strategies and methodologies used. Schultz and Slevin (1979) and Schultz and Henry (1981) classified implementation studies into not entirely exclusive categories: philosophical papers, cases, factor studies, model building, change process research, cognitive style studies, behavioral research, and institutional analysis. They stated,

> These schools clearly overlap, and most researchers are members of more than one camp. The key point is that the field of implementation research is changing over time. The implementation problem is changing and the methodologies used to study it are changing also.
>
> For all these schools, the general trends are toward such ideas as change, innovation, process, decision making, organizational effectiveness, situational generalization and intervening variables as parties in the implementation process (p. 10).

I believe that the implementation studies to date can be characterized as follows:

1. Case studies, including factors and change process (action research) approaches

---

[8] See Ginzberg (1979) for a discussion of the use of this model in implementation research.

2. Field studies, including factors and change process (model testing) approaches
3. Laboratory experiments, including factors and change process (model testing and protocol analysis) approaches

One recommendation on selection of research strategies and methodologies mentioned previously is to use a number of research strategies is to compensate for the limitations of each. Gibson (1975) suggested using multiple case studies and tailoring the results of one sample to the working hypotheses and instruments for the next. A good example of this approach is the field study by Chowdhury (1983), which tested the influence of the implementation risk factors and strategies suggested by Alter's (1975) case study on the success of manager-developed support systems. Both the Ginzberg (1979) field study and the Alavi and Henderson (1981) laboratory study utilized models discussed in the organizational behavior literature (Kolb-Frohman, Lewin-Schein) to describe implementation as a change process and to explain the reasons for successful implementation. The importance of creating a perceived need in the user was suggested by Hurst et al. (1983) on the basis of case studies and by Alavi and Henderson (1981) on the basis of a laboratory study. The role of user participation in the system design process was investigated by Alter (1978) using case studies, by Robey and Farrow (1982) in a field study, and by King and Rodriguez (1981) in the laboratory. The mostly corroborating evidence in these studies is an encouragement for the use of multiple approaches to study implementation.

The second suggestion for choosing a research approach is to examine the characteristics of the problem being researched. Some authors believe that the factors approach has not yielded any useful suggestions because

> implementation is a process. This cannot be stressed too much. One reason the factor studies have not found any general factors that affect implementation is almost certainly because the dynamics of the process swamp particular structural aspects of the situation. For example, it may well be that top management support is a critical facilitator in implementation because it provides a power base, credibility, and momentum for action. However, the behavior of the parties in the implementation can either erode or build on this support. What determines the quality of the outcome is the designer's ability to identify the key constraints in the situation, to then match the formal technology to those constraints, and to work with the people to whom they apply. This is a complex process and very few rules can confidently be applied (Keen and Scott Morton, 1978, p. 199).

If a researcher adheres to the process view of implementation or wants to investigate the dynamics of the process, then action research/participant observation approaches are appropriate (see Gibson, 1975). Another approach is to adopt a model of organizational change as a guide to study implementation either in the field (Ginzberg, 1979) or the laboratory (Alavi and Henderson, 1981).

I favor the second approach. Explanatory models, either adopted or built by conducting a series of field studies (Lucas, 1978), provide an understanding of how to increase the likelihood of successful implementation through the design process. The case/action research approaches, which have been employed in the pioneering studies of MSS by the academics who to a large extent have defined this field, have been useful vehicles for generating insights. However, as Gibson (1975) pointed out, it has not been possible to test models of implementation in the case studies he has conducted because of a number of unforeseen events. Therefore, the next logical step is to test the hypotheses generated from these case studies and the models adopted from other disciplines in the field or in the laboratory.

Issues suggested by Ginzberg (1979, p. 86) and Schultz and Slevin (1975, pp. 16-17) to characterize implementation studies could also be used to choose a research approach. If the focus is on the whole organization, the phases of the project's life over time are being considered, and the perspectives of the multiple participants are of interest, then case studies, field studies, and sample surveys have a comparative advantage over laboratory studies. Laboratory studies have been criticized for focusing on a narrow aspect of the implementation problem, such as model-user compatibility in terms of psychological characteristics (cognitive styles),[9] and for examining only a short time slice of an evolutionary process. However, even with a narrow focus, laboratory studies could provide valuable insights, because the proliferation of personal computers and distributed systems will allow more support systems to be built for individual managers and for only one user's area of responsibility.

The last suggestion for a research method is joint use of the factors and change process approaches. For example, Ginzberg (1979) used the change process models and organizational contingency factors to determine their influence on success. Robey and Farrow (1982) measured user participation, user

---

[9] Huber (1983) argued that the study of cognitive styles as a factor in decision support systems design is unlikely to reveal any new insights for building more effective systems. Designers of decision support systems would find this article and Robey's (1983) reply to it of interest.

influence on design, amount of conflict generated, and the degree of conflict resolution (a success measure) in each phase of the development life cycle (initiation, design, implementation) to explore the relationships of these four factors at different development phases and across phases. I believe that combining the two approaches alleviates some of the problems associated with use of the factors approach alone to study implementation.

The Manager-Computer Interface

Earlier I discussed the study of the manager-computer interface in terms of the role of intermediaries and the action language and presentation language alternatives. It is also useful to distinguish between interface characteristics that make the system simple to use and those that augment the manager's decision-making capabilities.

Stabell (1983), following Meador and Ness (1974), offered a more detailed interpretation of the interface: passive and active understanding of the system. Passive understanding relates to the mechanics of system use--operation of the terminal, input and output procedures, the syntax of the dialogue, and so on. Active understanding refers to utilizing the capabilities of the system as a decision aid; for example, what are the meaning and uses of the different functions provided in terms of the stages of the manager's decision-making process? According to Stabell, active understanding is concerned with design features that maximize the effectiveness of the manager's expenditure of mental energy in dealing with a problem. I would interpret active understanding as types of commands, information representation methods, and model interface options provided. For example, a command to perform sensitivity analysis could improve problem-solving effectiveness by allowing the user to test different alternatives.

Although researchers studying the manager-computer interface have in general used the same strategies and methodologies as those studying implementation, their emphasis has been different. The implementation studies have mostly examined groups or organizations; research on interface design has focused on the individual using the computer. Because the computer is always a party in the interaction, it can automatically track and capture the dialogue between itself and the user. Avoidance of the inaccuracy, bias, and variance in human observers and the ability to collect large volumes of data unobtrusively at low cost have led researchers to use this automatic recording option. However, as the studies discussed in this section indicate, subject preferences elicited through questionnaires, interviews, or protocol analysis have revealed insights unavailable from data captured by the computer. These two methods for collecting data are complementary; both are necessary.

Studies of passive understanding--the mechanics of systems use--have in general been conducted in the computer science and human factors disciplines. Studies of active understanding--improved decision-making effectiveness through better interface design--have been few. Most examples are found in the MIS literature and deal with the influence of different information representations (for example, graphical versus tabular) on decision effectiveness. There are some studies of how the interface between models and managers should be designed to enhance problem-solving abilities. The works by Botkin (1974) and Dos Santos (1982) on implementation research are also examples of improving effectiveness by providing special ways of manipulating models.

The studies relevant to the manager-computer interface discussed or referenced in this section are categorized in Table 3 according to research strategies and research emphasis--active or passive understanding. Some case studies that appear under both research emphasis categories were also discussed under implementation research. This indicates one of the advantages of the case approach--the opportunity to consider the full range of issues relating to design and implementation of MSS in one study.

Table 3. *Manager-Computer Interface Design Studies Research Strategies*

RESEARCH EMPHASIS	*Case Studies*	*Field Studies*	*Sample Surveys*	*Laboratory Experiments*
Passive Understanding (mechanics of system use)	Gerrity (1971) Carlson, Grace, and Sutton (1977) Keen and Gambino (1983)	Sondheimer (1979)	Sondheimer (1979)	Shneiderman (1978) Reisner (1981)
Active Understanding (using the system effectively)	Gerrity (1971) Scott Morton (1971) Keen and Gambino (1983)			Botkin (1974) Dickson, Senn, and Chervany (1977) Ghani and Lusk (1982) Dos Santos (1982)

Case Studies. Case studies on the user-computer interface have used a combination of traditional and action research approaches and have examined both passive and active understanding issues.

Carlson, Grace, and Sutton (1977) used the interactive Geo-Data Analysis and Display System (GADS) to study how nonprogrammers solve unstructured problems. The study sample consisted of 16 case studies involving over 100 users working on applications such as design of school boundaries, market analyses, and commercial site location. Data were collected by observers, automatic (computerized) tracing facilities, and follow-up questionnaires and interviews. The case studies generated a number of recommendations on the use of intermediaries, data display techniques, and data extraction techniques. For example, a "chauffeur-driven" mode appeared to be viable when problems were solved by committee or when there were time constraints for generating a solution, but success with this mode required the users to be present and interact with the system through the intermediary.

Gerrity (1971), in an action research study, designed and investigated the use of a prototype portfolio management system. He discussed how normative and descriptive specifications of portfolio managers' decision processes helped define the types of commands (operators) for the intelligence, design, and choice phases of the decision process. For example, computer tracking data showed extensive use of the graphic functions to obtain an overview of the portfolio structure at the intelligence phase of decision making.

Field Studies and Sample Surveys. Field studies can be used to identify the ways the MSS is operated, the types of commands and dialogue options favored by users, the dialogue features that are incorrectly used, and the personal reactions of users to the system.

Sondheimer (1979) conducted an elaborate field study combining sample survey, computerized data capturing, and questionnaire feedback methodologies. Through a sample survey he identified the kinds of features users desire in text editors. These features were added to the existing text editor and the enhanced system was released to a portion of the user community. Use of the enhanced text editor was monitored over nine months to study the changes in the number of users and rates of use. A questionnaire survey measured user satisfaction at the end of the study. Although the users had shown desire for additional features and expressed satisfaction with their implementation, only limited use of the enhancements was observed. Sondheimer concluded that users had developed strong personal styles of using the system and that introduction of new options must be carefully managed.

This study provides a good example of how multiple methods (questionnaires and computerized tracking) can compensate for some of the limitations of each. In this case the research methods reveal the differences between desired interface features, perceptions of their value after use, and actual use.

Laboratory Experiments. Many laboratory experiments have examined various aspects of the human-computer interface. Dickson, Senn, and Chervany (1977) summarized the methodology and findings of some of these in the MIS field. Reisner (1981) surveyed and evaluated the studies on query language interfaces conducted in the human factors/computer science field.

Ghani and Lusk (1982), working in MIS, investigated the impact of graphical and tabular representations on profit performance and decision-making time in a simulated inventory ordering decision setting. The subject population was divided into four groups: Group 1 worked with tabular reports in the first portion of the experiment and switched to graphical representation for the rest of the session. Group 2 started with graphical reports and switched to tabular reports. Group 3 used graphical representation and Group 4 used tabular representation throughout the experiment.

Data on profit and time performance were captured unobtrusively by the computer. Questionnaires were administered to elicit subject preferences for different presentation formats, and verbal protocols were used to understand subject decision-making behavior.

Although the profit and time data did not show any statistically significant differences, the opinions elicited from the subjects indicated why one representation method could be preferable over the other. Ghani and Lusk (1982) reported,

> It is interesting to note the verbal statements made by the subjects in explaining their preferences. Subjects who preferred the graphical representation emphasized the ease of perceiving relationships among the data and also that the graphics helped them to make faster decisions. Note the similarity of these statements to those reported by Business Week. Subjects who preferred the tabular representation emphasized the ease of obtaining exact values of the data. Those subjects who changed from a graphic to tabular representation complained that they found it difficult to visualize the relationships among the data from the tables. Those subjects who changed from a tabular to graphic representation complained that the graphics were overwhelming and confusing, and that they found it difficult to obtain exact values from the graphics (p. 277).

Shneiderman (1978), working in the human factors/computer science area, conducted an experiment to compare the relative advantages of natural and artificial query languages. Subjects were told about a department store employee data base and were asked to pose questions to help them decide which department to work in. One subject group posed their queries first in natural English, then using a subset of the SEQUEL query language; the order was reversed for the other subjects.[10] The queries were

---

[10] Reisner (1981) described a query language as follows: "A

(Footnote Continued)

graded as valid or invalid by the experimenter. Valid queries had to be answerable from the data base and relevant to the task of deciding which department to work in. No significant differences were found between valid English and valid SEQUEL queries. There were, however, fewer invalid queries generated by the use of SEQUEL, and the English-SEQUEL group had more invalid queries than the SEQUEL-English group.[11]

Laboratory experiments could be used to study both passive and active understanding issues. The study by Shneiderman dealt with passive understanding, making it easier for the decision maker to use the system. The Ghani and Lusk study showed how changes in information representation could increase or decrease the manager's understanding of the relationships between critical variables, an issue of active understanding.

Discussion. Carlson (1983, p. 86) observed that little research has evaluated the relative importance of the user interface with respect to the many other factors that influence the success of MSS. He believes that because the design of the interface will be more an engineering discipline than a science, experimental data will be important in understanding how its effectiveness could be improved. In my opinion one reason for the paucity of empirical research, especially in the administrative sciences, has been the belief that some interface approaches are inherently better than others and thus do not require

---

(Footnote Continued)
query language is a special-purpose language for constructing queries to retrieve information from a database of information stored in the computer. It is usually intended to be used by people who are not professional programmers. Query languages are usually high-level languages with a fairly limited number of functions. Thus they are small enough that experimenters can study an entire language in a reasonable time period" (p. 14). In SEQUEL (now known as SQL) data are assumed to be stored in the form of tables or "relations." As an example, the query for "Find the names of employees in Department 50" could be posed in SEQUEL as SELECT NAME/FROM EMPLOYEE/WHERE DEPARTMENT = 50."

[11] Shneiderman's (1978) analysis of the invalid queries revealed that when posing queries in English subjects let their imaginations go and came up with questions that were relevant but unanswerable from the given data base, such as "Do people like working in the department?" What are the personalities of managers?" It should be noted that Shneiderman pointed out a number of experimental issues that might have biased the results. This experiment is used for illustrative purposes and not as a conclusive study on natural versus query languages.

investigation. Natural language and color and graphics interfaces are examples of these areas. Bennett (1983) and Ramsey and Atwood (1979) refer to the notion that the real impact of managerial support tools will be seen only when managers can converse with the computer through natural language interfaces.[12] However, these authors also caution that the operational use of unconstrained natural language dialogues is not yet feasible because they require extensive knowledge of the task domain and are very expensive to use. Similarly, the trade literature contends that color and graphics are indispensable in information presentation, even though the empirical studies have not in general supported these claims.[13] Ives (1982, p. 22) referred to one researcher who believes that the "advantage of color is so obvious that no one bothers to prove it, and therefore the literature does not provide evidence that supports the conclusion."

Such claims may be valid. Most of the laboratory experiments, including the ones discussed in this section, have used task settings that involve relatively structured problems at the operational control level and therefore do not represent the task domain of MSS. This is especially true for improving active understanding, which is the role of the interface in increasing decision-making effectiveness. Most of the studies evaluating graphic interfaces have used graphical representations that are definitely inferior to state-of-the-art quality. There is, therefore, a need to replicate these studies in semistructured problem settings with the interface features available in the new color and graphics hardware.

The critical research question, aside from these methodological problems, is what types of methodologies and strategies are appropriate for conducting research on manager-computer interface design. One recommended approach, applicable to both field and laboratory studies, is multiple dependent variables (performance and preferences) and multiple methods (computer tracking and questionnaire or interview data) to measure them.

Case studies, and especially action research approaches, are more suitable to consider the role of the intermediary. The important interaction in these instances takes place between two or more people, rather than between the person and the computer. The working relationship between the manager and the

---

[12] Some critics (Hill, 1972; Shneiderman, 1978) argue that natural language interfaces may not be preferable in every situation.

[13] Ives (1982) provided an excellent review of the color and graphics literature.

intermediary develops a different character over time as both parties learn about the task at hand and each other's approach to problem solving. For this reason, longitudinal action research approaches should be used to capture the nature of this interaction.

The various action and presentation languages can be investigated in the field or the laboratory. I believe that field studies or field experiments are preferable to laboratory studies for considering the interface, because the computer can unobtrusively capture large volumes of data over time in natural settings. This is especially true for passive understanding issues, such as the types of languages that improve user efficiency, lead to fewer errors, and improve the speed of interaction. Field approaches would have stronger external validity than laboratory studies. Also, threats to internal validity, which are usually of concern in field settings, are fewer in this context because data can be captured objectively and measured accurately.

Studies investigating alternative interfaces to promote active understanding have been few. Furthermore, they have not examined the influence of the interface on decision-making effectiveness in depth. The typical study has measured the effects of alternative information representations on decision outcomes. This method is similar to the factors approaches discussed in connection with implementation studies. A more appropriate approach is to examine the process--why and how does the interface improve effectiveness. Protocol analysis and action research methods are recommended for this purpose. The work by Botkin (1974) is an example of protocol analysis in the laboratory to study active understanding. Based on the observed problem-solving approaches, Botkin suggested specific model manipulation commands and model features for improving the effectiveness of intuitive managers. Similar laboratory experiments could be conducted to study the way computer-based models are used in decision making. An understanding of how decision makers manipulate models--for instance, the order in which they change model parameters, how they conduct sensitivity analysis, and how they examine data generated by simulation runs--could reveal patterns of use that might assist in designing commands for interactive planning languages. Along the same lines, Ghani and Lusk (1982) elicited subject opinions to determine why different information representations are preferred.

Another approach to understanding the influence of the interface is to investigate its effect on different phases of the decision-making process. It is conceivable, for example, that graphical interfaces are helpful in highlighting problems at the intelligence phase, whereas tabular reports provide the exact figures needed to perform calculations at the choice phase. Scott Morton (1971) followed a similar approach to evaluate the benefits of a decision support system over a manual system.

The action research approach is also recommended for studying active understanding, because it brings the researcher closer to the user. The researcher learns users' reactions to different interfaces as data and command representations are designed and used and the quality of the interface is critiqued. This method provides a better understanding of how the interface improves decision effectiveness in a way similar to protocol analysis. The Gerrity (1971) and Keen and Gambino (1983) studies are examples of this approach.

Decision Processes

Stabell (1979, 1983) used the term decision research to label the activities associated with describing and evaluating decision making in unstructured tasks. He proposed a set of alternative models and methods for this research; a sample of these are listed in Table 4. These models and methods can be further classified according to the research strategies with which they are associated (see Table 5). The belief/attitude, interaction, and communication models have been used mainly in field and case studies to reveal the decision activities, information sources, and communication flows of managers. The algebraic and predecisional behavior models are more structured and examine one specific problem area and problem solver in detail. They are associated with the judgment task research strategy in laboratory experiments.

Table 4. *Decision Research Models and Methods*

Model	*Method*	*Level*	*Purpose*
Belief/Attitude	– Role Construct Repertory Interview – Critical Success Factors	Cognitive (focus on individual)	Determining Inputs
Interaction	Structured Observations	Organizational	Understanding manager-environment interaction, determining information sources
Communication	Sociometry	Organizational	Determining information flows
Algebraic	Regression Approaches	Cognitive	Policy capturing, determining inputs
Predecisional Behavior	– Protocol Analysis – Explicit Information Search – Eye Movement Data	Cognitive	Analyzing problem-solving behavior, determining information sources and information search patterns

Source: Adapted and modified from Stabell (1979, p. 38)

Table 5. *Decision Research Models and Associated Research Strategies*

	Research Strategies	
Model	*Case and Field Studies*	*Laboratory Experiments (Judgment Task Strategy)*
Belief/Attitude	Stabell (1974) Rockart (1979)	
Interaction	Mintzberg (1973, 1975)	
Communication	Farace, Monge, and Russell (1977)	
Algebraic		Libby (1981) Alavi and Henderson (1981)
Predecisional Behavior		Botkin (1974) Newell and Simon (1972) Payne (1976) Payne, Braunstein, and Carroll (1978) Libby (1981)

These methods can assist both the researcher who wants to model the process of decision making and the designer who wants to understand current decision-making activities. Because the studies discussed in this section are mainly interested in describing decision and information utilization activities, rather than evaluating and testing alternatives, I will emphasize how each model could be used to describe and understand decision-making activities to develop the design specifications for an MSS.

Case and Field Study Models. The belief/attitude model considers that the decision maker's beliefs about and attitudes toward objects in the decision situation are an important determinant of all facets of decision-making behavior (Stabell, 1979). Beliefs and attitudes are identified by asking the decision maker to evaluate or rank the relevant objects, such as sources of information, in the decision situation. One measurement method suggested by Stabell (1974) is the information sources role construct repertory interview (RCRI), an extension of a technique initially developed by Kelly (1955):

> The RCRI is a three step interview enabling the manager first to identify a number of sources he is familiar with; secondly, to identify important dimensions or attributes along which he perceives that the different information sources can be differentiated; and finally, to rate the different sources identified in the first step along the attributes identified in the second step on a five point scale. The output of the

> interview can therefore be viewed as a matrix of ratings of information sources along attributes (Stabell, 1974, p. 964).

Another method that could be considered in the same category bases information determination on management objectives. The critical success factors (CSF) approach is used to elicit information needs of executives at the management control level. Critical success factors are the limited number of areas in which results, if satisfactory, will ensure successful competitive performance for the organization (Rockart, 1979). These factors are determined as follows:

> The actual CSF interviews are usually conducted in two or three separate sessions. In the first, the executive's goals are initially recorded and the CSFs that underlie the goals are discussed. The interrelationships of the CSFs and the goals are then talked about for further clarification and for determination of which recorded CSFs should be combined, eliminated, or restated. An initial cut at measures is also taken in this first interview.
>
> The second session is used to review the results of the first, after the analyst has had a chance to think about them and to suggest "sharpening up" some factors. In addition, measures and possible reports are discussed in depth. Sometimes, a third session may be necessary to obtain final agreement on the CSF measures-and-reporting sequence (p. 85).

The <u>interaction model</u> focuses on the series of events and activities that define the processes of a decision maker's interaction with the organizational or external environment (Stabell, 1979). The method suggested is structured observation.[14] Mintzberg (1973) described the approach:

> Structured observation couples the flexibility of open-ended observation with the discipline of seeking certain types of structured data. The researcher observes the manager as he performs his work. Each observed event (a verbal

---

[14] Mintzberg (1973, Appendix B) discussed a number of other methods--including interviews, questionnaires, diaries, activity sampling, and unstructured observations--for analyzing managerial work. He rated each method according to its strengths and weaknesses and explained the reasons for choosing structured observation.

> contact or a piece of incoming or outgoing mail) is categorized by the researcher in a number of ways (for example, duration, participants, purpose) as in the diary method, but with one important difference. The categories are developed during the observation and after it takes place. In effect, the researcher is influenced in his coding process not by the standing literature or his own prior experience, but by the single event taking place before him. In addition to categorizing events, the researcher is able to record detailed information on important incidents and to collect anecdotal materials (pp. 231-232).

Mintzberg used this method in a field study to observe managerial activities. He kept a "mail record" that included information from letters, memos, reports, periodicals, and clippings. Each item was categorized according to the sender, attention given, purpose, and action taken. A "contact record" listed details on meetings, telephone calls, and tours and included the place, initiator, participants, duration, and purpose of each. Mintzberg (1975) provided a summary of the findings that describes the information-processing and decision-making roles of managers.

The communication model "considers the series of information exchanges between the decision maker and other sources of information in the decision situation. Thus while the interaction model focuses on events relevant to the focal decision maker, the communication model focuses on dyads consisting of an information source and information sink" (Stabell, 1979, p. 15).

Farace, Monge, and Russell (1977) proposed that the study of communication networks include the following concepts, whose behavior directly influences the organization's functioning: communication structure, communication loads, rates of message flow, and extent of message distortion.

An understanding of these concepts is important for designers. For example, message distortion could be reduced by having the manager access the status of key variables directly from a data base. Similarly, computer-based support systems could decrease communication loads by having filters (exception reports) and analytical tools reduce large volumes of data to a more usable set.

Sociometry (Stone, 1978) is the term that describes the data-gathering techniques useful in the study of communication and interaction patterns. Farace, Monge, and Russell (1977) referred to the following approaches to monitor communication networks:

1. The duty study: managers' records of their communication activities
2. Use of observers
3. The cross-sectional survey: interviews or questionnaires

of a sample of managers to identify the persons they communicate with and the functions and importance of these communications

4. Small-world techniques: tracking of a message destined for a specified receiver and tracing of the steps the message follows to reach this person

Laboratory Experiment Models: Algebraic. Brunswik's lens model (see Libby, 1981, for a detailed description) and the regression representation of the lens model have been used extensively in the accounting literature to describe a decision maker's judgment process. The decision maker is given some data (cues) and asked to judge or predict an event. For example, a loan officer is asked to predict business failures on the basis of accounting ratios (sales over current assets, current assets over current liabilities, and so on) for a number of businesses. The weights the decision maker assigns to the different accounting ratios are estimated using statistical regression techniques where the Y variable is the response (fail/not fail) and the X variables are the data provided (accounting ratios). The regression weights indicate which data elements were used, which were ignored (in other words, a zero or very low weight), and how the data elements were combined to make a judgment. Knowledge of the relative importance of individual cues in the judgment process and the functional form of the judgment rule can be a starting point for describing and evaluating decision processes. The regression representations are thus helpful for revealing the information sources used in the decision and for capturing policy.

Laboratory Experiment Models: Predecisional Behavior. The algebraic input-output methods are not, however, adequate to develop and test models of problem definition, hypothesis formulation, and information search in less structured contexts (Payne, Braunstein, and Carroll, 1978; Libby, 1981). Payne, Braunstein, and Carroll (1978) suggested two process tracing methods for identifying information use and decision processes: protocol analysis and analysis of information acquisition behavior.

Protocol analysis produces a transcript of the verbalized thoughts and actions of the subject, who has been asked "to think aloud" while performing the decision task. The methods used to analyze the protocol data are quite complex and time consuming. They are described by Newell and Simon (1972) and Payne (1976). The following quotation from Libby (1981) offers a short description of the analysis process:

> The taped protocol is then transcribed, and an attempt is made to break the protocols into short phrases containing what the coder believes to be a simple assertion. These phrases provide the unit of analysis for further processing and interpretation. They can either be directly coded as a computer program or classified into pre-determined formal

> categories for hypothesis testing. The categories are usually chosen to represent operations (e.g., information search) or knowledge states (e.g., current assets = $2.5 million) relevant to the researcher's hypotheses. The codings can then be displayed and used in a number of ways. Tree graphs and transition matrixes are particularly useful for testing hypotheses concerning the sequential nature of the process. Various frequency measures are used when cue importance is of interest (p. 77).

Verbal protocols provide data on both external and internal information search behavior. The second method, analysis of information acquisition, focuses on the subject's use of objective, external information. Two approaches are suggested for this method: explicit information search techniques and recording of eye movements. In the first approach, information acquisition is monitored by presenting the subjects with a decision task in which they are asked to search explicitly for information about available alternatives. For example, the task is the selection of a computer system; the alternatives are different vendors' proposals; and the attributes (dimensions) on which the selection is to be based are hardware and software characteristics, cost, vendor support, and so on. The subjects are instructed to request information from the alternatives-attributes matrix by specifying an alternative (for instance, vendor name) and attribute (for example, cost). Subjects are permitted to acquire as much or as little information as they want before reaching a decision. The data collected from these studies can be used to assess information utilization by measuring the types of attributes selected and the frequency of their selection. Moreover, the sequence of selections can be used to test different models of the decision process.

Eye movement data can be collected by using special eye movement recording apparatus or by analyzing videotapes. The objectives are similar to those of the explicit information search techniques--sequences of eye fixations and the duration of each fixation provide data on different processing strategies and relative information use, respectively. The special apparatus used is expensive and cumbersome, but videotaping could provide a less obtrusive data collection strategy than the explicit information search method.

Discussion: What Is the Value of These Methods to the Designer? The methods presented in this section are suggested as tools for both designers and researchers. The following discussion raises a number of questions in two general areas. In my opinion these questions have to be answered before the value of these methods for MSS design can be understood.

The methods proposed to perform descriptive modeling provide data on a wide range of managerial activities--from an overall view of organizational communication patterns to a detailed understanding of the decision rules followed to solve a particular problem. However, it is very unlikely that designers would use all or even a few of these methods because of time constraints and the obvious difficulties of getting managers to participate in the activities. Even if we take one method, such as protocol analysis, the sheer difficulty of analyzing the protocols (Simon, 1979) could be beyond the expertise of the average designer.

Some researchers have used the "intelligence-design-choice" paradigm (Simon, 1977) to guide their design activities. Gerrity (1971) illustrated how these categories helped him identify the potential operators needed to support decisions. Scott Morton (1971) used the paradigm to determine deficiencies in the existing decision-making process. Stabell (1983), although agreeing that these approaches provide a broad understanding of decision making, believes that methods to operationalize this understanding in a specific decision situation are also needed.

Except for one study by Munro and Davis (1977), which analyzed the quality of different "information requirements determination" processes, I have not found any studies that attempt specifically to test the value of these different methods.[15] I therefore believe that the following are some of the unresolved research issues in MSS design: (1) How does the designer choose the appropriate method or methods to guide the design activity? (2) What contextual variables guide this selection? (3) What kinds of research approaches are appropriate to evaluate the alternative methods?

Discussion: What Are the Comparative Strengths of the Different Methods for the Researcher? The experiments using the algebraic (regression) model have been criticized as suitable only for the study of structured tasks. In the typical experiment, the subject is given a set of information elements (independent variables) and one dependent variable to predict. Another criticism is that this approach is "largely useless for discovering and testing process models to explain what goes on between appearance of stimulus and performance of response" (Simon, 1976, p. 261). The explicit information search and eye movement fixation methods attempt to resolve this problem by tracing how information is being processed. However, in experiments using these methods the researchers specify in advance the information elements available to the subjects. Moreover, these methods do

---

[15] Verbal protocols have been used by a number of researchers as a basis for building computer models of decision behavior. These models have then been tested against the behavior of the human after whom they were modeled. The differences between the human and model performance were measures of the ability of protocols to capture human behavior.

not provide insights into the decision maker's use of information stored in internal memory, as the protocol analysis method does. Protocol analyses are suitable to study less structured tasks and generate more detailed data for analyzing decision processes. Simon (1979) raised a number of theoretical and methodological problems associated with the use of protocol analysis, including the objectivity and reproducibility of the coding of protocol data and the amount of effort required in coding.

The various methods used to study managerial behavior in the field--such as structured observations, activity sampling, diaries, interviews, and questionnaires--could also be criticized as research methodologies. Mintzberg (1973) evaluated these methods. He believes, for example, that structured observation is expensive but is perhaps the only method that provides a systematic approach to studying the parts of managerial activities that are not well understood. In contrast, questionnaires and interviews are more convenient to use, but provide data of questionable reliability because managers are poor estimators of their own activities.

Where will the major breakthroughs for more effective design of MSS come from? Will they be dependent on a better understanding of organizational decision making, or on advances in artificial intelligence and expert systems design? Gorry and Krumland (1983) and Reitman (1982) appear to be optimistic that artificial intelligence research will provide innovations to benefit MSS design, but they do not think these innovations will be available in the near future. Therefore, they anticipate that ad hoc development of MSS applications will remain the rule. They also state that many artificial intelligence researchers have recently turned to serious study of human problem solving to gain a clearer understanding of what knowledge is required and how knowledge is organized for various problem-solving activities. Thus, at least in the opinion of these authors, the methods for understanding decision-making processes (coupled with advances in artificial intelligence techniques) offer higher potential benefits for the design of MSS.

Conclusion

This paper has attempted to identify the research methodologies appropriate for conducting research in MSS by surveying the studies directly or indirectly related to this field. Because the selection of a research method depends on the research question, the first step was to determine the research areas that have received special attention in the literature. These were managing implementation, designing the manager-computer interface, and understanding decision activities--all closely related. The research strategies and methodologies that have been used in these areas range from case studies to laboratory experiments, and from studying a decision maker solving a given problem to determining communication links in an organization. In other words, no strategy or methodology for conducting empirical research seems to be excluded from the list. If we consider that MSS deal with organizations and individuals using computers to improve decision making, we will not be surprised to find all methodologies being used to study the wide range of research issues in the field.

In an attempt to be more specific, I have suggested which methodologies to use for particular research areas and issues; these recommendations are summarized in Table 6. In conclusion, I would like to offer a number of observations and raise some further questions.

Table 6. *Research Areas and Recommended Research Strategies*

		Research Strategies		
Research Area	*Research Focus*	*Case Studies*	*Field Studies*	*Laboratory Experiments*
Implementation:	– Dynamics of Change Process	*[A]	**[M]	*[M]
	– Organization; Various Phases of Project Life; Multiple Participants	*	*	
	– Single User; Individual Differences			*
Manager-Computer Interface	– Role of Intermediary	*[A]	*	
	– Passive Understanding		**	*
	– Active Understanding	*[A]		**[P]
Decision Processes	– The Decision-making Process			*[P]
	– Information Inputs; Information Utilization	*	*	*
	– Organizational Communications	*	*	

A: Action Research M: Guided by Change Models P: Protocol Analysis

*Recommended.
**Highly Recommended.

1. The case study/action research strategy has been the most commonly used. Pioneering researchers have used action research strategies to define this new field. Their studies have been valuable in discovering novel approaches to building computer-based MSS. They have covered a broad range of issues, including information requirements, implementation approaches, and interface design alternatives.

Have we reached a level in our understanding of MSS where the marginal knowledge contributed by case approaches is diminishing? I believe so. Except for a few instances, the insights and hypotheses generated in case studies have not been tested in the field or the laboratory. Thus, a model-building and testing stage is the logical next step.

2. Field studies appear to be useful for two purposes: (1) to test the value of different interface features by tracking actual use and collecting statistics on efficiency measures, such as error rates; and (2) to test the power of organizational change models to explain the implementation process and predict its success.

I found no examples of studies using the field experiment strategy. This is consistent with Van Horn's (1973) observations. Sample survey strategies do not appear to offer particular benefits for the study of MSS.

3. The laboratory studies to date have not contributed as much as they might have to our understanding of MSS for a number of reasons: (1) they have studied structured, operational-level problems; (2) they have not used state-of-the-art technology, for example in experiments studying color and graphics; and (3) they have not examined how a system supports the decision-making process. Laboratory studies that attempt to discover *why* a particular feature of a system leads to better decision making, similar to Botkin (1974), should be conducted. The match between the capabilities of the support system and the needs of the decision maker can be best understood by examining the process of decision making through methods such as protocol analysis.

4. Some researchers believe that only advances in artificial intelligence and our understanding of human information processing will lead to important breakthroughs. They think that until these occur MSS will be built in an ad hoc fashion. If we accept this argument, we should channel our efforts to study artificial intelligence. The question of what are the most promising areas of research in MSS should ultimately determine appropriate methodologies. I believe that we have not yet explicitly discussed this important question in the literature.

Bibliography

Alavi, Maryam; and Henderson, John C. "Evolutionary Strategy for Implementing a Decision Support System." Management Science, November 1981, pp. 1309-23.

Alter, Steven L. "A Study of Computer Aided Decision Making in Organizations." Unpublished doctoral dissertation, Massachusetts Institute of Technology, 1975.

_______. "Development Patterns for Decision Support Systems." MIS Quarterly, September 1978, pp. 33-42.

_______. "Implementation Risk Analysis." In The Implementation of Management Science, ed. R. Doktor, R. L. Schultz, and D. P. Slevin. Amsterdam: North-Holland, 1979.

_______. Decision Support Systems: Current Practices and Continuing Challenges. Reading, Mass.: Addison-Wesley, 1980.

Benbasat, Izak, and Dexter, Albert S. "Value and Events Approaches for Accounting: An Experimental Evaluation." Accounting Review, October 1979, pp. 735-749.

Bennett, John L.; ed. Building Decision Support Systems. Reading, Massachusetts: Addison-Wesley Publishing Company, 1983.

Botkin, James W. "An Intuitive Computer System: A Cognitive Approach to the Management Learning Process." Unpublished doctoral dissertation, Harvard University, 1974.

Carlson, Eric D. "Developing the User Interface for Decision Support Systems." In Building Decision Support Systems, ed. John L. Bennett. Reading, Mass.: Addison-Wesley, 1983.

Carlson, Eric D., Grace, Barbara F., and Sutton, Jimmy A. "Case Studies of End-User Requirements for Interactive Problem-solving Systems." MIS Quarterly, March 1977, pp. 51-63.

Chowdhury, D. K. N. "An Exploratory Study of Manager-developed Decision Support Systems." Unpublished doctoral dissertation, Simon Fraser University, Vancouver, Canada, 1983.

Churchman, C. West. "Theories of Implementation." In Implementing Operations Research/Management Science, ed. R. L. Schultz and D. P. Slevin. New York: American Elsevier, 1975.

Dickson, Gary W.; Senn, James A.; and Chervany, Norman L. "Research in Management Information Systems: The Minnesota Experiments." Management Science, May 1977, pp. 913-923.

Dos Santos, Brian L. "Aids for Model-oriented Decision Support Systems." Unpublished doctoral dissertation, Case Western Reserve University, 1982.

Farace, Richard V.; Monge, Peter R.; and Russell, Hamish M. Communicating and Organizing. Reading, Mass.: Addison-Wesley, 1977.

Gerrity, Thomas P., Jr. "Design of Man-Machine Decision Systems: An Application to Portfolio Management." Sloan Management Review, Winter 1971, pp. 59-75.

Ghani, Jawaid, and Lusk, Edward J. "The Impact of a Change in Information Representation and a Change in the Amount of Information on Decision Performance." Human Systems Management, December 1982, pp. 270-278.

Gibson, Cyrus F. "A Methodology for Implementation Research." In Implementing Operations Research/Management Science, ed. R. L. Schultz and D. P. Slevin. New York: American Elsevier, 1975.

Ginzberg, Michael J. "A Study of the Implementation Process." In The Implementation of Management Science, ed. R. Doktor, R. L. Schultz, and D. P. Slevin. Amsterdam: North-Holland, 1979.

Gorry, Anthony G.; and Krumland, Rand B. "Artificial Intelligence Research and Decision Support Systems." In Building Decision Support Systems, ed. John L. Bennett. Reading, Mass.: Addison-Wesley, 1983.

Hamilton, Scott; and Ives, Blake. "MIS Research Strategies." Information and Management, December 1982, pp. 339-347.

Hill, I. D. "Wouldn't It Be Nice If We Could Write Computer Programs in Ordinary English--Or Would It?" Honeywell Computer Journal, Vol. 6, No. 2, 1972, pp. 76-83.

Huber, George P. "Cognitive Style as a Basis for MIS and DSS Designs: Much Ado about Nothing?" Management Science, May 1983, pp. 567-579.

Hurst, Gerald E., Jr.; Ness, David N.; Gambino, Thomas J.; and Johnson, Thomas H. "Growing DSS: A Flexible, Evolutionary Approach." In Building Decision Support Systems, ed. John L. Bennett. Reading, Mass.: Addison-Wesley, 1983.

Huysmans, J.H.B.M. "The Effectiveness of Cognitive Style Constraint in Implementing Operations Research Proposals." Management Science, September 1970, pp. 92-104.

Ives, Blake. "Graphical User Interfaces for Business Information Systems." MIS Quarterly (special issue), December 1982, pp. 15-47.

Keen, Peter G. W.; and Gambino, Thomas J. "Building a Decision Support System: The Mythical Man-Month Revisited." In Building Decision Support Systems, ed. John L. Bennett. Reading, Mass.: Addison-Wesley, 1983.

Keen, Peter G. W.; and Scott Morton, Michael S. Decision Support Systems: An Organizational Perspective. Reading, Mass: Addison-Wesley, 1978.

Kelly, George A. The Psychology of Personal Constructs. New York: W. W. Norton, 1955.

King, William R.; and Rodriguez, J. I. "Participative Design of Strategic Decision Support Systems: An Empirical Assessment." Management Science, June 1981, pp. 717-726.

Kolb, D. A.; and Frohman, A. L. "An Organization Development Approach to Consulting." Sloan Management Review, Fall 1970, pp. 51-65.

Lewin, K. "Group Decisions and Social Change." In Readings in Social Psychology, ed. T. M. Newcomb and E. L. Hartley. New York: Holt, 1952.

Libby, Robert. Accounting and Human Information Processing: Theory and Applications. Englewood Cliffs, N.J.: Prentice-Hall Contemporary Topics in Accounting Series, 1981.

Lucas, Henry C., Jr. "Empirical Evidence for a Descriptive Model of Implementation." MIS Quarterly, June 1978, pp. 27-42.

Lusk, E. J. "Cognitive Aspects of Annual Reports: Field Dependence/ Independence." Empirical Research in Accounting, 1973: Supplement to Journal of Accounting Research, pp. 191-202.

Meador, C. L.; and Ness, D. N. "Decision Support Systems: An Application to Corporate Planning." Sloan Management Review, Winter 1974, pp. 51-68.

Mintzberg, Henry. The Nature of Managerial Work. New York: Harper and Row, 1973.

_______. "The Manager's Job: Folklore and Fact." Harvard Business Review, July-August 1975, pp. 49-61.

Munro, Malcolm C.; and Davis, Gordon B. "Determining Management Information Needs: A Comparison of Methods." MIS Quarterly, June 1977, pp. 55-67.

Newell, A.; and Simon, Herbert A. Human Problem Solving. Englewood Cliffs, N.J.: Prentice-Hall, 1972.

Payne, John W. "Task Complexity and Contingent Processing in Decision Making: An Information Search and Protocol Analysis." Organizational Behavior and Human Performance, December 1976, pp. 366-387.

Payne, John W.; Braunstein, Myron L.; and Carroll, John S. "Exploring Predecisional Behavior: An Alternative Approach to Decision Research." Organizational Behavior and Human Performance, February 1978, pp. 17-44.

Ramsey, H. R.; and Atwood, M. E. "Human Factors in Computer Systems: A Review of the Literature." U.S. Department of Commerce, NTIS AD-A075 679, 1979.

Reisner, Phyllis. "Human Factors Studies of Database Query Languages: A Survey and Assessment." Association for Computing Machinery (ACM) Computing Surveys, March 1981, pp. 13-22.

Reitman, W. "Applying Artificial Intelligence to Decision Support: Where Do Good Alternatives Come From." In Decision Support Systems, ed. Michael J. Ginzberg, W. Reitman, and E. H. Stohr. Amsterdam: North-Holland, 1982.

Robey, Daniel. "Cognitive Style and DSS Design: A Comment on Huber's Paper." Management Science, May 1983, pp. 580-582.

Robey, Daniel; and Farrow, Dana. "User Involvement in Information System Development." Management Science, January 1982, pp. 73-85.

Rockart, John F. "Chief Executives Define Their Own Data Needs." Harvard Business Review, March-April 1979, pp. 81-93.

Runkel, Philip J.; and McGrath, Joseph E. Research on Human Behavior. New York: Holt, Rinehart and Winston, 1972.

Schein, E. H. "Management Development as a Process of Influence." Industrial Management Review, Spring 1961, pp. 59-77.

Schultz, R. L.; and Henry, M. D. "Implementing Decision Models." In Marketing Decision Models, ed. R. L. Schultz and A. A. Zoltners. New York: North-Holland, 1981.

Schultz, R. L.; and Slevin, D. P. "Implementation and Management Innovation." In Implementing Operations Research Management Science, ed. R. L. Schultz and D. P. Slevin. New York: American Elsevier, 1975.

_______. "Introduction: The Implementation Problem." In The Implementation of Management Science, ed. R. Doktor, R. L. Schultz, and D. P. Slevin. Amsterdam: North-Holland, 1979.

Scott Morton, Michael S. Management Decision Systems: Computer Based Support for Decision Making. Cambridge: Harvard Business School, Division of Research, 1971.

Shneiderman, Ben. "Improving Human Factors Aspect of Database Interactions." ACM Transactions of Database Systems, December 1978, pp. 417-439.

Simon, Herbert A. "Discussion: Cognition and Social Behavior." In Cognition and Social Behavior, ed. J. S. Carroll and John W. Payne. Hillside, N.J.: Erlbaum, 1976, pp. 253-267.

_______. The New Science of Management Decision. Englewood Cliffs, N.J.: Prentice-Hall, 1977.

_______. "Information Processing Models of Cognition." In Annual Review of Psychology (1979), ed. Mark R. Rosenzweig and Lyman W. Porter. Palo Alto, Calif.: Annual Reviews, 1979.

Sondheimer, Norman K. "On the Fate of Software Enhancements." In Proceedings of the 1979 National Computer Conference. Arlington, Va.: AFIPS Press, 1979, pp. 1043-49.

Sprague, Ralph H.; and Carlson, Eric D. Building Effective Decision Support Systems. Englewood Cliffs, N.J.: Prentice-Hall, 1982.

Stabell, Charles B. "On the Development of Decision Support Systems as a Marketing Problem." In Proceedings of the International Federation for Information Processing 1974, Amsterdam: North-Holland, 1974, pp. 962-966.

_______. "Decision Research: Description and Diagnosis of Decision Making in Organizations." Institute for Information Systems Research, Norwegian School of Economics and Business Administration, Working Paper No. A-79.006, 1979.

_______. "A Decision-oriented Approach to Building DSS." In Building Decision Support Systems, ed. John L. Bennett. Reading, Mass: Addison-Wesley, 1983.

Stone, Eugene. Research Methods in Organizational Behavior. Glenview, Ill.: Scott, Foresman, 1978.

Susman, G. I.; and Evered, R. D. "An Assessment of the Scientific Merits of Action Research." Administrative Science Quarterly, December 1978, pp. 582-603.

Swieringa, Robert J.; and Weick, Karl E. "An Assessment of Laboratory Experiments in Accounting." Journal of Accounting Research, Vol. 20, Supplement 1982, pp. 56-101.

Van Horn, Richard. "Empirical Studies in Management Information Systems." Data Base, Winter 1973, pp. 172-180.

DISCUSSION: BENBASAT PAPER

Starting from Izak Benbasat's outline of three major fields of study and four research methods in management support systems (MSS), the group discussing his paper worked on two questions: What ought to be researched? How should the research be carried out? On the "what" front, six major topics were discussed: the type of individual to be studied, MSS as a communication device, the basic processes of management, individual versus group systems, fundamental versus "unique" segments of support systems, and the "value" of MSS. Some participants felt that MSS researchers would be more successful in researching the decision-making processes of managers at lower corporate levels. Not only these processes, but also the body of knowledge they require from the computer, are more easily determined. As one participant put it, "If the manager is a manager of a purchasing department, we know what he or she wants. There are part numbers and vendor numbers and various things that we can quantify in some sort of organized way. We can put together support systems for that kind of manager. It seems to me that this is quite different than putting together a support system for an executive vice president, who spends most of the time trying to figure out what the industry rumors are, and who he or she ought to pick for the next group vice president of a specific business unit." Others felt that supporting the executive is more challenging and more worthy of research.

It was pointed out that most support systems today have a very important "communication" component. In some systems the technology has been developed to allow managers to communicate numbers and pictures immediately. Even where this is not so, however, paper printouts or monitors are often used for group discussions. Participants felt that this communication process itself deserved more research effort.

Several participants stressed that although the ordinary MSS focus is on the "systems," the research focus should probably be more on the process or processes of management. As one noted, "What we are really looking at are the tools that influence deciding, thinking, communicating and motivating. It's a lot of the basic processes in management, ranging from structured to unstructured, that are being supported."

Another participant noted that "we know damn little about general managers or what their staffs do. The staff thing is important. We focus on supporting individuals and yet management teams work as groups. Therefore, it is not the processes of an individual we're after, but those of the management team. We don't know much about how these teams function."

Some participants believed that as systems proliferate in organizations, building unique systems to support each manager would be wasteful. The group felt a need to determine whether generic aspects among support systems could be identified. In this context the concept of a single "support system language" was raised.

The final research issue that concerned the group was defining the "value" of MSS. As one industry participant put it, "I'm under a lot of pressure for cost justification and ROI [return on investment]. I'll be darned if I know how to include in ROI analysis factors such as better accuracy, more timeliness, and a wider scope of information. The accountants can't quantify any of these. Any research that academics could do to attack this problem would be of great help to me." Others noted that in some organizations, which are highly cost conscious today, replacing even parts of systems with MSS is difficult. "Existing systems, because they've been there for so long, are perceived as part of the woodwork, as the drinking fountains, and as the established way of doing things. Nobody really looks at their costs. We need a way to justify our newer approaches."

Laced throughout the discussion was an assessment of research methods. Advocates of additional case studies, field studies, and, in particular, longitudinal studies spoke loudest and most often. Some noted that there was a progression from "a few case studies that would provide insight into what ought to be studied" to field studies that allow generalization on various aspects of MSS. As one participant stated, "I don't believe that you can get truth from one case or two cases. But you sure as hell can get some insights as to what you ought to look at in a following multisite field study."

The session moderator felt that he heard "a real emphasis on a number of case studies done in a longitudinal manner." And he pointed out that there was no consensus on research methods. Clearly, there was none.

Some real doubts were raised about case studies. One participant noted that he didn't "think we could learn anything from large comprehensive cases. We need a multiplicity of attacks on the problem." Others agreed. Some even doubted that there was much need for research in the MSS field. Citing VisiCalc, they suggested that one "just ought to put some kind of technology into the corporation because then it will pull some activity from people, and they'll start doing things." He wondered aloud whether the mere existence of some technologies might be crucial in getting an organization moving in MSS.

Laboratory studies did have their backers, although they were fewer in number. Most followed the arguments Benbasat made in his paper.

The closing moments of the session brought up several issues. Some argued for an "extension of the scope of the field" to include ethical issues. "We're going to get a lot of work stations on people's desks and they're going to be able to use them as an integral part of how they do their jobs. Therefore, we can meter down to the millisecond the way each person is doing something. That raises a terribly difficult organizational problem. Potentially, we have an unparalleled source of data about how people conduct their business. But does the organization want us to meter this?" It was also noted that the kinds of approaches proven in decision support systems "are now becoming relevant for traditional systems."

On a perhaps weary, perhaps insightful, final note, one researcher remarked that although Benbasat had "done a very useful job of structuring the key research questions and approaches that have been pursued, I found myself wondering why I am less interested in these questions today." His answer was that the field is changing so quickly that every month a new set of interesting research challenges are posed. It is not illogical to expect that the relevant research issues will change with the explosive growth in the use of MSS.

SOME REAL-WORLD ISSUES

Albert B. Crawford, Jr.

I have been asked to "identify all relevant and as yet unanswered research issues related to management support systems." In response, I would like to present some real-world issues that, from a practitioner's point of view, I believe deserve research attention. First, I will describe my business, the working environment and culture in which I am attempting to assimilate both significant behavioral change and information-age technology. In that context, I will outline Digital's strategic computing strategy, established in early 1982, in terms of which we are now creating active projects and ongoing operation plans. Finally, I will summarize what I see as some of the unresolved issues in management support systems on which research could help us attain our strategic objectives.

Corporate Background

Business Environment

Digital Equipment Corporation is approximately 25 years old and is still directed by its founders, who are, by background and inclination, engineers and entrepreneurs. We do make computing equipment, not tractors or toothpaste, and this significantly affects our internal computing plans. We have enjoyed a sustained high rate of growth in all desirable parameters. Further, until recently we have operated in a market niche that we created--the minicomputer market. To go after that expanding competitive market, and to capitalize on tax havens and tax sheltering opportunities, we have become multinational.

Organizational and Managerial Environment

Digital's culture continues to be entrepreneurial--to the extent that some 65,000 employees feel quite expert in applying information technology to their jobs. That is not our entire work force; some 4,000 employees admit they don't understand the technology and await direction and suitable tools.

The company's present organizational structure relies heavily on matrix concepts, which significantly increase information flow horizontally and vertically through multiple channels. Digital continues to be a single business entity; it does not have subordinate or wholly owned subsidiaries that merely roll up financial performance. To capitalize on the advantages of economies of scale and centrally directed product architecture, we have centralized engineering (or product development), research, manufacturing, sales, customer services, and overhead functions. This structure adds further to the extent of information flowing across organizational boundaries. Digital's environment--like those of most businesses these days, especially in the high tech industry--has been laced with great turbulence and continuing rapid change.

The Information Resource Management Function

Within Digital we have defined our function as information resource management. This picks up and reinforces the concept emerging from academia and general research that information should be considered a corporate resource and managed accordingly. But it also expands the boundaries of what had been called management information systems (MIS) to cover most applications of information technology to corporate problems--data processing, text and image processing (to include typesetting, a print plant, microfiche production, records administration, and videotext), office systems (to include mailrooms), all aspects of telecommunications (voice, data, and image), and process automation. The information resource management concept also gives the corporate function the responsibility for data resource management, still an ambiguous area, which I will discuss later.

In the short term, as in most large companies, those responsible for Digital's internal information systems have been confronted with growing backlogs of applications awaiting development; ever-increasing technical options; shortages of the skills required to plan and implement advanced information applications; mounting client or customer literacy; and the feeling of falling "behinder and behinder." In early 1982 it was painfully clear to me that the status quo was unacceptable and that corporate leadership in information management must strike off in a new direction with aggressive and imaginative plans.

The Digital Information Systems Vision

We decided in late 1981 to construct a "strategic computing vision" for the mid-1980s. Within Digital, visions are quite fashionable; one can stipulate and publicize a desired futuristic goal without having to define the specific tactics and strategies necessary to attain it. Such visions stir imagination and, with the proper "buy in," harness the organization to address particular accomplishments. The Digital information systems vision was pulled together as a straw; then some 35 decentralized group managers were brought together in a strategic planning session to hear the vision, refine it, and embrace it before we proceeded to the rest of the corporation and implemented strategic plans and programs.

The underlying premise of the vision was to make Digital information systems and internal use of Digital's products a strategic competitive edge for the company as a vendor. This would mean incorporating early use of mainstream products into the life cycle of applications development and operations to make the company both a testing ground for our immature products and a showcase for our full-blown integrated and advanced portfolio. A further intention was to encourage the MIS professional staff to accept more personal risk and become proactive in articulating and demonstrating our information technology projects' direct contributions to corporate business goals. In other words, the information resource management function would market itself internally as more than an overhead service, as a corporate function that could enhance product quality, profitability, and customer service and reduce product cost and time to market.

Dramatic shifts in the roles of information specialists and end users and in the physical placement of computer power were the basic elements of the vision. In short, it fully embraced application development without programmers, more popularly called end user computing (see Table 1). Architecturally, this would be accommodated by an extreme model of distributed processing--put computer power where it is needed. Further, the vision called for "wiring up" the corporation with both current and projected telecommunications technology. We would focus primarily on the offices and plants, but business units would also have to be tied together to facilitate information transfer.

Table 1. *Projected Shift in Digital's Applications Portfolio*

	1981	*1986-1988*
– Operational Control	80%	25%
Management Planning Control	15	60
Strategic Planning	5	15
– Transaction-driven	80	20
Decision Support Systems Packages	10	10
End-User Computer (Queries and Reports)	5	50
Process Automation	5	10
Knowledge- or Rules-based Packages	Pilots	10

Finally, the vision set forth a long-range objective: as the basic information structure was created and applications redesigned, we would provide intelligent filtering to reduce the volume of detail transactions and data dropped on decision makers. (Herbert Simon suggests that assimilating inferential processing and artificial intelligence techniques to mitigate the burgeoning information explosion is the most significant challenge facing the MIS profession in the 1980s and early 1990s.)

Most of today's business enterprises, and Digital is no exception, are strapped with very labor-intensive and usually obsolescent technologies and methodologies embedded in their business applications portfolios. (I use the phrase applications portfolio to encompass all aspects of information resources, primarily computing power and person power in the information skill set.) In early 1982 we found that approximately 80% of Digital's information resources were consumed in operating and maintaining ongoing transaction-driven or operational control systems, leaving little for management planning or strategic planning.

Therefore, it was obviously desirable to find dramatically different ways of developing and maintaining operational control systems so we could reallocate information resources to more strategically leveraged applications. The basic attractiveness of end user computing led us to hypothesize an order-of-magnitude increase in the degree to which end users would take care of their own computing needs (queries and reports), leaving professional programmers and analysts to concentrate on more advanced operational control systems or the decision support and management support systems that required specialized assistance. Information professionals would also have to be redeployed to evaluate, develop, and tailor generic software tools that would enhance end user computing and office systems. However, our projected rapid introduction of knowledge-based or rules-based packages would demand new skills and a degree of sophistication currently unavailable in the MIS work force.

Digital's business today moves on networks. Few, if any, business processes do not demand a coupling of telecommunications technology with the basic application or process. Given the current rate of growth in the use of personal computers (which we call professional work stations to suggest interconnection to the network), we forecast some 40,000 work stations within Digital by 1986. (We already have some 18,000 active subscribers on our internal interactive electronic mail system.) So we must come up with an active, reliable, and cost-effective network to meet this forecast and the many other emerging requirements for advanced telecommunications capability--digitized voice mail, videoconferencing, electronic interconnection with customers and primary vendors (which will supersede a good bit of today's current manual and paper mail), and down-line loading (electronic transmission) of software products to customers and our own field sites.

Research Recommendations

Social and Political Implications

Earlier I mentioned the projected shift in skill mix of information professionals. However, the industry seems almost afraid to acknowledge or confront the structural unemployment of indirect labor or knowledge workers implied by the heavy introduction of office information technology or the structural dislocation that may result from replacing expert people with expert systems.

In the same vein, Alvin Toffler talks of the "electronic cottage" as a 1990s reality that business and government must accommodate as traditional centralized smokestack industries disperse and information services expand. The technical, social, and political implications of managing the dispersed work force are not currently addressed in any of my plans.

Topical Areas

Turning back to a more narrow view of my problems and the demands of creating realistic strategic programs and practical operating projects that contribute to our vision, I see six topical areas in which research by informed and insightful academics might break through current roadblocks.

Information Architecture. The current methods--perhaps the current understanding--of breaking a business down into its relevant components and graphically or narratively portraying the significance of basic information flow are not suitable. I have been unable to articulate Digital's information architecture in a global form that senior management can understand and use to put into context the strategic implications of the vision. Either we get lost in the detail of boxes and arrows, or we have to deal with such a small piece of the business that we can no longer see interdependencies and opportunities to simplify organization or process. Even the phrase information architecture needs further rigor; like the phrase strategic planning, it has almost become content-free.

Data Resource Management. Intuition and some futurists (such as James Martin) lead us to conclude that an absolutely essential ingredient in reaching our vision is effective data resource management. Emerging concepts suggest that one way to break the current logjam in labor-intensive, error-prone applications development is to install and instill the disciplines of data analysis, data modeling, and active data directories or dictionaries. It also seems obvious that if we are to have some 40,000 knowledge workers--all with VAXs on their desks and potentially with access to both corporatewide and most external data bases--then we must build toward some form of harmonized data directories. How do we take the business itself and model it? (Is that information architecture?)

We still do not know how to take the overall picture and position it all the way down to basic shared data elements. My observation is that, as with the study of artificial intelligence, centers of research and expertise have been built up around data resource management concepts, each with its own semantics and favored processes. They only confuse the practitioner attempting to glean a "right" way to proceed. In my view, unrealistic expectations are being set today by the hype about what data resource management can do for the information manager. Practical research is required to move this area toward some standards and to take nontrivial applications all the way through the process to demonstrate how data resource management can work and show its payback in increased productivity and control over the information resource.

Network Management. As I indicated above, a critical success factor in my immediate future will be the creation and management of an extremely large network. Some research has been done on effective use of digital event simulation for voice network design and optimization. Similar work is in order now for very large data networks and, in fact, for the merging hybrid voice/data networks of the future. Network management tools are nearly nonexistent today. Research applying information technology to managing networks themselves, including work in expert-based techniques for network diagnosis and repair, would have great value.

Artificial Intelligence. I have no doubt that after three decades we are finally going to begin to harness some artificial intelligence techniques for business applications. Digital has already put into production its first expert-based application and has several others in the prototype and pilot stage. As we move artificial intelligence out of academia and the laboratory, what skills should we be planning for? Is there a logical partitioning of artificial intelligence into separate methods and technologies (for example, expert-based, knowledge-based, vision-based, and natural language systems)? Are new techniques required to extract rules or expert knowledge from the experts, or do these processes merely extend the current business systems analyst's interview and general analytic skills?

Project Life Cycle. The classic project life cycle for the large business-related, computer-supported application is well understood, but how does data resource management affect it? Has the sequence of functional spec, design spec, detail design, and, ultimately, system test and user test lost its practicality? How widely can prototyping techniques be used? Does artificial intelligence constitute a different project life cycle? In general, how do we properly accommodate user participation in designing these advanced information methodologies, so we can avoid the previous dead end of confronting users with automated solutions with which they have had no formative involvement?

Cost-Value Analysis. Finally, I submit that there has been little progress over the past decade in advancing the tools and techniques for assessing the value of proposed investments in information technology. If we believe that information should be managed as other corporate assets are, then we must proceed aggressively toward doing so. Getting beyond the qualitative or intuitive assessment of information technology and its impact on the business demands more rigor and meaningful quantification.

I hope that Digital's strategic computing vision is attainable. But recognizing that our goals are perhaps a bit "leading edge," I have to be willing to deal with some unknowns and the risks of proceeding without all the tools in hand. From my point of view, cohesive research in the areas cited above could decrease the unknowns, provide more of the necessary tools, and break down some of the existing barriers.

DISCUSSION: CRAWFORD PAPER

The discussion of Albert Crawford's paper was a very broad and thoughtful one. It focused on current research needs in the management support systems field from the practitioners' viewpoint, the kinds of studies academicians do best, and the mismatch between the two.

As a backdrop, the group generally recognized that not only has the technology changed rapidly in the past, but it will continue to do so. Thus, what is possible and practical in management support systems will continue to shift. The group also acknowledged that organizations' ability to understand and assimilate these changes moves at a much slower rate. Even though some business schools have done work on what future systems might be like, many participants felt that the problems posed by technological change and how they can be better managed would be highly valuable areas for business schools to investigate. For several reasons, however, the consensus developed that it would be quite difficult for the schools to do this work.

Crawford's paper was seen as an appeal for broad research in a number of areas to produce tentative, ad hoc answers almost immediately. The practitioners cried for insights into complex problems that they could use to evaluate the odds for success in today's pressing decisions. It was generally noted, however, that academicians have traditionally received the most payoff for narrow research on questions that are quite clearly defined. Practitioners who want to utilize the results of these confined studies must take a chance on generalizing them and bringing them up to a level where they can be helpful.

Conversely, for academicians to develop such powerful generalizations through in-depth research takes long periods of time, and the risks of failure are great. The group also noted that these risks are further compounded by the rapidly changing technology itself, which may make hard-won generalizations totally obsolete by the time they can be presented; the technological environment in which the research was done may no longer exist when a study is finally published.

Much discussion took place on the tensions between practitioners and academicians. The group came to no resolution of this problem, but the practitioners present strongly urged academicians to stress relevance more than academic respectability. On their side, the academicians pleaded for practitioners to understand the difficulties of executing the research they desire. They also outlined the special problems imposed by their academic settings, which prize specific, high-quality knowledge generation over voluminous generalization, which may appear superficial.

CONCLUSION TO PART I

John F. Rockart

As the sessions on management support systems (MSS) progressed, it became clear that there is an exceedingly long list of potential research issues in the field. However, the scope of these issues was even more striking than their number. The questions that surfaced can be organized in three quite different ways, each of which sheds additional light on MSS. They are the type of support provided, the perspectives of the three session papers, and the MSS process.

Type of Support

One way to consolidate the issues raised in the colloquium is to look at the primary type of support provided by MSS in the past, present, and foreseeable future (see Figure 1). In the past MSS software was developed primarily to support an individual involved in a particular task or set of tasks, which most often led to a decision (for instance, financial pro forma analysis or stock selection for a portfolio). The scope of MSS is now moving rather rapidly and appropriately from particular tasks to the multitude of tasks that an individual might perform, whether they are decision oriented or not. In short, MSS are supporting a person in all the things he or she does. Thus, today we see someone at a terminal using financial pro forma analysis, word processing, electronic mail, and other capabilities. Slowly but surely "integrated" software (Lotus 1-2-3, for example) and "window" software are being developed to further this movement.

In the long run, a third grouping of software and data availability will allow multiperson access to all corporate data bases, networks, and computer-based support to "integrate" the functioning of the organization as a whole. Thus, we are moving from single tasks to a collection of tasks performed by an individual to support for the set of functions and roles that compose an organization. Much of the colloquium discussion reflected this perspective on MSS evolution.

Figure 1. *Type of Support*

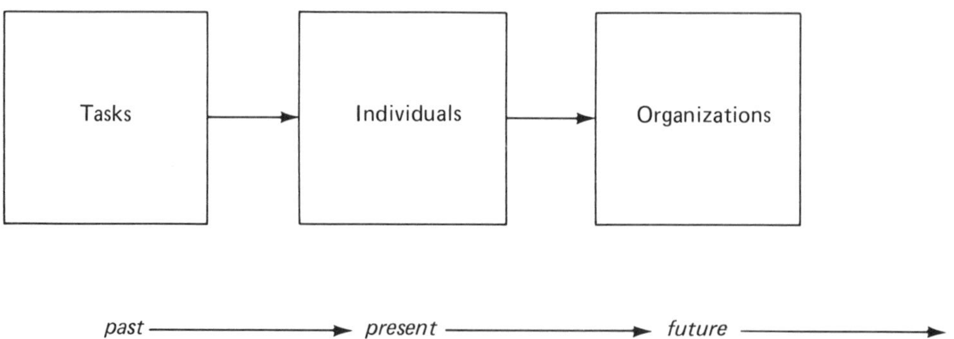

Figure 2. *Perspectives of the Papers*

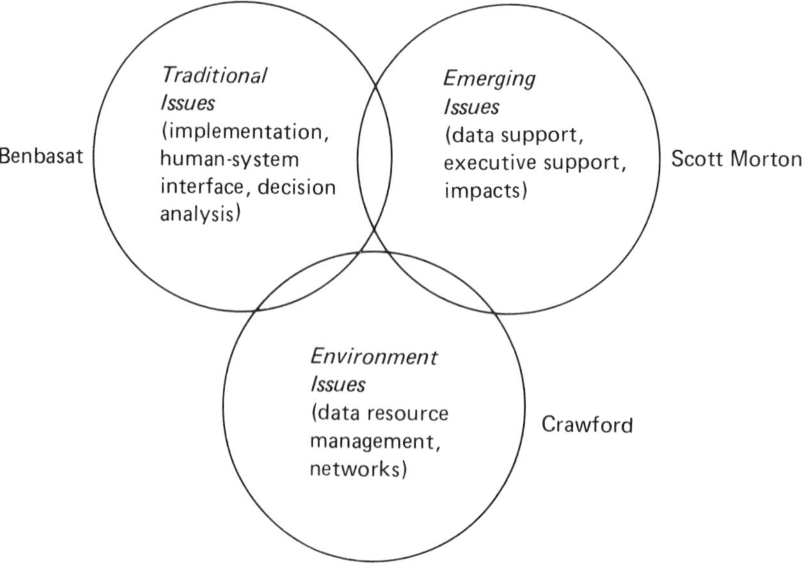

Perspectives of the Papers

The perspectives offered by the papers in this session are shown in Figure 2. Each paper took a vastly different approach.

Izak Benbasat discusses three areas of research that have become quite traditional aspects of decision support or MSS work: implementation, the human-system interface, and decision analysis. Although the history of the field itself is brief, these areas have "rich" traditions, within which an MSS researcher can pick a relatively narrow issue and build on the work of others. Their research questions are becoming better understood and, after a long series of case and field studies, reasonably well defined. They can be best researched today through rigorously designed, well- controlled academic laboratory experimentation.

Michael Scott Morton's paper broadens the consideration of MSS research to include what might be termed "emerging" issues. He emphasizes relatively fuzzy areas, such as data support and executive support, on which very little, sometimes nothing, has been written. He points out the breadth of the MSS field from an academic perspective, and the "white space" in his matrices of published research is a reminder that the field is both exceedingly large and rapidly expanding. It is increasingly evident that as the MSS field grows, new phenomena to research can be expected. Scott Morton raises, in particular, the issue of impacts of MSS, about which virtually nothing is known.

Albert Crawford takes an entirely different look at MSS. From the perspective of a practicing manager who must both ride and tame the end user computing racehorse, he focuses on learning more about the technical and organizational environment that will support MSS efforts and integration throughout the organization. He raises issues such as data resource management and the shape of network architecture, which must be understood if information systems management is to put in place the structure that will allow users to "do their own thing." Research on these large, difficult, and organizationally messy background issues is much more important to Crawford than increased understanding of the finer points of cognitive style.

These three views of MSS research are quite different, although clearly they overlap somewhat. They also reflect, although inexactly, the type of support perspective discussed in the previous section--the shift from task or decision support to support of individuals throughout an organization accomplishing corporate purposes corresponds to the flow from Benbasat to Scott Morton to Crawford.

The three session papers have much to say about research method. The studies Benbasat discusses are on specific problems that are defined narrowly enough to allow precise research in laboratories and well-designed longitudinal and cross-sectional field studies. Scott Morton's "white spaces" suggest that there are a number of areas in which we know little or nothing at present. They call for exploratory, often case study, research. Crawford, at the far end of the spectrum, opens up many difficult problems. The academic researcher who approaches them must use, at best, the methods of an anthropologist. At worst, the method is puzzle solving, based on scraps of data collected from a maze of contingent factors and assembled intuitively. Moreover, in these areas "quick hits" for aspiring scholars wishing to make their mark are unlikely. Yet these are significant problems, whose partial or complete solution will add greatly to the field. Will they also add to the store of intellectual knowledge? Or are they just consulting problems? Particular schools and researchers must answer these questions according to their research values and traditions.

Management Support Systems Process

As Figure 3 shows, the MSS process has six steps, which reflect a need to research all aspects of MSS planning and implementation. The many specific research issues raised during the colloquium could have been listed under the categories in either of the two preceding sections; but in my judgment the process focus allows the clearest groupings. Because the process steps are well known to MSS researchers, I will describe each only briefly.

Figure 3. *Management Support Systems Process*

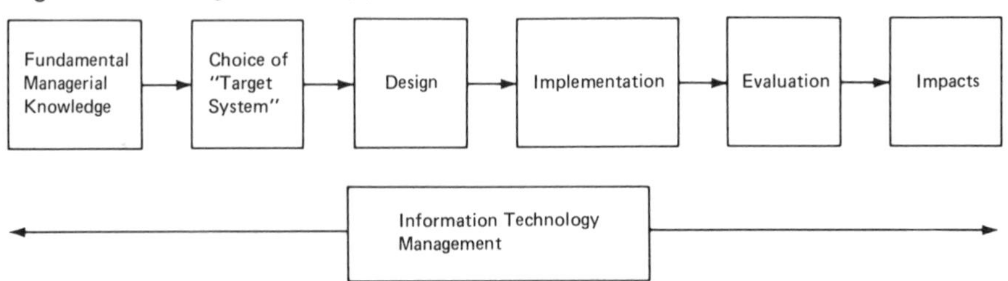

Fundamental Managerial Knowledge

If we are to install systems that support individuals and organizations, we must gain a deeper knowledge of how individuals function, managers manage, and organizations work. Research issues in this area include

1. What is the process of organizational decision making (as opposed to individual decision making)?

2. What are the most significant roles general managers play, and how can these roles be supported? Henry Mintzberg and John Kotter provide insights into this, but more detailed research is necessary.

3. How greatly do individual managers differ in their needs for various types of support? What causes these differences?

4. How will the "new information technology" change the processes, roles, and support needs of managers as communications and computer technology aimed at supporting them grows and matures over the next decade?

Choice of Target System

By any measurement, there are far too few personnel to accomplish all the systems development needed in MSS. Thus, the choice of which systems to develop is crucial. Among the research issues raised in this area are

1. Do executives, professionals, or middle management most warrant support? Should some work be done for each? Top executives have more personnel support available to them, yet their activities have greater impact on the organization. Alternatively, professionals are given less support and have a clear need for analytic tools. How do information systems managers (and researchers) choose to allocate MSS development among these groups?

2. Should there be a shift in emphasis from supporting analysis to supporting the availability of text, documents, and so on?

3. Should the communication process, in which managers appear to spend a significant amount of time, be a major focus of MSS effort?

4. What is the value of the MSS group being proactive? Should it seek out and attempt to prioritize opportunities for effective MSS support? Or should it merely react to user-stated needs?

5. Should more research be aimed at the infrastructure of MSS? In particular, this would involve work on

   - The process of managing the data resource
   - A network architecture to deliver data and computing power effectively and efficiently

Design

Analysis and design of MSS have long been an area of active research. As the field has progressed, however, several new issues have become clear. These include

1. What are the differences among varying types of MSS?

   - What are the unique characteristics of decision

support and executive or organizational support systems?
- How is supporting an individual different from supporting a group?
- What is the role of noninteractive as opposed to the more generally accepted interactive environments?
- How are task-specific and manager-specific tools different from each other?

2. As the technology changes, how should the human-computer interface change? Is there an ideal interface?

3. How much of MSS can be prepackaged?

   - Which aspects of MSS are generic across functions and levels?
   - What functions must be packaged in general flexible tools?
   - What is the effect of individual managerial styles on the generality of MSS software?

A significant number of the analysis and design issues raised during the colloquium concerned better understanding of basic MSS functions that might be included in "standard" tools for a particular managerial role (such as financial manager, divisional manager, or general manager).

Implementation

Although implementation is also a standard area for MSS research, it continues to generate significant research issues. Among these are

1. How are initial adoption decisions made?

2. How does one catalyze organizationwide acceptance of MSS products? Of equal significance, how does one manage MSS acceptance, especially during periods of rapid change (such as the current personal computer inundation)?

3. How long does it take individuals to learn to use various types of systems? What is the individual learning cycle for integrating the use of several different MSS packages? Is there a point at which MSS cross over from occasional use to become "part of the working fabric"? What causes this? How long does it take? What are the differences in the learning and acceptance process for various types of MSS?

All these questions concern individual learning. The same questions apply to organizational learning.

4. What types of support are necessary for effective use of decision support, executive support, and data support systems? How much of the support should come from within the user group and how much from the information systems department?

5. What are the primary elements of "user friendliness"?

Evaluation

Research topics on evaluation of MSS are also numerous. They range from the effectiveness of MSS to efficiency concerns, including cost-benefit justification. Some of the issues include

1. How are MSS changing decision processes?

2. How are MSS changing the ways work is carried out, including the roles of particular individuals?

3. What are the success measures for MSS? Is there a generic set?

4. When, if at all, is traditional cost-benefit analysis applicable?

5. What are the appropriate means of assessing the "value" of MSS in qualitative terms? How can one communicate this evaluation to senior line executives?

Impacts

All the traditional questions concerning the impacts of computers on organizations were raised about the impacts of MSS. Many felt, however, that the existence of widely accessible information data bases plus the software to manipulate the data will provide more opportunities for future organizational change than have been evident in the past, when computers were utilized primarily for paperwork processing applications. Thus, the need for studies of organizational impacts is greater today than ever before. Research questions are

1. Do MSS make more fluid organizational hierarchies possible?

2. Can MSS reduce or replace staff personnel? Line personnel?

3. Are the levels at which decisions are made changing? Are they apt to change further? In which direction?

4. In what ways are roles within organizations affected by MSS?

5. What are the overall impacts of MSS on organizations in terms of structure, roles, educational levels needed, and other generalizable characteristics?

Information Technology Management

The entire process of selecting, designing, and implementing MSS must somehow be "managed." The information systems department is totally uninvolved in the management of some systems today. However, the availability of MSS has raised a number of significant information systems management needs on which research must be done. Among these are

1. An evolutionary model or scenario of MSS-driven end user computing as it will be in a few years

2. An understanding of data resource management

3. Effective management of the interface between information systems and users

4. New chargeback policies

5. Monitoring of MSS use to provide data for MSS planning

6. Reorganization of the information systems function to serve end users as effectively as possible

7. Effective management of a network consisting of telecommunications, computer engines of various sizes, and data storage

PART II

INFORMATION SYSTEMS TECHNOLOGY AND ORGANIZATION

INTRODUCTION TO PART II

Richard O. Mason

Computers and information systems do not operate in isolation. Information technology is always part of a larger sociotechnical system, which is composed of hardware, software, data, organizational rules and procedures, and people. All these factors affect the organization's performance and, in turn, are affected by information technology policies.

Understanding better this matrix of factors and the mutual dependence between organizational performance and information systems (IS) technology was the purpose of the sessions on IS technology and organization. The topic is immense, both in the number of dimensions and the pertinent levels of aggregation. Yet the problem is significant, and it presents many opportunities for fruitful research. As our knowledge about information technology has improved, corresponding knowledge about its impact on people, organizations, and society has accreted at a much slower rate.

This gap is unfortunate, because most organizations that acquire information technology and systems do so to improve their overall performance. They seek more effective strategies, higher profits, lower costs, more efficient operations, and other competitive advantages. They want to avoid disgruntled employees, alienated customers, unpaid suppliers, and technology-shy managers. To achieve these goals, an organization's migration from one system to another must be smooth and economical. It should not unduly disrupt the business's primary functioning. This means that the new technology must become part of the organizational culture. It must be accepted, adapted, and adopted by the people of the organization.

People are involved in all aspects of an IS--its hardware, software, data, rules, procedures, and, of course, its other people. Each change in the system potentially affects them. So it is important to consider people in designing systems and in researching them.

Among the roles people play in an IS are

Perform systems analyses
Design systems

Write programs and operating programs
Provide data
Process data (in other words, perform "human information processing")
Supervise information processing
Use data
Communicate data
Manage with people who use data

This list can be extended easily. However, just these few items reveal some important points. One is that <u>all</u> these activities must be carried out satisfactorily (or better) if the organization is to perform well. These activities can be either what Kurt Lewin calls "supporting forces," which help the organization achieve its goals, or "resisting forces," which are barriers to progress and excellence. Their role in an organization is further complicated by the trends toward telecommunications, distributed computing, personal computers, dispersed word processors, and interorganizational information-sharing systems. There is seldom a single identifiable locus of control for aligning these activities as supporting forces.

Each activity must also be dealt with at various levels of aggregation. Among those to consider are

The individual--psychological level
The small group--social psychological level
The organizational unit--suborganizational level
The organization--closed-organizational level
The organization's stakeholders--open-organizational level
Society--sociological and political level

Attention, of course, must be paid to each of these levels as systems are designed, installed, and evaluated.

This leads to a rather enormous agenda of research topics in the area. Just these two lists suggest many questions for which answers are not currently available. The colloquium could only deal with a few. One of them, and an excellent place to start, is, By what methods are these questions to be researched?

Karl Weick's paper responds to this question. It is concerned with the role of theory in selecting a methodology for research and how theory and method are related. Weick first boils this complex problem down to a simple but highly useful 2 x 2 matrix. One dimension involves a choice about people: Either people are basically alike, or each person is unique. The other dimension involves a choice about research method: Either the method is extensive--selective examination of many subjects--or it is intensive--detailed examination of few subjects. This matrix yields four possible combinations, which Weick describes. He then fleshes these options out in a detailed examination of the role of a priori assumptions in organizational research and analysis.

Within this framework, however, many different research methods are available to the management information systems researcher. Weick examines briefly the 27 identified by J. D. Douglas. These methods form a continuum ranging from purely rational mathematical models on one end to Husserlian analysis of unconscious experience on the other. All are potentially relevant to this research area. The methodological choice turns on the trade-off the researcher is willing to make between capturing "free-flowing existence" (that is, experiential reality) and establishing "control" (that is, systematic direction of the research). The result of Weick's analysis is a menu of methodologies for research on information technology's impact on organizations.

Allan Mohrman and Edward Lawler open their paper where Weick left off by evaluating the research published to date on the impact of IS technology on organizations and summarizing its findings. One insight pervades their conclusions. Information technology impacts are predominantly situational, not generally inherent in the technology and not universal in their manifestations. Consequently, a contingency theory is called for. In response, the authors seek to identify both the dependent and independent variables in various contexts. With respect to one important dependent variable, "quality of change," they suggest a threefold categorization based on the extent of the social system affected by the change. To analyze the independent variables, they draw on a theory of information processing and measurement to identify the critical information activities that have potential organizational impacts.

There is a rather deep psychological argument buried in Mohrman and Lawler's work. Information technology does not necessarily and causally lead to either a more rigid social order or more expansive social freedoms, as some sociologists have argued. Instead it is the mind that is affected. People associated with the new technology change their mental sets, their cognitive behavior, and "their patterns of attention, learning, and mental engagement." These changes in mind lead to different individual choices and, hence, to organizational impacts. The possibilities are numerous and largely unbridled. What is called for is a better understanding of mind as the mediating force between information technology and organizational impact.

Everett Rogers, in contrast to Mohrman and Lawler, takes a decidedly sociological view. He argues--in part on the basis of a study he and Judith Larsen did on high technology firms in the Silicon Valley--that information technology results in new types of bureaucratic arrangements, which differ substantially from those

Max Weber envisioned for an industrial society. New organizations created around microcomputer-communications networks are characterized by "a major deemphasis of formal organizational structure as a guide to human behavior, a management style that rewards performance generously, and a flourishing system of horizontal information-exchange networks."

The consequences of this technological innovation can be evaluated in three binary dimensions--desirable or undesirable, direct or indirect, and anticipated or unanticipated--yielding eight categories of consequences. Greater office productivity falls within the high-order "desirable, direct, and anticipated" category, whereas decreased employment, especially for older female office workers, is a low-order "undesirable, indirect, and unanticipated" consequence. Furthermore, Rogers points out that the range of impact of the new information technologies is far greater than that of previous technologies. Time, space, and organizational hierarchy no longer serve as major barriers to change.

These three papers can be read as a discussion. Weick poses the question, What is the appropriate methodology for studying the impact of technology on organizations? Both Mohrman and Lawler and Rogers respond to this query. The responding authors single out concepts and approaches they have found useful. Their approaches are informative, but not definitive. As the paper discussions and part conclusion indicate, there is ample opportunity for readers to contribute to the discussion as well. This is an embryonic field, and there is much research to be done.

THEORETICAL ASSUMPTIONS AND RESEARCH METHODOLOGY SELECTION

Karl E. Weick

Here, in the words of a practicing administrator, is the phenomenon of interest to me in this paper:

> I am influenced by personal experience, even in this still unautomated world, of the power of the measurable to dwarf the nonmeasurable. I recall times when I have criticized some forecast or estimate for omitting some variable which must obviously be relevant to the result and have been answered--"We couldn't include that; we couldn't put a value on it." And if I objected--"But by omitting it, you have valued it at zero; and you know that is the only value it _cannot_ have." The answer--given in the sad, patient voice which the professional keeps for the amateur--would be--"No; we haven't valued it; we have only _omitted_ it." And then, triumphantly--"Look, one of the footnotes says so."
>
> I fear the alluring possibilities of automating decision processes, first, because the decisions which lend themselves to be so treated are decisions about the best means to reach given ends, where the criteria by which means are judged best are given, like the "ends," at the outset. I believe that no important decisions are of this type and that those which appear to be so usually conceal more important questions which ought to be dealt with first. I fear that automation will further bury these essential issues. Intractable problems are usually solved by being re-stated; their "facts" are found to be irrelevant. Vast, vested interests resist such re-statements; and I fear that automation will make these vaster still. Most of all, I fear the possibilities of automatized decision making, because I believe that the criteria which determine decisions are only

---

I am grateful to Larry Williams for his input on some of the issues discussed.

> evolved by the process of decision itself and that this process, so tedious and necessarily only half-conscious, will be further jeopardized by the appearance of the new technique and the new mystique, with its panache of certainty (Vickers, 1967, pp. 144-145).

Are Vickers's fears warranted? In which organizations, at which levels, and for which problems are his concerns well founded? Vickers speaks of displacement of words and pictures by numbers, simplification, redefinition of problems, decision types, trial-and-error learning, vested interests, and the ease with which people can be romanced by technology. For those who wish to study technology and organizations, Vickers's concerns compress into the warning "efficiency gains should be findings rather than assumptions." The purpose of this paper is to address the question of appropriate methodology for studying the impact of technology on organizations. Choice of methodology can well mean the difference between objective findings and self-confirming prior assumptions.

By _appropriate methodology_ in the context of management information systems (MIS) research, I mean two things. First, we need methods that generate theories, ideas, and hypotheses rather than test them. Neither organizational studies nor MIS studies have well-developed theories, but theories drive all other stages of inquiry, so it is crucial to improve them. Second, we need methods that enlarge the limited set of limited theories we currently apply to organizational situations. I will argue that MIS researchers tend to see rationality everywhere, partly because their prior beliefs assume rationality and partly because the methods they use preserve these prior beliefs. Appropriate methodology becomes whatever theoretical and methodological choices compensate for the restricted ideas that MIS researchers impose on organizational questions.

The Role of Theory in Methodology Selection

The argument that theory is an integral part of appropriate methodology is grounded in several assumptions. By _theory_ I mean an inference from data or observations suggesting a general principle that lies behind them as their cause, their method of operation, or their relation to other phenomena. To theorize about technology and organizations is to relate two quite different domains, which share few common terms (examples of terms they do share are _queue_, _program_, _subroutine_, and _storage_).

Everyone has theories (Wegner and Vallacher, 1977), but these theories are usually specific and implicit. They often are used only once, depend on commonly accepted ideas, contain little abstraction and no clearly formulated logical structure, are difficult to express in words (like a horseplayer's "hunches"), are formed by a solitary rather than a social process, take time to build, and are based on minimal reflection and a limited range of concrete experience and data.

To develop more appropriate methods is partly to transform implicit and specific ideas into something more explicit and general. Organization theorists are likely to have implicit theories about technology, a topic they know less about, just as technology theorists are likely to have implicit theories about organizations, about which they know less. These implicit theories impede understanding; they act as blind spots.

Because believing is often seeing, implicit theories become undeliberated assumptions, which are imposed and appear to be self-confirming. People see what they expect to see. The problem is, they never learn what they have overlooked. And often in issues as complex as technology and organization, the determinants that are ignored explain the strange variation of the variables that are noticed. Error is simply an indication that too little implicit theory has been made explicit, contestable, and correctable.

Theories do make a difference in observation, as is evident in this description by Kling (1980). Suppose someone wanted to analyze the consequences of computing.

> Shall we start with <u>social groups</u> connected by <u>channels of communication</u>, <u>cooperatively striving</u> to satisfy <u>common goals</u>? Shall we further assume that the social <u>world in which</u> computing is used is relatively well ordered, with participants adopting stable <u>roles</u> and acting in accord with stable <u>norms</u>? Or shall we <u>start</u> with <u>social groups</u>, <u>in conflict</u>, which manipulate available <u>channels of communication</u> and messages to gain more <u>valued resources</u> than their competitors? Moreover, shall <u>we assume that</u> <u>roles</u> are <u>fluid</u>, that lines of action are <u>situated</u>, and that <u>rules</u> and <u>norms</u> may be selectively <u>ignored or renegotiated</u>? In any <u>case</u>, how do goals arise among social groups or in organizations? How do they influence the modes of computing adopted, and the ways that they are used? Are <u>goals</u> to be viewed as the sum of <u>individual preferences</u>, <u>reflections</u> of <u>economic relationships</u>, the <u>negotiated agreements among interested parties</u>, or as convenient <u>fictions retrospectively formulated to make</u> sense of <u>ambiguous streams of events</u>? (p. 62).

Each underlined word or phrase in this quotation is an idea that punctuates the problem of technology impact differently, and this punctuation is no less influential if it is inadvertent. The underlined words and phrases and the relations among them are some of the prior beliefs that control what people regard as significant. They serve as blinders, too, in the sense that whichever combination of ideas one chooses in the preceding paragraph, those that one excludes will be treated as variables with a value of zero.

Theories also affect how people inquire (Rose, 1967). If one imagines that human behavior is a response to a stimulus, then the experimental method, requiring that behavior be measured before and after application of the stimulus, will be the only procedure judged relevant. If one believes that tendencies to act are manifestations of internal pressures, then factor analysis rather than the experimental method must be used to discover in which concrete behaviors the tendencies are found.

The danger in applying beliefs to method choice with no deliberation is that hypotheses are never tested. Instead, the methods logically produce findings that confirm the hypothesis. Experiments will support stimulus-response theories, factor analysis will find universal factors in a wide variety of behaviors, and deep analysis will uncover unconscious motives.

> We note the higher order of animal studied by psychologists of learning whose theories favor more complex patterns of learning than those whose theories favor less complex patterns (apes as compared to rats or pigeons). . . . In the many "community power" studies conducted since the early 1950's, those using some kind of Marxist theory invariably find a partially hidden "power elite" of businessmen in American society, while those who follow a pluralist theory find the businessmen competing for power and influence with certain other segments of the community. The former tend to use the "reputational" method; the latter use the "decisional" method (Rose, 1967, 213-214).

Beliefs limit what people see and how they look. This cannot be avoided, because simplification is universal. But a single set of homogeneous simplifications or the illusion that one is free of beliefs can be prevented. In this context, it is interesting to reflect on Art Turner's comment that faculty in the Harvard Business School "have a certain distaste for overelaborate theorizing" (Sonnenfeld, 1982, p. 121). If believing is seeing, then Harvard faculty should either have difficulty seeing anything in those dense case studies they produce; or what they see should be one of two things: essentially private, eclectic, and shifting, or else consistent, but unexplicated and unmodifiable. For example, the assumption that businesses are run from the top down is preserved by using as data conversations with "key managerial informants." The assumption that organizations are systems is maintained by case studies in which there is no unexplained variance.

The ways beliefs affect what researchers see and how they look can be summarized by Marceil's (1977) extension of the distinction between nomothetic and idiographic inquiry. Nomothetic methods seek general laws and use only procedures admitted by the exact sciences. Idiographic methods--such as history, biography, and literature--seek to understand some particular event. Marceil clarifies the important point that in most debates over which method was better for what purposes, people tended to confound a theoretical issue and a methodological issue. If the two are separated, options become clearer. The method issue is, Does the most fruitful mode of research involve selective examination of many subjects or intensive examination of a few? The theory issue is, Are people basically alike or basically unique? These two issues yield the following combinations:

	Theory Assumptions	
Method Assumptions	A. People are more alike	B. People are unique
A. Selective examination of many subjects	AA	AB
B. Intense examination of few subjects	BA	BB

The AA combination is exemplified by the Aston studies (Pugh, 1981) and by the bulk of data DiMaggio and Powell (1983) use to support their idea that organizations mimic one another. The peculiar AB combination can be seen in the work of population ecologists (Freeman, 1982; Aldrich and Mueller, 1982), who assume that organizations have unique configurations of resources, although they survive and disappear in clusters. The BB combination is exemplified by case studies such as Krieger's 1979 observation of the unique transition of a counterculture radio station into a commercially successful operation or McFarland's 1979 study of innovation in a metropolitan hospital. And the BA combination is shown by Miles's 1982 examination of three cigarette manufacturers, who serve as prototypes for understanding organizational learning, diversification, and adaptation in general.

It is difficult to do MIS research within this framework, and the reasons for this are instructive. Assumptions about uniqueness are seldom stated, which makes it hard to choose a column. Because specific organization theories are seldom used to analyze the results, it is impossible to see whether observations are being treated as prototypes or unique cases. Research conducted so far tends to be intensive (Row B) rather than extensive (Row A), but the reader is left to puzzle over how representative the case study is or what it is presumed to represent.

The close relationship between a priori theory and method choice can be illustrated by Marceil's diagram. Assumptions about homogeneity often guide people to adopt what <u>seems</u> to be the appropriate method (just as the belief in stimulus-response images leads researchers to do what seems like the "natural" thing, a laboratory experiment). The assumption that people are basically alike is turned into a self-fulfilling prophecy when investigators observe many people on a few variables, just as the assumption that people are unique gains support when one person or organization is examined in depth. Both strategies are self-sealing. They add incremental information, but they lend themselves to circular arguments and no surprises.

Potentially more information lies in the off-quadrant combinations. Treating a single observation as if it were a universal (BA) and reading survey results in terms of their measures of dispersion (AB) rather than their measures of central tendency (to show how organizations are different), can break the normally close relationship between believing and seeing and increase the odds that new information will be discovered.

Two additional characteristics of theories complement the point that the choice of theory makes a difference: all theories are limited; and all theories are correct.

Theories are limited because none can be acceptable in terms of all the following: generality, accuracy, and simplicity. At most, any theory can meet only two of these criteria. General accurate theories are complex, general simple theories are inaccurate, and simple accurate theories have no generality (Thorngate, 1976; Weick, 1979, pp. 35-42). When MIS researchers try to improve their inquiry by a more deliberate choice of theory, they will be only modestly successful, because any theory they choose will be inadequate. The art in choosing a set of beliefs to control seeing and observing is to sacrifice the least crucial dimension. If the ability to generalize among situations is crucial, then the investigators must decide whether accuracy or simplicity is more dispensable. If researchers want complete accuracy in a theory, then they will have to forgo either generalizing to other organizations or working with a simple set of ideas that colleagues will comprehend and appreciate.

Given these limitations, it makes sense to shift the trade-off depending on the stage of the inquiry. The sequence is a matter of taste as long as researchers use different sets of trade-offs over the course of their research. I tend to start with general simple ideas (such as loose coupling, enacted environments, or a cause map), so I will see something common in a variety of settings, though I will not have great precision. Once I have found a crude regularity across different settings, I must decide whether to sacrifice generality in the interest of making the simple formulation more accurate or to sacrifice simplicity in the interest of making the general formulation more accurate. Because I prefer generality and am tolerant of complex explanations, I tend to continue the refinement process. I take the initial general simple explanation and make it more accurate, which necessitates further qualification, differentiation, and specification of boundary conditions--all of which involve greater complexity.

The moral for MIS researchers is that no theory will be fully satisfactory. But one must resist the resulting temptation to discard all theories. The fact that any single theory proves inadequate should not be used to indict an entire field, because no theory, regardless of its field, can override its inherent limitation. The fault lies with epistemology--if fault must be found--not with soft science, subjective data, or imprecise words.

Even though all theories are limited, all theories are also correct, a position recently articulated by McGuire (1984) under the label *contextualism*. He argues that empirical confrontation is not a test of whether a theory is correct; rather, it is a discovery process: to make clear what the theory means, disclose its hidden assumptions, and clarify the conditions under which it is true or false. Through a series of studies, one seeks to establish the theory's pattern of adequacy, that is, to articulate the settings in which its inevitable misrepresentations are tolerable or intolerable. One by-product of this point of view is the implication that pilot studies that fail are far more important than the final sanitized procedure that eventually shows the effect. Lurking in those "failed" preliminary studies are hints of the conditions under which the hypothesis does not hold.

A related way of explaining that all theories are correct is Riskin's (1970) discussion of conceptual laws, described by Schwartz and Jacobs (1979): "Ordinarily, one has a hypothesis, knows pretty well what it means, and wants to know if it is true. Here, one has a hypothesis, is pretty sure it is true, and wants to know what it means (wants to know *what* is true). In order to answer this question, he treats his hypothesis as a conceptual law and puts a bit of knowledge beyond question for a while in order to see where it leads" (p. 327). A conceptual law serves as a scheme of interpretation rather than as an empirical law. It is so crucial because many patterns cannot be found *unless* one believes or knows that they are already there. A conceptual law sustains knowing long enough for observers to find what they know.

Conceptual laws are ways to search the world. They are believed in for reasons not obvious to the observer (I'm right about something, but I don't know what it is), and their outcroppings are discovered rather than predicted. They are attempts by the observer to impose distinct, strong images onto the world that affect seeing. Such attempts, however, are dismissed by those preoccupied with falsification and negation (see Armstrong, 1980, for an example).

So, whatever despair one might feel upon learning that no theory is perfect can be balanced by the more upbeat point that all imperfect theories are correct. One simply has to discover where theories make correct predictions.

Appropriate Theories

Several taxonomies of organization theory reveal the options open to MIS researchers (see, for example, Benson, 1983; and Morgan, 1980), but the most useful summary is in Kling (1980). He argues that there are two basic theories used to analyze computing in organizational settings--systems rationalism and segmented institutionalism--and within each category there are three variants (see Table 1).

Systems rationalist perspectives assume consensus on goals relevant to computer use, view efficiency as a predominant value, focus attention on the user more than on the context in which the user operates, assume a top-down view of change and implementation, and treat the formal authority structure as an accurate map of the way activities are carried out.

Segmented institutionalist perspectives assume that conflict is more common than consensus, that definitions of the situation are multiple, that goals are diverse, that implementation is affected by vested interests and power, that relevant social forms consist of much more than task groups, and that technology can take on a variety of meanings.

These summaries reveal that differentiated options are available for conceptualizing organizations. In the context of appropriate methods, the key points are that most MIS researchers have an image of organizations more like the left half of Table 1 than like the right half; and that their view is more like the far left column (rational) than like the far right column (class politics). Researchers in MIS will "see" rational organizations when they ask top-level informants about common tools, tasks groups, strategies of implementation, anticipated resistance to change, and coordination.

Rational images enable observers to see how key social actors measure, comprehend, analyze, and act sensibly in a complex world and how computing can be embedded in organizational operations and management control systems within well-specified organizational boundaries. Systems rational explanations work best when applied to situations involving relatively few social groups that are relatively well controlled by agents with centralized authority (Kling, 1980, p. 100).

These rational images are not adequate when systems boundaries become larger and include vendors, consultants, service providers, programmers, data entry staff, legislative oversight groups, public interest groups, and others. When computing is seen in context, the effects of technology on organization can be understood as what happens when diverse lines of action, originated by groups who see things differently, become married to hardware, which by itself does nothing to anybody.

The general body of assumptions about organizations described so far can be illustrated by McKenney's (1979)

Figure 1. *Theoretical Perspectives Adopted by Social Analysis of Computing*

	Systems Rationalism			*Segmented Institutionalism*		
	Rational	*Structural*	*Human Relations*	*Interactionist*	*Organizational Politics*	*Class Politics*
Technology	Equipment as instrument	Equipment as instrument	Equipment as instrument/ environment	"Package" as milieu	Equipment as instrument	Equipment as instrument
Social setting	Unified organization 1. The user 2. Tasks and goals 3. Consistency and consensus over goals (assumed)	Organizations and formal units (e.g., departments) 1. Formal organizational arrangements 2. Hierarchy of authority, reporting relationships	Small groups and individuals 1. Task groups and their interactions 2. Individual needs 3. Organizational resources and rewards	Situated social actors 1. Differentiated work organizations and their clientele 2. Groups with overlapping and shifting interests 3. Participants in different social worlds	Social actors in positions 1. Individual/groups and their interests	Social classes in stratified system
Organizing concepts	Rationalization Formal procedures Individual ("personality") differences Intended effects (assumed) Authority Productivity Need Cost benefit Efficiency Task "Better management"	Organizational structure Organizational environment Uncertainty Standard operating procedures Organizations' resources and rewards Uncertainty absorption Rules Authority/power Information flow	Trust Motivation Expectations and rewards Job satisfaction (subjective alienation) Self-esteem Leadership Sense of competence User involvement Group autonomy	Defining situations Labeling events as a social construction Work opportunities/ constraints Power Career Legitimacy Social world Social conflict Interaction Role Negotiations Orientation Arenas	Work opportunities/ constraints Power Social conflict Legitimacy Elites Coalitions Political resources Bargaining Power reinforcement Gesture	Ownership of means of production Power Social conflict Alienation Deskilling Surplus value
Dynamics of technical diffusion	Economic substitution—"meet a need" Educate users A good technology "sells itself"	Attributes of 1. Innovation 2. Organization 3. Environment	Acceptance through participation in design	Accepted technologies preserve important social meanings of dominant actors	Accepted technologies serve specific interests	Accepted technologies serve dominant class interests
Good technology	Effective in meeting explicit goals or "sophisticate" use Efficient Correct	Helps organizations adapt to their environments	Promotes job satisfaction (e.g., enlarges jobs)	Does not destroy social meanings important to lower level participants, public, and underdogs	Serves the interests of all legitimate parties and does not undermine legitimate political process	Does not alienate workers Does not reproduce relations
Workplace ideology	Scientific management	Scientific management	Individual fulfillment through work	Individual fulfillment through evocation of valued social meanings	(Several conflicting ideologies)	Worker's control over production

Source: Kling (1980).

investigation of the assimilation of computer systems by the Forest Service. His assumptions about organizations are evident in instances such as these.

1. "Learning has occurred when a 'critical' set of individuals begins to rely on a new concept for managing others" (p. 14). This statement suggests a top-down image of the organization and a dominant coalition.

2. "Our focus is not the complex tapestry of interpersonal transactions that occurred to accomplish change. During our visits we obtained a rich store of vignettes on turf protection and power rivalries. We often observe groups of managers in small, isolated communities, and, at times, such protection and rivalry can be vivid. However, we feel those individual affectations balance out over a long period" (p. 29). This description reveals a preference for the left half of Kling's taxonomy.

3. Reversions to earlier technologies are attributed to an insufficient number of enthusiasts, replacement of people in the critical set, or the loss of allies (p. 38), never to inadequate technology, poor design, resistance to deskilling, or any other explanations that might be more social and admit a more diverse set of agendas.

4. McKenney notes that the supervisor who introduced a new budget system "felt the PPB system offered a means to implement an MBO process" (p. 16). This is a superb example of a choice becoming a garbage can into which a variety of issues are dumped, although this possibility clashes with systems rational assumptions.

5. Organizational learning is described as a threshold process determined by individual processes. A social explanation for this same pattern is just as plausible: adoption does not occur until gatekeepers who control important incentives endorse it, after which learning is swift. The smoothness of learning is then predicted by who learns what, in what order.

6. Forests are described as arenas in which many people are waiting to tell foresters how to use their resources, yet this context is dropped, possibly because there is no place for it in systems rational analysis.

7. McKenney describes the effect of the computer system as follows: "These facts had always been taken into account, but in an experiential process that relied upon the judgment of persons who had cruised the land, not on formatted data" (pp. 8-9). This suggests a trade-off of efficiency for accuracy and detail.

8. The analysis is introduced with a general organizational framework (p. 10)--Leavitt's (1965) suggestion that tasks, structure, people, and technology are interrelated. McKenney's ambivalence toward this specification is evident in the statement that "the independent variable is task and the dependent variables are people, structure, and technology. This dependence is not a classic, rigorous, knee-jerk response but an interaction that can be managed" (p. 10).

The emphasis on "managing" Leavitt's world suggests rational imagery. But Leavitt proposed that these four properties of organizations were interdependent and that causation among them was reciprocal rather than linear: "These four [variables] are highly interdependent . . . so that change in any one usually results in compensatory (or retaliatory) change in others" (p. 1145). A crucial insight is lost when the four variables are partitioned into independent and dependent variables. The whole point of the right side of Kling's table is that organizational actions have unintended consequences, action evokes reaction, plans and designs are undermined, technology affects structure and people, and these effects then reverberate back and change the technology. The power of Leavitt's analysis lies in the suggestion of circular causation, an insight that is lost when a more linear rational view is adopted. Variables do not remain partitioned into independent and dependent groups when multiple interests are activated. We need to preserve these differences to understand how and when technology has its impact and what its effects are.

In summary, McKenney has implicitly incorporated several rational assumptions about organizations into his analysis (for instance, implementation is a top-down process, goals are shared, resistance is a problem of learning). The organizational framework he uses, which is potentially capable of showing the segmented character of organizations, is dropped shortly after its emphasis on reciprocity is misrepresented. Explanations that give prominence to power, politics, negotiation, and social processes are undeveloped. If implementation of technology in the forest simply involved a few groups and centralized authority, the rational framework would be sufficient. However, because the case also contains a mixture of standardization and decentralization, diverse interest groups, ambitious foresters, more legislative oversight, increased dependence, and ambivalence toward the technology itself, sole reliance on the systems rational perspective excludes much of what is happening. A compensating set of beliefs are needed to uncover these additional dynamics.

Appropriate Methods

Definition of Methods

Methods are simply ways to systematize observation. By systematized observation, I mean sustained, explicit methodical observing and paraphrasing of social situations in their naturally occurring contexts. Let me break this definition down into its components:

Sustained. Systematic observation involves prolonged, continuous watching to discover recurrent events, specify the sequence of events, and trace the wider effects of local disturbances.

Explicit. Explicit procedures are self-conscious, public, open and contestable, fully and clearly expressed, and capable of reconstruction. They make meaningful replications and return trips possible.

Methodical. Inquiry that is methodical adheres to an orderly sequence of data collection procedures, including planned improvisation and revision on the basis of accumulated experience and feedback.

Observing. Observing is examining steadily and in detail the stream of events toward which attention is directed. The essence of standardized observing is described by Barton and Lazarsfeld (1969): "A careful observer who is aware of the need to sample all groups in the population with which he is concerned, who is aware of the 'visibility bias' of the spectacular as opposed to the unspectacular case, who becomes intimately familiar with his material over a long period of time through direct observation, will be able to approximate the results of statistical investigation" (p. 188).

Paraphrasing. Paraphrasing an observation is labeling events that have been extracted from a stream so that a more limited and explicit set of meanings become attached to them. All products of observation involve simplification, editing, imposed meaning, and omission. Systematic observation has traditionally meant the use of preformed categories. In many ways the goal of observation, understood as paraphrase, is to destroy the a priori categories of the observer and to suggest more valid replacements.

Social Situations. A social situation involves an interaction among a place (any physical setting, for example, a bank window), actors (people who are present in the setting doing something, such as newcomers), and activities (individual acts that fall into recognizable patterns, for instance, making small talk with the bank teller).

Naturally Occurring Contexts. A naturally occurring context is an uncontrived environment that is examined to see what is going on. This observation allows one to ask how and why these things are going on. Schwartz and Jacobs (1979) use the example of the botanist to contrast contrived experimental settings and uncontrived natural settings.

> The botanist would hardly search out the indigenous growth of a new land by growing his own plants in his greenhouse and observing the results. The analogy of this, for the sociologist, is to start out with a common sense concept such as impression formation and then construct an experimental mockup, and treat the results as an indication of the way people actually do business in social life. Such a procedure will never do (p. 303).

The typical MIS study of technology impact compromises one or more of these seven components. It is crucial to assess the costs of these compromises.

Perhaps the most essential dimension is sustained inquiry, because this enables observers to detect patterns and notice just how many different actors are affected when technology is introduced. The importance of sustained inquiry is implicit in Kling's (1980) argument that it is less accurate to call computing a tool than a package. The image of a tool suggests a simple, controllable device that has a specific, local impact. The metaphor of a package suggests more: "In the case of computing the package includes not only hardware and software facilities, but also a diverse set of skills, organizational units to supply and maintain computer-based services and data, and sets of beliefs about what computing is good for and how it may be used efficaciously" (p. 79).

The complex relations among multiple actors in a computer package will not be discovered unless observation is sustained for a long time. Furthermore, the temptation to substitute linear causal statements of reciprocal causation is less intense the longer one watches. Sustained watching reveals effects that turn into causes. Glassman (1973), for example, has suggested that if researchers remained in organizational settings for longer periods, they would be less likely to see disconnected events and loose coupling and more likely to see patterns that simply are slow to unfold.

The single most informative article I studied while preparing this paper was Mann and Williams's (1960) description of what happened when electronic data processing equipment was introduced into a large electric light and power company. They began with data on employees of the accounting department, the principal site of the transition, 6 years before the changeover began and continued to collect data for 5 years while the technology was put in place. Although these data did not consist of direct observation throughout the full 11 years, constant scrutiny enabled the researchers to see the same things happen over and over, to observe diffusion and delayed effects, and to discover just how many people actually were affected by the change.

In terms of paraphrasing, MIS researchers need to adopt organization theories to which they are not accustomed, so they can see something other than common-sense rational processes. This can be accomplished by choosing research team members with different perspectives (Wax, 1979), or even by turning the tight coupling between believing and seeing on its head.

If believing controls method choice (stimulus-response theories "require" experimentation), then adopting a method that "fits" a specific theory might induce the corresponding theory. The person who believes in inherited tendencies but wants to counter that bias can either try to think like a behaviorist or try to use the methods of the behaviorist on the chance that doing so will make a behaviorist theory seem more plausible. The investigator who is dissatisfied with the restrictions of a systems rational point of view might either study interactionist theory or use the methods of the interactionist on the chance that they will reveal phenomena that could only be understood by an interactionist theory. The reverse--an interactionist using surveys, structured interviews, time-lapse photography, unobtrusive measures, or archival records--could induce an appreciation for efforts rationality that the interactionist might not achieve by simply attempting to understand the words and notation used by systems rationalists. Next to sustained observation, careful attention to paraphrasing is most necessary to improve our understanding of technology impact.

Observation of social situations rather than solitary action is crucial, because so much of what happens in organizations is communication among people. To sit quietly for hours interviewing one key informant is to forgo the crucial data on how that informant actually confronts others about different issues. Peter Drucker's marvelous conversation with Martin Coyle captures the essence of this point.

> Martin Coyle, the head of Chevrolet, always preached with great unction. Once when I was sitting in his office listening to his favorite sermon of the beatitudes of decentralization, the teleprinter in the corner of the office next to a big brass spitoon began to yammer. "Pay no attention," Coyle said, "It's only the Kansas City plant manager letting me know he's going out to lunch," and continued the sermon on the complete freedom by local managers (Peters, 1979, p. 54).

Neither explicit procedures nor methodical inquiry is quite as important as sustained watching and careful attention to paraphrase. Explicitness is a precondition for replication, cumulation, and criticism, but the understanding of technology does not seem sufficiently developed to warrant these advanced stages. Methodicalness, likewise, becomes crucial when replication occurs or the observer fears either missing something crucial or having to account for observer effects.

The current questions in MIS research are what is going on, and how can that be understood as a joint technology-organizational issue. Addressing the most severe threats to internal and external validity is important, but first one has to grasp a significant phenomenon, which usually requires intense observing with relatively crude tools. And there is always the risk that the phenomenon singled out is actually a phantom of the observation process. It all depends on whether one views Type I or Type II errors as the more severe fall from grace.

Methodological Options

Any method that contains some of these seven properties will be more systematic than one that contains none of them. The specific methodological options open to MIS researchers are summarized in Douglas's list, reproduced in Table 2.

Table 2. *Continuum of Free-Flowing Existence to Controlled Observations*

Everyday Life Social Experience and Thought	1	Unconscious Experience
	2	Subconscious Experience
	3	Dreams
	4	Conscious Experience
	5	Practical Thought and Action
	6	Diaries and Memories
	7	Travelogues
	8	On-Site Field Studies and Reports
	9	Systematic Reflection
	10	Philosophical Thought
Field Research Participant Field Research	11	Depth-Probe Field Research
	12	Investigative Reporting, Detective Work
	13	Covert Field Research
	14	Overt Journalism and Police Work
	15	Overt Field Research
Nonparticipant Field Research	16	Discussion Research (free-flowing), In-Depth Interviews
	17	In-Depth Interviews with Flexible Checklists of Questions
Controlled Experimental Methods	18	Natural Experiments
	19	Preprogrammed Interviews (statistical)
	20	Official Data and Business Analysis Reports
	21	Judicial Investigations (operating under rules of evidence)
	22	Business Studies (statistical)
	23	Panel (test and retest) Studies
	24	Laboratory Experiments
	25	Questionnaires and Polls
	26	Computer Simulation Studies
	27	Mathematical Models

Source: Douglas (1976)

As one moves down Douglas's list, observation involves more control and more preconceived categories and is less inductive and holistic.

Although the fit is by no means perfect, the systems rational perspective tends to be associated with higher-numbered methods on Douglas's list, whereas the segmented institutional perspective tends to be associated with lower-numbered strategies. Crucial overlap between the two ways of viewing organizations occurs in the middle range--Methods 11 through 17--and studies of these types may hold the greatest promise for combining the best that each perspective has to offer.

Observers should adopt methods that are less compatible with their theoretical leanings so that they can discover new properties of organization-technology interactions. Systems rational theorists should use lower-numbered methods; segmented institutional theorists should use higher-numbered methods. Low-numbered strategies tend to uncover conflict, multiple definitions, and coalitions, whereas high-numbered strategies tend to reveal common understandings, task-related issues, and authority structures.

It is impossible in a short paper to describe several specific methods, but I do want to emphasize three methodological points, because they tend not to be mentioned in discussions such as this. They are investigative observation, the use of prototypes, and assessments of meaning.

Investigative Observation. The context within which technology has its impact is thick with politics, advocacy, sunk costs that need to be justified, careers on the line, embarrassment at an inability to cope, excessive claims of vendors, solutions to problems that never needed solving, and repeated discovery that people and structures are not all they seemed to be. Because so much is at stake in these situations, conventional social science methods that presume cooperation, openness, and candor may not work. Instead, one may need to assume that conflict is the rule and use an investigative journalism model (Guba, 1981; Douglas, 1976) rather than an anthropological framework. In the anthropological model, the observers are outsiders who gather information by gaining cooperation from marginal members whose interests are defended. In a journalistic model, observers try to get behind fronts, look for internal contradictions, and assume conflict between the observers and the observed (see, for example, Dalton, 1959). In this model observers seek to expose those they study.

Clearly, investigative observers and cooperative observers make different assumptions. Investigative observers presume that people hide and lie and that those who cannot lie and conspire tend to lose the competition. Suspicion, their guiding principle, translates into two attitudes: Where there's smoke, there's fire; and there are always far more immoral or shady actions going on than meet the eye. The suspicious stance may provide, by its self-fulfilling nature, an inexhaustible supply of clues that it is warranted. Having assumed that people have things to hide and are competitive, the investigator may provoke behaviors that seem to confirm this prediction and solidify the resolve to probe.

However, to presume that what distinguishes investigative research from collaborative research is its heavy-handedness and paranoia is to neglect the patience, persistence, cross-checking, and triangulation required to learn things. Naturalistic observers, by definition, are reluctant to meddle and eager to believe what they see and hear. They trust time, triangulation, and tact to penetrate fronts. Investigative observers differ in degree rather than kind from their naturalistic colleagues. Their suspicion occurs earlier and is sustained longer.

The lengthened period of suspicion leads investigative observers to bring in more informants (while fully believing none of them), to assess whose interests are best served by which definitions of the situation, and to assume that there are more rather than fewer distinct alliances and points of view in any setting. The imagery of cohesion and cooperation is suspect. Instead, observers presume the existence of fragments, weak ties, and units that only intermittently function like systems. Ethnocentrism is the rule, but it is presumed to characterize quite small units.

To invoke investigative assumptions is not necessarily to moralize about humankind. Rather, it is to recognize that ambivalence may be the optimal compromise for observers and participants when individuals are complicated and capable of sustaining simultaneous psychological opposites (such as love-hate and warmth-coldness), and when they have vastly different abilities to marshal and use power. To take situations and contexts seriously is to recognize that conflicting interests are woven into them.

Use of Prototypes. The use of prototypes in MIS research is straightforward. A number of strong organizational studies in the literature can serve as models for efforts to incorporate organizational variables into technology studies. My favorites are Mann and Williams's (1960) deatailed description of the multiple effects when data processing equipment was introduced in a power company, Meyer's (1982) multiconcept, multimethod study of three quite different ways hospitals in San Francisco adapted to an unprecedented doctors' strike, Blau and Alba's (1982) combination of qualitative and quantitative description to trace the networks that allow a complex child-care center to function, and Egelhoff's (1982) thoughtful analysis of how the information demands of various multinational firms' strategies are satisfied more or less successfully by the organizational structures through which the information must funnel.

To use one of these as a prototype, one becomes immersed in the study and then tries to think about his or her own problem just as the study's authors thought about theirs. Initially, one tries to think about a problem of technology impact as if one were Mann and Williams, Meyer, Blau and Alba, or Egelhoff--perhaps going so far as to substitute in their article nouns that are appropriate for the site and problem one is contemplating. Every time Meyer mentions "hospital," for example, one could insert "Forest Service," "employee relations department," or "tanker-fleet mix," and then watch the variables interact within a structure already developed by someone else. As an alternative, one could study the prototypes and then immediately write items, a proposal, a description, or a line of reasoning for one's own project. Some of the structures one read about would influence the ways one then described one's proposed work. It is also possible to design a study deliberately to duplicate a prototype, paying special attention to precisely those places where this is impossible, because they may embody some of the crucial boundary conditions that limit the generality of the prototype's ideas.

Obviously, there are far more ways to use prototypes than this. My point is that it is difficult to adopt a new set of beliefs which provide counterpoint to a well-rehearsed, seemingly valid set of ideas. Systematic use of prototypes that incorporate perspectives applied infrequently in MIS research might help overcome these problems.

Assessments of Meaning. It seems difficult to uncover what meaning participants actually attach to technology. Research by Boland and Day (1982) looks like a promising way to solve this problem. They used a series of "phenomenological interviews" to track one year in the life of a programmer-analyst who was hired by a credit union to develop an inventory system and a loan application processing system. The interviews uncovered a surprising number of issues in systems design that had never had been known to exist. For example, numerous design decisions involved moral choices, such as when the designer was requested to design user friendly systems that turned out to be systems which allowed poorly paid, low-talent people to replace higher-paid, more talented people (p. 19).

Boland and Day are experimenting with the top portion of Douglas's list in pursuit of themes on the right end of Kling's chart. And they are discovering, in the process, meanings that lie behind the patterns Mann and Williams observed, meanings that elude systems rational inquiry. This work also represents sustained, methodical paraphrasing in an emergent social situation between interviewer and interviewee that promoted understanding of the other social situations the interviewee faced. Over a year each session was used to deepen themes introduced at a prior session. Because the interviews did not occur in the credit union and the description of method does not allow for replication, the initial work is less explicit and less natural than it could be. But I presume the authors would say that their work will become more explicit, observational, and natural once they know what to look for.

Conclusion

The question of the appropriate methodology for studying technology impact is woven into issues of theoretical substance much more tightly than people might realize--or prefer. What people "see" when they use various methods is largely a function of their prior beliefs or what they expect to find. Researchers in MIS usually expect to see rational systems, and they usually find them. What they fail to see is that additional processes and variables affecting technology impact lie outside their rational combination.

This paper has argued that prior theoretical beliefs impede understanding of technology impact and that the appropriate remedy is intentional adoption of theories and methods which enlarge the set of events observers look for in organizations.

The crux of my concern is that the comfort MIS researchers feel with rational models, measurement, and order will tempt them into the following illogic:

1. Every real phenomenon can be measured
2. If it can't be measured, it's not real
3. If it can be measured, it is real

Blunt measures, narrow measures, and nonmeasures poke holes in this reasoning. Nevertheless, the imagery is seductive. Application of this illogic, especially when the issues in technology and organization are at a formative stage, could make it impossible for us to learn about this important area.

If we stretch our definitions of what an organization is and what constitutes an acceptable research method, then whatever falls within these <u>wider</u> definitions becomes the appropriate preconception and the appropriate methodology to study issues of technology impact. This broader approach is much more likely to help MIS researchers see their subject more accurately.

Bibliography

Aldrich, H.; and Mueller, S. The evolution of organizational forms: Technology, coordination and control. In B. M. Staw and L. L. Cummings (eds.), Research in Organizational Behavior. Vol. 4. Greenwich, Conn.: JAI Press, 1982, pp. 33-87.

Armstrong, J. S. Advocacy as a scientific strategy: The Mitroff myth. Academy of Management Review, 1980, 5, 509-511.

Barton, A. H.; and Lazarsfeld, P. H. Some functions of qualitative analysis in social research. In G. J. McCall and J. L. Simmons (eds.), Issues in Participant Observation. Reading, Mass.: Addison-Wesley, 1969, pp. 163-196.

Benson, J. K. Paradigm and praxis in organizational analysis. In L. L. Cummings and B. M. Staw (eds.), Research in Organizational Behavior. Vol. 5. Greenwich, Conn.: JAI Press, 1983.

Blau, J. R.; and Alba, R. D. Empowering nets of participation. Administrative Science Quarterly, 1982, 27, 363-379.

Boland, R. J.; and Day, W. A phenomenology of system design. Unpublished manuscript, University of Illinois, May 1982.

Dalton, M. Men Who Manage. New York: Wiley, 1959.

DiMaggio, P. J.; and Powell, W. W. The iron cage revisited: Institutional isomorphism and collective rationality in organizational fields. American Sociological Review, 1983, 48, 147-160.

Douglas, J. D. Investigative Social Research. Beverly Hills: Sage, 1976.

Egelhoff, W. G. Strategy and structure in multinational corporations: An information-processing approach. Administrative Science Quarterly, 1982, 27, 435-458.

Freeman, J. Organizational life cycles and natural selection process. In B. M. Staw and L. L. Cummings (eds.), Research in Organizational Behavior. Vol. 4. Greenwich Conn.: JAI Press, 1982, pp. 1-32.

Glassman, R. B. Persistence and loose coupling in living systems. Behavioral Science, 1973, 18, 83-98.

Guba, E. G. Investigative journalism. In N. L. Smith (ed.), New Techniques for Evaluation. Beverly Hills: Sage, 1981, pp. 167-262.

Kling, R. Social analysis of computing: Theoretical perspectives in recent empirical research. Computing Surveys, 1980, 12, 61-110.

Krieger, S. Hip Capitalism. Beverly Hills: Sage, 1979.

Leavitt, H. J. Applied organizational change in industry: Structural, technological, and humanistic approaches. In J. G. March (ed.), Handbook of Organizations. Chicago: Rand McNally, 1965, pp. 1144-70.

Mann, F. C.; and Williams, L. K. Observations on the dynamics of a change to electronic data-processing equipment. Administrative Science Quarterly, 1960, 5, 217-256.

Marceil, J. C. Implicit dimensions of idiography and nomothesis: A reformulation. American Psychologist, 1977, 32, 1046-55.

McFarland, D.E. Managerial Innovation in the Metropolitan Hospital. New York, Praeger, 1979.

McGuire, W. J. A contextualist theory of knowledge: Its implications for innovation and reform in psychological research. In L. Berkowitz (ed.), Advances in Experimental Social Psychology. Vol. 16. New York: Academic, 1984.

McKenney, J. L. A field study on the use of computer-based technology to improve management control. Harvard Business School Working Paper 79-46.

Meyer, A. D. Adapting to environmental jolts. Administrative Science Quarterly, 1982, 27, 515-537.

Miles, R. H. Coffin Nails and Corporate Strategy. Englewood Cliffs, N.J.: Prentice-Hall, 1982.

Morgan, G. Paradigms, metaphors, and puzzle solving in organization theory. Administrative Science Quarterly, 1980, 25, 605-622.

Peters, T. J. Structure as a reorganizing device: Shifting attention and altering the flow of biases. Unpublished manuscript, McKinsey & Co., 1979.

Pugh, D. S. The Aston program of research: Retrospect and prospect. In A. H. Van de Ven and W. F. Joyce (eds.), Perspectives on Organization Design and Behavior. New York: Wiley, 1981, pp. 135-166.

Riskin, S. R. Reasonable accounts in sociology: Some problems in the logic of explanation. (Doctoral dissertation, University of California, 1970). Dissertation Abstracts International, 1971. (University Microfilms, No. 71-9249).

Rose, A. M. The relation of theory and method. In L. Gross (ed.), Sociological Theory: Inquiries and Paradigms. New York: Harper & Row, 1967, pp. 207-219.

Schwartz, H.; and Jacobs, J. Qualitative Sociology: A Method to the Madness. New York: Free Press, 1979.

Sonnenfeld, Jeff; and Steckler, Nicole, eds. "The History of Applied Organization Study at Harvard: A Conference Examining Agendas of the Past and Agendas for the Future," May 21-22, 1982 (unpublished manuscript).

Thorngate, W. Possible limits on a science of social behavior. In L. H. Strickland, F. E. Aboud, and K. J. Gergen (eds.), Social Psychology in Transition. New York: Plenum, 1976, pp. 121-139.

Vickers, G. Towards a Sociology of Management. New York: Basic, 1967.

Wax, R. H. Gender and age in fieldwork and fieldwork education: No good thing is done by any man alone. Social Problems, 1979, 26, 509-522.

Wegner, D. M.; and Vallacher, R. R. Implicit Psychology. New York: Oxford, 1977.

Weick, K. E. The Social Psychology of Organizing, 2d ed. Reading Mass.: Addison-Wesley, 1979.

DISCUSSION: WEICK PAPER

The discussion of Karl Weick's paper opened with the observation that the author is offering a trilogy of criteria for evaluating methodologies:

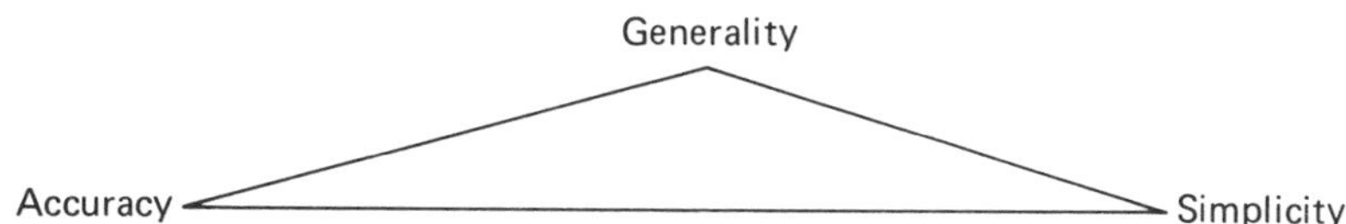

All three can seldom be achieved simultaneously (a business executive remarked on the similarity to the old market research saw "I can provide you data cheap, fast, or good. Pick two!"). In his paper Weick favors generality, but several executives argued that they would opt for simplicity.

This led to the point that not only do researchers emphasize different criteria than do businesspeople, but different organizations and units within an organization do as well. One executive commented, "What engineering thinks is super, perfect, 'cheezy,' marketing thinks is dumb." This suggests the need for a cultural perspective, but the problems raised by such an approach are many. They are as much communication issues as information or decision issues. First, each organization possesses a different set of values. Next, there is a need for a variety of filtering mechanisms. (One executive remarked, "I'm getting entirely too much data. I can't process it all. I don't know how to shut off the data that's irrelevant or the data that's overkill. Nor do I know how to let through the data that is relevant to what I'm looking at.")

The crucial management problem that emerged in discussion is not to manage the amount of change but rather to cope with its first derivative--the rate of change. The rapid migration in one organization, for example, from 600 terminals to 1,400 and then to 3,200 eventually exceeded top management's ability to deal with the change. This was in part because of cultural barriers. The new technology meant that negotiations could take place and agendas be set without going through the traditional organizational hierarchy. (Note the similarity to the observation in Everett Rogers's paper). These new networks present a new organizational dilemma. The intent is to link as many people together as possible. However, as people are added, the number of different values, backgrounds, styles, and jobs is increased. With this expansion, communication problems are exacerbated.

Issues concerning information sharing also came up. Does everybody get everything? This seems infeasible, yet little research has been done on criteria for exclusion from or inclusion in information-routing systems. Several questions can be asked. On the one hand, who should decide which people do and do not share in information? On the other hand, should people be forced to accept information sent to them? Some people want to "drop out" of their organizations' data-sharing system. One executive reported that she is being deluged with requests for unlisted numbers on her firm's electronic communications system so members can avoid electronic junk mail and information overload.

A major substantive issue was raised that any research methodology should address: How is information technology changing the allocation of authority, responsibility and work within organizations? This is the eternal concern of centralization versus decentralization. Descriptive, predictive, and normative considerations were raised by the group. Is distributed computing clustered in local networks linked to international telecommunications networks reducing the need for middle managers? Will the trend toward increased user involvement in systems design, programming, and data management result in further decentralization of the firm? Should decentralized control of corporate decision making and hence of information systems be encouraged? This last question sparked an exchange on the problems of managing large, unwieldy companies and the stifling of innovation in centralized bureaucracies.

In terms of research, the need to use a variety of theories and methods was stressed. The group focused on Weick's statement, "People see what they expect to see. The problem is, they never learn what they have overlooked." More interdisciplinary research is called for to overcome this limitation. This necessitates changes both by researchers--who must learn to work with (and tolerate) colleagues from different disciplines--and by companies--who must provide access to a <u>team</u> of researchers. As one person observed, "It's hard enough to get one researcher into a corporate site. How are we ever going to get several in?" One possibility is for researchers to "tool up" in more than one discipline, but this is only partly feasible. A suggested alternative was to send just one well-trained observer into the company and have him or her record observations in minute detail. This "data base" of observations could then be analyzed from the points of view of a variety of disciplines.

A REVIEW OF THEORY AND RESEARCH

Allan M. Mohrman, Jr.
Edward E. Lawler III

Technologies and organizations are both human contrivances (Katz and Kahn, 1978). And many of the ways people look at and react to the world are socially learned. Consequently, the question of how information technology (IT) affects organizations and human behavior is a question of how people--individually and socially--reconstruct their organizations and behaviors to fit with the technologies. But it doesn't end there. Because technologies are socially constructed, they can be reconstructed as well. Thus, our working assumption in this paper is that IT has impacts, but they are evolutionary, developmental, and reciprocal--the technology is also affected.

A number of theoretical and empirical research studies have been done on IT's effect on organizations. However, not all relevant topics are addressed in the existing literature. There are several reasons for this. First, although much of the literature is recent, it is rapidly being outdated by advances in the technology itself. We have, for example, little reason to believe that the impact of a mainframe will be similar to that of a network of professional work stations. Second, much existing research fails to consider what is known from organization theory about organizational growth and development and how context factors influence "planned change."

We will begin this review by surveying some current thinking on the types of changes that planned change programs like IT might produce. Then we will consider previous research. Finally, we will present a theoretical point of view on organizations to help integrate the research findings and guide future studies.

Throughout the paper we assume that whatever impacts the new technology has will not change the basic nature of human beings. Its impacts will be on human contrivances and social and personal constructions. When these change, people's relationships to them will be affected, but those relationships will be determined by the nature of humanity. The question is, and always has been, Which phenomena are caused by the fundamental characteristics of human beings, and which are part of the contrivances?

Information Technology and Change

Sources of Change

Three sources of uncertainty and change are associated with information technology. First, the technology itself is still evolving. We and our organizations will be confronted continually with unforeseeable, or at least unforeseen, technology changes.

Second, whenever IT is implemented in an organizational setting, it, like any other organizational change, creates short-term ambiguity and uncertainty accompanied by unanticipated organizational responses.

A third source of change stems from the technology itself and will be present even when the first and second sources disappear. In most implementations of a technology, at least the technology itself is relatively static. The uncertainty lies in the human and organizational contexts--how people will respond and how organizational structures and practices will change. With IT, however, this uncertainty is compounded by the technology's ability to be adapted to feedback. *The technology itself can be changed by those using it.*

There are four orders of information feedback in goal-oriented behavior and technology (Schoderbek, Kefalas, and Schoderbek, 1975).

No Feedback. In situations with no feedback the technology produces an output based on original input. No goal-oriented functioning occurs. Output is completely determined by the input and the technology.

First-Order Feedback. In first-order feedback output is adjusted on the basis of feedback about how closely it is corresponding to its goal. The goal and the technology remain constant; level of output varies to keep the system in a goal-oriented equilibrium.

Second-Order Feedback. The preprogrammed technology and goals change in second-order feedback according to circumstances. Essentially, the technology has multiple functions with switching rules activated by feedback. Goals and technology are contingent on the situation, but in a predetermined way.

Third-Order Feedback. In third-order feedback the technology is adapted to achieve new goals. Feedback provides the inputs for these adaptations of goals and technology, neither of which were predetermined or preprogrammed.

Feedback can be performed in a number of ways, through various technologies or through human agents. All technologies are parts of systems with all four feedback states. Most industrial technologies, for instance, are relatively inflexible once installed. Either they have no third-order feedback loop in an organizational setting or they require much time for adaptation. On the other hand, there is always a larger system in which a third-order feedback loop leads to redesign and evolution of industrial technologies. Eventually, all technologies can be changed to achieve different goals. The important determination is in the locus of the feedback loops.

The development of IT has allowed third-order feedback at the user level. This is made possible by increased multifunctionality of the technology, flexible hardware configurations, and accessible and flexible software. Up to now the technology has been generally configured for use by particular organizational units and roles for specific purposes (for example, word processing by secretaries or computer graphics by designers). Although we have ample evidence that the technology frequently engenders interdependencies among organizational functions (Whisler, 1970), in the past there were few linkages among different technological functions and organizational roles. Word processing technologies used by secretaries could not access data analysis technologies used by professionals, for instance. But networks linking specialized applications and multifunctional work stations are now available to all office roles. The potential result is increased flexibility in how the organization and individual can choose to use the technology in relation to roles and task structures. The degrees of variation and the prospects for continuing change are greatly increased (Bjorn-Andersen et al., 1979). Unlike many industrial technologies, IT can literally be designed and redesigned by users--especially through software but also in component configurations (Johnson, 1983; Johnson and Rice, 1983).

Kinds of Change

The paradox of researching IT impacts is that the installation of IT may involve many fundamental changes, and the more fundamental the change the less its nature can be known beforehand. If they are unable to anticipate changes, researchers do not know what to look for and measure as bench marks. Furthermore, the very natures of the measurement and what is measured are subject to change and may muddy the water by affecting the change that is being studied. To cope with this issue, the literature on organizational change has articulated different kinds of change--alpha, beta, and gamma--and offered ways of measuring them (Golembiewski, Billingsley, and Yeager, 1976; Terborg, Howard, and Maxwell, 1980).

Alpha change refers to changes in level of phenomena while the type, dimensions, and criteria for evaluating the phenomena remain constant. People who contemplate the productivity impacts of IT usually have an alpha change of preexisting outputs in mind.

Beta change occurs in situations where the dimensions and type of phenomena remain the same but the criteria or calibrations used to evaluate and measure them change. For instance, one might expect IT to open new levels of output potential so that what used to be considered very high output would become moderate. The technology would bring with it a new standard for evaluating output, although the kind of output might remain essentially the same.

Gamma change reflects changes in worldview and reality so that phenomena before and after change are not directly comparable. Not only might things be done in different ways because of the technology, but they might come to seem different in nature and therefore be evaluated in new ways.

Introduction of a new IT into an organization can produce alpha, beta, or gamma change. Recent studies suggest that IT produces more than alpha change. The research so far has usually focused on the alpha change associated with IT; as a result it may well have missed IT's most important impacts. Readers of studies in this field should remember that different kinds of change in addition to the one researchers have considered may be occurring.

Research on IT

We begin our survey of research on IT where others have ended. Rather than review studies that have been included elsewhere, we will summarize the earlier research and then focus on three recent studies that break new ground.

Earlier Findings

Research reports and reviews of impact research have made the following points:

1. Research results are mixed and even contradictory (Bikson and Mankin, 1983; Edstrom and Nauges, 1975). The organizational impacts of IT are not deterministic, and as a tool or network of tools we can adapt IT to support a number of organizational forms (Bjorn-Andersen and Eason, 1980; Sorenson, 1982).
2. We need to frame our research and its results in theory so we can make some progress toward explaining and usefully understanding them (Kling, 1980a).
3. We need to conduct our research in a way that recognizes and is designed to deal with difficulties in assessing IT impacts (Kling, 1980a).
4. The implementation process has more impact than the nature of the technology (Bikson and Mankin, 1983), and some say participative methods should be used in designing and implementing IT (Bjorn-Andersen et al., 1979).
5. Impacts depend less on the nature of the technology and more on the human choices that designers and managers make and the models of human beings they use (Bjorn-Andersen and Eason, 1980).

6. The impacts of IT are best understood as political in source and nature (Kling, 1979).
7. The major individual and organizational issue in the study of IT is the balance between freedom and order (Tricker, 1980).
8. The impacts of IT are best understood in terms of the technology's cybernetic nature; the basic cybernetic issue is control (Hirschhorn, 1981).
9. As the technology advances, the freedom available to designers will increase and any deterministic aspects of IT will be lessened (Bjorn-Andersen et al., 1979).
10. The "effects" of the new IT can only be understood in specific applications of microelectronics to organizations. The basic technology has no characteristic effect (Songeard, 1982).

Taken together, we believe these points provide clear guidelines for further research. First of all, we can see that the technology itself is undeterministic, that this is so because of the large element of human choice involved in how IT is applied, that consequently each application has a number of idiosyncratic (or organization-specific) aspects, and that these idiosyncrasies can lead to contradictory results. On the other hand, it is equally clear that we need more theoretical underpinnings to help us generalize beyond our atomistic knowledge of IT impacts in unrelated situations and that these theoretical models need to address the themes running through most past research studies: the cybernetic and rationalistic nature of the technology, the political nature of its impacts and the choices made, the role of participation in these choices, and, finally, the tensions between freedom and order (or autonomy and control or decentralization and centralization) that the technology brings forth.

In summary, we need a model for the organizational impact of IT that is based on an understanding of how human beings tend to construct their organizational worlds by making basic human choices between freedom and order. The model must incorporate the roles of elements such as participation, technology, and politics in these choice processes. Before we propose a model, however, let us summarize some recent research.

Current Studies of Office Technologies

Three recent studies of the new office technologies reflect both the researchers' responses to new technological developments and grounding in previous research on the impact of IT on organizations. The work of Allan Mohrman and Luke Novelli, Tora Bikson and colleagues, and Bonnie Johnson and colleagues provides examples of current research in the field.

Mohrman and Novelli (1982, 1983) looked at the alpha, beta, and gamma effects of freestanding multifunctional word processors and professional work stations in an office environment that includes about 80 managers, professionals, and secretaries. The majority had dedicated work stations; some professionals shared work stations. Alpha, beta, and gamma changes in perceived individual effectiveness were measured with two questionnaires, one at the time of implementation and the other after one year of use. The first survey listed job activities and asked the respondents how effective they were at each (T1). The second repeated the list and the question (T2), but also asked respondents to recall their effectiveness at the time of the first questionnaire (Memory).

If answers to the T1 and Memory questions were not different, then the researchers assumed that no beta and gamma changes took place and that the T2 responses revealed alpha change. If T1 answers and memories were different, the researchers reasoned that the frame of reference had changed, either because of the scale shifts associated with beta change or through a more fundamental gamma change of worldview that redefined the activities and therefore the nature of effectiveness in doing them. Beta change was gauged by comparing the T1 and Memory answers to see the direction of scale shift. Gamma change was tested for by comparing factor analyses of the T1, T2, and Memory responses. Similar factor structures would indicate no gamma change. If the T2 and Memory structures were similar to each other but different from T1, a gamma change would have taken place. If gamma change had occurred, then any measured beta change would have been caused by a fundamental change in the nature of the activity and would not be simply a scale shift.

Table 1 summarizes Mohrman and Novelli's findings. It compares three factor analyses of perceived effectiveness--at T1, at T2, and by Memory--to test for gamma change. If there was no gamma change, all activities would be grouped in factors that would fall along the major diagonal of the matrix. Each cluster of activities is also marked to indicate whether it showed no change, alpha change, or beta change in effectiveness measures. As can be seen, four activities (filing, searching files, handling mail, and collating) showed no change in effectiveness and always factored together. The technology was not often used for these. Four other activities--writing, calculating, preparing presentation materials, and proofing--showed alpha changes. Most respondents had had previous experience (vicarious or direct) in using computer-based technology for these activities (secretaries had used an earlier generation of word processors from another vendor and some professionals had done programming). So it appears that respondents had already adopted evaluative standards appropriate for the technology in these cases. The new implementation, nevertheless, further reoriented the way people thought about these activities, especially in relation to all the other activities. In general, when the technology was used to mediate activities it was accompanied by a gammalike

Table 1. *Mohrman and Novelli Study: Comparison of Factor Analyses of Perceived Activity Effectiveness*

Post Factors T2

Pre Factors T1	A	B	C	D	E
1	Filing Searching, Pulling files, Handling mail, Copying, collating, sorting $\Delta \equiv \phi$			*Record keeping $\Delta \equiv \beta$	
2		Using telephone Conferring Meeting $\Delta \equiv \beta$	**Writing, composing $\Delta \equiv \alpha$		
3			Reading $\Delta \equiv \beta$		
4			*Creating designing conceptualizing *Analyzing, reviewing $\Delta \equiv \beta$	*Scheduling, keeping calendars *Planning, organizing $\Delta \equiv \beta$	**Preparing presentation materials $\Delta \equiv \alpha$
5			*Calculating $\Delta \equiv \alpha$		**Proofing, correcting, revising $\Delta \equiv \alpha$

Then Factors T2 Memories of T1

**Over 85% use technology for this activity

*Over 33% use technology for this activity

$\Delta \equiv$ kind of change
$\phi \equiv$ no change
$\alpha \equiv$ alpha change
$\beta \equiv$ beta change

redefinition of activity effectiveness. Further, people's memories of these activities before the technology's introduction for the most part retain this new view.

Table 2 repeats the final T2 groupings of the activities with tentative titles. It shows how respondents saw effectiveness to have been impacted (their memory of effectiveness is compared with the present). It also classifies these activities according to their information systems levels (Marsh and Mannari, 1981). Besides yielding activity groupings more in line with information systems models, the new technology seems to have increased the effectiveness of people doing the activities, at least from their new perspective.

Because of beta shifts within the gamma change, comparing T2 with T1 ratings (not shown) provides quite different results. This comparison makes it seem as if technology did not change or even lessened effectiveness. Actually, definitions of what is effective changed, so in most cases the new criteria of

Table 2. *Mohrman and Novelli Study: Activity Groupings*

	Factor Groupings of Activities	*Significant Change in Perceived Effectiveness*	*Information Systems Levels*
	1. *Handling Information*		
	Filing	o	
	Searching, pulling files	o	Technical
	Handling mail	o	
	Copying, collating, sorting	o	
	2. *Reformatting Information*		
**	Preparing presentation materials	+	
**	Proofing, correcting, revising	+	
	3. *Analyzing and Giving Meaning to Information*		
**	Writing, composing	+	
	Reading	o	Semantic
*	Creating, designing, conceptualizing	+	
*	Analyzing, reviewing	+	
*	Calculating	+	
	4. *Managing Intentions through Information*		
*	Record keeping	o	Influence
*	Scheduling, keeping calendars	+	
*	Planning, organizing	+	
	5. *Communicating Information*		
	Using telephone	+	Channels
	Conferring	+	of Communi-
	Meeting	+	cation

* = Over 33% of respondents use work station to do this activity.
** = Over 85% of respondents use work station to do this activity.
\+ = $P \leqslant .05$ for paired T-tests comparing T2 levels of perceived effectiveness with memories of T1 levels of effectiveness.
o = No significant change in perceived effectiveness.

Source: Mohrman (1983).

effectiveness were more stringent. From their new perspective, people rated their former effectiveness in an activity significantly lower.

Because individuals tend to see the past with their present perspective, they may be blind to the important differences between their old and new views. But these perceptual changes can have real impact on not only the content of people's jobs but the relationship among their roles. For instance, some activities in the office (for example, preparing presentation materials, proofing, record keeping, scheduling, and planning) came to be more equally performed by all roles (Mohrman, 1983). This suggests that when users regroup activities conceptually they will eventually regroup them behaviorally and structurally.

We cannot be sure what caused the gamma change Mohrman and Novelli measured. Many of the changes can just as easily be ascribed to the implementation approach and the nature of the technology. For instance, the freestanding work stations were made available to <u>all</u> personnel without prejudice. Then all employees were encouraged to adapt the technology to their tasks. Frequent formal and informal opportunities were created to share ideas and issues, make suggestions, and solve problems. As users gained experience they could change the nature of the distribution of technology as well as the social and organizational arrangement. Employees who were both technically and interpersonally skilled acted as resources for the others. In short, everything was conducive to creating and fostering gamma change. Although we know that gamma change occurred in this case, we need multiple cases to determine how much it happens in general, and to what extent it is caused by the technology or the implementation choices.

Bikson and her colleagues (Bikson, 1981; Bikson and Gutek, 1983; Bikson and Mankin, 1983) have researched the contributions of organizational context, and especially the implementation process, to technology impacts. They have focused on advanced office systems. Their sample contained 26 organizations equally divided between manufacturing and service. These were represented by 55 "offices" or work groups ranging in size from 4 to 37, with an average of 10. The offices were "early adopters" of the new office-oriented IT and were divided into four categories based on their organizational missions: management and administration; text-oriented professionals; data-oriented professionals; and secretarial, clerical, and technical support.

Questionnaire, interview, and documentary data were collected. Sixty-seven percent of the 530 respondents used a computer-based technology during their regular work. This usage was relatively uniform across all job categories except executives, whose usage was 36%.

The researchers gathered additional data on the information activities for which people used the technology, employing a list similar to Mohrman and Novelli's. Factor analysis of these data revealed four factors that were roughly comparable to the four types of offices in the sample. Clerical and administrative activities were together in the first factor. The second factor included text creating and text altering activities. The third and fourth factors, programming and computation and filing, manipulation, and distribution of numeric data, respectively, were activities associated with data-oriented professional offices. Although to some extent the distribution of activities reflected role and office differences, all activity groupings were performed by all types of offices and all role classifications. These results are very similar to Mohrman and Novelli's.

To date, Bikson and her colleagues have focused on two kinds of impacts: satisfaction with the technology and work performance. They factored various features of the technology on the basis of respondent satisfaction. Four factors emerged: functionality, equipment performance, environment, and interaction. Respondents were most satisfied with functionality--the technology's capability for alteration, entry, storage, error detection, and so on. They showed low satisfaction with equipment maintenance aspects of equipment performance, but high satisfaction with quality of video and print output. Environmental features, such as the arrangement and comfort of space and furniture tended to foster low satisfaction. The lowest satisfaction, however, stemmed from interaction features--computer response time and the operating manual. (Type of dialogue with the computer was generally satisfying.) Of the four factors, only functionality "predicted" how much the technology was utilized and integrated into the individuals' regular work flow. Only functionality and environment were associated with overall satisfaction with the technology.

The respondents felt the technology, once utilized, positively affected every aspect of work performance. This was so for speed, quantity, type, and quality of work done by the office as a whole and was even more true for productivity and quality of individual performance.

Two organizational characteristics affected implementation of the technology. The first was variety in work; in this sample broad jobs facilitated implementation. The second was the organization's orientation toward change. A problem-solving and positive approach aimed at doing what is achievable was found to be important.

Overall, these results paint a rather positive picture of acceptance and functionality of the new technology in office settings. At least in these early adopting units, a problem-solving and multifunctional (as opposed to fragmenting) approach resulted in success--in terms of both implementation and subsequent performance. We do not know, however, whether this spirit will prevail in future applications or what the long-term effects of this technology will be.

Johnson and her colleagues (Johnson, 1983; Johnson and Rice, 1983; Rice et al., 1983) have been investigating the degree to which a "reinvention" process, when allowed to occur after initial implementation, leads to certain organizational impacts. In addition, they are interested in the variation in impacts depending on how the process takes place. They started with a narrowly defined form of the technology, word processing. Their findings indicated that word processing has come to be increasingly integrated with other office and organizational IT.

Thus, they are being empirically driven to a more broadly defined technology, similar to that studied by Bikson and her colleagues.

For their study of 200 word processing units, Johnson and her colleagues collected interview data structured around a sociotechnical systems approach. They focused on the "effective use of word processing," which they defined as an "increase in capability directed toward organizational mission." Specifically, they wanted to know if the technology was being used for tasks that would be "impossible or impractical without it." In this sense, they were looking for gamma changes, not efficiency-oriented alpha changes in effectiveness.

For the most part they found that efficiency was the major reported benefit of the technology--remember, however, Mohrman and Novelli found that respondents often were blind to gamma changes. Johnson and her colleagues rarely saw the technology being used to increase organizational capability. When they did find such improvement in effectiveness beyond efficiency, the following principles were in operation:

1. Involve people jointly in changes of technology: Most technology changes were unilaterally initiated by management; however, when operators were jointly involved in changing their own jobs, they developed uses of the technology (tracking loan authorizations or establishing coordination mechanisms, for example), that increased organizational capability.

2. Encourage experimentation: Few units encouraged experimentation, but when they did--by allowing time to play with the technology and showing appreciation for new methods--capability was extended.

3. Maintain flexible procedures: Units in the study typically started with substantial flexibility. This impeded efficiency, so pressure emerged to decrease flexibility. Nevertheless, within some degree of necessary routinization, flexibility produced expanded capability. Means of achieving flexibility include direct contact between word processors and authors, and authors' use of the technology.

4. Increase the "response repertoire" and information of employees: Vendor training has generally been inadequate; the most useful training has been employees instructing one another.

5. Promote self-regulation of employees: Employee self-regulation happens in at least two ways. The first is associated with the nature of the technology; it allows employees broader responsibility for document creation and for each document as a whole. The second is related to control and monitoring systems that regulate performance. Organizations showing high capacity involved employees in developing performance measures to encourage motivation.

6. Build discretion into the job: Seldom was the technology installed to increase quality of work life or enrich jobs. Nevertheless, some situations did seem to engender increased discretion, creativity, autonomy, and ability to work on

whole projects without interruption. When increased discretion resulted, personnel administration typically would not accept it as a job dimension involved with word processing. Higher capacity was associated with situations where pay systems reflected increased discretion.

7. Encourage communication: Although respondents generally felt that relationships and communication with co-workers were motivating sources of creativity, problem solving, and quality of work life, word processing centers tended to foster a sense of isolation from the rest of the organization that had to be overcome. Conversely, distributed word processing hindered communication among peers. Communication was seldom encouraged, but when it was--either formally or informally--it was associated with more capabilities.

One implication of these findings is that the kinds of impacts organizations experience depend on what they want and expect. Most of these word processing units, it seems, implemented the technology as a means to accomplish existing performance needs more efficiently. Most realized these goals. A few, however, achieved increased capabilities not originally envisioned. Focusing on either type of impact may blind one to the other, because the methods for achieving and the criteria for measuring each stem from different logics of organizational effectiveness.

Summary. Taken together these three recent studies raise many important points. First, IT has often been successfully used to automate predefined activities efficiently and productively. This depends on a rationality that combines the technology's capabilities with the flow of the activity. Technical rationality affects the users' worldview, the nature of their work, and eventually the technical relationships among individual tasks, jobs, and roles. The way this rationality is incorporated into organizational arrangements is variable, as is the meaning individuals ascribe to it. In general, users are satisfied with the technology and are able to employ it. Whether the technology brings capabilities that are not possible without it depends on the extent to which individual users can be involved in a continuing process of sociotechnical systems design in which the technical rationality is applied to new activities that in turn can yield a reinvention of the technology--third-order feedback and gamma change. Without such an involving and evolving process, the tendency is simply to use the technology for more efficient performance of predefined activities.

Integrative/Disintegrative Model

We offer the following model, which we call the integrative/disintegrative model, as a heuristic for interpreting research on IT impacts (see Figure 1). It is based on considerable previous study of how organizations evolve and operate (Bikson and Gutek, 1983; Etzioni, 1961; Galbraith, 1977; Katz and Kahn, 1978; Ouchi, 1981). It assumes that the fundamental organizational choice is how to integrate the organization's needs with those of individuals and individual units. Human beings tend to adopt three modes of organization to integrate a system: utilitarian, authoritative, and normative.

Figure 1. *Integrative/Disintegrative Model of Organization Modes*

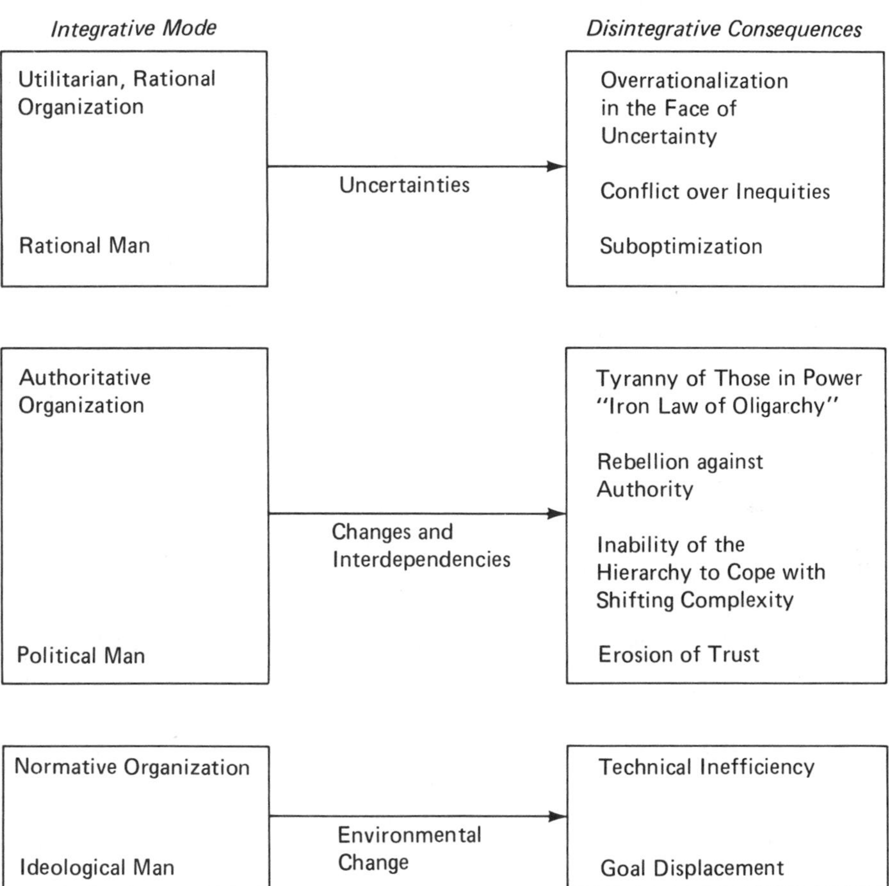

Each mode follows a different logic and flows from a different set of assumptions about why and how human beings behave. Paradoxically, each approach engenders a characteristic disintegrative reaction that threatens the integration it seeks. Each organizational mode complements the others; it deals with their disintegrative consequences but fosters yet another set of disintegrative forces through its own weaknesses. Because of this, we usually find all three forms of organization in any situation, although one or two are usually stressed more.

Utilitarian Mode

The first mode of organization uses a utilitarian and goal-oriented logic. Organizational tasks are rationally configured in the attempt to optimize achievement of organizational goals. The same characteristics are assumed of people employed in organizations: that they are rational, utilitarian, and goal oriented. Because individual and organizational goals are not assumed to be the same, the utilitarian rationality is used to set up ways to integrate organizational and individual needs. Employees receive inducements they value in exchange for contributions that the organization values (Marsh and Mannari, 1981). The feasibility and efficiency of this organizational mode depend on the degree to which inducements and contributions and the logic of how contributions combine to achieve organizational goals can be specified. The organizational rationality is related to the technologies used and their underlying logic.

The utilitarian approach breaks down when its assumptions cannot be met. Uncertainties and ambiguities caused by lack of knowledge and information can prevent specification. Overspecification runs the risk of appearing and being irrational. Ambiguities about contributions increase the probabilities that actors will perceive inequities between their own inducement-contribution exchanges and those of others. Inability to specify the relationship between individual contributions and organizational goals leads to suboptimization. Thus, uncertainties can result in disintegrative, segmented concerns and conflicts unless an integrative approach can be found to deal with them.

Authoritative Mode

The integrative organizational approach traditionally used to deal with the ambiguities of the rational mode is legitimate authority (Galbraith, 1977). This assumes that within certain bounds people are willing to give authority to others, especially in situations of ambiguity. The bases on which such authority is granted may vary--organizational position, expertise, personality, organizational experience, democratic election--but the important thing is that people will give authority to others. Those given authority are allowed to make decisions in the ambiguous realms, and thus to control the relevant actions of others. Their power can be extended to establishing goals for others. Authority also lies in the way decisions are made (Bjorn-Andersen and Eason, 1980; Easton, 1965), including determining who should be placed in authority positions. Because of the way authority is related to uncertainty, legitimate authority structures in organizations can complement the utilitarian organization. Many aspects of the authoritative decision-making structure nevertheless reflect other influences, such as historic sources of power and conventional notions of governance.

Because authority is granted by organizational actors carrying out the decisions made by those in authority positions, it is subject to change by them. An obvious source of such change is a change in the rational organization that would shift the areas of ambiguity. Existing authorities may not be willing to participate in such a shift, because authority positions often become bases of power that exceed the authority granted. An "iron law of oligarchy" often prevails; those granted authority can use it to perpetuate and even exacerbate the uncertainties at the base of their authority as well as to acquire other sources of power. When this happens the integrative balance between the needs of the organization and those of the individuals in it is tipped so that the decision-making process attends to the needs of only some organizational segments. People rebel when the power structure is out of balance with the authority necessarily granted to complement the rational organization. Support for the authoritative decision-making system breaks down, and demands on it escalate (Easton, 1965). The more frequently changes occur and the more uncertainty there is, the more exacerbated this dynamic becomes.

Typically, the uncertainties authority deals with are exceptional cases that cannot be specified or anticipated in the task definitions at lower levels. Authority breaks down when it is unable to handle the uncertainties that are passed up the hierarchy.

One important source of these uncertainties is increasing interdependencies among organizational tasks. As interdependencies increase, performance of tasks becomes more contingent on what is done and how it is accomplished in other tasks. Authority figures are assumed to know the contingencies of multiple tasks and therefore to make decisions based on this knowledge. But as interdependencies increase, task contingencies overload authorities' cognitive capabilities. The hierarchy's inability to cope with this shifting complexity undermines its authority. One solution can be to create tools and understanding that allow one to cope with the uncertainty by specifying the contingencies and the decision rules to deal with them--a rational, utilitarian approach. The other remedy is to absorb the uncertainty in a much different way, through normative organization.

Authority breaks down when the variety of needs and values come to be differentially considered because power is differentially aggrandized by those in authority positions. Those granting authority will no longer trust that those in authority are operating in their interests or the interests of the organization as a whole. On the other hand, those in authority will tend not to trust that other organization members will act according to what they consider to be organization needs and will escalate controlling behaviors accordingly.

Normative Mode

Utilitarian and authoritative integration depend on the existence of underlying norms--reciprocity in the utilitarian mode and legitimacy in the authoritative (Ouchi, 1981). Utilitarian integration breaks down because it is either impossible or too expensive to specify and measure contributions and inducements to set up an equitable exchange in which both individual and organizational needs are met. Authority breaks down when either those granting authority or those in authority positions do not trust the others to consider their needs or the needs of the organization. The alternative integrative approach in these cases is to bring individual needs, goals, and values and those of the organization into alignment with each other. In addition, these values and norms must be internalized by all, and all must trust that the others have done so. Among the methods for achieving this mode are socialization processes and consensual and participative processes. The vehicle for normative integration is a common culture with norms of behavior, beliefs, and values that are not dictated by utilitarian or authoritative logics but by tradition and informal social processes leading to social conformity.

Normative integration breaks down because of environmental change. Traditional ways of doing things that may once have been best do not always remain so. Organizational and technological contrivances in the environment are subject to change. Organizational output can result in environmental feedback that leads organizational actors to question the organization's goals and methods. Success of competitors can cause the organization to question its technology. As knowledge and techniques evolve in the environment, they supply new models of rationality that people compare with those (implicitly) in use in their organization. Disintegrative conflicts arise between segments of the organization which adhere to the status quo and segments which claim that normative organization has displaced and obscured its original goals and that practices are accepted only because they are normal and are no longer judged on their efficiency and effectiveness. A growing push for understanding and clarifying the goals of the organization and for explicating and rationalizing its practices evolves.

All three integrative and disintegrative modes are at work at all times in all organizations. Each integrative mode complements the others. Organizations vary in the degree to which they stress one or more integrative approaches, and disintegrative issues likewise vary among organizations, parts of organizations, and individuals.

Applying the Model to IT

Rob Kling and Walt Scacchi (1982) developed a framework for classifying research on the impact of IT that partially corresponds to the integrative/disintegrative model. They divided the research into two general theoretical perspectives: those assuming "systems rationalism" and those assuming "segmented institutionalism." The former approach stresses the integrative uses of the technology; the latter stresses that IT must deal with a reality in which disintegrative social forces are always present. The technology might integrate organizational segments, but it can also exacerbate disintegration.

Research on the roles of computer-based modeling (Dutton, 1983) has derived a similar typology. Models can be classified in terms of how they affect the various modes of integration. They can be used "rationally" to provide information that guides decisions according to the accepted utilitarian rationality. They can be used "technocratically" or "bureaucratically" to legitimate proposals or adopted policies. Finally, they can be used "consensually" as bases for interactive building of common beliefs and norms.

The technology can be directly used to impact any of the integrative or disintegrative modes in Figure 1, and it can have indirect effects by engendering organizational activity in the other modes. Depending on what antecedent conditions exist in the organization and on which we choose to focus, the technology will generate some immediate effects. For instance, if the organization has been in a state of high normative integration that fostered growing disintegrative concerns about technical inefficiency, then a rational system could have immediate integration effects. These, however, might have disintegrative consequences that would drive or perhaps be preempted by changes in authoritative integration. Eventually, there will be a series of direct and indirect consequences, both integrative and disintegrative in nature. And they will be further modified by reactive or anticipatory organizational responses.

Using the Model to Interpret Impacts

Much of the theorizing about and research on the impact of automated technology has focused on the integration of the individual with work and the organization. Often the focus has been on the disintegrative side, especially alienation of individuals from the organization and their work.

Jon Shepard (1971) compared the alienation of white- and blue-collar workers in jobs representing various stages of the automation continuum. His dependent measures of alienation, drawn from the classic sociology literature, fit into our model.

Instrumental work orientation refers to the degree to which workers labor for the money only, and is a consequence of the utilitarian organization. In addition, this orientation forecasts worker focus on economic inequities and the disintegrative conflicts it engenders.

Powerlessness is the lack of influence over their own labor that workers feel. It reflects a source of illegitimacy of existing authority structures if the areas of powerlessness result in an inability to meet the individual's personal or task needs. Powerlessness is the result of granting authority.

As operationalized by Shepard, normlessness refers to the extent to which workers consider authority illegitimate. Normlessness would indicate the degree of the authority structure's disintegration.

Self-evaluative involvement is the extent to which workers derive an identity and status from the work as opposed to the nonwork aspects of their lives. This reflects how much workers are normatively integrated with the organization.

Meaninglessness refers to workers' ability to make rational sense of how their jobs integrate with the others in the organization and contribute to the goals of the organization or the organizational unit. Meaninglessness signals a disintegrative breakdown from an extremely normative state and lays the groundwork for a positive, rationalizing impact of the technology.

Shepard looked at the effects of automation or integrating alienation by comparing blue- and white-collar workers who had automated jobs with those who had mechanized or traditional jobs. Two kinds of jobs were created by computer automation: jobs monitoring automated processes, which were found in both blue- and white-collar settings, and white-collar jobs dealing with computer software. Shepard's findings are summarized below.

1. Half or over half of all white-collar clerks with either traditional or mechanized jobs showed alienation of all kinds. Mechanized blue-collar workers showed considerably more alienation in all forms than did white-collar workers.

2. Blue- and white-collar workers who had jobs involving the monitoring of automated equipment showed converging degrees of less alienation.

3. Except in the case of white-collar powerlessness, where no differences were noted (60% for both mechanized and automated), both blue- and white-collar monitors of automated equipment were less alienated than any workers with mechanized jobs. Not only did they have less alienation, but both blue- and white-collar monitors showed similar levels (30%-50% depending on the type of alienation).

4. In another form of job created by automation, computer software, only a minority of workers showed powerlessness (10%) and instrumental work orientation (20%). Only one-third reported job meaninglessness. People in these jobs showed normlessness (33%) and self-evaluative involvement (60%) comparable to automation monitors.

Shepard's results lend credence to the notion that automated jobs will increasingly involve processing information in second- and third-order feedback loops and will therefore narrow the differences between blue- and white-collar work. Workers in the automated settings of his sample tended to be more integrated with the organization than those in mechanized settings. Their levels of integration with job and organization were closer to those of craftspeople, who were also included in the study. Others have reported similar findings (Hirschhorn, 1981; Hull,

Friedman, and Rogers, 1982; Zuboff, 1982). Nevertheless, Shepard's work also shows that significant percentages of people in automated settings are just as alienated as the majority in mechanized settings. And many other studies have shown automation to be more alienating in some situations (Bjorn-Andersen et al., 1979).

We can partially predict the impacts of the technology through the integrative/disintegrative model. To some extent the seemingly contradictory results of various studies can be explained by the fact that they represent impacts in different integrative and disintegrative stages.

The obvious starting point is the rational, utilitarian organization. Often the primary intent of IT is to affect this mode. Intentions can be at two levels: either the technology is used to bolster the existing rationality in the organization, or it is used to change it, to install a new view of how to design the organization rationally. As Mohrman and Novelli (1983) make clear, even when the technology is implemented to augment existing organizational roles and no attempt is made to influence the rationale behind those roles, the organization's rationality can eventually change.

The technology, in its particular hardware and software combinations, embodies knowledge and its underlying rationality. Its strengths are speed and reliability in performing complex logical maneuvers (Whisler, 1970). Therefore, we would expect its most direct impacts to be on the rational and utilitarian forms of organization and individual behavior. Many of the reasons for adopting IT in the first place are such expectations, and the bulk of the research literature reports on the generally positive impact of IT on organizational rationality and utility.

For instance, a study of the impact of computer systems (ranging from real-time, on-line to batch) in five banks in four countries (Bjorn-Andersen et al., 1979) yielded the following generally applicable findings: error detection by computer replaced detection by people, there was faster error feedback, the clerk job became more structured and programmed, much learning about the technical system occurred on the job. A general narrowing of the clerk job was matched by some workers' satisfaction with the technology and interest in it. In this case, the technology is making some positive rational and utilitarian impact. On balance, it is serving the existing rationality of the banks rather than bringing in a new one. Johnson's (1983) findings are similar.

The effects of the new rationality, or the responses to it, depend on the state of the organization at the time of implementation. If, for instance, an organization's normal practices and traditions are not leading to success in the environment and technical inefficiencies are becoming salient, then the effect of the new rationality, provided it attends to the inefficiencies, will be accepted. Ken Eason (1980), for example, found that IT changed managers' perceptions of their jobs' complexity and nature. This improved view of their tasks led to new ideas and new methods. Managers saw all these results as useful progress from their previously poorly understood roles. In this context, they evaluated the standardizing and routinizing nature of IT positively. These attributes clarified the managing role and fostered development.

But even favorably received and useful changes in the rational structure must be followed by adjustments in the organization's other integrative modes. And each of these commensurate adjustments will be driven by the disintegrative forces that arise out of the others. For instance, Eason also found that the nature of the IT's rationality not only elucidated the managers' jobs but also made information available to subordinates that clarified their perceptions of their roles and the relationship of their roles to those of the managers. This increased information and understanding led to an argument--based on the resulting redistribution of sources of uncertainty, inequities, and suboptimizations--that in certain areas subordinates should be more involved in decision making. Thus, the new rationality began to drive a new authority structure by questioning the legitimacy of the old and proposing a replacement.

Even though the IT is, on the surface, a rational intervention, its uses and effects can occur in the other integrative modes. For instance, IT is frequently employed to bolster a disintegrating authority structure, through increased monitoring of subordinate performance, for example. It is important to distinguish between the technical rationality of the monitoring and its authoritative uses. It may well make technical sense--consistent with the new rationality--to centralize certain kinds of performance information, to achieve economies of scale, perhaps by processing the information centrally. As Derek Stone's (1975) research shows, however, it is a mistake to assume that centralization of information is tantamount to centralization of authority and control. Stone reported that, despite the advice of consultants, an organization wisely refused to use information centralized for efficient processing to make decisions. Decision making was left decentralized. Centralization of the routine created more local time for attention to management issues. The results included lower costs, increased customer service, and, in general, better local management that was able to respond to local issues. Local issues were the sources of uncertainty upon which management authority was legitimated.

Rationalization brought with IT can also affect the normative mode of integration. Perhaps the most common example of these effects is when IT is used to fragment jobs on the basis of an analytical rationale. Although this might make utilitarian sense--as long as compensating attention is given to rationally integrating these differentiated parts--it can undermine normative integration. People develop a level of integration and involvement with their jobs that is based in part on socially learned characteristics of the tasks. Job fragmentation can disrupt these modes of integration and undermine the organizational culture (Argyns, 1971). If, however, the organization is already strongly based on a rationality, and especially if that rationality has reached or exceeded the limits uncertainty places on it, then a further intervention--for instance, fragmentation of existing tasks--will foster or strengthen the disintegrative forces that evolve out of extreme rationality (Bjorn-Andersen et al., 1979).

Conclusions and Implications

Figure 2 displays the major relationships we have identified so far. It shows that the impact of the particular IT is a function of the nature of the organization in which it is installed as well as of the implementation process. The research quite consistently points out that involvement of employees is key to a successful implementation. This finding seems to hold for all types of technologies. The effects of the nature of the organization are much more complex. Organizational nature moderates the impact of particular technologies, so unless the type of technology and the nature of the organization are specified in terms of the integrative/disintegrative model, the organizational impact of the technology is not predictable.

Figure 2 also shows two feedback loops. The one from organizational impact to the nature of the organization highlights the point that IT can change the state of an organization. Specific predictions about how this will occur require knowledge of the technology and the existing organization. The feedback loop to the technology itself highlights the cybernetic nature of IT. Again, a specific prediction requires knowledge of the technology's starting point. However, this argument suggests that, in general, organizations will gravitate toward higher and higher levels of technology.

The cybernetic nature of IT and its adaptability to third-order feedback loops imply that adaptive and participative research techniques are appropriate for assessing the impacts of IT (Elden et al., 1982; Mohrman and Novelli, 1982). In fact, the same rationale can be used to argue that organizational use of and response to the technology should also be adaptive and participative (Bjorn-Andersen et al., 1979). These normative statements are not mere indications of a value stance independent of the technology; they reflect the technology's impacts. Indeed, we find examples again and again in the literature of IT creating a pressure for increased participation and adaptation, either as a reaction to an inappropriate application that purposefully limits such participation, or as a natural extension of an implementation that allows such participation to take its course.

Figure 2. *Effects of Information Technology*

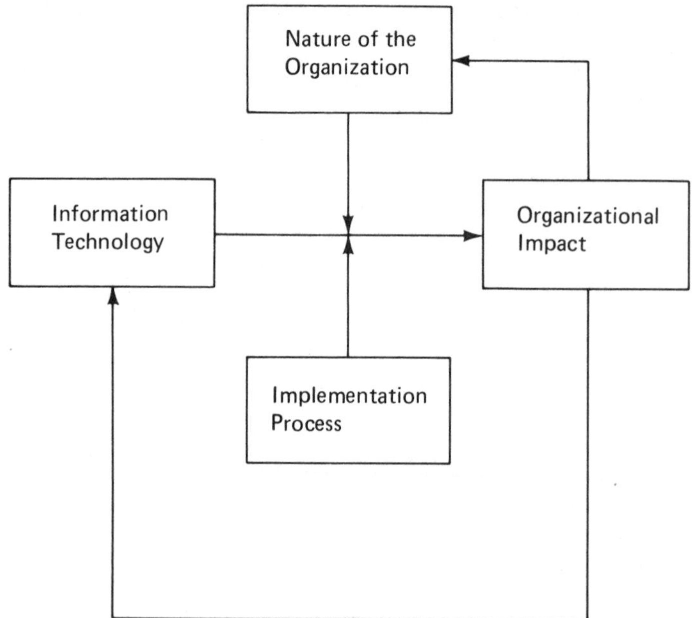

The impact of IT is not toward more order or more freedom; this debate is a fruitless one--the technology can be utilized to support either. Research is replete with examples of both. As our knowledge of organizations establishes, every approach to organization is a two-edged sword that carries the means of its own destruction. The impact of IT is to sharpen the sword. It exacerbates the potential negative and unintentional consequences of the positive and intentional "cuts" it makes. This is because the technology highlights not physical activity or interpersonal behavior, on which previous iterations of organizational models have concentrated, but cognitive behavior, "patterns of attention, learning, and mental engagement" (Zuboff, 1982) that are more and more being recognized as fundamental to understanding much of organizational behavior. Information technology is providing organizations with a higher-order test of their ability to balance their needs and goals with those of the individuals within them.

Bibliography

Argyris, Chris. "Management Information Systems: The Challenge to Rationality and Emotionality." Management Science, February 1971, pp. B-275 - B-292.

Bikson, Tora K. "Electronic Information Systems and User Contexts: Emerging Social Science Issues." Rand Paper Series, p-6690, September 1981.

Bikson, Tora K.; and Gutek, Barbara A. "Advanced Office Systems: An Empirical Look at Utilization and Satisfaction." Rand Note N-1970-NSF, February 1983.

Bikson, Tora K.; and Mankin, Don. "Factors in Successful Implementation of Computer-based Office Information Systems: A Review of the Literature." Mimeo, Rand Corporation, 1983.

Bjorn-Andersen, Niels; and Eason, Ken D. "Myths and Realities of Information Systems Contributing to Organizational Rationality." In Human Choice and Computers, 2d ed., A. Mowskowitz (ed.), New York: North-Holland, 1980.

Bjorn-Andersen, Niels; Hedberg, Bo; Mercer, Dorothy; Mumford, Enid; and Sole, Andreu (eds.). The Impact of Systems Change in Organizations. Alphen aan den Rijn, The Netherlands: Sijthoff & Noordhoff, 1979.

Briefs, Ulrich. "The Effects of Computerization on Human Work--New Directions for Computer Use in the Work-Place." In Human Choice and Computers, 2d ed., A. Mowskowitz (ed.), New York: North-Holland, 1980.

Cheney, Paul H.; and Dickson, Gary W. "Organizational Characteristics and Information Systems: An Exploratory Investigation." Academy of Management Journal, March 1982, pp. 170-184.

Deutsch, Steven. "Unions and Technological Change: International Perspectives." In Labor and Technology: Union Responses to Changing Environments, D. Kennedy, C. Craypo, and M. Lehman (eds.). University Park, Pa.: Pennsylvania State University, 1982.

Dutton, William. "The Role of Computers in Decision Making." Presented to the National Computer Conference, Anaheim, Calif., May 18, 1983.

Eason, Ken D. "Computer Information Systems and Managerial Tasks." In The Human Side of Information Processing, Niels Bjorn-Andersen (ed.). New York: North-Holland, 1980.

Easton, David. A Systems Analysis of Political Life. New York: John Wiley & Sons, 1965.

Ebizawa, Eiichi. "Office Automation Systems and Organizations' Responses to Them: A Summary Report on a Survey of Three Different Types of Organizations." Mimeo, University of Oregon, 1983.

Edstrom, Anders; and Nauges, Louis. "Discontinuities of Computerization--A Study of French Companies." In Information Systems and Organizational Structure, E. Grochla and N. Szyperski (eds.). New York: Walter de Gruyter, 1975.

Elden, Max; Havn, Vidar; Levin, Morten; Nilssen, Tore; Rasmussen, Benta; and Veium, Knut. Good Technology Is Not Enough. Trondheim, Norway: Institute for Social Research in Industry (IFIM), 1982.

Etzioni, Amitai. Complex Organizations. New York: Free Press, 1961.

Fadem, Joel A. "Automation and Work Design in the United States." UCLA, Center for Quality of Working Life, Working Paper 43, 1982.

Galbraith, Jay R. Organization Design. Reading, Mass.: Addison-Wesley, 1977.

Giuliano, Vincent E. "The Mechanization of Office Work." Scientific American, September 1982, pp. 149-164.

Golembiewski, Robert T.; Billingsley, Keith; and Yeager, Samuel. "Measuring Change and Persistence in Human Affairs: Types of Change Generated by OD Designs." Journal of Applied Behavioral Sciences, April-June 1976, pp. 133-157.

Gutek, Barbara A. "Effects of 'Office of the Future' Technology on Users: Results of a Longitudinal Field Study." In Work, Organizations, and Technological Change, G. Mensch and R. Niehaus (eds.). New York: Plenum, 1982.

Hackman, J. Richard; and Oldham, Greg R. Work Redesign. Reading, Mass.: Addison-Wesley, 1980.

Hedberg, Bo. "Computer Systems to Support Industrial Democracy." Presented to the International Federation for Information Processing Conference, Vienna, April 1974.

__________. "Using Computerized Information Systems to Design Better Organizations and Jobs." In The Human Side of Information Processing, Niels Bjorn-Andersen (ed.). New York: North-Holland, 1980.

Hirschhorn, Larry. "The Post-Industrial Labor Process." New Political Science, Fall 1981, pp. 11-32.

Huber, George. "Organizational Information Systems: Determinants of Their Performance and Behavior." Management Science, February 1982, pp. 138-155.

Hull, Frank M.; Friedman, Nathalie S.; and Rogers, Theresa F. "The Effect of Technology on Alienation from Work." Work and Occupations, February 1982, pp. 31-57.

Ives, Blake; Hamilton, Scott; and Davis, Gordon B. "A Framework for Research in Computer-based Management Information Systems." Management Science, September 1980, pp. 910-934.

Johnson, Bonnie McDaniel. "Innovation in Word Processing." A series of project reports, Institute for Communication Research and Policy Conference, Annapolis, April 1983.

Johnson, Bonnie McDaniel; and Rice, Ronald E. "Policy Implications in Implementing Office Systems Technology." Presented to the 11th Annual Telecommunications Research and Policy Conference, Annapolis, April 1983.

Katz, Daniel; and Kahn, Robert L. The Social Psychology of Organizations, 2d ed. New York: John Wiley & Sons, 1978.

Kensing, Finn. "The Trade Unions' Influence on Technological Change." Presented to the 10th World Congress of the International Sociological Association, Mexico, August 1982.

Kling, Rob. "The Impacts of Computing on the Work of Managers, Data Analysts and Clerks." University of California, Irvine, Public Policy Research Organization, Working Paper, WP-78-64, 1978.

__________. "Social Issues and Impacts of Computing: A Survey of North American Research." University of California, Irvine, Public Policy Research Organization, Working Paper, January 1979.

__________. "Social Analyses of Computing: Theoretical Perspectives in Recent Empirical Research." Computing Surveys, March 1980a, pp. 61-110.

__________. "Social Issues and Impacts of Computing: From Arena to Discipline." In Human Choice and Computers, 2d ed., A. Mowskowitz (ed.), New York: North-Holland, 1980b.

Kling, Rob; and Scacchi, Walt. "Computing as Social Action: The Social Dynamics of Computing in Complex Organizations." Advances in Computers, Vol. 19, 1980, pp. 249-327.

__________. "The Web of Computing: Computer Technology as Social Organization." University of California, Irvine, Public Policy Research
Organization, Working Paper, WP-175-25-161, 1982.

Lucas, Henry C., Jr. "Measuring Employee Reactions to Computer Operations." Sloan Management Review, Spring 1974, pp. 59-67.

__________. "Performance and Use of an Information System." Management Science, April 1975a, pp. 908-919.

__________. "The Use of an Accounting Information System, Action and Organizational Performance." Accounting Review, October 1975b, pp. 735-746.

Mann, Floyd C.; and Williams, Lawrence K. "Observations on the Dynamics of a Change to Electronic Data-Processing Equipment." Administrative Science Quarterly, September 1960, pp. 217-256.

March, James G.; and Simon, Herbert A. Organizations. New York: John Wiley & Sons, 1958.

Marschak, Jacob; and Radner, Roy. Economic Theory of Teams. New Haven: Yale University Press, 1972.

Marsh, Robert M.; and Mannari, Hiroshi. "Technology and Size as Determinants of the Organizational Structure of Japanese Factories." Administrative Science Quarterly, March 1981, pp. 33-57.

Mason, Richard O. "Measures of Information Output." UCLA, Study Center in Public Services Management and Policy and Information Studies, Information Systems Working Paper 12-77, 1977.

Meyer, Marshall W. "Leadership and Organizational Structure." American Journal of Sociology, November 1975, pp. 514-542.

Meyer, N. Dean. "Human Resource Issues in Office Automation." Research Report, Diebold Group, 1981.

___________. "Office Automation: A Progress Report." Office: Technology and People, March 1982, pp. 107-121.

Mohrman, Allan M., Jr. "The Impact of Information Processing Technologies on Office Roles." University of Southern California, Center for Effective Organizations, Publication G 83-2 (33), 1983.

Mohrman, Allan M., Jr., and Novelli, Luke, Jr. "Adaptively Learning about the Impacts of Information Processing Technologies in the Office." University of Southern California, Center for Effective Organizations, Publication G 82-8 (27), 1982.

___________. "Three Types of Change in the Automated Office." University of Southern California, Center for Effective Organizations,
Publication G 83-5 (36), 1983.

Mowskowitz, A. Human Choice and Computers, 2d ed. New York: North-Holland, 1980.

Ouchi, William G. "Markets, Bureaucracies, and Clans." Administrative Science Quarterly, March 1980, pp. 129-141.

_______. Theory Z. Reading, Mass.: Addison-Wesley, 1981.

Pava, Calvin H. P. "Socio-Technical Design for Advanced Office Technology." Harvard Business School, Working Paper, HBS 82-75, 1982.

___________. Managing New Office Technology: An Organizational Strategy. New York: Free Press, 1983.

Rice, Ronald E. "The Impacts of Computer-mediated Organizational and Interpersonal Communication." In Annual Review of Information Science and Technology, M. E. Williams (ed.). White Plains, N.Y.: Knowledge Industry Publications, 1980.

___________. "Media Style and Organizational Use of Computer-based Communication Systems." Mimeo, University of Southern California, Annenberg School of Communications, 1983.

Rice, Ronald E.; and Case, Donald. "Electronic Message Systems in the University: A Description of Use and Utility." Journal of Communication, Winter 1983, pp. 131-152.

Rice, Ronald E.; Johnson, Bonnie McD.; Kowal, Deborah; and Feltman, Charles. "The Survival of the Fittest: Organizational Design and the Structures of Word Processing." Paper presented at the Academy of Management annual meeting, Dallas, August 1983.

Rice, Ronald E.; and Rogers, Everett M. "New Methods and New Data for New Media." In The New Media: Uses and Impacts, Ronald E. Rice et al. (eds.). Beverly Hills, Calif.: Sage, 1983.

Salancik, Gerald R.; and Pfeffer, Jeffrey. "A Social Information Processing Approach to Job Attitudes and Task Design." Administrative Science Quarterly, June 1978, pp. 189-203.

Schareck, Bernard; and Barton, Ewald. "Comments on the Influence of Information Technology on Organizational Structure in Insurance Industry." In Information Systems and Organizational Structure. E. Grochla and N. Szyperski (eds.). New York: Walter de Gruyter, 1975.

Schoderbek, Peter P.; Kefalas, Asterios G.; and Schoderbek, Charles G. Management Systems. Dallas: Business Publications, 1975.

Schultz, George P.; and Whisler, Thomas L. (eds.). Management, Organization, and the Computer. Glencoe, Ill.: Free Press, 1960.

Seligman, Ben B. "The Impact of Automation on White-Collar Workers." In Automation, Alienation, and Anomie, S. Marcson (ed.). New York: Harper & Row, 1970.

Shepard, Jon M. Automation and Alienation: A Study of Office and Factory Workers. Cambridge, Mass.: MIT Press, 1971.

Sorenson, Knut Holtan. "The Impact of Technology upon the Development of Industrial Democracy." Paper presented at 10th World Congress of the International Sociological Association, Mexico, August 1982.

Sorge, Arndt; Hartmann, Gert; Warner, Malcolm; and Nicholas, Ian. "Technology, Organization and Manpower: Applications of CNC in Manufacturing in Great Britain and West Germany." In Information Society: For Richer, for Poorer. N. Bjorn-Andersen, M. Earl, O. Holst, and E. Mumford (eds.). New York: North-Holland, 1982.

Stableski, Joan. "Is Office Automation Hazardous to Your Health?" World of Work Report, April 1983, pp. 29-30.

Steinfield, Charles. "Uses and Impacts of Electronic Mail." Paper presented at the National Computer Conference, Anaheim, Calif., May 1983.

Stone, Derek. "Changes in Organizational Design Induced by the Introduction of Computerized Information Systems: A Longitudinal Study in the Electricity Industry." In Information Systems and Organizational Structure, E. Grochla and N. Szyperski (eds.). New York: Walter de Gruyter, 1975.

Szell, Gyorgy. "New Technology and Activation of Workers in Self-Management." Paper presented at 10th World Congress of the International Sociological Association, Mexico, August 1982.

Terborg, J. R.; Howard, G. S.; and Maxwell, S. E. "Evaluating Planned Organizational Change: A Method for Assessing Alpha, Beta, and Gamma Change." Academy of Management Review, January 1980, pp. 109-121.

Traesborg, Michael; and Bjorn-Andersen, Niels. "Micro-Electronics and Work Qualifications." Report for the International Institute of Vocational Training, Berlin, 1981. Summarized in the ISRG-Newsletter (Copenhagen School of Economics and Business Administration), June 1982.

Tricker, Robert I. "Order or Freedom: The Ultimate Issue in Information Systems Design." In The Human Side of Information Processing, Niels Bjorn-Andersen (ed.). New York: North-Holland, 1980.

Uhlig, Ronald P.; Farber, David J.; and Bair, James H. The Office of the Future. New York: North-Holland, 1979.

Walton, Richard E.; and Mela, Wendy. "New Information Technology: Organizational Problem or Opportunity?" Mimeo, Harvard Business School, Division of Research, 1981.

Warnecke, H. J.; Bullinger, H. J.; and Haller, E. "Effects of Social, Technological, and Organizational Changes on the Labor Design as Shown by the Example of Microelectronics." Stuttgart, Germany: Fraunhofer-Institut fur Productionstechnik und Automatisierung, 1981.

Weick, Karl E. The Social Psychology of Organizing, 2d ed. Reading, Mass.: Addison-Wesley, 1979.

Whisler, Thomas L. The Impact of Computers on Organizations. New York: Praeger, 1970.

Williams, Trevor. "Learning to Manage Our Futures." University of
Southern California, Seminar presentation, 1983.

Zuboff, Shoshana. "New Worlds of Computer-mediated Work." Harvard Business Review, September-October 1982, pp. 142-152.

DISCUSSION: MOHRMAN AND LAWLER PAPER

What is organizational impact? How is it measured? These are the questions that dominated the early discussion of Allan Mohrman and Edward Lawler's paper. It was pointed out that the authors make a critical assumption: "Information technology impacts on people. People, in turn, impact on organization." This, it was stressed, is an argument from the premise of technological determinism. Might it be the other way around? That is, Do people get new ideas and then acquire the type of technology they want? or, Do organizations change and then acquire the technology they need? It is likely that all these are possible, but that technology is still the prime driving force. Technology, especially microelectronic technology, is also inherently uncontrolled. It's like the old Persian adage, "Once the camel gets his nose under the tent, there is no stopping the rest of him, humps and all, from coming in too."

This led to a discussion of organizational learning and the need for models of organizational learning and organizational change to study the impact of IT. Starting with its point of entry into an organization, the impacts of IT ripple throughout. Impact, it was argued, does not diffuse in a linear path or even in a well-behaved geometric progression. Rather it moves in a series of concatenated cause-and-effect chains, each building on and multiplying its predecessor, yielding first-, second-, third-, and nth-order effects. This presents a knotty methodological problem for researchers, because it is extremely difficult to trace and record the time-space path of such impacts.

Another problem is that impact, however it is propagated, is hard to measure. It takes a comprehensive theory of organization, a well-conceived measure of performance, and a finely calibrated instrument to gauge impact. None of these is available today. But such research tools are needed to deal with the fact that IT is itself more malleable by the person it affects. One participant set up a contrast: "A Chevy assembly line isn't very alterable by the person who is working on it, nor is the management system that is constructed around it." Personal computers and word processors, on the other hand, are inherently alterable, and people change them to suit their needs. One executive said, "Those guys, no matter how constrained the technologies seem to be [change them]. With word processors, you find those people are just inventing all sorts of uses for them that were never even envisioned by the people who put them together."

This malleability is one of the reasons for the mosaic of feedback loops that characterizes the propagation of impact. As a result, we lack clear points of stability from which analysis can depart. The impact of automobiles, for example, can be traced from roads and highways. But the things that are analogous to highways for IT, whether wires or software connections, are not concrete. They can be changed, reprogrammed, and reconfigured.

Longitudinal studies--lasting, say, five or more years, as the classic Mann and Williams study did--were offered as a research possibility. Everyone agreed that they were important and desirable and that incentive systems should be developed to encourage them. Over time the small sorties of change are muted and only the strong, permanent trends emerge. But even over extended periods of time, malleability presents a new dimension of concern. The phenomenon of interest is changing itself, taking qualitative leaps. This calls for broad theories and highly sensitive instruments. Perhaps the notions of alpha, beta, and gamma change will have to be expanded to include at least omega change.

What is the most reliable source of data on change? Is it subjective or objective? Mohrman and Lawler employ a subjective source. The people affected were asked to report whether life was better for them or not. But the possibility was raised that these users might have convinced themselves that the changes had occurred for the better simply as an adjustment to their new environment. Cognitive dissonance, as Leon Festinger called it, results in users changing their attitudes and values to make them psychologically consistent with the behaviors required by altered circumstances.

With all these barriers, why are we interested in measuring impacts? Is the motivation "organizational greed," as one person suggested--that is, learning better how to manipulate others? Or is the impetus scientific? Are we really trying to "find some truths, to stumble onto science so that we will be able to train better 'organizational engineers'?" Whatever the motivation, research should produce reliable guides to action. This, of course, raises the moral issue with which Mohrman and Lawler begin their inquiry: to achieve a balance between freedom and order.

A SOCIOLOGICAL RESEARCH PERSPECTIVE

Everett M. Rogers

Probably the most important single change in organizations in the past century is now under way: the impacts of new communication technologies. These innovations involve applications of the computer to problems of organizational communication.

Information technologies are founded on advances in semiconductor chips, particularly the microprocessor, which puts the control functions of a computer on a silicon chip. Invention of the microprocessor in 1971 by Ted Hoff, then at Intel Corporation in Santa Clara, California, facilitated the miniaturization of computer power, sharply reduced the price of computing, and caused rapid diffusion of computers among the public (Rogers and Larsen, 1984). The microprocessor, along with the prior invention of the transistor in 1948 at Bell Labs, must rank among the most important technologies of the twentieth century. Both are today involved in the new information technologies that are affecting organizations. The spread of microcomputers and other microelectronics technologies constitutes an information revolution, through which the United States, Japan, and most of Western Europe are rapidly becoming an information society.

Microcomputers are affecting homes, schools, factories, entertainment, and especially the office. Because computers are information tools, they are being utilized wherever information is input, processed, or output. Organizations are basically communication bodies (with the special characteristic of a rather high degree of formal structure, such as that imposed by authority and hierarchy), so they are natural sites for the application of a communication technology.

Considering this natural fit, it is actually surprising that office automation has not had an even greater impact to date. But although at least 20% of U.S. businesses have adopted some kind of office automation, the rate of adoption has recently slowed down (Uttal, 1982). Three general factors account for this trend.

1. Although office automation promises to increase productivity, such improved performance, if it does occur, is difficult to measure. Organization leaders have to adopt these expensive technologies largely on faith. The advantages of office

automation have often not been great enough to convince organizations to make the sizable initial investment they require. A respondent in one survey of users of office technologies (Johnson and Rice, 1983) described the difficulties of measuring their benefits: "Measurement of work activity gets to be a little strange sometimes. You can take 1½ hours to write a glossary that will do the job; another person will take 3 hours each time to do it manually. It doesn't make any difference to the administration because it only sees the number of pages and the number of lines. No account is made of time required or time saved."

2. Serious transition problems have often occurred in organizations that introduced the new information technologies. The basic requirements for proper implementation (employee training, for example), the extensive changeover that the new systems demand, and the seriousness of their negative consequences (such as possible unemployment of office workers), all augur against facile adoption. In fact, I believe that implementation is one of the main problems of organizations that have tried to adopt office automation.

3. Finally, computer-based office automation technologies have many shortcomings: user unfriendliness, relatively high cost, and rapid technological change (which means that an organization must constantly purchase new machines to keep up to date).

Despite these hindrances, however, office information technologies have the potential for major impacts on organizations, the first signs of which already exist. This paper will utilize concepts from social science fields such as communications, sociology, and organizational behavior to help explain these impacts. Office automation today seems to be having important desirable, direct, and anticipated effects, but I expect that it may also lead to an expanding set of undesirable, indirect, and unanticipated consequences (Rogers, 1983).

Background

We can distinguish three main eras of computers in organizations. The first was the era of the mainframe computer, which began in the 1950s. Organizations used mainframes for data analysis, payrolls, data processing, and other heavy "number-crunching" functions. The mainframes often cost more than a million dollars each, and only a small number of skilled experts were allowed in the air-conditioned rooms in which they were housed. Users were forced to go through intermediaries. What mainframes could do was often quite different from what users wanted them to do. Further, the language of computer programmers was entirely foreign to the organizational officials who wanted to use the computers. And managers soon found that computer costs were an escalating and uncontainable budget item.

In short, this era was not a very happy time for computers in organizations. But everyone agreed that, like it or not, computers were essential to modern organizations.

The second computer era began in the mid-1960s, when minicomputers started to replace mainframes for certain purposes. A DEC (Digital Equipment Corporation) PDP could function outside an air-conditioned room and only took up about as much space as a refrigerator. Minicomputer operators still had to be highly skilled, but many of them were simply engineers or scientists, rather than Ph.D.'s in computer science. The minis were much easier to program and use, so more individuals became users. Minicomputers (and mainframes, which were still around) performed about the same number-crunching functions as their predecessors had. The real computer revolution was still in the future.

Then came the microprocessor and the microcomputer it made possible. The first crude micros were sold to hobbyists in 1975. Some observers could see what was coming. Theodor Nelson, in his book Computer Liberation (1975), claimed that the microcomputer was about to end computer domination by lab-coated specialists. He predicted that micros would decentralize and democratize organizations. Indeed, some of what Nelson anticipated has come to pass, and more of his optimistic scenario may be coming in the near future. On the other hand, the present era of microcomputers in the office has also experienced many disappointments, which Nelson did not foresee.

To a large extent computers have become a regular part of office furniture and have proven less threatening to managers, secretarial workers, and other employees than might have been expected. But the ubiquity of microcomputer technologies in organizations could not have been anticipated, even a few years ago. Perhaps the biggest single surprise is the way computers have become tools of communication.

In the typical organization with office automation today, introduction of the new technologies began with a decision by one or a few managers to purchase word processing equipment that could raise the productivity of the secretarial force. In a survey of 200 organizations, about two-thirds of the units said they initially adopted computer technologies for word processing and repetitive typing (Johnson and Rice, 1983). The equipment might consist of a word processor costing approximately $15,000 or, more recently, a microcomputer with a word processing software program, costing $5,000 or less. Very soon managers began to compose their communications on the word processing equipment instead of drafting documents by hand or machine and asking their secretaries to produce the final copies. Then the secretaries complained that they could not get access to the word processing equipment, creating pressures to purchase more machines. The trend toward a computer or a terminal on every employee's desk had begun.

Next, organizations started to understand that computers are not only stand alone means to create written messages, but also communication networking tools. Enter applications such as electronic messaging, computer bulletin boards, and computer newsletters. These uses for the new information technologies are now exploding. Uttal (1983) estimates that about 12,000 microcomputer networks existed in 1982, but that this number will swell to 110,000 by 1987. A compelling reason for this increase is that the costs of peripherals such as printers and hard disk drives can be shared among all members of a network.

The trend toward using office microcomputers as networking devices actually represents a complication for the gradual introduction of such technologies in an organization. A useful strategy is to launch the innovation on a pilot basis (Meyer, 1983) so that organization members can have more realistic grounds for evaluating the technology. But pilot projects are difficult when the micros are used for network communication rather than for stand alone functions, because even the smallest pilot must consist of the entire network.

The innovation process for office automation in an organization typically involves several stages: getting management support, setting up a pilot operation, and then diffusing computer use throughout the organization. A recent survey of 35 U.S. and Canadian firms found that organizations required, on average, three or four years to pass through these stages (Meyer, 1983). Implementation is usually led by an entrepreneurial champion for the new technology; this individual often becomes the head of the organizational unit responsible for the innovation once it is adopted.

Most computer designers believe that faster is better. So the pell-mell race in computer design is to create machines with greater power, larger memories, and faster response time. A much better computer, in the eyes of most users, would be friendlier (that is, easier to begin using and simpler to apply to everyday problems) and lower in cost. The exact future of this third era of microcomputers in organizations is somewhat cloudy, because the technology itself and the uses to which it is put continue to change.

Impacts

There are many ways to classify the consequences of a technological innovation; Rogers (1983, pp. 380-391) suggests a threefold typology.

Desirable consequences are the functional effects of an innovation on an individual or a social system. Undesirable consequences are its dysfunctional effects.

Direct consequences are the changes in an individual or social system that occur in immediate response to an innovation.

Indirect consequences are the changes that result from the direct consequences of an innovation.

Anticipated consequences are changes caused by an innovation that are recognized and intended by the members of a social system. Unanticipated consequences are changes that are neither intended nor recognized.

A usual investigative approach is to gather data about the impacts of a technological innovation by comparing a system on certain variables before and after the introduction of the new technology (pre-post evaluation). There are many difficulties with social science research on the consequences of innovation. Basically, our research methods are not very successful in studying a process that extends into the future. Most social research methods work best as rearview mirrors; only under special conditions can we adapt them to predict phenomena. One means of studying the impacts of new information technologies is to investigate advanced organizations in which these innovations have been used and then extrapolate from them to other organizations. In fact, this is the basic design for most consequences studies on office automation cited in this paper.

Laura Murphy's (1983) study of two organizational units, one utilizing a centralized computer system (a minicomputer and terminals) and the other using decentralized, stand alone microcomputers, is an example. The main function of both technologies was word processing. Murphy found that the similarities of impacts in these organizations were greater than their differences. Both experienced the advantage of eliminating tedious retyping of reports and other documents with each successive revision. Employees were generally satisfied with their technologies in both organizations; they commented on the "fun" of working with the equipment. But the capacity for easy revision could also lead to an endless series of versions of a document. Murphy found that both organizations she studied suffered from poor documentation of computer procedures, with much criticism of the training and users' manuals, and from a lack of adequate training. Similar findings have been reported by other investigators. The grand visions of a happy, electronically connected community were hardly being realized in these two organizations, but employees were basically satisfied with their equipment, and their quality of work life seemed to have improved.

The impacts of office automation cannot be fully understood without also considering the current home computer revolution. Sales of home computers in 1983 represented a doubling over 1982 sales, which were double those of 1981. Today 10% of American homes have at least one microcomputer. One of their main uses (in addition to playing video games) is word processing, often in connection with work (Rogers et al., 1982).

In some cases this use amounts to teleworking, with an employee working at home on a microcomputer or terminal for at least several days a week (Olson, 1983). Trips to the office for conferences and other personal discussions still seem to be important socioemotionally for most employees. In most current cases, however, an organizational member simply works at home for a few hours a night. In these situations the addictive power of computing becomes a problem. The typical workaholic can now easily spend more hours of work per day by working at home. This desegregation of work and home poses difficulties for many people, who have yet to find effective means of managing these dilemmas. They will be even more serious by 1990, when about 50% of U.S. households are expected to have microcomputers.

Figure 1 shows the numerous other impacts of new information technologies on organizations. Computers can be used to supervise employees very closely. For example, in some organizations a supervisor monitors the number of keystrokes per hour made by each employee in a word processing pool; an automatic warning message is printed on the screen of an employee whose performance is not up to standard. In contrast, computers can be utilized as tools for employee independence and responsibility, allowing an individual to work with great autonomy. The choice between such antithetical uses of the technologies depends on how an organization decides to implement its new tools.

Figure 1. *Possible Organizational Impacts of the New Information Technologies*

More desirable, direct and anticipated impacts

More undesirable, indirect, and unanticipated impacts

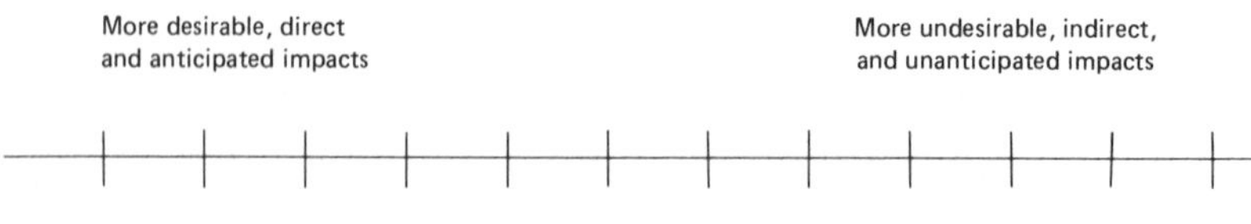

Possible Impacts

- Greater office productivity
- New industries (software, computer magazines, retail stores, and microcomputer manufacturers)
- Work role changes for male bosses and female secretaries
- Closer supervision (with computers) of computer-using employees
- Information overload
- Ability to work at home
- Higher status for secretarial workers
- Rise of computer networks
- Invasion of privacy
- Decreased employment, especially for female office workers
- Computer crime

An interesting experiment in office automation is occurring at Apple Computer Inc. of Cupertino, California. A few years ago the top officials at Apple did away with secretaries and typewriters. Each employee has an Apple computer on his or her desk and another one at home; all are expected to prepare their own documents. Every 15 or 20 employees have one "area assistant," who provides certain administrative-secretarial services, such as taking telephone messages, arranging meetings, and so on. Essentially, Apple has used computer technology to create a rather high degree of autonomy among its professional employees. It has also eliminated most of the usual tasks of secretaries. One of several motivations for banning typewriters and secretaries was to foster greater occupational equality among Apple employees. But that consequence is part of a much larger potential impact of the new information technologies--they may "disorganize" organizations in certain important ways.

One significant consequence of office automation is changes in social status. Often managers and executives gain status by using computers, and certainly clerical staff do. Some high-level officials, however, perceive computer use as typing, which they consider a low-status job. A survey of 530 employees in 26 organizations found that executives were much less likely to be using computers than were employees in other work categories, such as managers, secretaries, or clerks (Bikson and Gutek, 1983). When a high-status individual in an organization shows that he or she supports the new technology, much of the resistance to office automation is likely to melt (Eveland, 1983). For instance, when an electronic messaging system was introduced at Stanford University a few years ago, a photograph of President Donald Kennedy using the system was published in the university newspaper.

New Organizational Designs in High Technology Firms

About 80 years ago the eminent German sociologist Max Weber published his important analysis of human behavior in organizations, centering on the concept of bureaucracy. The types of organizations he had in mind included government agencies, industrial manufacturing firms, religious groups, and the military. Weber argued that the essence of organizational behavior revolves around elements such as rules and regulations, division of tasks, and a hierarchy of formal positions that contributes to rational efficiency in performing organizational functions. He stated, "The decisive reason for the advance of bureaucratic organization has always been its purely technical superiority over any other form of organization" (1948).

Without doubt, Weber's conception of bureaucracy was an accurate synthesis of efficient organizational structure and behavior for the prototypical firms of the early industrial era. And many present-day industrial and business organizations are closely patterned after his mold. But such bureaucratic behavior and structure do not fit the realities of high technology firms in the current information society. They certainly do not apply to the particular scenario of the future represented by Silicon Valley microelectronics firms (Rogers and Larsen, 1984).

The Silicon Valley firms have many employees with two, three, or more bosses; other employees may not even know who their bosses are. These organizations are managed as if people mattered, on the assumption that if employees feel satisfied they will perform well with little direct supervision. Such an organizational style, enabled in part by the new information technologies, would make Max Weber shake his head. A new type of organizational arrangement is being pioneered in high tech microelectronics companies--they have a major deemphasis of formal organizational structure as a guide to human behavior, a management style that rewards performance generously, and a flourishing system of horizontal information-exchange networks. All this is occurring in the context of vigorous competition for continuous technological innovation in the industry and a high degree of work involvement (to the point of workaholism), at least among professional employees.

The production of information technology is becoming more important in the U.S. economy, and many new firms are starting up (fueled by large amounts of available venture capital). The high technology culture of Silicon Valley, now spreading to a dozen or so other emerging centers in the U.S. (including Dallas, Phoenix, Route 128 [near Boston], Salt Lake City, the Research Triangle [Chapel Hill, Durham, and Raleigh], and Minneapolis), may gradually infect all of American private industry.

That is a possible future impact of producing the new information technologies. Now let us examine the future impacts of the new technologies on the organizations that use them.

The Restructuring of Organizational Communication

The new information technologies allow the restructuring and/or destructuring of organizational communication. "The Office of the Future concept is not just the automated office or the electronic office; rather, it is one in which new technologies give senior management the opportunity to consider entirely new approaches as to how best to organize, manage, and control the enterprise" (Strassmann, 1980). This kind of impact is very grand, and at present only a rather vague, hazy vision. We cannot now point to an organization that has utilized the computer-based technologies to create really new alternatives in organizational form, communication, and structure. But the potential exists. Here are some examples.

- In a recent evaluation of an electronic messaging system in one large organization, we found that much bypassing of layers in the hierarchy occurred. Workers sent many copies of a message, in part because it was so easy to do so--"Just push the 'send' button." Such electronic networking systems decrease the influence of organizational hierarchy on communication patterns; they are usually highly decentralized systems in which messages flow with few constraints.

- Two managers, one sitting beside a pool in Los Altos Hills, California, and the other in Austin, Texas, write a joint memo about plans for collaboration between their divisions. At one point they ask another individual at company headquarters (in Sunnyvale, California) to produce a set of color charts and insert them in their memo. All their communication is via computer terminals. In fact, the two managers have not met since they were introduced at a company beer-blast five years ago. Yet they talk with each other, by computer network, at least once a week.
- A large German bank provides full services to about 40,000 customers by means of the Bildschirmtext system, a videotext service begun in 1980. All banking is done via computer terminals, telephone lines, and home television sets. No bank buildings, no vaults, no tellers. The electronic bank has only 39 employees--a president, a secretary, 37 computer programmers, and, of course, one big computer (Rogers and Picot, 1984). Because of its lower overhead costs, the bank can pay 1% higher interest on deposits than other German banks.

These examples show how the new information technologies can overcome the usual limitations that time, spatial distance, and organizational hierarchy impose on communication patterns. I think that organizations will never be quite the same again. The new information technologies will help us change our conception of what the work organization is, and can be. They will free us from conventional thinking about our relationships with work associates and lead us to question how essential it is to be with them in the same place at the same time. Out of the present groping explorations of information technology applications may come a new type of organization that is particularly suited to the emerging information society.

Research Implications

Most of the rather modest number of past research studies on the impacts of new information technologies on organizations were essentially pre-post evaluations. In fact, most such evaluations are after-only designs. These studies are a type of variance research, in which an investigator analyzes the interrelationships among variables at one point in time (Mohr, 1982). A variance approach is appropriate for identifying covariances among variables, but a different approach--process research--is best for determining the time order of events in a process, such as the consequences of information technologies in an organization. To date, we have slighted process research because our graduate training in methodology, our statistical tools, and our theoretical approaches have steered us mainly toward variance studies. But a great many research problems are simply not amenable to a static, cross-sectional approach; they require process studies.

Some of the process problems involving the impacts of information technologies on organizations are (1) the stages in the innovation process for an organization--initial awareness of an information technology, the decision to adopt, implementation, and eventual routinization (so that the innovation is no longer distinguishable from usual procedure); (2) the process of reinvention, in which an innovation is modified by the members of an adopting organization as they implement it; and (3) the direct and indirect consequences of an information technology over time.

Further, we should investigate the negative, as well as the positive, impacts of the new technologies. Although most employees using the new office automation technologies are satisfied, others complain of "terminal illness"--sore backs, eyesight problems, and the like--from working at a computer (Makower, 1981). Is there anything to these complaints? Some negative impacts of the new technologies on the organization and society include (1) unemployment (especially in middle-class occupations such as clerk and middle manager), (2) deskilling (in which computers allow less educated individuals to do work previously accomplished by professionals), and (3) information overload (in which individuals are inundated with more information than they are able to handle). These impacts deserve study too; past research on computer consequences has displayed a pro-innovation bias (Rogers, 1983).

More fundamentally, future study should determine whether the new information technologies are the cause, or just a catalyst, of change in organizations. The social changes occurring in organizations today probably have multiple roots; they are most likely not just the consequences of computer-based technologies.

What are the implications of the shift from use of computers as stand alone number crunchers and word processors to their employment as interpersonal communications channels (Rogers and Rafaeli, 1984)?

The new communication technologies in organizations allow us to gather new kinds of data, and to analyze them in novel ways. One example is computer-recorded data about how extensively a computer-based office technology is used by individuals or organizational units. The computer component in the new communication systems provides their interactivity, their humanlike ability to conduct a "conversation" with the user. This component can also keep a record of every use. Although there are obvious ethical and analytical ramifications of using such data, I think they represent an improved approach to investigating the social impacts of the new technologies on organizations (Rice and Rogers, 1984).

Finally, we are beginning to realize that the computer-based technologies can provide freedom from the constraints of time and place on person-to-person communication. How can this asynchronous and space-freeing quality best be utilized in new work arrangements? That, indeed, is the meta-issue for the future of the new information technologies.

Bibliography

Tora K. Bikson and Barbara A. Gutek, Advanced Office Systems: An Empirical Look at Utilization and Satisfaction (Santa Monica, Calif., Rand Note N-1970-NSF, February 1983).

Daryl Chubin et al., Trends in Computers and Communication: The Office of the Future (Atlanta, Georgia Institute of Technology, Technology and Science Policy Program, Report, 1983).

J. D. Eveland, "Social Dimensions of Changing Office Technology," Journal of Clinical Computing, 11 (1983): 201-208.

Bonnie McD. Johnson and Ronald E. Rice, "Redesigning Word-Processing for Productivity," in R. Vondran (ed.), Proceedings of the American Society of Information Science (Washington, D.C., 1983).

Joel Makower, Office Hazards (Washington, D.C., Tilden Press, 1981).

N. Dean Meyer, "The Office Automation Cookbook: Management Strategies for Getting Office Automation Moving," Sloan Management Review, 24 (1983): 51-60.

Lawrence B. Mohr, Studying Organizational Behavior (San Francisco, Jossey-Bass, 1982).

Laura Murphy, The Impacts of Word-Processing at Stanford University: A Comparative Study of Centralized and Decentralized Word-Processing Systems (Stanford, Calif., Stanford University, Honors thesis, 1983).

Theodor H. Nelson, Computer Liberation (Schooleys Mountain, N.J., Ted Nelson, 1975).

Margrethe H. Olson, "Remote Office Work: Changing Patterns in Space and Time," Communications of the American Academy of Management, 26 (1983): 182-187.

Ronald E. Rice and Everett M. Rogers, "New Methods and New Data for the Study of New Media," in Ronald E. Rice et al. (eds.), The New Media: Uses and Impacts (Beverly Hills, Calif., Sage, 1984).

Everett M. Rogers, Diffusion of Innovations (New York, Free Press, 1983).

Everett M. Rogers and Rekha Agarwala-Rogers, Communication in Organizations (New York, Free Press, 1976).

Everett M. Rogers and Judith K. Larsen, Silicon Valley Fever: Growth of High-Technology Culture (New York, Basic Books, 1984).

Everett M. Rogers and Arnold Picot, "The Impact of New Communication Technology," in Everett M. Rogers and Francis Balle (eds.), The New Media in America and Western Europe (Norwood, N.J., Ablex, 1984).

Everett M. Rogers and Sheizaf Rafaeli, "Computers as Communication," in Brent Rubin (ed.), Information and Behavior (New Brunswick, N.J., Transaction, 1984).

Everett M. Rogers et al., The Diffusion of Home Computers (Stanford, Calif., Stanford University, Institute for Communication Research, Report, 1982).

Paul Strassmann, "The Office of the Future: Information Management for the New Age," Technology Review, 82 (1980): 55-56.

Bro Uttal, "What's Detaining the Office of the Future?" Fortune, May 3, 1982, 176.

_______, "Linking Computers to Help Managers Manage," Fortune, December 26, 1983, pp. 145-150.

Max Weber, The Theory of Social and Economic Organization, translated by A. M. Henderson and Talcott Parsons (New York, Oxford University Press, 1948).

DISCUSSION: ROGERS PAPER

"I was holding all aces, but what was the game?" This quotation from Joan Didion's Play It As It Lays, brought up in the discussion summary, captures the tenor of the entire discussion of Everett Rogers's paper. The group acknowledged that the new information technology is powerful, but that it is very difficult to identify the arena in which its power is unleashed and the path of its impact.

Does anyone care? Is information technology impact research worthwhile from the point of view of high technology managers? There was no consensus on these points. Most participants agreed that such studies were basically interesting, but some executives took the position that they were of no real concern to their businesses as they knew and understood them.

Others dissented. They stated that managers, at least those who are purchasing or deploying information technology, should have some idea of what they are getting and what its likely organizational consequences will be. Other sources of information--the news media, manufacturers, and consultants--are not wholly adequate. Neutral, academic studies are also needed. Research on useful strategies for implementing information technology and systems is needed to allay fears of potential failure and to help managers make sharper and smarter decisions. University-based research, this dissenting position argued, is the best place to obtain such knowledge.

This led one researcher to ask, "When do businesses come to universities?" and to answer his own question by stating that they come after they are already committed to building large-scale information systems. These businesses request studies of the systems they are building so that they will understand them better. But in some cases, it is too late to do such research. Many profitable avenues may have been foreclosed before the researchers come on board. So, it was argued, university researchers should be more proactive in finding workable research sites if they expect their studies to influence management decision making.

The discussion turned to an attempt to identify the different ways information technology and systems can bring about organizational change. Four areas emerged. First, information systems can affect decisions. Decision support systems and operations research models are intended to do this. So are command and control systems and, in fact, many data base systems. Second, they can serve as catalysts or facilitators. Electronic mail is an example. It changes the communication patterns among people--who talks to whom about what and when, where, and how they do it. This, in turn, leads to more profound changes in the organization itself. Third, the new technology can be used as an excuse to make adjustments that could have been made without it; we can call this technological rationalization. Many inventory control and financial management systems do this. Their installation forces a routinization of reporting and an emphasis on control that could have been achieved by manual approaches. Finally, there is the "halo" (or is it the "scapegoat"?) effect. The performance of an information system in one area is attributed without direct causal connection to another area. To wit, "The problems on your statement are due to a computer error."

The fact that all these sources of impact work together in a sort of mélange complicates the problems of measurement and attribution. One researcher offered a colorful and useful metaphor. When electricians are troubleshooting circuits, they frequently apply a voltmeter to measure the current. They know, and researchers on information systems in organizations must determine, Where do you put the alligator clips? Do you measure individuals, work groups, or organizations; do you sweep customers, suppliers, and other stakeholders into the analyses? What is the organizational analogue to the volt or the ampere? Whatever it is, it must be sensitive to many things. Among them are changes in the character of jobs, shifts of secretaries from typists to coordinators and schedulers, relocations of work from office to home, modification in the volume and type of communications, redistribution of power and authority, and adjustments in the allocation of organizational resources. A common theme in all these changes is the potential for redistribution of control of the organization.

The discussion ended with a sobering observation. The group had created a matrix of about 40 cells, each representing a class of research that might be undertaken. Someone noted that there were only about 36 scholars currently working in any of these areas and that any one area had enough unresolved questions to tax the capabilities of all three dozen. The optimistic note, of course, is that there is plenty of room for many research careers in this vast, still largely uncharted field.

CONCLUSION TO PART II

Richard O. Mason

The range of research opportunities in organization and information systems technology is staggering, as the papers and the discussions in this part suggest. Throughout the colloquium, however, a few recurrent themes and concerns emerged. Most of these were not presented as refined, well-honed research projects. Though cogent, they were more flickers of insight than clearly specified programs of inquiry. They are, however, a sort of Rorschach test for the field, because they identify the crucial dimensions of concern from which research frameworks may be built.

Two clear needs were identified. They are important precursors of any further development of impact research.

One is the need for a taxonomy of information technology (IT). The field needs a theory of technology and a classification scheme that will permit (1) similar groupings of hardware, software, data, rules, procedures, and people to cluster together (for example, personal computers are different from large mainframes, local networks are different from worldwide networks and stand alones, and integrated data bases are different from collections of independent files); and (2) different groupings to be clearly distinguishable from one another. Good classification practice also requires that the categories be readily assignable (in other words, have clear differentia), mutually exclusive, collectively exhaustive, and nonvacuous. Some progress is needed on this score so that researchers can identify and describe the independent variable (stimulus, or treatment) that presumably is responsible for the impact.

In addition to needing a better understanding of the thing doing the impacting, we must also be clearer about the thing that is impacted. An important research choice is what unit or units of analysis should be used to record the impact. All levels seem to be relevant and useful. Among the options are

Individual
Work group
Department
Organization
Organization stakeholders, such as customers and suppliers

Interorganizational groupings

- Linked directly through networks
- Coordinated through trade associations or cartels

Society

This leads to a series of more specific research questions on various aspects of the topic, which were gleaned from the colloquium and its activities. Each is offered as a "springboard" for thought.

Impacts on Individuals

1. How does IT affect existing jobs and job holders?
2. How might it affect the design of jobs? How does this relate to the tasks within jobs?
3. What is the effect of IT on the quality of work life? Does it enrich or deplete jobs? Is this a matter of choice--that is, dependent on various design options--or is it predetermined? What are the measures? Individual perception or actual performance?
4. How, in turn, do people affect IT? How pliable is it? How does its malleability by individuals relate to quality of work life, organizational performance, and the distribution of organizational control?
5. Are there demographic factors, such as age, that affect individuals' learning, acceptance, and performance with respect to IT?
6. What new skills are required to use IT effectively or to coexist with it?

Communication and Social Consequences for Work Groups

1. How does IT affect work relationships?
2. Does a new type of social life develop around IT?
3. What happens to communication interactions? Is there more horizontal networking? More vertical networking? An increase or decrease in volume of communications?
4. How can the fact that many systems cut across traditional organizational boundaries to form new work groups best be utilized? How can communication be facilitated among diverse cultures, each with different goals, values,beliefs, and expectations?
5. How can information sharing be managed? When should information move from one place to another? When not? Who should have control?
6. How do individuals and groups filter the information coming to them? How should they? What are the implications for information overload and the paucity of relevant information?

Effects on Organizational Structure

1. What is the effect of IT on organizational size and composition? Does it shrink organizations? Eliminate clerical staff? Eliminate middle management? Eliminate top-level executives? Expand technological jobs?
2. How does IT affect patterns of authority, responsibility, and accountability? Does it lead to flatter organizations? More matrix organizations with increased horizontal communication in a vertical bureaucracy?
3. How adaptable are old organizational structures to the implantation of IT? Do new structures emerge, or do the old survive by developing new channels of communication?
4. Do organizational structures exist that maximize the beneficial impacts of IT? Are they always small autonomous units? If so, how are large organizations composed of many such units to be managed?
5. Does IT change people's images of their organization and its structure?
6. Is overall workplace control tighter or looser as a result of IT?
7. How is control redistributed? Who benefits?
8. How is IT related to organizational uncertainty? Is it a cause? A remedy?
9. Specifically, how does electronic mail affect organizations and their communications?

Conditions of Organizational Change

1. Why are some organizations more resistant to the introduction of IT than others?
2. What factors account for adoption and use of IT? Culture? Market position? Design? Level of control? Strategy? Structure? Systems?
3. How is IT used to implement corporate policy (implicitly or explicitly)? Are there "hidden policies" or values embedded in IT adoptions?
4. Are there recognizable differences between organizations that are moving from the base of an old embedded system to a new system and those that are acquiring IT for the first time? How significant is the amount of difference (the degree of change) between the base and the new IT? Does the number of previous changes make a difference; that is, do organizations gain experience in IT transition? Are there preferred patterns of migration?
5. Is there a proper tempo for IT-induced organizational change? Can it be too slow? Too fast? How does one manage it? What are the risks?

6. How is the rate of change measured?
7. Which among the following characteristics influence the adoption or adaption of IT within organizations?
    - History
    - Stage of growth in life cycle
    - Values, culture, goals
    - Strategy
    - Size
    - Industry
    - Structure
    - Location
    - Personalities of key leaders
    - Uncertainties of market, technology, or science base
    - Position as early or late adopter

Organizational Costs and Benefits

1. How is the value of information technology and systems to be measured?
2. How is their true and full economic cost to be calculated?
3. Does IT help an organization cope better with societal complexity? If so, how is this advantage valuated?
4. How dependent is the actual securing of IT benefits on the assumption that workers are dedicated and positively motivated? Will they use IT creatively and constructively in the best interests of the organization?
5. Are information and IT strategic resources? If so, do the benefits outweigh the costs, given a strategic vision?

Social Implications

1. Is there a need for a national IT policy, as suggested by Edward A. Feigenbaum and Pamela McCorduck in *The Fifth Generation* (Reading, Mass.: Addison-Wesley, 1983)?
2. In the United States emphasis is placed on the role IT can play in improving productivity. In Europe the primary concern is job creation and employment. Which is in the best national or social interest? What is the overall effect of IT on employment (taking into account reemployment and net unemployment)? What is the effect of IT on national productivity? Is there a need to advise governments on retraining needs?
3. How do IT policies, programs, and experience differ among nations?
4. What new policy issues arise in the information society? Do we, for example, need a new ethics of information?

These questions (and more) beg for study. To be answered adequately, they must be considered by means of a carefully designed system of inquiry. That is, reliable research methods must be employed. This need places several burdens on the IT researcher. First, many of the questions in this field require interdisciplinary research. Virtually every basic discipline is involved--logic, arithmetic, geometry, kinematics, mechanics, electronics, physics, biology, psychology, social psychology, sociology, management theory, organization theory, politics, and ethics. This calls for a renaissance person and a holistic perspective. It also calls for supreme methodological judgment. The methods appropriate to one discipline are rarely applicable without modification in another. The IT researcher must go a step further to construct from the methodological materials of various disciplines a cohesive and sound research design. No mean task, but essential.

In this difficult undertaking the researcher should answer several questions. All of these were discussed in one way or another during the colloquium. After each, I have mentioned a few of the specific aspects brought up during the sessions.

1. What are the goals of the research?
   - To gain understanding
   - To yield new products
   - To construct better systems
   - To contribute to science
   - To gain tenure
2. How is goal achievement performance to be measured?
   - By publication
   - By a well-functioning system
   - By answers to questions
3. Who is the client for the research?
   - Academia
   - Practitioners
   - Others
4. What are the constraints under which the research must operate?
   - Budget
   - Time
   - Access to suitable sites
   - Acceptance by colleagues
5. What are the essential components of the research design?
   - Which basic disciplines should be involved?
     - Logic to ethics
   - Which approach is best?
     - Normative
     - Predictive
     - Descriptive
   - What will be the source of data and experience?

    - Models
    - Prototypes
    - Cases
    - Experiments
    - In situ studies
    - Longitudinal versus cross-sectional work
  - How will the data be collected?
    - Observation (unobtrusive versus participatory)
  - How will the data be analyzed?
    - Qualitative versus quantitative
    - Rational (formal models) versus empirical
  - How will the results be communicated?
    - Publications
    - Education (workshops, conferences)
    - Direct conversation with colleagues

6. Finally, one might ask, What will we know when the research is completed? How generalizable is it, and to what populations will it apply? Is it epistemologically sound, that is, if a corporation acts on it can they expect to achieve the predicted results?

PART III

MANAGEMENT OF THE INFORMATION SYSTEMS RESOURCE

INTRODUCTION TO PART III

Gordon B. Davis

The data items collected and stored by an organization represent an organizational resource. They are converted to information by information processing. Basic information processing functions can be performed manually; however, the capabilities of computers establish broader boundaries for the information system (IS). Our vision of what an IS should be and should do has been greatly enlarged by what computers can accomplish.

Information supplied by the information processing system can aid organizational transactions, operations, management control, planning, and decision making. The IS is a support system for the organization. Its subsystems provide support for various organizational functions and activities. Conceptually, there are transaction support systems, operations support systems, management control support systems, planning support systems, decision support systems, and so on. But the physical implementation of IS frequently merges these different elements into single applications, obscuring the fact that an information system is a multidimensional support system.

The IS is a significant organizational resource. It is static to the extent that it codifies and institutionalizes the use of data in organizational procedures and functions, preserving organizational learning and transmitting it to new employees. But the IS is dynamic when it is used to create new and improved procedures, functions, and services.

The objectives of this part are to examine the issues and research questions in management of the IS. The underlying concept is that the IS is a resource and should be managed as such. The IS may be a fairly insignificant item on the balance sheet; only its equipment is usually shown as an asset. But there is general recognition that a well-designed portfolio of properly implemented IS applications and a well-trained IS staff represent an intangible asset of far greater real economic value. This was illustrated recently when a financial organization renegotiated a merger offer downward after assessing the information systems of the organization it was acquiring.

The following is a framework for management of the IS resource:

Organization
- To provide effective service to users
- To maintain efficient internal operations

Planning
- To support organizational goals and objectives
- To use information technology efficiently

Development
- To meet user requirements
- To utilize development resources efficiently

Personnel
- To select and train staff effectively and efficiently
- To motivate and develop staff effectively and efficiently

Operations
- To function efficiently
- To satisfy user needs effectively

This framework illustrates the omnipresence of both effectiveness and efficiency objectives in management of IS. Effectiveness applies to meeting organizational (user) information needs; efficiency is measured by the resources required to meet these needs. Management is difficult because user needs are frequently not well defined, so there is no effectiveness context within which to judge efficiency.

The papers in this part focus on three significant aspects of this area:

Information systems planning (on the basis of a development stages theory)
Management of IS personnel
Management of the IS function

The first paper, by Richard Nolan, explores the need for a theory by which to understand past and impending changes in the IS organization and the structure of the information system. The observed transition from data processing-driven to user-driven IS calls for a theory. Nolan's stages theory of IS organization and management change, published ten years ago, has been the most significant theory in IS management; it provides the basis for his current discussion.

The second paper, by Daniel Couger, explains the forces that are changing management of IS personnel. Recruitment, training, motivation, and supervision processes are all affected by these changes. Couger is well qualified to speak in this area; he and Robert Zawacki have conducted the most extensive data-based research on motivational factors for IS personnel to date.

Finally, Carl Reynolds's paper introduces a practitioner-oriented conceptual framework for management of the

IS function: the information system can be understood as a business within an organization, having all the functions of an autonomous business-- production, marketing, finance, and so on. This paper reflects the experience of a thoughtful IS executive.

Readers of these papers and the accompanying discussions should seek to formulate their own answers to certain fundamental questions:

1. How do computers and communications technology and their rapid change affect the management of IS?

2. How does management of IS differ from management of other functions in an organization?

3. What dynamic interactions between the organization and the IS (as a support system) affect management of the IS resource? In particular, how does the diffusion of information technology and information processing expertise within the organization affect the organization and management of the IS resource?

4. What are the significant aspects of motivation and management of IS personnel?

This part intends not only to examine issues and questions, but also to identify research that will lead to improved organization, procedures, and practices for the management of information resources.

MANAGING THE ADVANCED STAGES OF COMPUTER TECHNOLOGY: KEY RESEARCH ISSUES

Richard L. Nolan

The machines of the Industrial Revolution were all important breakthroughs. But the "revolution" was not the machines, it was the economic and social changes that affected how and where work was done. Some see the impact of the computer as an electronic revolution (Diebold, 1983). Again, though, it is clear that the revolution is not the computer but the resulting economic and social changes that affect how and where work is done. A major aspect of these changes has been the recent evolution of the computer industry from simply a capital goods industry, which supplied expensive computers to centralized computer departments, to a consumer product industry as well. The impact of this evolution on how and where work and play are done creates the key management issues for the 1980s.

Research and Accelerating Change

Alvin Toffler (1980), Peter Drucker (1980), and John Naisbitt (1982) have observed that the single most important characteristic of computers is the increased rate of change they foster in society and organizations. This accelerating change has affected the codification of knowledge and theory concerning the management of computer technology in organizations in three ways. First, the importance of the computer to industry and the shortage of people who have the training and experience to work with it have escalated salaries, making it difficult for academic institutions to attract qualified staff in the field. Second, rapid technological progress has shortened the time from research to application, causing codification of practice into journal articles and books to fall further and further behind. Third, although exploratory research, such as casewriting and surveys, is still necessary, universities and academic journals have an inherent bias against these methodologies. Thus, promising academicians often become frustrated by the lack of appropriate journal outlets and peer acceptance of their work. While these factors will inevitably change, practitioners and academicians are playing important roles in the development of the body of knowledge on management of computer technology.

The need for computer management principles is great, and researchers must carefully guard against pressures to attempt premature predictive theory formulation. At present only the rudimentary foundation exists for a normative, or predictive, theory on computer use in organizations. Even the terminology abounds with imprecision. Therefore, research activities must first support a formative period during which the variables exerting major influence on management of the computer are identified, their behavior and interrelationship determined, and their generality and major determinants assessed.

The Stages Theory of Computer Growth

The study of computer use in organizations is a recent offshoot of organization theory (Nolan, 1973). The stages theory of computer growth is based on identification of an S-shaped learning curve of technological assimilation.[1] The learning curve, manifested by a company's annual expenditures on computer technology, proposes to reflect the company's organizational learning of how to incorporate computer technology to carry out business functions more effectively or efficiently. To date the theory has been supported in studies conducted by universities, IBM, and Nolan, Norton & Company.[2]

Stages theories have proven particularly useful for developing knowledge during the formative periods of diverse fields, for example, in the studies of biological growth, economic growth, and galaxies. Such theories are based on the premises that elements in systems move through a distinct pattern of stages over time and that these stages can be described. Simon

---

[1]Hamilton and Ives (1982) identified the stages theory (as presented in Gibson and Nolan, 1974) as one of the 15 most cited management information systems articles among researchers in the field.

[2]Empirical validation studies of the stages theory have been conducted at Stanford by Henry Lucas and the University of British Columbia by Robert Goldstein. The theory has led to a major doctoral study on the construct of organizational learning at the University of Massachusetts. Walter Carlson reported on a 1976 IBM study on the stages theory at the International Federation of Information Processing Societies Conference in Toronto, August 1977. More than 200 Nolan, Norton & Company studies have empirically supported the S-shaped learning curve phenomenon of computer expenditures. The firm has built a data base on attributes of the four growth processes as they evolve through the stages.

Kuznets (1965, pp. 213-216) states two guidelines for a stages theory--(1) the characteristics of each stage should be distinct and empirically testable; and (2) the analytical relationship of any stage to its predecessor or successor should be well defined: it must be possible to identify what processes cause an element to move from one stage to the next.

My original statement of the stages theory of computer growth was based on the learning curve reflected through the data processing (DP) budget (Nolan, 1973). I hypothesized that three growth processes underlay organizational learning--control tasks, organizing tasks, and planning tasks. By 1979 I had identified six stages of growth and found that four growth processes were more useful for understanding the organizational learning: applications portfolio, resources (technology and personnel), management (organization, planning, and control), and user awareness (Nolan, 1979).

The Advanced Stages: Recharting Research

During the early 1980s it became clear that computer expenditures were accelerating and growth was being driven not by DP technology but by user-oriented computer technologies. In 1982 and 1983 Nolan, Norton & Company conducted research with approximately 40 of its clients on the resurgence in computer expenditure growth and the factors driving that growth. This program, which came to be known as "Recharting DP to the Advanced Stages," led to refinement of the stages theory and to six findings that raise important issues in management of computer technology (Nolan and Norton, 1982).

Finding 1: Period of Technological Discontinuity

Large companies are struggling with the organizational problems of "technological discontinuity" as they make the transition from the DP early stages curve to the advanced stages curve.

Figure 1 shows the technological discontinuity period, which began around 1980 and will probably continue through 1985. Personal and institutional barriers to the divestiture of an ongoing technology to make way for an improved technology are not novel organizational phenomena.

For example, by the mid-1950s it was clear that the next generation of airplanes could not rely on the internal combustion engine. Boeing and Douglas made the transition to the turbojet (the second technology curve) earlier than Lockheed. As a result, Boeing and Douglas reaped the benefits of the turbojet technology earlier and dominated the commercial airplane market. They were on the steep part of the second curve while Lockheed was on the flat part. Other examples include Michelin and radial versus bias-ply tires and steam-powered versus sailing ships.

Figure 1 *Stages of Computer Growth*

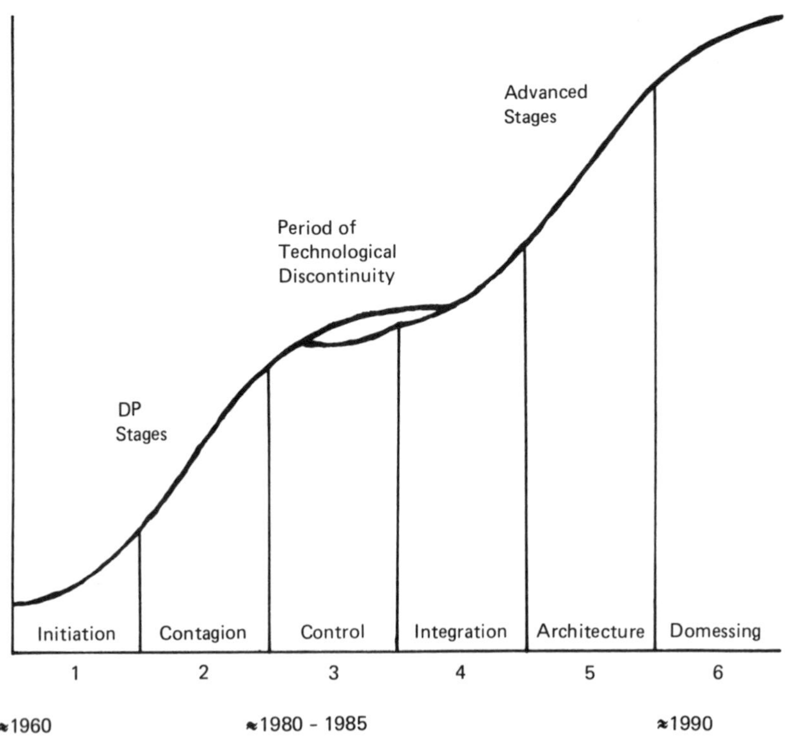

Internal DP departments appear to be experiencing a similar discontinuity in making the transition to the diversified user-oriented computer technologies of the advanced stages. The problems are sometimes subtle, such as responding to office automation or personal computers by zealously building information centers rather than truly assessing the unique attributes of new technologies (such as bubble memory, control, and cost) and aligning them with the organization's business objectives.

The main barrier to the transition is often the internal organization itself. It knows the older, more mature technology, while the less mature, new technology is by definition associated with problems.

Related Research Issues. Major issues surround understanding the current period of technological discontinuity and finding effective ways to manage the transition. Important research questions are

- What is the most effective role for the DP department

during technological discontinuity?

- How long does it take to move through technological discontinuity, and what are the major activities that must be accomplished?

- To what extent must Stage 3 controls and applications be in place before entry into technological discontinuity can be a constructive evolutionary process?

- What kind of computer functional executive leadership is most effective during technological discontinuity?

Finding 2: Shift to User Computing

Computer expenditures in large companies from 1980 to 1990 will increase six- to eightfold, compared with about fivefold from 1970 to 1980, but the computer topography will shift dramatically to user computing.

Figure 2 shows a representative expenditure projection and profile from our research. The cases generally showed DP expenditures doubling or tripling. User computing, however, was predicted to increase from 20 to 25 times. The number of telephone handsets was projected to halve by 1990 and their function to be integrated into personal computing/office automation products. Clearly, new organizations, different from the existing centralized DP departments, will emerge to manage user computing.

Related Research Issues. Major issues in the shift to user computing include identifying organization structures appropriate for managing user computing and further analyzing the 1990 computer product topography. Important research questions are

- What controls, standards, or guidelines result in effective user computing from an overall company perspective?

- What is the relationship of user computing to DP over time?

- Who should be accountable for the types of user computing and user computing as an overall phenomenon?

- How does user computing evolve?

Finding 3: Executive Leadership

Senior management is looking to the corporate DP department for leadership to manage the technologies of the advanced stages.

Once expenditures on office automation and/or personal computers reach significant levels, members of senior management

Figure 2. *Representative Computing Expenditures*

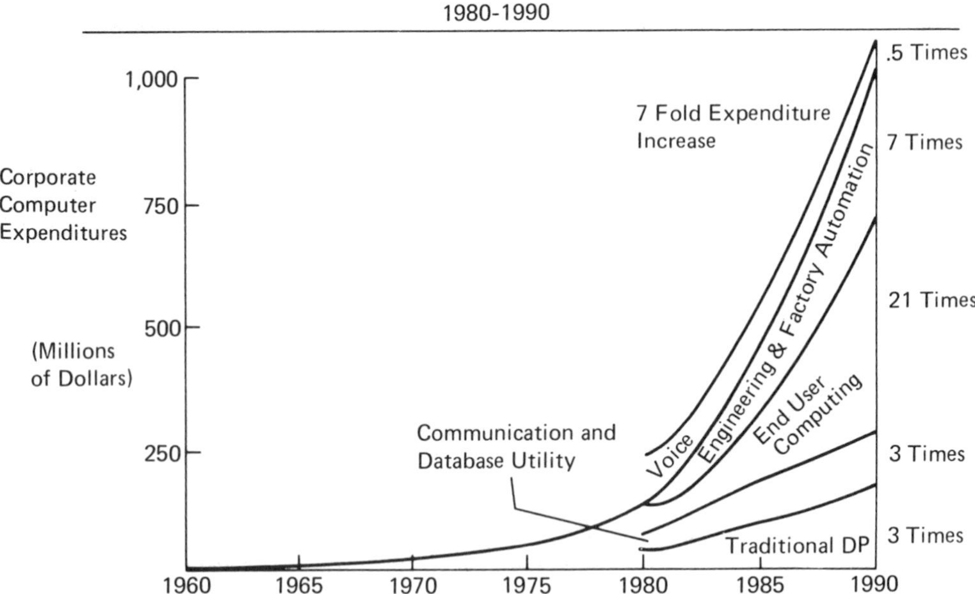

consistently turn to their DP management for leadership and control. Increasingly, executive-level steering committees have been formed to provide corporate direction and ratify proposed guidelines and standards.

Further, once the broader role of communications is recognized and the implications of the AT&T restructuring are realized, senior management will look to the DP manager to deal with communications as well. For the first time communications is appearing as a significant element on corporate DP organization charts.

Related Research Issues. A significant issue for DP management is determining how to make the transition from department manager to executive. Important research questions include

- What are the executive functions of computer functional leadership in the advanced stages?

- Where will the computer functional executives in the 1980s come from?

- What should be the role of executive steering committees?

- How do companies structure and charter these committees to make them work effectively?

Finding 4: Computer Architecture Planning

Companies are fundamentally shifting their computer planning from narrowly focused DP planning to enterprisewide computer architecture planning. Currently, DP applications portfolios are reasonably well developed, but they are built on a hollow foundation of data bases and communications. For example, Figure 3 shows a company with seven applications portfolios and five niches identified: office automation, data processing, personal computers, robotics, and computer-aided design and manufacturing (CAD/CAM).

Each of the applications portfolios corresponds to the major organizational unit of the company that requires horizontal management of a computer architecture product. For example, the large data processing and office automation applications portfolios and the personal computing portfolio correspond to the corporate organizational unit supplying centralized computer services to corporate functions and three product divisions. The CAD/CAM applications portfolio corresponds to the engineering division. The other data processing and office automation applications portfolios and the robotics portfolio correspond to the company's major manufacturing division.

Although the corporate computer functional executive does not have direct-line responsibility for the division's applications portfolio, he or she has dotted-line responsibility and, very clearly, is relied on to guide effective use of the merging technologies. Perhaps even more important, this executive is directly responsible for building and managing the company's data and communications utility to give optimal support to both short- and long-term development of all the company's applications portfolios. The computer architecture strategic plan is the main management vehicle by which the corporate computer functional executive can ensure effective integration among the applications portfolios and among the existing products on the computer architecture product spectrum.

Figure 4 shows the target--the company's computer architecture strategic plan. The applications portfolio niches oriented to existing products along the computer architecture product spectrum have lost their identity through integration, leaving six applications portfolios that correspond to the company's organization. In addition, the company's data and communications utility foundation has grown stronger. The current, rather emotional issues of centralization versus decentralization-- direct-line responsibility for managing the resources of the overall computer architecture--will become

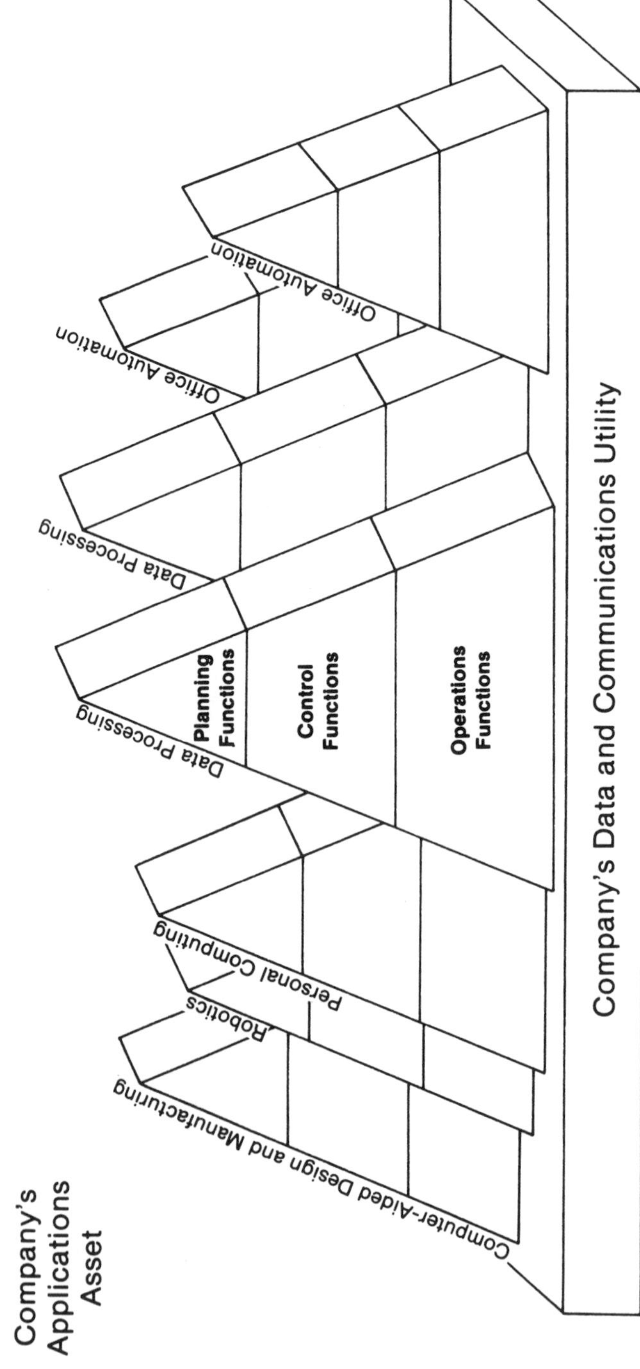

Figure 3 *Existing Computer Architecture*

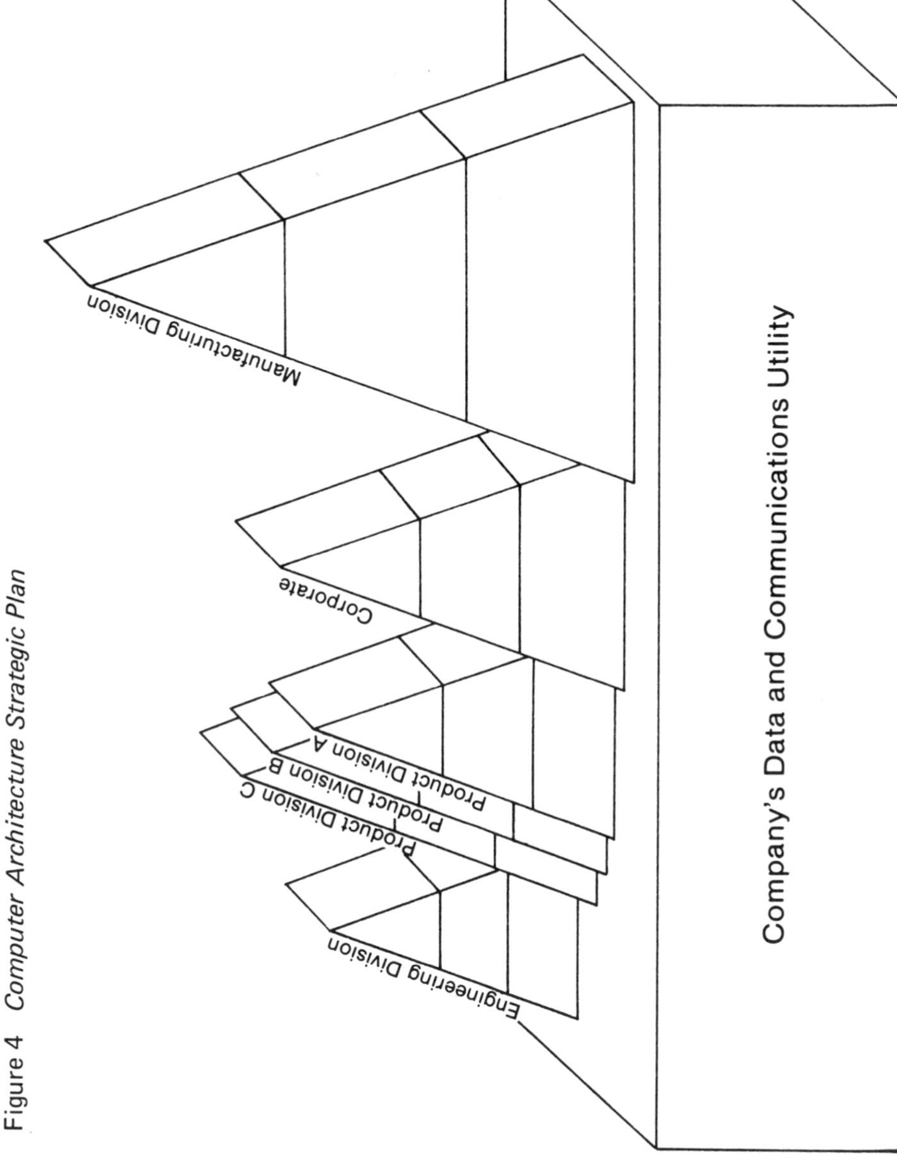

Figure 4 *Computer Architecture Strategic Plan*

obsolete. The computer will become an organizational phenomenon that is used with other technologies to support virtually every aspect of the business.

Related Research Issues. A major issue in computer architecture planning is investigating the fundamental changes in company planning--from organizing DP computing to building a computer technology foundation to support business strategies. Important research questions are

- How should existing computer planning processes change to enable effective computer architecture planning?

- What are the appropriate roles for the DP manager, the executive steering committee, and users in computer architecture planning?

- What are the key management processes involved in implementing a computer architecture plan?

- What should be included in the plan?

Finding 5: Horizontal versus Vertical Management

The existing products along the computer architecture product spectrum are currently being managed "horizontally," but there is a growing realization that "vertical" management is required.

The computer architecture product spectrum in Figure 5 shows two communications/data product spectra (voice/data and graphics/data) and multiple applications/data product spectra according to industry. Levels of communications/applications cross-integration in the products are illustrated by the bands of technology circling the spectra. This shows, for example, a need to integrate CAD not only along the graphics/data product spectrum, but also with factory automation along the cross-integration communications/applications spectrum. This somewhat involved but more comprehensive computer architecture product spectrum permits us to address the issue of horizontal versus vertical management more effectively.

The computer architecture product spectrum includes both relatively mature products, such as data processing, and immature products, such as personal computers. Although sound management control practices have been generally worked out for the mature products, they are rudimentary for most of the immature products. Also, various products along the spectrum affect different groups in a company. Some represent users' first major experience with computer technology.

The tendency, then, is to manage new, immature products independently, or horizontally. There is much justification for horizontal management. Users have their hands full just figuring

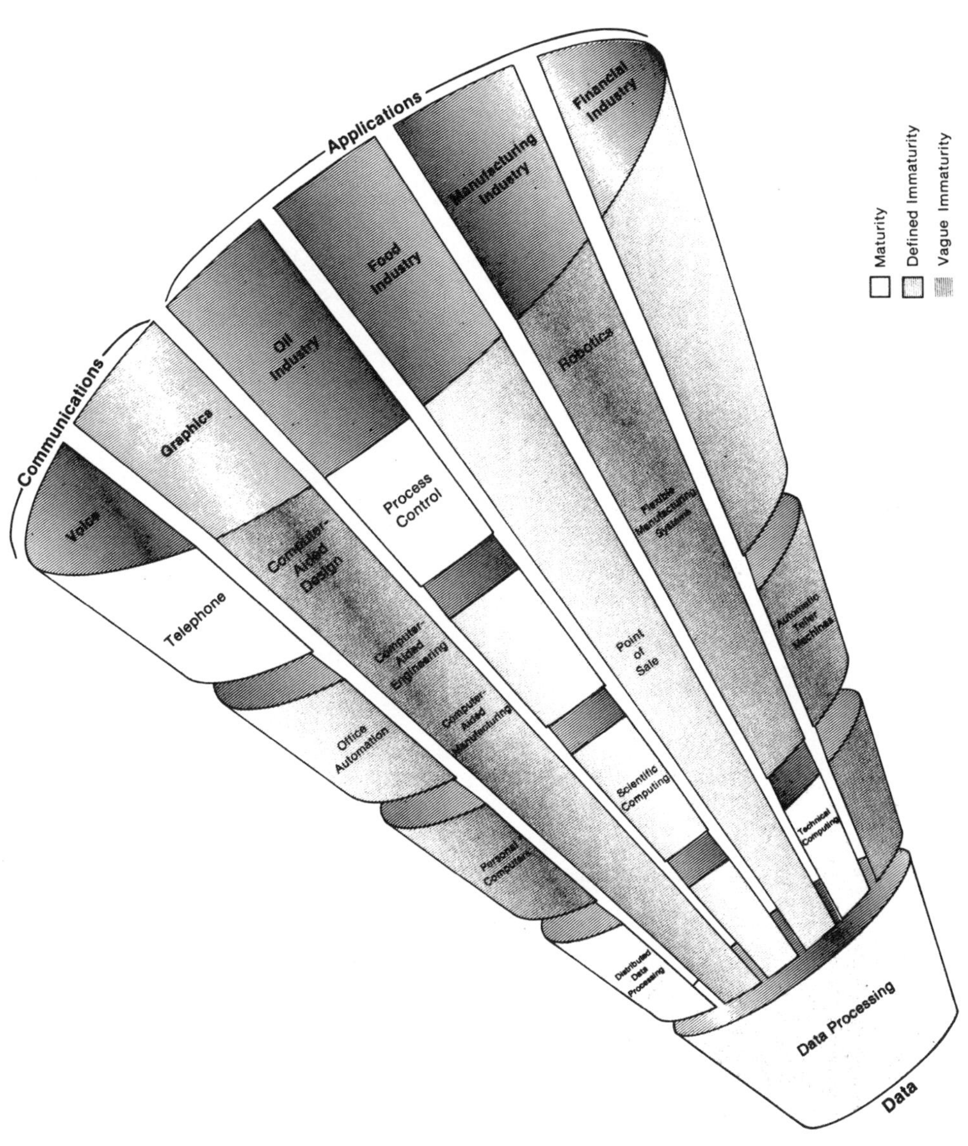

Figure 5 *Computer Architecture Product Spectrum*

out how to apply the new technology and have little time left to worry about the longer term. The DP department may be consumed with its own management problems, or its proposed management approach may not be appropriate. Vendors market their products for limelight, short-term benefits instead of their longer-term role in the company's computer architecture.

These conditions have influenced the technical possibilities for integration and how integration is occurring. Consider, for example, voice and data. Both IBM and AT&T have the wherewithal to develop, market, and install the integrated technology. Further, the economic stakes and business advantage are high enough to motivate companies to pursue voice/data integration.

However, there are many products on the spectrum between voice and data. Voice/data integration, in effect, means integration of the products between as well. Adjacent products on the spectrum are already being integrated: voice is being integrated with office automation, office automation with personal computing, personal computing with distributed computing, data processing with distributed computing. But in most cases these levels of integration have been achieved with difficulties in technology and organizational change. The more diverse the product technologies and vendors, the greater the technological problems of integration. The larger the independent investment in relevant products along the spectrum and the more departments involved, the harder the organizational problems.

Horizontal management is needed to react to the new products, but vertical management is essential to ensure that appropriate products along the spectrum can be effectively integrated through the longer run.

Related Research Issues. Significant issues are associated with understanding horizontal and vertical management strategies and their implications for the optimal balance between centralization and decentralization. Important research questions are

- How should a company organize through time to manage product spectra effectively?

- How and when can products be projected to fill in the product spectra identified?

- How and when should a company begin focusing on vertical as well as horizontal management of a product spectrum?

- What are the relationships among the product spectra?

Finding 6: Pragmatic Operating Strategies

Corporate DP managers who are being asked to lead the

transition to the advanced stages recognize the need for integration, sense the technological problems, and are inclined toward their existing vendors and vendors who have the capability to meet their companies' needs over the long term.

Most large organizations have relatively savvy DP managers at the corporate level. Most of these managers have the ability to become computer functional executives and lead the advanced stages. They are asking the right questions and developing pragmatic operating strategies. Their questions include the following:

- Does the vendor have the technical and financial strength to provide the advanced stages products I need?

- Does the vendor have a product strategy that will provide the levels of integration our businesses require?

- Is the vendor a "safe" choice in respect to senior management's perceptions, and can I make a good business case to support my choice if things go awry for a while?

Related Research Issues. Interesting issues concerning operating strategies involve comprehending the impact of information management industry structure and determining effective business strategies for both emerging firms (Altos, Fortune) and established firms (IBM, DEC, AT&T). Important research questions are

- What are the fundamental vendor strategies available to the computer functional executive?

- How does the executive assess the risks of alternative vendor strategies?

- What role should senior management play in determining vendor strategies?

To provide validation evidence for our recharting findings, I cross-analyzed the key issues we identified with those found in two other recent studies. One was conducted by the Conference Board with about 300 chief financial officers and management information systems (MIS) executives. The other was carried out by the Society for Information Management among its membership of over 800 practicing MIS managers. The tabulation of key issues is shown in Table 1. Although there is a reasonable mapping of the key issues among the studies, the stages theory seems to facilitate a uniquely useful perspective on the recharting issues.

Table 1. *Reconciliation of Nolan, Norton & Company Recharting Findings with Conference Board Top Ten Management Issues and Society for Information Management Survey*

Recharting Research Findings	*Conference Board Top Ten Computer Management Issues*	*Society for Information Management Survey*
FINDING 1: Technological Discontinuity Transition to Advanced Stages	7. Integration with strategic planning	2. Facilitation of organizational learning and usage of information systems (IS) technologies 15. Planning and management of the applications portfolio
FINDING 2: Shift to User Computing	1. Personal computing 4. Office automation (OA) 9. Software: make versus buy	3. Facilitation and management of end user computing 6. Improved software development and quality 12. Development and implementation of decision support executive information systems 13. Increased understanding of the role/contribution of IS 17. Impact of artificial intelligence 18. Effective use of graphics
FINDING 3: Executive Leaders in Managing the Advanced Stages	6. IS personnel	4. Measurement and improvement of IS effectiveness/productivity 5. Specification, recruitment, and development of IS human resources 7. Alignment of IS organization with that of the enterprise 11. Information security and control 14. Determination of appropriate IS funding
FINDING 4: Building of the Organization's Computer Architecture		1. Improved IS planning 8. Integration of DP, OA, and telecommunications 9. Planning and implementation of a telecommunications system 10. Planning, implementation, and management of OA 16. Effective use of the organization's data resource 19. Management of data and document storage
FINDING 5: Horizontal Versus Vertical Management of Emerging Diversified Technologies	2. Centralization/decentralization 5. Value of information 10. Education of management in use, value of information	
FINDING 6: Technological Simplification of Diversified Technologies	8. Introduction of new technology	
OTHER	3. Security and control	

Sources: The 1983 Conference Board Survey on "Ten Top Computer Issues," Management Information, New York: The Conference Board; and "Research Study Results Identify Key Issues," *Members Forum, Society for Information Management,* No. 2, 1983.

The Nolan, Norton & Company recharting findings indicate that most large companies have entered a "window" that began in 1980 and will probably last through 1985, a fundamental transition in their use of the computer. From a stages theory perspective, the window can be thought of as the technological discontinuity of moving from the DP-driven early stages to the user-driven advanced stages. Important research issues for the 1980s center on leadership and effective management of this transition.

Bibliography

Diebold, John. "Where We Are Heading in the Age of Automation." Management Review, March 1983, pp. 9-15.

Drucker, Peter E. Managing in Turbulent Times. Cambridge: Harper & Row, 1980.

Gibson, Cyrus F.; and Nolan, Richard L. "Managing the Four Stages of EDP Growth." Harvard Business Review, January-February 1974, pp. 76-88.

Hamilton, Scott; and Ives, Blake. "Knowledge Utilization among MIS Researchers." MIS Quarterly, December 1982, pp. 61-77.

Kuznets, Simon. Economic Growth and Structure: Selected Essays. New York: W. W. Norton, 1965.

Naisbitt, John. Megatrends: Ten New Directions Transforming Our Lives. New York: Warner Books, 1982.

Nolan, Richard L. "Managing the Computer Resource: A Stage Hypothesis." Communications of the Association for Computing Machinery, July 1973, p. 99.

_______. "Managing the Crisis in Data Processing." Harvard Business Review, March-April 1979, pp. 115-126.

Nolan, Richard L; and Norton, David P. "Recharting DP to the Advanced Stages." Stage by Stage, Autumn 1982, pp. 1-4.

Toffler, Alvin. The Third Wave. New York: William Morrow, 1980.

Appendix

Recharting Data Processing to the Advanced Stages Program

Nolan, Norton & Company has a unique position in the industry. Our methodologies for planning and managing computer technology are deeply rooted in academia, and our client base provides a cross section of industry and organization levels that ensures a focus on current issues and leading-edge practices. The professional associations we have built in our research and education programs give us access to the best current thinking in universities and a stimulus for contributing to an evolving profession and body of knowledge.

Through our consulting organization, we launched our Recharting Program to gain an understanding of issues facing organizations as they move into the era of the advanced stages. The first phase of the program was a series of five conferences, which were supported by research programs such as our multiclient study on office automation, casewriting, management seminars, and clients' special interest groups. Table A-1 lists the U.S. participants; Table A-2 lists participating European companies. The six findings in this paper are derived from the overall Recharting Program in the United States and Europe.

Table A-1

U.S. Participants

Advanced Systems, Inc.
Albany International--PPG
Amerada Hess Corporation
American Airlines, Inc.
American Bell
American Standard, Inc.
Amoco Oil Company
Anaconda Minerals Company
Associates Bancorp, Inc.
Associates Commercial Corporation
AT&T
Bank of America
BASF Wyandotte Corporation
Battelle Northwest
Bigelow Company
Boeing Computer Services, Richland
Bronson Methodist Hospital
Burns and Roe, Inc.
Burroughs Wellcome Company
H. E. Butt Grocery Company
Canada Systems Group
Cenex
C-I-L, Inc.
Commercial Shearing, Inc.
Connecticut General Life Insurance
Connecticut Mutual Life
Crown International, Inc.
Department of Energy
DuPont
Emerson Electric Company
First Boston Corporation
Flexi-Van
General Dynamics
Gillette Company
Golub Corporation
GTE Service Corporation
Heublein, Inc.
Humana, Inc.
IBM Corporation
ITT
S. C. Johnson & Son, Inc.

Table A-1 Continued

Lehman Brothers Kuhn Loeb, Inc.
Liberty Life Insurance Company
Management Decision Systems, Inc.
McKinsey & Company, Inc.
Merck & Company, Inc.
Merrill Lynch & Company
Morgan Guaranty Trust Co. of New York
Morton Thiokol, Inc.
New England Telephone Company
Northern Trust Company
Northwestern Bell Telephone Company
Northwestern Mutual Life
Norton Company
Oscar Mayer Food Corporation
Pacific Northwest Laboratories
PepsiCo, Inc.
Phillips Petroleum Company
Ralston Purina Company
R. J. Reynolds Tobacco International
Rockwell Hanford Operations
Royal Trust
Scott Paper Company
Serviologic Corporation
Simpsons-Sears Ltd.
Social Security Administration
SOHIO
South Hills Health Systems
Sun Company
Super Valu Stores, Inc.
3M Company
TRW Tool Division
UNC Nuclear Industries
United Virginia Bank
Westinghouse Hanford Company
Wisconsin Power & Light Company

Table A-2

European Participants

Beecham Group PLC
BOC Limited
C. T. Bowring and Company Limited
British Gas Corporation
Citibank NA
Colonial Mutual Life Assurance Society Ltd.
Ford Motor Company Ltd.
Kongsberg Vaapenfabrikken
Lloyds Corporation
London and Manchester Assurance Company Limited
London Transport Executive
Morgan Grenfell and Company Limited
Occidental Systems, Belgium
Prudential Assurance Company Limited
Rank Xerox Limited
Rolls-Royce Limited
Scandinavian Airlines (SAS)
Shell International Petroleum Company Limited
Standard Telephones and Cables
TI Info and Computing Centre

DISCUSSION: NOLAN PAPER

Participants in the discussion of Richard Nolan's paper accepted the historical fact that his stages theory has been a powerful, intuitively satisfying aid to understanding the changing information systems (IS) management environment. Nolan noted the theory's descriptive nature and his attempt to achieve generality, simplicity, and accuracy. His taxonomy of stage (growth process) characteristics has been altered over time, but always within the basic model of an S curve. The discussion focused on the "real" nature of the process summarized by the stages theory and the theory's relevance for the future. The usefulness of the stages theory as a contingency theory that predicts or specifies alternative outcomes was also considered.

Participants generally agreed that there are multiple growth or change curves representing shifts through time and organizational strategies. The group also considered the fundamental forces causing the S curve. Major topics in this part of the discussion were the nature of organizational learning and the concept of an organizational shift as opposed to a technology shift.

Organizational learning was identified with learning by individuals and the learning transmitted to new employees (and reinforced in present employees) by formal procedures, standards, forms, display screens, training, supervision, and informal training and culture. Information systems require an information processing discipline at both the individual and organizational levels. The discussion questioned whether the processes organizations need to achieve a required level of information discipline for a given degree of system complexity exist. For example, is experience with transaction systems (transaction discipline) a prerequisite for successful implementation of data base systems (data discipline)? Some suggested that experience and discipline with automation is the critical element. One participant commented that the discipline for some new systems requires unlearning the lessons of older systems. Others submitted that concepts of diffusion, innovation, and technology transfer explain this kind of organizational learning better than learning theory.

The discontinuities in the ways organizations use and manage IS were examined in terms of organizational shifts rather than technology shifts. Involvement of management and diffusion of technology among users introduce fundamental changes in organizational behavior. Will users as systems developers and managers need to go through the same stages as centralized systems have? Participants noted that user stages will be somewhat different. Questions of control and the degree of organizational slack necessary for innovation were also raised.

The nature of future stages was discussed in terms of the user-oriented stage and the emergence of an information architecture to guide development and support user-developed systems. The boundaries of IS are changing and roles are shifting. Some participants called for more descriptive research to define clearly what is happening.

The net result of this discussion was an awareness that Nolan's stages theory, however useful in earlier practice, now must adjust to a number of issues concerning underlying phenomena, multiple curves, organizational learning, and stage-based management and organization. The new conditions posed by diffusion of IS technology and the emergence of user-dominated systems call for research to aid current and future management of the IS resource.

RESEARCH ISSUES IN INFORMATION SYSTEMS PERSONNEL MANAGEMENT

J. Daniel Couger

I will begin this paper with my projections of changes in the information systems (IS) profession over the next decade, the consequences of those changes for the overall IS management functions, and their resulting research issues. Then, because other contributors to this part discuss the first three research areas, I will concentrate on the last: improved personnel management techniques.

Overview of IS Management Issues

1. Changes that will precipitate new demands on managers of IS technology:

   - A company's competitive success will be so dependent on up-to-date technology that only technology-wise managers will progress to top management positions. As a consequence, the IS manager's superiors will be more knowledgeable in technology.

   - The user-managers of the next decade will be M.B.A.'s who used the computer as a natural and integral part of their educational program. Consequently, the IS manager's peers will also be more technologically knowledgeable.

   - The aura of the new IS profession will have worn off, and its managers will face the same problems as their peers have in older disciplines. The need to distinguish true motivators from more disenchanted subordinates will be imperative.

   - Both hardware and personnel will be increasingly distributed--physically, if not organizationally--in the camp of the user.

   - The impact of systems will be more integrally tied to company success.

2. Consequences:

   - Managers of IS will be held more closely accountable by technology-wise superiors and user-peers.
     - Scheduling will have to be more precise.
     - Project control will have to be more effective and efficient.

   - Planning will have to be more accurate and for a longer range.

   - New approaches for management of remote hardware and personnel will have to be developed.

   - System errors will have more far-reaching effects.

   - Personnel will be less motivated unless the motivational environment can be enhanced.

3. Resulting research issues:

   - Improved planning methods and models--especially for longer-range planning--must be developed.

   - More accurate techniques for both schedule and cost estimating will be needed.

   - Behavioral and quantitative approaches to project management will have to be developed.

   - Improved personnel management techniques will be required in the following areas:
     - Recruitment and selection
     - Motivation
     - Performance measurement
     - Supervision and leadership
     - Goal setting and feedback
     - Career path guidance

The Changing IS Personnel Environment

Four major factors will necessitate new IS personnel management focus in the next decade. First, the nature of IS work itself is changing. For the typical firm using IS, the principal work is no longer development of new systems, but maintenance of old ones. Labor dollars spent on maintenance are already more than 50% of the personnel budget according to Boehm (1981). Elshoff (1976) indicated that the figure for General Motors is about 75% and that GM's are fairly typical of large-business software activities. The average life of a system has increased from three years in 1960 to five in 1970 and eight in 1980 (Lyons, 1980).

The impact of this trend is particularly significant because maintenance work is generally regarded as unchallenging compared with new development. The following quotations are representative of programmer and analyst views of maintenance: "Traditionally, program maintenance has been viewed as a second class activity, with an admixture of on-the-job training for beginners and of low-status assignments for outcasts and the fallen" (Gunderman, 1978). "Analysts and programmers generally view the maintenance function as an inferior, noncreative, nonchallenging activity" (Liu, 1976).

The second factor affecting motivation and productivity is the greater availability of software packages. These increase programmer and analyst productivity despite the heavy modification necessary to tailor some packages to a company's specific needs. Further, they are being implemented sooner than internally developed systems. Nevertheless, modification is another form of maintenance. It is adaptation of others' work and is, therefore, less creative and less challenging.

The third factor in IS personnel management is the emergence of the information center concept. Users are being armed with higher-level languages, simplified model-building capabilities, and their own data bases. They are handling an increasing share of their own systems development. This trend relieves IS management of pressure, but it deprives programming and analysis staff of opportunities to work on some interesting decision support systems. (A complete discussion of the information center can be found in Hammond, 1982.)

The fourth factor affecting employee motivation is the availability of macrolanguages and applications development facilities. These innovations greatly simplify the tasks of design and programming. They allow IS management to respond more quickly to demands for services, but they require less skill from programmers and analysts.

Although the overall effect of these four changes will be higher output per programmer or analyst, this will be accompanied by a reduction in job satisfaction. As a result, IS managers will have more personnel problems.

Robert A. Zawacki and I have measured the effect of one of these factors on IS personnel--maintenance. The dramatic reduction in motivation related to increased maintenance activity we found is shown in Figure 1.

The data for this graph were derived from the Couger-Zawacki data base of more than 6,000 people in the IS field. It is doubtful that each of the other three factors has a negative motivational impact as significant as that of maintenance. But even if their combined effect was no more than that of maintenance, the total result would be of great consequence.

Managers in IS need special preparation for these new motivational problems.

Figure 1. *Effect of Percent of Maintenance on Job's Motivating Potential*

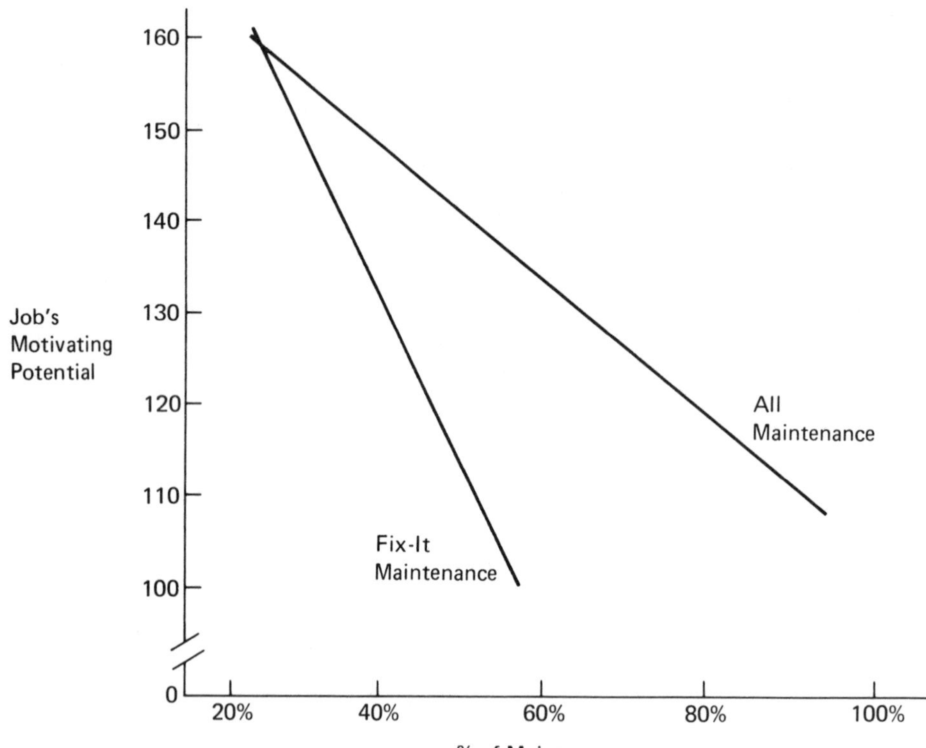

The Impact of Change on IS Personnel Management

The four major changes in the IS environment will affect six personnel management activities: recruitment and selection, motivation, performance measurement, supervision and leadership, goal setting and feedback, and career path guidance.

Recruitment and Selection

As the IS field stabilizes and approaches maturity, some of the problems more traditional disciplines have experienced will emerge. For example, the issues associated with recruitment and selection will change. Previously, only personnel with minimal qualifications were available. Internal training programs and on-the-job performance weeded out the undesirables. That costly process must be improved. Programmer aptitude tests offer a new approach. They have high validity for predicting both success in training and on-the-job proficiency (Schmidt, Gast-Rosenberg, and Hunter, 1980). Even though equal employment opportunity considerations have made it more difficult to use these tests, the effort is justified by the correlation between test results and on-the-job performance.

Unfortunately, satisfactory aptitude tests for systems analysts have not been validated. I participated in a 1982 conference, sponsored by the Institute for Certification of Computer Professionals, to try to define the field and the content for certification (see Cotterman et al., 1981). The select group of academicians and practitioners at that gathering could not agree. They recommended that development of certification exams be delayed until the field matured and concurrence could be reached on what knowledge was required to be a successful systems analyst. These conclusions are surprising, because national curriculum guidelines for the profession were published by the Association for Computing Machinery in the early 1970s (for graduate curriculum see Ashenhurst, 1972; for undergraduate studies see Couger, 1973). They were also recently updated (see Nunamaker, Couger, and Davis, 1982). These guidelines have been utilized in more than 100 universities (Nunamaker, 1981) to develop IS programs.

Research Issues. Further research is required on knowledge and performance criteria for systems analysts to strengthen the recruitment and selection process.

Motivation

Fitz-enz was the first to attempt to relate prior motivation research to the IS field. He replicated the Herzberg studies with a survey of 1,500 IS personnel (Fitz-enz, 1977). The factors most important to participants in his study were (in order of importance): (1) achievements; (2) possibility for growth; (3) the work itself; and (4) recognition. Couger and Zawacki (1980) utilized the Job Diagnostic Survey of Hackman and Oldham (1975, reliability and validity proven) with our data base of more than 6,000 people in all areas of IS. This generic instrument was expanded to include a number of IS-specific areas and was revalidated in 1976. It subdivided the Herzberg category of "the work itself," analyzing the correspondence of more than 40 variables to intrinsic motivation of the job. The key job dimensions identified were skill variety, task identity, task significance, autonomy, and feedback. The motivating potential score of the job was computed from survey variables and compared with an individual's growth need strength.

Earlier work had concentrated on relating job characteristics to job satisfaction (see, for instance, Awad, 1977; Woodruff, 1980). Our work showed that job satisfaction is an output of a good motivational environment, not an input, as was previously hypothesized. Job satisfaction is a by-product of a productive environment. This conclusion was substantiated by the research of Bagozzi (1980). It is surprising, therefore, to see the continuing emphasis on sensitivity analysis performed against the job satisfaction variable (for example, in the 1983 study by Goldstein) instead of against productivity.

Couger and Colter (1983) considered the changing nature of IS work. Our research indicated that maintenance activity can be restructured to make it challenging. We identified ten organizations in which the maintenance productivity was satisfactory and examined their motivation environments in depth. We used two research instruments: the Couger-Zawacki Diagnostic Survey and the Structured Interview Questionnaire on Motivation. We obtained a total of 555 usable responses from the survey. And we interviewed a sample of 104 people, including 43 supervisors, whose assignments ranged from 0% to 100% maintenance.

Our research showed that the key to motivation is matching the richness of the job to the individual's need. Two elements must be assessed: the job's motivating capacity, and the individual's capacity to be motivated. The proper match is the key to productivity, and supervisors have all the factors for that match under their control. We developed 14 application cases representing the maintenance environment in government and industry. One or more should apply to the maintenance situations of most settings.

Research Issues. The work I have recounted substantiates and enhances the job enrichment and job enlargement research of earlier decades. It also proves that the negative effects of a continuously changing technology can be altered. Nevertheless, further studies are needed to measure the specific impacts of changes in the work environment and to determine counteractive measures when these changes decrease motivation.

Performance Measurement

Professionals in IS are highly goal oriented and consequently desire both quantitative and qualitative performance measurements. Such measurements remain imprecise devices for most programming and analysis work. Although the literature is filled with discussions of models and metrics for software estimating and reporting (see, for instance, Basili, 1980; Jones, 1981), there is little evidence that more than a few companies have implemented these techniques. Recent surveys show that managers rely principally on schedule compliance to measure performance in both new development and maintenance (Couger and Colter, 1983).

Managers have also utilized qualitative performance measures. Solid work has been under way for some time to improve the reliability of this judgment process. It is referred to as behaviorally anchored rating scales. These scales are developed from critical incidents, ranging from particularly good to particularly bad incidents. Behavioral scientists then assist in developing dimensions of performance. Job characteristics and performance expectations determine the number of dimensions.

Arvey and Hoyle (1974) worked with IS management to develop appropriate behaviorally anchored rating scales for systems analyst and programmer-analyst jobs in a specific organization. First, they identified 12 behavioral dimensions: possessing technical knowledge; planning, organizing, and scheduling; maintaining customer relations; providing supervision and leadership; training others; performing documentation; maintaining communications; assessing customer needs and providing recommendations; demonstrating job commitment and effort; debugging; doing program and/or systems modification and/or development; and conducting presentations. They next developed seven to nine items (anchors) within each dimension to describe behaviors that evidenced gradations from very poor to very good performance. The results increased the consistency of managerial ratings.

A similar approach was developed by Beatty, Schneier, and Beatty (1977). Their system, behavioral expectation scales, defined anchors in terms of what an employee could be expected to do. They derived 16 behavioral dimensions: coding programs, understanding and implementing program specifications, knowing existing software and its applications, showing dependability, being receptive to feedback and willing to make changes, performing documentation, debugging, understanding the scope of a project outcome, solving problems, using job control language, working with others, demonstrating professional growth, working with clients, planning and scheduling projects, designing systems, and coordinating. The study produced mixed results. One positive outcome was increased agreement on performance between supervisors and subordinates. This area is still controversial (see Glueck, 1982), but most researchers agree that qualitative performance scales aid performance evaluations, because they focus on actual behaviors rather than on traits.

Research Issues. Continuing research is needed on quantitative and qualitative performance measures. Testing of existing scales in industrial situations is particularly necessary.

Supervision and Leadership

Many studies have been conducted on management and leadership--both within and outside the IS field. The most frequent type of IS leadership study concerns qualities essential to effective managerial performance. For example, Elliott's study of IS managers (1975) identified the following characteristics, in order of importance: (1) ability to relate to others; (2) capacity to deal logically with difficult problems; (3) skill in planning, organizing, and controlling the work of the department; (4) willingness to understand and employ new techniques; (5) capacity for coping with new situations; (6) ability to relate to the specialist staff; (7) sufficient technical knowledge of equipment and systems; (8) knowledge about the business operations of the firm; and (9) discretion and tact with users. Fourteen skills were isolated from a list of 99 in a study of IS managers by Benbasat, Dexter, and Mantha (1980). Generalist aptitudes, such as human and organization skills, were rated above technical abilities.

Goldstein (1983) examined IS managerial roles in reducing goal conflict and role ambiguity. He used Bowers and Seashore's (1966) supervisor and peer leadership characteristics scales and the role conflict scales developed by Rizzo, House, and Lirtzman (1970). Goldstein found strong correlations between role ambiguity and job satisfaction and slightly weaker correlations between role conflict and job satisfaction. These results support Bostrom's (1981) findings concerning IS personnel as well as the more general findings of House and Rizzo (1972).

Research Issues. The studies cited show substantive progress in determining what is important in IS supervision and leadership. However, much more work needs to be accomplished in the "how to" areas.

Goal Setting and Feedback

The importance of participation in goal setting and feedback on goal performance to IS personnel at all levels was revealed by Couger and Zawacki (1980). We found that participation was satisfactorily achieved, but feedback was not. The quality of feedback was negatively correlated with job level (it was poorest for programmers, best for vice presidents and directors), but its quality was perceived to be unsatisfactory at all levels.

A one-to-one session between worker and supervisor is the key approach to goal setting and feedback. However, the quality circle can improve employee participation in these processes. The first research on quality circles in IS departments was reported by Couger (1983). A quality circle is a team composed of eight to ten volunteers working to identify problems and to develop and implement solutions. Special techniques are used in both problem analysis and solution. My research showed that quality circles are beneficial both for participation and feedback and for resolution of important technical and environmental problems. They are also quite cost effective.

Research Issues. Continued research is needed on specific procedures for effective goal setting and on improved methods for feedback on goal performance.

Career Path Guidance

Changes in approaches to systems development will have a critical impact on the IS professional career path. The short-range effect is mostly negative--displacement of thousands of programmers because users are developing their own applications. The positive aspect is an expanded career path for some IS professionals. Not only will they continue to have access to the career paths presently open to them, but they will have a new multichannel path available in the user area. Users will be able to perform many application generator tasks, but other tasks will require the expertise of professional IS personnel. Software identification, selection, implementation, and maintenance; user training; and consultation when problems arise or seldom-used functions are necessary are examples. Users and user-managers will also need assistance in selecting personal computers, identifying internal and external data bases, and determining when to utilize IS staff and when to have users develop applications.

Positions are now being created in each user area for advisers to perform these functions. These professionals will have the opportunity to move up the career path within the user function, because they will be expert on computer use for a specific application area. As computer use becomes more pervasive, individuals in these positions will have a "leg up" on their user-colleagues for promotion into user management, because even greater computer utilization will be desired by higher managers.

The magnitude of the short-run problem of handling displaced applications programmers was illustrated by one of the IS directors attending this colloquium. He said to his discussion group, "Help me with some career path planning for the 3,000 COBOL programmers that will no longer be needed in my company."

The displacement cannot be resolved within the IS function. Some programmers can be transferred to the user area as user advisers. But, unfortunately, only a few will qualify for these new jobs, because the personality traits they require for success are not the same as those needed to be a successful applications programmer. The majority of displaced programmers will require an occupational shift. To lessen the problem, IS managers need immediately to turn off the hiring spigot so they can minimize the buildup of personnel in this category.

Research Issues. Researchers can perform a valuable function by analyzing the characteristics of applications programmers and comparing them with the traits of workers in other occupations. This will help identify where career crossovers would be easiest.

Conclusion

The changing IS personnel environment during the next decade will result in reduced motivation, and, hence, lower productivity unless IS management initiates specific remedies.

The procedure for enhancing work is equally applicable to all four problem areas outlined previously: increasing maintenance activity, greater use of package software, more systems development by users, and increasing use of macrolanguages and applications development facilities.

Managers can improve motivation by enhancing the other four core job dimensions to offset the reduction in skill level. The net effect is a job as rich as the previous one, although changed substantially. Most individuals will find the work challenging, but some will not. Personnel with a macroperspective will be much more motivated in such an environment, where the task identity and task significance core job dimensions are enhanced. Personnel with a microperspective (high tech orientation) are more centered on the skill variety dimension. The recruitment and selection process must be refined to differentiate these people.

The effective IS managers of the next decade will need good behavioral skills to match their technical competence. Research shows that once they see the need, IS managers can quickly assimilate behavioral techniques and apply them well. Managers in IS are well aware of the necessity to retool continually in the technical area. Research can continue to help managers develop and apply appropriate proactive as well as reactive skills.

Bibliography

Arvey, R. D.; and Hoyle, J. C. "A Guttman Approach to the Development of Behaviorally Based Rating Scales for Systems Analysts and Programmer/Analysts." Journal of Applied Psychology, February 1974, pp. 61-68.

Ashenhurst, Robert L., ed. "Curriculum Recommendations for Graduate Professionals in Information Systems." Communications of the Association for Computing Machinery, May 1972, pp. 363-398.

Awad, E. M. "Job Satisfaction as a Predictor of Tenure." Computer Personnel, Autumn 1977, pp. 7-10.

Bagozzi, R. Causal Models in Marketing. New York: John Wiley and Sons, 1980.

Basili, Victor, R., ed. Models and Metrics for Software Management and Engineering. Los Alamitos, Calif.: Institute of Electrical and Electronics Engineers, Computer Society Press, 1980.

Beatty, R. W.; Schneier, C. E.; and Beatty, J. R. "An Empirical Investigation on Perceptions of Ratee Behavior Frequency and Ratee Behavior Change Using Behavioral Expectation Scales (BES)." Personnel Psychology, Winter 1977, pp. 647-658.

Benbasat, I.; Dexter, A. S.; and Mantha, R. W. "Impact of Organization Maturity on Information System Skill Needs." MIS Quarterly, March 1980, pp. 21-34.

Boehm, Barry. Software Engineering Economics. Englewood Cliffs, N.J.: Prentice-Hall, 1981, p. 18.

Bostrom, R. P. "Role Conflict Ambiguity: Critical Variable in User-Designer Relationship." Proceedings of the Seventeenth Annual Computer Personnel Research Conference, 1981, pp. 88-112.

Bowers, D. G.; and Seashore, S. E. "Predicting Organizational Effectiveness with a Four-Factor Theory of Leadership." Administrative Science Quarterly, 1966, pp. 238-263.

Cotterman, W. W.; Couger, J. D.; Enger, N. L.; and Harold, F. System Analysis and Design: A Foundation for the 1980s. New York: North-Holland, 1981.

Couger, J. Daniel, ed. "Curriculum Recommendations for Undergraduate Programs in Information Systems." Communications of the Association for Computing Machinery, December 1973, pp. 727-749.

______. "Circular Solutions." Datamation, January 1983, pp. 135-142.

Couger, J. Daniel; and Colter, Mel A. Motivation of the Maintenance Programmer. Colorado Springs, Colo: CYSYS, Inc. (Box 7345, 80933), 1983.

Couger, J. Daniel.; and Zawacki, Robert A. Motivating and Managing Computer Personnel. New York: John Wiley and Sons, 1980.

Elliott, C. "Qualities of a Data Processing Manager." Data Management, January 1975, pp. 35-37.

Elshoff, J. L. "An Analysis of Some Commercial PL/1 Programs." Institute of Electrical and Electronics Engineers Transactions on Software Engineering, June 1976, pp. 113-120.

Fitz-enz, J. "Who Is the DP Professional?" Datamation, September 1977, pp. 125-128.

Gilb, Tom. Software Metrics. Cambridge, Mass: Winthrop, 1977.

Glueck, W. F. Personnel. Plano, Tex.: Business Publications, 1982.

Goldstein, D. K. "A Further Examination of the Determinants of Job Satisfaction in Programmer/Analysts." MIT, Center for Information Systems Research, Report WP96, February 1983.

Gunderman, Richard E. "A Glimpse into Program Maintenance." Datamation, June 1978, p. 99.

Hackman, J. R.; and Oldham, G. R. "Development of the Job Diagnostic Survey." Journal of Applied Psychology, April 1975, pp. 159-170.

Hammond, L. W. "Management Considerations for an Information Center." IBM Systems Journal, No. 2, 1982, pp. 131-161.

House, R. J.; and Rizzo, J. R. "Role Conflict and Ambiguity as Critical Variables in a Model of Organizational Behavior." Organizational Behavior and Human Performance, Vol. 7, 1972, pp. 467-505.

Jones, Capers. Programming Productivity: Issues for the Eighties. Los Alamitos, Calif.: Institute of Electrical and Electronics Engineers, Computer Society Press, 1981.

Liu, Chester C. "A Look at Software Maintenance." Datamation, November 1976, p. 5.

Lyons, M. J. "Structured Retrofit--1980." Proceedings of Share 55, 1980, pp. 263-265.

Nunamaker, Jay F., Jr. "Educational Programs in Information Systems." Communications of the Association for Computing Machinery, March 1981, pp. 124-133.

Nunamaker, Jay F., Jr.; Couger, J. Daniel, and Davis, Gordon B., eds. "Information Systems Curriculum Recommendations for the '80s." Communications of the Association for Computing Machinery, November 1982, pp. 781-806.

Rizzo, J. R.; House, R. J.; and Lirtzman, S. J. "Role Conflict and Ambiguity in Complex Organizations." Administrative Science Quarterly, Vol. 15, 1970, pp. 150-163.

Schmidt, F. L.; Gast-Rosenberg, I.; and Hunter, J. E. "Validity Generalization Results for Computer Programmers." Journal of Applied Psychology, December 1980, pp. 643-661.

Woodruff, C. K. "Data Processing People--Are They Satisfied/Dissatisfied with Their Jobs?" Information & Management, December 1980, pp. 219-225.

DISCUSSION: COUGER PAPER

There was no disagreement in the discussion of Daniel Couger's paper about the importance of personnel concerns. The exchange centered on issues of motivation in terms of maintenance, career path planning and new positions, selection of personnel, and productivity.

Underlying the discussion was an untested assumption that maintenance of software is not challenging or interesting. This led to consideration of how either to make it more interesting or to reduce the amount of maintenance activity necessary. One approach is to transfer programming of minor enhancements, such as new reports, to the users. Another is to identify the components of job satisfaction and build jobs that are more satisfying.

Career path planning is an area that needs research. Career paths must be more clearly defined, especially for information systems (IS) professionals working in user areas. The distinction between users and IS professionals is obscured when analysts are given long-term assignments in user areas. Concurrently, users may become proficient with IS technology and seek career path opportunities that utilize a combination of functional area knowledge and technological skill. Job content for IS professionals is also changing; there is more emphasis on supporting end users and being part of an organization and less on being a technician without commitment to the organization as a whole. New skills are required to help end users build systems rather than to build them alone.

Career path planning also relates to selection of personnel. Research is needed to identify the skills required to support changing IS roles and the educational experience necessary for new IS positions.

The group felt that productivity, generally related to efficiency, was not as important as effectiveness. The major concern in IS is to be effective--to provide the "right" service and the "right" information to aid the organization. Only in IS operations or routine processing is efficiency a major consideration. Performance measurement elicited mixed reactions from session participants. If the function is operating smoothly, performance measurement is not significant; the search for performance metrics begins when things are not going well. A more significant performance issue is how to translate organizational goals into individual performance goals and measure their accomplishments.

THE CORPORATE INFORMATION SYSTEMS BUSINESS

Carl H. Reynolds

The delivery of information systems (IS) services within even a modest-sized company is an endeavor that has all the characteristics of a business. The analogy is straightforward: the functions of the host business and the users are the market and customer; the various collections of services, reports, and applications constitute the products; terminals and communications, and trucks and messengers make up the distribution system; the computers, peripherals, and system and applications software are the factory; the applications programming department is the research and development organization. And all these must be managed and accounted for with the familiar financial, legal, personnel, and executive functions.

In many companies this collection of activities has become an enterprise comparable to the corporate profit centers. No other staff function in a business has this nature, and that is one major reason why IS managers and their corporate superiors have so many difficulties in developing an effective relationship. Even if one does not operate IS as a business, the analogy gives a useful framework in which to examine the IS function.

Thus, this paper will look at each area of the IS business and outline its major problems. The paper reflects what I believe are the most pressing IS management concerns. However, IS is unique in each environment, and the relative importance of these problems will vary widely between organizations.

All of us must deal constantly with two fundamental kinds of problems: relevance and productivity. Most of the information and advice directed at IS managers addresses the problems of productivity. There are hundreds of course offerings on programmer productivity, for example, but I consider these exercises in microproductivity. We must consider what I call <u>macroproductivity</u>, the relevance of information systems. In fact, the overriding problem of IS today is relevance. The arcane nature of the IS world keeps out the users, and the thrill of technological discovery and achievement keeps the minds of IS practitioners focused inward. The result is that IS managers need to spend almost all their energies making sure that IS plans are relevant to the needs of the business and are executed in a relevant way.

Hughes Aircraft Company

The ideas expressed here are the result of my 12 years in a unique IS environment. Hughes Aircraft is a privately owned defense contractor engaged primarily in electronics research, development, and manufacturing. Its products range from small, inexpensive items, such as fiber optic cable connectors, to large, million-dollar items such as guided missiles and communications satellites. The Department of Defense is Hughes's principal customer, but each of its areas presents a different set of technical and marketing requirements. To cope with this diversity, Hughes has adopted a highly decentralized organization. Each of its six main divisions, called groups, operates like an independent profit center. There is, however, a large amount of intergroup work transfer, which generates considerable interdependence.

In 1971, in response to the recession of 1969-70, Hughes centralized data processing onto two IBM 360/165s. At that time the company had sales of about $1.5 billion and 29,000 employees. In 1975 we started to decentralize IS operations, and today our central operation accounts for about 40% of the IS dollars spent. Hughes is now a $4.5 billion company and has over 60,000 employees.

Several characteristics of the Hughes environment have had a great impact on IS. First, Hughes people and corporate management are highly technical. A third of the employees and most of the top management have degrees in the physical sciences or engineering. Thus, they are inclined to push the state of the art. Second, having these decentralized groups so geographically centralized (80% of Hughes employees are located within 35 miles of Los Angeles International Airport) keeps the conflict between the two ways of operating always in focus. Finally, the decentralized management philosophy really dominates Hughes's corporate life. The centralization in 1971 was an anomaly that we are working our way out of while trying to retain its advantages.

Today, IS structure at Hughes is a combination of centralized, decentralized, and distributed. If one wishes to centralize, it is easy to define what to do. Once one is centralized, however, decentralization poses such a bewildering array of alternatives that it is extremely difficult to define and maintain a clear course of action. The goals of decentralization are not so obvious, and its benefits are usually intangible. Centrally, we operate two Amdahl 5860s and an Amdahl V-8; we also have two distributed networks--one of HP 3000s and one of IBM 4341s. Within the groups there are an IBM 3081, a 3083, a 3033, and several 4341s. In addition, the groups operate a large number of VAXs and other DEC machines, as well as

Hewlett-Packard and PRIME hardware. There are over a hundred computing centers utilizing equipment valued at $250,000 or more.

This is the background that has generated the ideas I will discuss here.

The Business Analogy

Production

We include under the heading of production all IS activities that are required to produce routinely expected results: the running of scheduled production jobs; the availability of time-sharing services; the distribution of printed and microfiched reports; and the maintenance of existing programs. We also include the operation of the computer and communications facilities required for these services. The advent of on-line systems, the use of remote job entry networks, and the tremendous concentration of jobs processed into small physical and geographic volumes has made it much more difficult to know what is going on, and has made the operations manager's job more and more complex. In 1972 we had two IBM 165s and 70 disk drives in the space where today we have two Amdahl 580s, a 470/V8, and 204 disk drives. In other words, in one room we have gone from 4 million instructions per minute to 28, and from 7 billion bytes of on-line storage to 64 billion.

Three areas of major concern exist in this new environment. First, it is difficult to understand and measure performance. Results are known only remotely from the computer room. There are many technologies and organizations in the long chain of actions between submission of a piece of data and the report of its results. Second, management has a difficult time understanding the productivity of this operation; and, finally, planning for the future is becoming more difficult.

Measuring performance of the computer center has never been an easy task. Over the past decade the idea of measuring and reporting on such things as on-time report delivery, batch job turnaround, and terminal response time has become widely accepted. There are, however, two difficulties with this approach. The most obvious is that service now depends on an ever-increasing number of criteria. Network availabilities must be measured. And we have a wide variety of services, for which different service levels are required. For example, small, open-shop jobs must be treated differently from very large, number-crunching tasks.

The second difficulty is the lack of standards of acceptability. Thus, in the most fundamental activity of all IS organizations, quantitative measurement of the value of the product still poses a challenge. In addition to understanding the system's performance, one needs to be able to measure the cost of the system to measure its productivity. I will discuss some financial aspects of this problem later. The point here is that the factory of today's IS business has few if any rules of thumb for determining the adequacy of its performance. As more and more ways to implement a given production load become possible, having confidence that one is at least close to efficient is more and more difficult. For example, what is the cost/value/efficiency of one 12-million-instructions-per-minute installation versus several 2-million-instructions-per-minute ones?

Planning for factory capacity has always been, in my experience, the balancing of two points of view. One is that the work load expands to fill the available capacity. The other is that use of computers is a rational, predictable human activity. From this perspective, if planning is done properly, the right capacity will be available at the least cost. The latter is the more satisfying to believe, and some of us have a tendency to attribute the apparent accuracy of the former idea to the fact that our planning is poorly executed.

To date most capacity planning is what might be called microplanning. That is, the minutiae of machine operations are examined, summed, and extrapolated, and used as the basis of a "five-year plan." There are, however, some difficulties with this procedure. For one thing, an existing capacity limitation will limit the utilization of one or more of the forecast elements, thus biasing the prediction. More important, these analytic techniques usually ignore what is really driving the work load, namely the relationship between the cost of people--which has been steadily increasing--and the cost of computing--which has been steadily going down (see Benjamin, 1982, for one examination of this problem). Although detailed system simulations are great for understanding the impact of specific system configuration changes, they don't tell us much about how or why the work load is going to grow or what capacity is going to be needed. In other words, we need a macroplanning capability. This perspective must relate the needs of the business in comprehensive terms to the capabilities of the technology. Too often, the detailed techniques of today's capacity planners produce only disembodied numbers, which do not easily correspond to the business planning process. Further, we need to plan in terms related more to the business than to computing. At present, for example, our greatest planning need is for reasonable, defendable space forecasts. Space has become a bigger limiting factor for us than money.

Before we leave the IS factory, one other change needs to be mentioned. That is the growing prevalence of the multivendor environment. Many of my peers, for good reason, stick to one major vendor, usually IBM. At Hughes we have historically looked for just the product we want and learned to live with several vendors. In fact, at present we deal with 200 vendors. There will be more and more opportunities in the future to face this situation, especially now that the telephone industry is entering the world of IS. Ways to approach the multivendor environment and the impact of different strategies for managing it are issues that few have considered.

Research Recommendations. What are the correct measures of production performance, and what are the appropriate levels of those parameters? How can we measure the cost effectiveness of a production operation? What is the translation between user needs and hardware, software, and facilities requirements? How can we manage multivendor IS environments, and what are the consequences of various acquisitions strategies?

Research and Development

One can consider research and development as two separate activities. I put the design and implementation of new applications in the development category, because these efforts are very similar to the design and development of hard products. It takes the same sort of creativity to conceive of good new systems, and the same sort of discipline to produce strong, reliable implementations, as it does to produce a new computer. This issue is somewhat clouded by the fact that after a system is developed, there is no manufacturing cost. The cost of running an application in production is not the same as the cost of replicating a hardware product, and these costs do not exert the same influence on design. Nevertheless, good applications development requires knowledge of the technology and understanding of the market requirement beyond mere lists of users' desires.

New applications development is the most important task of IS. This is despite the fact that in most organizations true development is a relatively small percent of the programming/systems staff effort. It is true that maintenance and "small improvements" to existing systems are very important, but this is at least partly because of the lack of really effective development methodologies. Development seems to be moving in two directions--fourth-generation languages and packaged methodologies.

The more exciting development area today is the promise of fourth-generation languages, corporate data bases, and user programming. No IS organization will survive long without embracing these approaches. The assumption that all the necessary data are available and all we need is a good way to manipulate them raises a problem, though. This is certainly a good assumption in many cases; for example, personnel systems already contain more information than any collection of standard reports could ever analyze. At Hughes we are trying to use FOCUS to develop a system of data analysis that will be timely and effective for first- and second-line supervisors, for whom analyzing standard personnel data is not the primary function. It is certainly easy and rewarding to provide support for the administrative functions. It is more important, but harder, to solve the larger problem. For example, the line manager may be in desperate need of a manpower-job cost system that can only be obtained from a new time-card system.

Fourth-generation languages also lead easily to the notion of prototyping systems as a way to avoid paper analyses in new situations. Prototyping undoubtedly has its place. Our experience to date, however, is that it is most useful when users do their own programming. They do not, then, keep track of the cost of all their false starts and rewrites. When we have tried to do prototyping for users, with little of the usual data and systems analysis, we have had difficulty. We find that we often cannot respond to the changes in direction prompted by a user as he or she becomes more familiar with the problem. Further, the user cannot understand the delays and costs such changes cause.

The issue of development methodologies also needs review and understanding. There are several such canned approaches to development, and the Department of Defense is promoting a similar approach to the development of "embedded" software. Embedded software is an integral part of the hardware that the Defense Department buys, for example, the software in the guidance computer of a missile. Without contesting the need for discipline in the development process, one has to wonder about some things, though. Could VisiCalc have been developed by the use of SDM-70? Doesn't there need to be more flexibility in the approach to development to allow valuable undocumented concepts, such as VisiCalc, to be pursued? Development methodologies must both be adaptable to a variety of requirements and reflect the underlying character of the organization they serve. They cannot be used for every development, and they are not a substitute for well-trained staff (though they certainly are a good way to train a staff).

Finally, there is the matter of relating development activity to the needs of the business--the matter of relevance. So far we have been talking about the problems of implementation, but deciding <u>what</u> to develop is the crucial issue. In my experience, this is where we waste the most effort and get the least guidance from the technologies. The work of McFarlan et al. (1982) seems to be of the greatest importance in this respect, but we practitioners need considerably more help. We not only have to know what to do, but we also need help involving the users. It took several years for one of our division managers to decide that a reasonable production control and manufacturing inventory system was a better way to cut costs than reduction of his data processing effort.

In this day of increasingly rapid technological change, carrying out applications development using known and understood tools and implementation vehicles is not enough. Not a year goes by without a whole set of new products, software approaches, and enticing slogans appearing to challenge existing solutions to systems requirements. Keeping abreast of these changes; sifting through the evidence to select out a few important, relevant possibilities; and then trying to introduce these options into use is a bewildering task for IS managers. It was difficult enough when IS managers were expected to evaluate innovations in their field. Today, many other members of the corporate team have decided they can assess these new possibilities better. This adds to the velocity of the development effort, if not to its clarity.

The IS manager must select system designs from alternatives that vary from the traditional, central IBM processor to personal computers and expanded word processors. Each alternative has pluses and minuses, advocates and foes. Doing research on the best approach to office automation, electronic mail, or personal computing seems to boil down, really, to trying <u>some</u> of a selected <u>few</u> varieties in <u>some</u> likely situations. The problem, of course, is in picking the numbers to substitute for "some," "few," and "some." It is difficult to keep one's perspective in this new arena. Decisions on big machines tend to be reasonably well documented and are usually cost-justified in the light of a range of alternatives. Picking a personal computer, or a word processor, however, easily becomes a matter of taste. There is nothing wrong with this approach to R&D in these areas, but IS people will have to learn to live in a more democratic environment. We can afford to allow the users a few mistakes at $10,000 to $20,000 per machine.

<u>Research Recommendations</u>. In the choice between the laissez-faire of the fourth-generation, user-managed development and the use of structured disciplines, which works when? How can we determine which development problems are most relevant to the business? Are research errors--doing too much or doing too little--very costly?

<u>Finance</u>

The most basic way that IS is like a business is its intrinsic financial basis. Even if users are totally unaware of the costs, sooner or later each IS organization will be judged by the perceived value of its results against its (known) cost. Yet this is the area in which I often feel least adequate. Three principal financial issues are troublesome to the practitioner: acquisition analysis, cost accounting, and financial evaluation of existing applications.

<u>Acquisition analysis</u> has two parts. What do we need to acquire? And how should we finance the acquisition? Everything I read about acquisitions seems to assume that the first question has been answered correctly. Certainly, that ought to be true before a purchase is made. However, most managers are much more comfortable with reviewing the details of a lease-buy analysis and discussing the ownership of the investment tax credit than they are with the details of vendor or model selection. A financial analysis based on three-, four-, or five-year projections gives credibility to the whole process. I have always

wanted to do a historical review of different acquisitions scenarios. In my paranoid dreams, there are only two outcomes--either there was a strategy I missed that would have saved hundreds of thousands of dollars, or I spent endless hours of study only to find out that a small error in system tuning (model selection) completely overshadowed all the expected savings of a clever leasing scheme. This dilemma is sharpened by the fact that hardware is now only about 40% of the IS budget, so acquisition errors, relatively, are cut in half.

The area where errors seem most costly is setting realistic depreciation schedules. For example, it is possible to purchase for $450,000 a hardware-software system to do project control. Of that price, $350,000 is for software you cannot resell. What should the depreciation schedule be for the acquisition? What should the life of an IBM personal computer, total cost including software of $10,000, be? Of an IBM 3081? It seems that as the product introduction cycle gets shorter, we may have to shorten the depreciation lives of our equipment.

Cost accounting is another area of concern. A chargeback system can have many goals. At Hughes we have always said that users should pay for the resources they consume or prevent others from using. This is in keeping with our distributed management approach. Users, in principle, are free to get their IS wherever they want to, so this policy is intended to give them data for a sound economic decision. However, it is difficult to do accurate cost accounting; if such accounting is accurate, it is complicated. If it is complicated, then it may help the IS manager run his or her business, but it will probably confuse users and not help them run theirs. To date, the only cost accounting effort I am aware of is based on minute technical analysis of the workings of the hardware. Perhaps the problem would yield more easily to the efforts of accountants than to those of systems programmers.

The next problem is accounting for the lower and lower priced computers. Managers will probably not try to allocate their personal computers among the various contracts they work on. These costs may go into the direct hourly rate of users or, more likely, into the general overhead, like rent. Now we put in a local area network and buy a few Winchesters and a laser printer. We have quite a powerful computer system at a modest price. But how do we compare the cost of an application on this system with that of the same application on the central machine? The users will say that the incremental cost is zero. Generally, they have no idea what it costs to run such a system, or they only consider the most obvious elements of cost. It appears that there will have to be new controls or new approaches to keep the growing overhead costs visible. On the other side of the coin, this partial cost concealment may accelerate removal of small jobs from the large machines.

The final financial problem I would like to raise was articulated for me only last year by McFarlan et al. (1982). That is the problem of financially evaluating the portfolio of existing applications. This portfolio is usually considered a drag by IS managers. Its real financial value is set by the cost of replacing it, which puts IS in the same boat as the American steel industry vis-a-vis the Japanese, because at some point the portfolio may need large-scale modernizing. Deciding how much to invest in keeping the old systems running and when to replace them has always been an operational problem. I feel that systems are usually replaceable only under the most dire circumstances, and that one ought to keep maintenance as low as the screams of users will allow. However, that may be a reactionary view. McFarlan et al. (1982) suggest that a proper financial evaluation of the portfolio will shed some light on this question.

Research Recommendations. How should acquisitions be evaluated? How important is the financial acquisition (lease, buy, rent) method? Can we properly account for services provided by central computers, especially compared with distributed minis and micros? Is there an accounting method for deciding when to replace an old system?

Marketing

As do many technically oriented businesses, IS often fails to emphasize marketing. Everyone knows the need to sell their point of view and ideas, but a broader range of activities also needs to be carried out. One role of the marketing function is to define the sphere of operation for the organization. Many IS organizations can exert quite an influence on what services they will provide or avoid providing. One interpretation of critical success factors is that they spell out a marketing strategy, a way of focusing efforts toward a limited set of important objectives (Martin, 1982). Another marketing function is defining the needs of the users as they relate to specific program or services packages, a function we can call product planning.

These are not very original ideas, but their importance is growing as computer knowledge and usage spreads, greatly multiplying the opportunities and increasing the internal competition. It is clear that in most cases the IS group is going to lose market share, even though it may grow in size. At Hughes, for example, we have gone from over 95% of the market to about 40%, even though we have quadrupled in size. This means not only that IS management may feel some urgency about picking their strategy, but also that a view somewhat independent of the entrenched, internal IS bureaucracy is needed. It may have been true at one time that what is good for the IS organization is good for the company, but it certainly is not self-evident now.

Another current condition also relates to marketing. There are many three-headed IS organizations now--they consist of communications, applications development, and operations. Often each of these departments operates fairly autonomously. Applications develops its systems using the standard, available hardware-software architecture. Operations sees that these applications run, and the communications department is called on when lines need to be installed or fixed. However, many new opportunities can be overlooked with this approach. Integrating the capabilities of these three areas to serve a broad company need requires that they work together more closely and flexibly than they are used to.

We have begun to talk about "marketing programs," in which a set of technical capabilities is tied together in a temporary matrix management arrangement. The marketing organization keeps the technical departments focused on a joint problem to be solved. This cross-discipline management is needed because new approaches are often in conflict with the way things have always been done; often some plans may not seem reasonable from the unique viewpoint of one IS department.

One example of such a program is the use of an asynchronous network to support companywide Information Management System (IMS) data base applications. Hughes has lots of 3270 terminals, but we have even more ASCII terminals. We also have some corporatewide applications with low connectivity, or usage. Our internal packet network is ideal for connecting the corporate computer to such terminals on a switched rather than hard-wired basis. However, one has to design the application so it will work with the ASCII terminal, not just with the 3270. There are many detailed problems in making the application, IMS, the ASCII terminals, and the packet network do what the user needs. Without integrating the efforts of all our technical departments and keeping them focused on the desired end result, we would get nowhere.

If there is a marketing organization, it may be a good place to define performance standards. In the past the operations group at Hughes has had that responsibility. Standards tend to be established in times of stress and poor performance, and so reflect performance possibilities rather than values that relate to the nature of usage. This procedure can either give less service than is needed and available or raise costs higher than necessary.

The most interesting thing about the marketing function of an internal IS department is the definition of its mission. People in IS "marketing" positions easily become imbued with the enthusiasm of marketing, which may not be what is needed. Some organizations will require tremendous skill just to acquire resources for some minimum penetration of the possible IS need. Others will need to define limits and avoid the temptation to spread too far. A lot of literature in the past has discussed selling oneself and the IS profession. There may now be a need to adapt more of the business-defined marketing disciplines to IS.

Research Recommendations. What motivates users to get involved? Can simple goals be stated for IS as a business in view of the conflict between satisfying a user and constraining the IS budget? How can the business-defined marketing disciplines be adapted to make IS more effective?

Personnel

People are, of course, the only major problem and opportunity in IS. Hardware, although expensive, can be managed and fixed, and software sooner or later works. But people are what put it all together. The advent of fourth-generation languages, the rise of the packaged software industry, and the use of remote diagnostics are all aimed at lessening our dependence on an ever-increasing number of people with ever more esoteric technical skills. But at any point in time the information services of a company can be no better than the people who provide them. The things that concern me most about personnel are the seeming shortage of leaders, the difficulty in evaluating performance and productivity, and motivation of high producers.

The preponderance of activity in most IS organizations is maintenance of existing systems. In some cases large, basic applications may be 10 or 15 years old. These systems, of course, require continuous attention and actually are continually modified and extended to meet changing requirements. Doing such work takes many skills and great patience, and often the effort can be quite creative. In these tasks, however, the environment is almost completely defined. The rules of the game are very specific, even though they leave room for quite a lot of action.

Maintenance work is very different, however, from what is required to meet the pressing new demands on IS. The big growth in IS work arises from the relative change in people-computer costs that the technology is creating. Each time the hardware-people cost ratio goes down, a whole new layer of human activity becomes subject to economic automation. This results in new applications requirements, not just more of the old. But our existing staffs do not have the skills and attitudes needed to deal with new applications. The biggest single problem they need to adjust to is a very unstructured environment. No longer are they hemmed in by the established demands of a huge paper-people-machine system that has been running "this way" for years. No longer are they constrained to using the same hardware-software system that has served the entire company centrally since the advent of 360.

Of course, much of what we do is rearrange and reanalyze our existing applications data in new ways, which is so easy to do that we are busy passing that responsibility on to the users. Really new applications, however, are susceptible to many different approaches and raise new problems. In new situations users are not very clear about the solutions they really want. Often, too, the users are involved with data processing for the first time and have gained their technical knowledge solely from TV ads.

Finding enough people with skill in the necessary technologies, the aptitude and knowledge to do a full-fledged system design, and the leadership to structure a concrete task out of these amorphous building blocks is very difficult. My immediate staff and I spend a lot of our time trying to recruit these geniuses from outside, in the not-too-likely expectation that they are more easily found out there than inside. One reason we go outside is that everyone on our current staff who we think can handle these assignments is already overcommitted. Another reason may be that we believe that the missing ingredient of leadership might be more likely to be found in an adventuring job changer than in a worker who is content with the status quo--that thought shouts for attention. In brief, the demand for systems leaders is growing at an even faster pace than the demand for programmers, at least on a percentage basis. The shortage may even be as important a factor in the increasing applications backlog as the lack of programmer productivity tools.

The problem of programmer productivity has been receiving a lot of attention ever since I can remember. In 1963, when I was in charge of programming at IBM, the office of the president of IBM hired a sociologist from Princeton to study the matter in my organization. He took time samples of programmers in various activities. After several months, in a thesislike document, he reported that programmers worked 18% of the time. I thought my career was over until one of my staff found an article reporting a similar study at Bell Laboratories, which concluded that engineers worked only 12% of the time. Because engineers, after salespeople, were the standard of excellence in those days, I was saved.

Unfortunately, I have not seen any much more relevant work in the 20 years since then. People discuss lines of code per hour as though producing lines of code was the main thing programmers did. In fact, only 20% or so of a programmer's time is spent coding. Proponents of this metric account for this by specifically including or excluding different pieces of the other 80% of the effort it takes to produce a line of "debugged" code. The problem is that a line of code has no intrinsic value, and its relative value has yet to be determined.

It makes a reasonable amount of sense to talk about such things as pounds of steel per man-hour. One pound of steel is roughly interchangeable with many other pounds of steel, produced by other people, in other places. But a line of code is of no use anywhere but where it is created, and even if it works it may be worth nothing, or it may be worth a fortune. Would you rather have my entire accounting system code, perhaps 500,000 lines, or the rights to Pac-Man, which cannot be a very big program? Although that example is extreme, the principle is valid. When the value of a program can be understood, we will be able to judge the value of its creators. Until then, we must be content with realizing that lines of code averages are useful as estimating rules of thumb. But management should know what a programmer's productivity is, and programmers themselves deserve to be measured properly. I believe that the best go mostly unheralded; they are appreciated only by the project team members they save.

Motivation of personnel is obviously one of the central responsibilities of management. There has been a fair amount of research on the factors that motivate IS workers, and I am ashamed to say that I cannot cite it. Most of the studies I recall have centered on the uniqueness of the programmer's personality. However, it may not be true that the key to understanding personality is the key to motivating the person. I am sure that such understanding is important, even crucial, to motivate a particular individual. But the problem of running an 800-person organization is how to motivate most of the people, most of the time, without any significant personal contact.

I believe that accomplishment is what really motivates people. We need to understand Theory X and Theory Y, and the latest word from Japan, and this is especially necessary when the environment permits little individual sense of accomplishment. However, the important thing is to allow achievement. The opportunity is now with us, in all the new technologies, to restructure jobs so that individuals can in fact see the impact of their work on the host organization. People who can see that their efforts make a difference almost always seem to work harder. This is both a major argument for decentralization and a major force in making decentralization come about.

Research Recommendations. Is there an evolution in the assumed career paths within IS? How can IS people with leadership capabilities be found? How can we measure the value of a program? Of a programmer? What is the real source of satisfaction in IS? Does it support IS objectives? How can we restructure jobs with the new technologies to allow people to see the impact of their work?

Planning and Control

Nowhere is the idea that IS is a business within a business more apparent than in the overall management of the enterprise. Establishing plans, measuring performance against them, and taking corrective action are obviously the bases of all management. The special problems of IS that trouble me the most are integrating IS plans with those of the host organization, developing plans in the same terms in which performance is reported, and undertaking long-range or strategic planning.

Everyone knows that business and IS plans should be built together, and some organizations seem to establish that integration explicitly. There are, in fact, many organizations in which IS is a major element of the business plan. But in many others the connection is very tenuous. However, it is still a long way from knowing you're part of a cash cow company to giving an order to the local IBM salesperson or defining a new application. The biggest barriers seem to be that users are slow to conceive of IS as a solution to their real business problems, and that IS is unable to discern real business problems to work on. I have always put the major share of the blame on the former reason, but a recent experience may indicate that IS contributes to the difficulty by continuing to use the same old approaches, regardless of the problem.

At Hughes we recently needed to improve our company income tax forecasting ability. The stakes are very high because changes in the tax law dramatically affect government contractors. Our financial planning group, which has a small but very bright computing staff for normal decision support work, needed access to special runs of the basic accounting systems. These, in a $4.5 billion company, are many, large, and complex. The IS organization responded to their requests, but with some reluctance. We did not really see the urgency of the situation, especially because a new long-range task force was concurrently being developed to replace the entire system. The irony is that the best long-term plan is to address the immediate issue vigorously. This will respond to the urgent tax problem and allow the corporate staff, which is relatively new and does not know the long-range needs, to gain more insight into what they should do over the long range than they could obtain from elaborate lists of user requirements. Perhaps this also illustrates that long-range planning, like happiness, cannot be achieved by direct pursuit.

We at Hughes may be unique in our inability to plan and report performance in the same terms. Our internal IS has been patched together from the existing company overhead accounting system and programs built under crises to solve a series of major deficiencies. In addition, the data collection systems for both manpower and machine resource expenditures are only marginally satisfactory. The shoemaker does in fact have a hard time shoeing his children, but in the case of IS this difficulty hurts the whole business.

The organization of our planning effort is a problem, too. If it is put in the administrative department of IS, then the day-to-day pressures to give answers usually dominate whatever planning and development methodology skills the group has, and the patchwork continues to worsen. If the effort is placed in the development departments, then the talent has a way of getting assigned to "more important" user work. In any case, the administrative underpinnings of IS in both financial and management control areas are shaky.

Finally, long-range, strategic plans cause me almost as much guilt as security. (By the way, I just noticed that I do not consider security one of my major problems. I can only pray that I am correct.) We do five-year manpower and capital forecasting, and five-year applications revenue forecasting. Because so much IS activity is maintenance, a huge percentage of what we are doing today will be going on in 1987 no matter what we do now. From a percentage point of view, these forecasts are fairly good. But they don't reflect missed opportunities. They do not tell us what we might have done with just a modest redeployment of resources.

A large part of the problem is that users in general do not have much idea where they want to be in five years either. I suspect the key to long-range planning is going to be finding out how to limit the scope to the planning attempt. All parts of an organization may not need a real five-year plan, no organization may need one every year, and setting goals may not be a democratic procedure. Some of these ideas seem to be coming out now, but IS managers could use a lot more specific guidance.

Research Recommendations. What is the state of the art of management information systems in the IS function? How can we develop and justify a capital expenditure plan? What is an effective long-range plan?

Summary

In summary, I would like to see research point in two directions. First, IS professionals need help to adopt the existing body of management knowledge specifically to their operations. Case studies need to be developed, for example, that illustrate management principles in IS situations, even though these principles themselves are already well known. Second, non-IS managers, perhaps a much larger audience, must somehow learn to cope with two businesses--the organization they are running or helping to run, and the IS business within it. The goal is to integrate these two businesses so that IS will be efficient, effective, and, above all, relevant.

The problems of IS do not really seem to be very different from the problems of any business. I have managed several different kinds of activities, including large engineering organizations, large software projects, large software organizations, and, currently, a large information services organization. At the management level, the problems are all basically the same. There is, of course, much to know about what is being managed, and, as the old saying goes, to be successful you have to know the territory. But IS is different in one major respect from the other activities I have been responsible for. The environment in which IS usually operates has little if any understanding of the breadth of its operations or the fact that it is indeed a business within a business. The staffs of many corporations consist of specialists chosen for technical knowledge rather than for line management experience. One instance in which this can be a problem is the large percentage of IS organizations that reside in the corporate financial function and are, consequently, managed by people who are seldom experienced in systems development, task management, and technological evaluation.

In closing, I am reminded of the problem that the coming of the information age is said to present: what to do with all the man-hours freed from mental and physical drudgery by automation. I submit that there are two ways to use up all that time which could be challenging, entertaining, and perhaps rewarding. First, give everyone a personal computer. Second, ask them what the problems of IS are.

Bibliography

Benjamin, Robert I. "Information Technology in the 1990s: A Long-Range Planning Scenario," MIS Quarterly, June 1982, pp. 11-31.

Martin, E. W. "Critical Success Factors of Chief MIS/DP Executives," MIS Quarterly, June 1982, pp. 1-10.

McFarlan, F. Warren; Nolan, Richard L.; Norton, David P.; and Rogaw, Bruce J. "Linking Information System Strategy and Business Strategy." Distinguished Lecture, Boston, April 13-14 1982.

DISCUSSION: REYNOLDS PAPER

The thesis of Carl Reynolds's paper is that administering information systems (IS), at the managerial level, is identical to managing a business. Information systems managers must understand IS technology, but the rest of their managerial problems are the same as those of other managers. One difficulty unique to IS management is communicating with staff specialists in the organization, especially those in the functional area in which the IS operation resides, who lack line management experience and practical understanding of development, task management, and technological evaluation. Some participants challenged Reynolds's thesis by pointing out the unique characteristics of IS as a technology-based support system for other organizational functions. The qualities that make IS different from production, marketing, finance, and other business functions need to be researched.

The issue of the interests of IS managers was raised. Information systems managers who have come up through operations and development probably like technology. Their careers in IS may indicate more interest in solving problems with technology than in being entrepreneurs. This may be reflected in a preference for analysis and avoidance of strategic risk.

The changing role of the IS manager also received attention. The main IS managerial problem used to be reliable production performance. But users have become accustomed to excellent performance, high reliability, and rapid response; they take transaction processing and traditional report production for granted. Organizations are now looking for applications and facilities that address organizational problems. One participant felt that the paper addressed the problems of a centralized data processing shop but did not consider installation of end user facilities and use of computers on the factory floor--computer support for all functions of the organization.

The extent to which the IS manager should be involved in identifying and estimating benefits from IS applications was a point of controversy. One view was that assessing benefits should be the responsibility of users; the other was that the IS executive should deal with benefits (as well as costs).

Another area of contention was performance measures for information processing. Some viewed with favor measures that would, for example, establish whether a data processing installation is a low-cost producer; others felt that these are most suited to traditional, centralized shops and are counterproductive in a user-oriented environment. Questions were also raised about what constitute valid performance measures and what standards can be applied. A unit of output for data processing similar to the standard case measurements used in a manufacturing plant is needed. Participants suggested that excellent information systems should be studied the way Thomas Peters and Robert Waterman had examined "excellent" companies in their book, In Search of Excellence.

One participant classified computer installations into three categories: the generalized, centralized installation; the specialized installation serving a small group; and the personal computer. Criteria for selecting among these alternatives must be identified by research.

Decentralizing computing was a recurrent theme. Some participants favored complete user freedom; others called for control over decentralized efforts. Those who wanted to let users have complete freedom felt this would promote innovation; those who advocated more control pointed out the incompatibilities that result from freedom and inhibit exchange of data. But all participants recognized the need for an information processing infrastructure. If it is not provided by the IS functions, users will have to build it.

A theme running through the entire session was the effect of end user computing and user-developed systems on the IS manager's job. Discussion on this topic mirrored the centralization-decentralization comments, but there was general agreement that the next stage in IS is end user systems.

CONCLUSION TO PART III

Gordon B. Davis

Management of a business's information systems (IS) function is interconnected with management of its organizational functions. Some in the IS field are concerned that business schools have not done all they should to make computers and IS a part of the knowledge of every functional specialist. The academic area of IS has been better at teaching and researching algorithms than at researching and teaching systems analysis.

Information systems (especially management of the IS resource) as a research area is more closely related to organizational behavior, management, sociology, and psychology than to computer science. Information systems is an organizational rather than a technical or mathematical discipline. Most vital, interesting IS problems are related in some way to the human-system interface, the organization-system interface, and the design and implementation of IS that support organizational systems and individuals in organizational roles. This suggests that research in management of the IS resource should be multidisciplinary and apply related bodies of knowledge. Descriptive surveys and case studies are needed to document existing behavior and provide a basis for further theory development and experimental research. Longitudinal studies, over a number of years, are also needed. For all of these, the difficulties of data collection and the fact that so many objects of research are "moving targets" must be overcome.

A common theme affecting research in management of IS was the trend toward end user computing in its various manifestations: distributed systems, personal computing, fourth-generation languages, user-developed systems, and so on. End user computing affects a wide range of planning, development, evaluation, and management issues. A dichotomy seems to be arising between centralized systems that have significant control over the organizational systems and centralized systems that are merely service nodes for users. The contingencies that support the alternatives being used need to be researched.

The range of research topics suggested in the colloquium discussions illustrates the richness of opportunities. In some academic fields, research has been so extensive that innovative topics are difficult to find; in IS the pie is full of research plums, a scholar need only put in a thumb to get one. The following lists of questions are summarized from the discussions and are by no means exhaustive. They reflect a blend of traditional concerns, such as performance measures; new topics, arising from the changing organizational structures and dynamics of end user computing; and traditional topics in new contexts, such as personnel motivation in an environment of heavy maintenance. Finally, the transition problems themselves provide a rich source of research topics.

Information Systems Planning (Stages Theory)

There is a deeply felt need among practitioners for more research on planning for IS, especially in light of current rapid changes. Although the Nolan stages theory has been accepted as a useful hypothesis for planning, questions have been raised about its applicability as a contingency theory that can be used to predict outcomes or specify alternatives. Some specific research questions on this topic are

1. How can the stages be measured?
2. Does the stages theory apply to all organizations?
3. Under what conditions can stages be skipped or shortened?
4. What conditions are necessary for "stage" learning to occur?
5. Given multiple curves, does experience at one level of automation ease the learning process for another level?
6. How can an organization synchronize multiple learning curves?
7. Is organizational learning as observed in the stages analysis a generalizable theory that extends beyond IS?
8. Do user-area systems need to go through the same stages as centralized systems?
9. What is the best balance between control and organizational slack for innovation?
10. How are IS boundaries and roles shifting?

We are in the midst of a transition process that presents challenges to both practitioners and researchers. New organizations need to be designed, new organizational controls instituted, new management practices used; and all this must produce systems that effectively support organizational needs.

Management of IS Personnel

End user computing is an important consideration for management of IS personnel. The job content for IS professionals is changing; there is greater need for supporting end users and commitment to the organization. Some research questions are

1. What are the career path options for IS personnel? Which of these should organizations offer?
2. Can maintenance of IS be made more challenging?
3. How is prior research on job satisfaction relevant to IS personnel?
4. What is the effect of rotating IS personnel into functional areas?
5. What causes IS personnel turnover?
6. How does organizational structure affect IS job design?
7. Are project teams working on "whole jobs" more effective than the present distribution of tasks in IS departments?
8. Can the maintenance function be transferred to end users?
9. How adaptable are IS personnel?
10. Can traditional systems development personnel work with end users and staff information centers?
11. What characteristics are required to be a boundary spanner and handle role ambiguity and conflict in working with users?
12. What tasks are being or should be turned over to end users?
13. What is the organizational role and impact of "information engineers" developing expert systems?
14. How can the contribution of IS personnel to the goals of the enterprise be measured?
15. What skills and educational experience are required to support changing IS roles?

Management of the IS Function

End user systems also influence research topics in management of the IS function. Issues of centralized versus dispersed information capabilities and centralized versus decentralized control are fundamental. Suggestions for research on user involvement and the changing role of the IS executive are made within this context. Some research questions are

1. How can IS managers respond to the demands of general management?
2. How can IS managers respond to changes in organizational behavior?
3. What can IS managers do to bridge the communications gap with management and other users?
4. How can IS be communicated as a solution to business problems?
5. How can IS managers discern real business problems

that are amenable to IS solutions?

6. How can IS managers do internal IS research?
7. How can organizational mission be incorporated into performance measures for IS?
8. How can IS management become more proactive in corporate strategic planning?
9. What differentiates "excellent" IS operations from ordinary ones?
10. How can IS managers organize for rapid IS change?

PART IV

INFORMATION SYSTEMS TECHNOLOGY AND CORPORATE STRATEGY

INTRODUCTION TO PART IV

Robert L. Ashenhurst

The basic notion that corporate strategy and information systems (IS) strategy should be linked closely is an old, powerful, and enduring one. As Richard Mason notes in his first paper, the antecedents of today's thinking go back to the beginning of the twentieth century. Since then a steady profusion of books and articles by academicians and practitioners have discussed how this linkage might take place. Almost exclusively, the generators of this work have been individuals who have strong familiarity with and affinity for IS technology and its applications. Individuals with a broader perspective and those in disciplines other than IS have shown much less interest; consequently, a great deal of the writing about IS-corporate strategy linkage was excessively mechanical and consisted of ad hoc prescriptive formulas based on rather narrow views of corporate strategy and organizational dynamics.

This part of the colloquium was organized with the belief that these difficulties have begun to be overcome and that linkage represents not just an area where exciting work has been going on over the past several years, but a subject on which major advances in thinking will take place in the next decade. Indeed, we believe that this work will provide the context within which all the issues raised in this volume can best be addressed.

For better or worse, corporations have strategies (either explicit or implicit). Likewise, IS groups within these corporations have strategies (explicit or implicit). Understanding how these two sets of strategies can evolve in a way that is mutually supportive and contributes to the overall good of the corporation was the purpose of this part. The following papers contain numerous examples of how IS technology has (often accidentally) profoundly affected the strategy and overall effectiveness of a corporation. In a similar, and better understood way, awareness of a corporation's goals and strategy has affected the direction of its IS area's technology applications.

General questions the papers raise for the researcher are

1. How can the linkage between IS strategy and corporate strategy be improved in different types of settings? What variables and issues must be considered?

2. How can environments where this linkage is critical and those where it is not be distinguished?
3. What disciplines and frameworks can best illuminate the nature of this relationship?

The first paper, by Richard Mason, sets the context for the area. Describing the history of information and information technology, Mason reveals how we got to our current position. He sketches the histories of information technology, information theory, and organizational structure and strategy, showing the early concepts in each and how they have evolved. Today, he notes, although they came from different backgrounds, technology, organizational structure, and concepts of information and strategy have converged; they are almost indistinguishable from one another.

The second paper, also by Richard Mason, poses the more difficult question, Where do we go from here? Building on the well-described American Hospital Supply Corporation example, Mason suggests two ways of addressing the topic. The first is stakeholder approaches (stakeholders are people inside and outside an organization who have a "stake" in the business). Examples of these approaches are Michael Porter's competitive strategy framework (discussed in greater detail in Warren McFarlan's paper) and strategic assumption surfacing and testing methods. The second way of studying linkage is business analysis approaches. In contrast to the stakeholder approaches, which primarily look outside the organization to identify opportunities for response, business analysis approaches begin with the people and characteristics of the business itself to seek new ways of evolving strategies. Examples of these approaches applied to the IS-corporate strategy linkage include critical success factors, business systems planning, architecture planning, two cultures, product portfolio and life cycle, industry analysis, value added, and IS risk assessment.

The third paper, by Warren McFarlan, sets forth "five broad avenues along which research needs to be done." These are how IS technology can be used as a competitive weapon (building on Michael Porter's work), how the competitive environment influences IS strategy, how corporate style and culture affect IS strategy development, the challenges of organizational learning, and the problems and opportunities posed by use of information systems as products.

Together these papers provide several important impressions. First, in the very recent past new frameworks have genuinely shaken up prior thinking and offered the opportunity for significant progress in management practice. For the first time, a broad bridge is being constructed between different management disciplines. Second, there is an enormous opportunity for researchers to help clarify what this means to practitioners. Their work will be long and arduous but of great value.

A HISTORICAL OVERVIEW

Richard O. Mason

Converging Forces

Strategy begets structure. Structure, in turn, begets the need for administrative information. The chain of information dependency, so fresh when Alfred Chandler (1962) first proposed it, is insufficient to describe business in 1983. Chandler studied the American industrial enterprise as it emerged during the first half of the twentieth century. Today American business has changed. We are in the midst of an information age. In most contemporary organizations information is climbing up the chain of dependency. In some the thrust of information is so powerful that the converse of Chandler's logic also holds: Information systems beget strategy.

Several historical processes have brought us to this point. Among these, three forces account for most of the convergence of business strategy with organizational structure and information systems. They are

1. Rapid innovation of new information technologies
2. Widespread creation of new ideas and concepts about information itself
3. Extensive development of new information-intensive organizational forms and business strategies

During the last 75 years these forces have moved rapidly and reciprocally. Today they are nearly fused.

The relationships between information technology, information ideas, and forms of human organization have been close since the beginning of civilization. About 100 years after the birth of Christ, for example, the invention of paper had major social implications for the Chinese communities where it occurred. The new technology led to publication of the first dictionary and the first pharmacopoeia, thereby converting private, oral knowledge into public, written knowledge. In the process a boost was given to alchemic research and to the development of new educational institutions. About 1,500 years later the same social processes were put to work again in Mainz, Germany. Johann Gutenberg's printing press reduced reliance on penmanship, eliminated many scribes' jobs, and lessened the importance of the oral tradition. In return, it opened up new avenues for public education and made possible the proliferation of libraries.

What distinguishes these two information innovations of the past from those of the modern era? The difference is that paper and the printing press were introduced into essentially information-alien societies. They were pioneering technologies that encouraged new concepts and organizational forms, but they were comparatively slow to germinate and be diffused. The pace of society was slower. The predominate societal concerns were agriculture and the creation of fledgling cottage industries.

This, of course, has changed. The special character of our time, circa 1984, is that we are an information society, one in which concerns about information dominate those about agriculture and industry. For the first time in the history of the world, a few developed countries devote nearly one-half of their economic product to information-related activities. Today in the United States, the premier information society, over half of those employed are engaged in some form of information occupation.

As social commitment to the production of information expands, so does the quantity of information itself. It is estimated, for example, that the Library of Congress, first established in 1800, doubled in size during the 34 years from 1933 to 1966. It doubled again during the 13-year period 1967 to 1979, and it is expected to double a third time between 1980 and 1987. This exponential growth in information content places the Library of Congress's current data base at somewhere near 16 x 10 words.

The increased availability of information and business's demand for it are reflected in capital expenditures. In 1982 U.S. business devoted <u>half</u> of its capital spending to computers, instruments, and electronic and communications systems. This is compared with approximately one-quarter in 1972 and one-third in 1977 (David, 1983). This trend shows no signs of abating, and it suggests that information technology and systems have become a primary factor in business strategy.

As the demand for information and information technology has expanded, so have the businesses that supply them. AT&T, IBM, Xerox, RCA, NCR, Times-Mirror, Dun & Bradstreet, McGraw-Hill, CBS, Time-Life, Digital Equipment, Apple, and a host of other companies are all products of the information age. Most have grown substantially in sales and asset size during the last few decades, and many are quite profitable. Collectively they have changed the nature of American industry.

How did we reach this point? What role have the three historical forces previously identified played in this revolution? And, most important, what does all this mean now for corporate strategic and information systems planning? These are the questions that concern me in this paper. My discussion begins with a brief review of the three historical forces as they unfolded at the beginning of the twentieth century. I chose 1908 as the focal date, the year the Harvard Business School was founded. Significant changes have taken place in information technology, information concepts, and organization theory and practice during the 75 years since this pivotal event.

InformationTechnology

In 1908 the age of electronics was just dawning. Dr. Lee De Forest had invented the first three-element vacuum tube less than two years earlier. Researchers at AT&T were actively seeking improvements that would enable the tube to amplify signals in long-distance telephony. Within five years they were successful. In 1913 the first vacuum tube in commercial service was installed on AT&T's line between Baltimore and New York.

Alexander Graham Bell had invented the telephone in 1876, but by 1908 the Bell system had only a little over 3 million phones in service, and the independents collectively had a little under 3 million. Most businesses of any size had a telephone, but service was poor. There were few interconnecting lines between telephone companies, long-distance circuits were terribly ineffective, and coast-to-coast service was technologically impossible. Local calls were the order of the day.

The office equipment in use by a typical turn-of-the-century business included William Burroughs's Registering Accountant adding machine, Dorr Felt's hand-driven Comptometer, manual Remington typewriters, and NCR cash registers. Most bookkeeping was performed manually in bound loose-leaf journals and on ledger cards stored in trays. Rudimentary punched-card equipment had been introduced. Herman Hollerith, inspired by Joseph Marie Jacquard's automated loom, had employed it in the 1890 and 1900 U.S. censuses. But as of 1908 there were no significant applications of punched-card data processing to business problems.

Yet to come was Thomas Watson's founding of the International Business Machines Corporation in 1924, and it would be 29 years before Professor Howard Aiken of Harvard would collaborate with IBM to make the first fully automatic calculator--the Automatic Sequence Controlled Calculator, or Mark I. From Aiken's time on, however, the pace of innovation in information technology picked up dramatically, stimulated in large measure by the information requirements of the Second World War.

J. Presper Eckert and John Mauchly demonstrated the Electronic Numerical Integrator and Calculator (ENIAC) in 1946. Also that year John von Neumann and others published a paper advocating the now-fundamental concepts of the binary number system and the stored program in computer design. And Chester Carlson invented xerography. Then Bell Laboratories developed the transistor in 1947. Color television was introduced in the United States, and the first UNIVAC was installed at the Bureau of the Census in 1951. A few years later Russia launched Sputnik (1957); the United States in turn launched Telestar in 1962. Portable video recorders were made available in 1968. Microelectronic chips came into widespread use in 1970. Quickly thereafter fiber optics, videodisks, TV computer games, and inexpensive home or personal computers became available.

Today a vast array of information input, output, storage, and handling devices are available, most of which can be linked together by extensive communications networks. As a result, businesses and individuals have access to incredible amounts of current and archival information. Moreover, this technological innovation continues to flourish. As it has grown more pervasive, so too have the concepts for employing it.

Concepts of Information

In 1908 the intellectual idea of "information" was only rough-hewn. According to the Oxford English Dictionary, the word information was first used in the sense of knowledge communicated about facts, events, and subjects--that is as "news"--in 1450. Only, however, at the beginning of the twentieth century did information begin to assume its current connotation, that is, as something that could be symbolized, unitized, stored, and processed as a separate entity.

To be sure, many leaders from the beginning of time have intuitively understood that information had value and could be used as an aid in conducting one's affairs. Jakob Fugger, the founder of the great German house of Fugger, certainly did. In the middle 1500s his family's interests ranged from their headquarters in Augsburg to China, Peru, and all of Europe. To keep in touch with their widespread business interests, Fugger and his nephew Anton established a worldwide news-reporting service in which Fugger's agents were required to write letters on critical political and economic events occurring in their areas of responsibility. These were collected, interpreted, analyzed, and summarized in Augsburg and sent out with conclusions and instructions to each of the business's agents. This information strategy helped Fugger build a dynasty. The Fuggers' exclusive information permitted them to move more rapidly in the mercantile world than their rivals. This degree of information acumen, however, was rather rare among businesspeople of the time. Even in 1908 there was neither the technology nor the conceptual apparatus to treat information as a strategic resource and manage it accordingly.

One necessary component for the emergence of information as a resource was the development of classification systems. Melvil Dewey's decimal system, originally proposed in 1876, was in widespread use by 1908, and it continued to proliferate as the great era of public library expansion was completed. By 1908 collection of documents and accumulation of knowledge were beginning to require a new system of classification. The Library of Congress's initial proposal of 1904 was being considered, but it would be some time before the LC system was to find widespread use. Simultaneously, accounting classifications were being considered and beginning to be standardized. In 1906 the Interstate Commerce Commission supplemented its rules to include a uniform system of accounting reports. This was the first time a common classification was used for financial accounting information.

Many businesses in 1908, however, were little affected by these events. They were not deeply involved in classifying, storing, and retrieving information. Indeed, one of the topics of the day was the "slip system" of accounting. In this system a facsimile duplicate of each posting made to the journal of original entry was prepared with carbon paper. Then the duplicate rather than the "official" entry was used to post to ledgers and other books of account. This was one of the first instances of the now-common notion that information can be separated from its original accounting source, symbolized, and then processed as a "thing in itself."

The idea that information about industrial work and operations might be collected and analyzed on a scientific basis was also just beginning to blossom in 1908. Since 1878 Frederick W. Taylor and his followers had been conducting studies at the Midvale Steel Company. The management community, however, was not awakened to concepts of scientific management until 1911, when Taylor's _Principles of Scientific Management_ was published. It was followed by a series of well-publicized hearings at the Interstate Commerce Commission on the efficiency of railroads and in the House of Representatives on the effects of Taylor's system on the Watertown Arsenal. Despite the publicity Taylor's concepts were only slowly adopted by American industry.

One student of the office, however, Carl C. Parsons, was enamored with Taylor's principles. In 1918 he published _Office Organization and Management_, in which he argued that the principles of scientific management could be profitably applied to office workers to improve their accountability and their ability to produce the records, reports, and statistics necessary for managers to make intelligent decisions.

The "statistics" to which Parsons referred were very rudimentary by current standards. The theory of statistics available in 1908 and its application to decision making were still in embryonic form. A statistical historian, Maurice G. Kendall, picked 1890 as the approximate year in which modern statistics began. Adolphe Quetelet's and Francis Galton's ideas were in the air by then. They led Karl Pearson to formulate his _Grammar of Science_, with which the concept of statistical inference was born, in 1892. By 1908 Pearson's notions of frequency curves, chi-square, and the Pearson product moment correlation coefficient, _r_, had been introduced in the scientific literature, although they were not widely employed in business decision making.

But 1908 proved to be an important year for the application of statistical concepts to business. William Sealy Gosset, an Oxford-educated student of Karl Pearson working at the Guinness brewery in Dublin, Ireland, became interested in the problem of drawing accurate information from small samples of data. In 1908, under his preferred pseudonym "Student," he published "The Probable Error of the Mean" and "Probable Error of a Correlation Coefficient." By relating these notions to the normal distribution, he laid the conceptual foundations for the Student's *t* distribution and testing procedure. This test, later explicated and popularized by R. A. Fisher, is undoubtedly the most widely used method of statistical inference available today. It is used pervasively in business information systems and in business decision making.

Then in 1910 A. K. Erlang, a Danish mathematician working for the Copenhagen Telephone Company, made another significant contribution to the use of statistics as a source of business information. Erlang applied a probability model to the incoming calls at the central office of the telephone company to estimate average waiting times for customers and idle times for operators. Queuing theory was thus conceptualized and applied for the first time to a business problem.

About 1915 several authors acting independently applied elementary differential calculus to inventory cost data to derive an economic lot size equation that would minimize the sum of carrying costs and holding costs. The early formulas only worked when demand was known and constant. However, in a series of articles in the *Harvard Business Review*, R. H. Wilson popularized and extended this inventory optimization model. Information for business decision making was becoming more analytical.

Also in about 1915 R. A. Fisher, anticipating Claude Shannon by some 30 years, formulated a new concept of information. In a series of papers he argued that the variances calculated for a statistical sample provided a definite amount of information for estimating parameters. Fisher continued to consider sample data from the point of view of the information it contained. His classic work on experiment design was published in 1925.

By 1925 Walter A. Shewhart had joined Bell Laboratories and formulated his concepts of the statistical control of quality. He reasoned that if data collected on the attributes of the output suggested that their deviations from a statistical standard were random and hence inseparable from the common distribution, then the production process could be judged "in control." If these deviations were "too far" from the mean, however, managers should undertake a search for their "assignable causes." From 1925 to 1958 Shewhart elaborated on these notions and saw them applied to a variety of other areas, such as reliability testing, life testing, acceptance sampling, and process control.

In 1928 the link between information and decision making was drawn tighter. That year Jerzy Neyman and Karl Pearson's son Egon began to unfold a theory of statistical tests; essentially it compared the probability of acquiring given data under one hypothesis with the probability of acquiring it under an alternative hypothesis. Statistical decision making, they argued, could not be conducted "in vacuo." Instead it must be done by comparison with other alternatives. The criteria of power, relative efficiency, and optimality of tests were thereby derived.

Equally significant was John von Neumann's 1928 publication, "On the Theory of Games of Strategy." This paper proved for the first time the now-famous min-a-max theorem. This idea also spawned Abraham Wald's work on multiple decision spaces, risk functions, and weighting schemes, which culminated in his <u>Statistical Decision Functions</u>, published just before his death in 1950. In this book Wald set forth many of the initial concerns that underlie contemporary decision theory.

Meanwhile, in 1944 von Neumann and Oskar Morgenstern published <u>Theory of Games and Economic Behavior</u>, which laid out the basic concepts of game theory and influenced decision theory. Their original work applied decision theory to situations in which there was a conflict of interest among parties or nature was an opponent. The more recent works of R. Duncan Luce, Howard Raiffa, Robert Schlaifer, and Jacob Marschak have extended these concepts. Today they are used by practicing managers throughout the world.

Meanwhile, at Bell Laboratories, Claude Shannon began to think about information in terms of applied probability theory. He proposed that information be treated like a physical quantity, such as mass or energy, and that it be measured in terms of negative entropy by means of the logarithm of the probability of events. This concept was published with an insightful introductory essay by Warren Weaver in <u>Mathematical Theory of Communication</u> (1948).

Shannon and Weaver's concept played a central role in Norbert Wiener's <u>Cybernetics: Or Control and Communication in the Animal and the Machine</u>, also published in 1948. Wiener's important contribution was to relate information specifically to the attainment of social goals. His simplest model has four elements: sensors, which determine the state of a system; goals, which specify desirable states; error detectors, which measure deviations from goals; and, finally, effectors, which apply power to the system to close the gap between its current state and its goals. This basic cybernetic framework still underlies most management information systems.

The link between information and decision was further joined by the development of linear programs and George B. Dantzig's simplex algorithm for solving them. After 1951 linear programs became practical methods for allocating resources to maximize an organization's objectives in light of limited resources and other constraints. Around this time, Tjalling C. Koopmans, L. V. Kantorovich, Harold W. Kuhn, and A. W. Tucker also contributed to the origins of mathematical programming.

These concepts of information and decision soon found their way into educational programs for managers. The first graduate program in operations research was at the Case Institute of Technology. Pioneering textbooks by Morris and Kimball and by Churchman, Ackoff, and Arnoff emerged. Today most students of management are required to have some exposure to management science and its application to business. Furthermore, most students are taught computer programming and information systems principles. As a result, concepts of information developed during the last 75 years are becoming commonplace.

Organizational Structures and Strategies

In 1907 Theodore Vail joined AT&T for the second time and became its president. The company was on the brink of disaster. Its stock, which had sold as high as $186 a few years earlier, had fallen to a low of $88. With a remarkable turnaround strategy, Vail quickly refinanced the company. Then, in a move that would have a far-reaching impact on the information age, he consolidated AT&T's research and development into one organization. That organization ultimately became Bell Laboratories. By 1908 Vail was making progress with his other major influence on the era. He understood the essentially public and monopolistic aspects of information services--in this regard he agreed with J. P. Morgan, his backer--and he pushed for a regulatory umbrella to protect AT&T's monopoly. This pursuit cost him the divestiture of Western Union and a prohibition against acquiring any more independent telephone companies, but it allowed him to expand the Bell system, especially its long-lines capability, much further.

As Vail was restructuring AT&T, William C. Durant was conceiving a new kind of corporation. On September 16, 1908, he formed the General Motors Corporation. By bringing together a group of automobile manufacturers, including one run by Louis Chevrolet, he started a chain of events that would change the nature of organization, management, and strategy in the United States. The modern corporation, as Alfred P. Sloan described it in *My Years with General Motors*, arose out of Durant's entrepreneurial beginnings. It was more fully formulated around 1920. That year GM faced an economic slump and an internal management crisis. The response, led largely by Sloan, was to develop a coordinated, decentralized organization with clear lines of authority and responsibility. Two information concepts figured prominently in this reorganization--coordination by committee and management through financial and statistical controls. The committee structure provided for communication among disparate functions within the company. The control system, installed initially by Donaldson Brown and Albert Bradley, provided "significant facts" about the business to be used in strategic business decision making, especially in times of crisis.

While Durant was putting together a vertically integrated, diversified firm, which offered a variety of automobiles, Henry Ford was pursuing a more concentrated strategy. In 1908 Ford produced the first Model T. Fifteen million Model Ts would eventually be sold during the car's 19-year product life. With Ford's low-priced, mass appeal automobile came the concepts of the mass production assembly line and high minimum wages.

Another precursor of modern management concepts was the idea of mass marketing. In 1891 Sears, Roebuck & Co. published its first catalog. By 1908 Sears and Montgomery Ward and Company were well established, bringing isolated, rural America a variety of merchandise at comparatively low prices. Taking advantage of low postal rates and good postal service, mail-order operations transmitted large amounts of information about their businesses--advertisements, product descriptions, and forms and procedures for placing orders--directly into customers' homes. The establishment of the parcel-post system in 1913 facilitated the expansion of mail-order business and improved order deliveries. Not until 1925, when the automobile was in widespread use, did Sears, Wards, and others begin their major geographic expansion by establishing multiple retail store outlets. Today the retail outlet trend is abating as toll-free telephone numbers, computer-processed credit card billing, and the possibility of videotext in the home make mail-order systems attractive once again.

Meanwhile, as the Harvard Business School was evolving a curriculum to educate managers for industry, a person whose ideas would eventually have a profound impact on that curriculum was just preparing for his own career. In June 1909 Chester I. Barnard entered the employ of AT&T as an engineer. He rose rapidly; in 1927 he became the president of Jersey Bell. A deeply reflective student of management, Barnard evolved a theory of organization that began with the individual and his or her inducements to participate in the organization. He considered next how groups are organized to encourage cooperative behavior, and from these considerations he derived the following functions of the executive, outlined in his 1938 book, The Functions of the Executive:

- To formulate and define the objectives of the firm
- To promote the acquisition of the efforts needed to reach these objectives
- To provide a system of communication for all members of the cooperative enterprise

In formulating his theory, Barnard was influenced by Elton Mayo, an Australian-born Harvard professor who had been trained as a psychologist. Mayo had helped design the studies conducted from 1924 to 1933 at the Western Electric Company plant at Hawthorne in which a joint Harvard and Western Electric team researched the factors in the workplace that affect the morale and productivity of workers. Mayo and his colleagues stressed the need for human relations in management based on their observation that workers form a culture of their own. Further, they believed that workers and managers participate in this culture at an emotional level as well as at logical and psychological levels. Accordingly, sociological concepts are required to understand group process in the workplace, and individual psychological concepts are needed to understand people's wants, motives, drives, and personal goals. Because both types of concepts are operating in the workplace, both are necessary to manage effectively. T. N. Whitehead's Leadership in a Free Society (1936), Fritz Roethlisberger and William Dickson's Management and the Worker (1939), and George C. Homans's The Human Group (1950) grew out of this important research program at Hawthorne. Collectively, these works had a profound influence on the way people think about organizations and how they might be managed.

As industrial leaders were creating the modern corporation in North America, Max Weber, the German scholar who pioneered sociology, was delineating the theory of bureaucracy on the European continent. In 1908 he had just begun his empirical study of industrial workers for the Association for Social Policy and had begun to publish works on the methodological problems he had encountered. From 1910 to 1914 he worked on his theory of bureaucracy as a formal, technical, rational, yet indispensable form for meeting the mass administrative needs he observed in his day. There is a pervasive tension in Weber's view between the needs of the individual and those of organized social institutions. He considered this tension inevitable, however, because large governments and large industrial enterprises have several requirements to function properly. Their main requirement is a permanent staff of professionals organized into a hierarchy and applying impersonal, uniform rules to individual cases. He called this form the "ideal bureaucracy." Weber's work The Theory of Social and Economic Organization was interrupted by World War I and never completed. It was not widely known in the United States until 1947, when A. M. Henderson and Talcott Parsons published a translation and other sociologists, such as Ed Shils, began to interpret it.

While America was interpreting Weber's views on formal bureaucracy, Philip Selznick was identifying bureaucracy's limits. Formal organizations "never succeed in conquering the non-rational dimensions of organizational behavior" (1948, pp. 25-26). With Selznick's work, Mayo and Roethlisberger's concern with the informal organization and the functioning of small groups was beginning to find its way into sociologists' theories of bureaucracy as well.

Herbert A. Simon, who was deeply influenced by Chester Barnard, published Administrative Behavior and Models of Man, Social and Rational in 1957. These were followed the next year by James G. March and Simon's Organizations and in 1963 by Richard Cyert and March's A Behavioral Theory of the Firm. These works focused again on the potential for rationality in organization. Organizations are composed of people with disparate personal goals, but they resolve this conflict in two ways: by forming coalitions around dominate organizational objectives and by encouraging participation in organizational decision-making processes that seek to achieve these objectives. For Simon, the decision is the basic unit for the analysis of organizations. The need to decide creates a problem that is resolved through a search for acceptable, "satisficing" solutions and is refined through adaptive learning. This theory fully integrates communication and information processing into the theory of organizations.

Paul Lawrence and Jay Lorsch's 1967 piece, Organization and Environment, is among the first books to deal explicitly with information and communication problems. The organizational design problem as they see it is to "differentiate" the organization's tasks into manageable, accomplishable subtasks based in part on predictability of performance and then to "integrate" these subtasks into a structure that will ensure successful completion of each whole task. Finally, successful differentiation and integration of tasks require coordination through information and communication.

A few years later Henry Mintzberg discerned the impact of information processing activities in his detailed study of five chief executive officers. Originally published as a Ph.D. dissertation in 1968, this study was extended significantly in The Nature of Managerial Work (1972). The managers Mintzberg studied were "information processing systems," nerve centers who acquired information from the external environment and internal operations, processed it, selectively disseminated it to subordinates and to outsiders, and used it in making decisions and formulating strategy. Jay Galbraith, in his book Organization Design, made information, communication, and coordination the pivotal concepts for the design of organizations. In his view information consists of uncertainty reduction, as Shannon, Wiener, and others theorized. Moreover, organizations are designed to cope with uncertainty, just as classical management and organization theory purport. This led Galbraith to his basic proposition: "the greater the uncertainty of the task, the greater the amount of information that has to be processed between decision makers during the execution of a task" (1977, p. 36). Incidentally, Lawrence, Lorsch, and John Morse's research substantiated this proposition. This need for information requires data that have been processed through several different information functions: coded and classified into relevant categories, organized into data bases of adequate scope, disseminated to decision makers on a timely basis, and integrated into a decision-making process.

Jeffrey Pfeffer, observing many of the same phenomena, focused on a different aspect of them in Organizational Design (1978). Because information processing is fundamental to the functioning of an organization, it becomes the primary source of organizational power. Whoever controls information by selecting, filtering, processing, and distributing it acquires social-political power. Centralized information centralizes power, distributed information decentralizes power. Furthermore, the information system itself determines the criteria for evaluation of performance and for distribution of rewards and punishments. Information systems implemented with an increasingly sophisticated information technology permit the kind of monitoring necessary to convert the control of information technology and systems into a source of substantial organizational power. Dale E. Zand drew many practical implications from this point of view in his recent Information, Organization, and Power: Effective Management in the Knowledge Society (1981).

Some of our assumptions about the role of information in organizations are being challenged by recent developments in organization theory. By looking at organizations as ecological entities that change through evolutionary process, theorists such as Karl Weick (The Social Psychology of Organizing, 1979) and James March (Ambiguity and Choice in Organizations, with Johan P. Olsen, 1976) have proposed "loosely coupled" and "garbage can" models of organization. The idea is that organizations should be composed of relatively independent units. Each unit should be infused with autonomy and entrepreneurship and should experiment on a trial-and-error basis and create mutations that, if they prove successful, will help evolve the organization into a new ecological niche. This concept flies in the face of the more rational decision models and the highly centralized cybernetic control information systems they suggest. In an important way, however, information is even more fundamental to the loosely coupled systems model. An information systems network is the "coupler" in a loosely coupled system, and each subunit needs its own distributed processing capability to engage intelligently in the kind of experimentation the model calls for. A key notion in Weick's and March's models is that an organization must import substantial amounts of information from its environment, process it on a local basis, and use it to make decisions that will improve the organization's relationship with its environment. This idea of effectively relating an organization to its environment is also central to the concept of strategy.

At the same time men like Vail, Durant, Ford, Du Pont, and Julius Rosenwald at Sears, Roebuck were evolving new business strategies, researchers and educators were trying to understand the phenomena that underlay their strategies. Education for future managers was the primary goal, but as of 1908 the concept of "strategy" as a tool of business was not very well formulated. Strategy in those days generally meant a way to gain superiority in athletic or military endeavors, and the concept seems to have drawn heavily on the combative concepts of a Prussian general named Karl von Clausewitz, who in 1830 published <u>On War</u> and <u>Principles of War</u>.

The identification of strategy as a formal business concept probably emerged around 1911, when a course in business policy was offered for the first time at the Harvard Business School. Men like A. W. Shaw, Melvin T. Copeland, and George Albert Smith, Jr., pioneered the idea. In 1927 Edmund P. Learned joined the faculty and began a 40-year career shaping the field. The more inward-looking notion of "business policy" characterized Harvard's earliest efforts. The more outreaching, aggressive concept of strategy emerged after the Second World War. After that developments came rapidly, especially as the idea of strategy was merged with the concept of corporate planning. World War II alerted many managers serving in the armed forces to the need for long-range planning, especially with respect to material and manpower. After the war they sought to take those ideas back into their organizations.

Henri Fayol's classic on planning, <u>General and Industrial Management</u>, was translated from the French original in 1949. That seemed to prompt a flurry of activity. George Steiner, drawing on his experience at Lockheed Corporation, published <u>Managerial Long Range Planning</u> in 1963. In 1965 Learned, together with C. Roland Christensen, Kenneth R. Andrews, and William D. Guth, published the first text to treat strategy as a full-blown business topic, <u>Business Policy: Text and Cases</u>. In the same year Igor Ansoff published <u>Corporate Strategy: An Analytic Approach to Business Policy for Growth and Expansion</u>, in which he proposed one of the first comprehensive conceptual and methodological frameworks for "solving the firm's <u>total</u> strategic problem." Also in 1965 Robert N. Anthony published <u>Planning and Control Systems: A Framework for Analysis</u>, in which he identified three levels of planning--operational, managerial control, and strategic--similar to the sociological distinctions made by Talcott Parsons. He further argued that each of these levels places its own unique demands on the firm's information system. In 1965 very little work was under way to apply information systems and technology to the strategic level of managerial decision making, but it was not long before this changed.

George Steiner updated his view on strategy in a classic state-of-the-art summary book entitled <u>Top Management Planning</u>, which was published in 1969. Kenneth Andrews summarized the Harvard experience in 1971 in <u>The Concept of Corporate</u>

Strategy. Meanwhile, the literature started to abound with articles and books.

C. West Churchman's The Systems Approach (1968) and The Design of Inquiring Systems (1971) provided a philosophical base for applying systems concepts to problems of strategy and of information systems. Russell Ackoff further operationalized his and Churchman's notions in A Concept of Corporate Planning (1970) and Redesigning the Future (1974).

Meanwhile corporations and consulting firms were developing their own approaches. Bruce Henderson and the Boston Consulting Group staff published Perspectives on Experience in 1968. This book, based on a series of empirical studies, argued that as volume of sales goes up, costs per unit go down because of the accumulated experience of the firm. Thus a drive for market share can lead to an increase in profits and increased cash flow, unless of course the capital demands of growth deplete the business's resources. This last observation led to the now-famous fourfold classification of business units as stars, cash cows, question marks, or dogs, based on their growth (demand for cash) and relative market share (supply of cash).

Meanwhile, planners at General Electric were creating their own approach. One result was the GE Stop/Go planning grid, a popularization of which was published in Forbes on March 15, 1975. The grid is a nine-part matrix that classifies a business by its relationship to GE's business strength on one dimension and its industry's attractiveness on the other.

One problem facing planners is the lack of data on characteristics and performance of businesses operating in a defined product-market area, a so-called strategic business unit. In response to this need, early in 1972 the Marketing Science Institute at the Harvard Business School, with the encouragement of GE, organized the Profit Impact of Market Strategies (PIMS) project, which collected a large data base of information on over 100 companies operating over 1,000 strategic business units. These data can be analyzed by means of regression models. In 1974 Sidney Schoeffler, Robert Buzzell, and Donald Heany reported on the early findings of the PIMS project. Among their generalized conclusions were that strategic business units with higher market shares tend also to have higher pre-tax returns on investment than their competitors, and that units with high intensity of investment are often less profitable than those with lower investment-to-sales ratios. Schoeffler and his associates are still engaged in this line of research at the Strategic Planning Institute.

The methods of the mid-1970s focused on just a few variables and gave little consideration to the competitive dynamics of the industry. In 1980, however, Michael Porter's book Competitive Strategy changed that. Drawing on economists' conceptualization of industrial organization, Porter identified a series of determinants for the intensity of competition in an industry and the likelihood of a particular business's survival. Essentially, he outlined five main considerations: the degree of rivalry among existing firms, the relative bargaining power of the firm's buyers, the relative bargaining power of its suppliers, the threat from possible substitute products or services, and the threat of new entrants as dictated by entry and exit conditions. Firms that can manage these dimensions and get the dimensions working in their favor can gain power in their environment. Survival and higher profits ensue.

One feature common to all considerations of strategy, policy, and organizational structure is their basis on assumptions about the principal parties and players in the organization's game. Agents from within and outside the organization take actions that collectively produce the organization's outcomes. These agents are referred to as *stakeholders*, and the assumptions made about them are basic units for strategic planning and focal points for information systems design. During the past few years, Ian Mitroff, James Emshoff, Ralph Kilmann, Vincent Barabba, and I have developed methods for surfacing, testing, and prioritizing strategic planning assumptions. This approach was published by Mason and Mitroff in *Challenging Strategic Planning Assumptions* (1981). This book also demonstrated how argumentation analysis can be applied to each strategic assumption to identify the information requirements for supporting it. The results have been used at several organizations to specify the relevant information technology and delivery system.

Current Convergence

When the Harvard Business School was founded in 1908, information systems were in their infancy. Electronic technology was in its early stages. Theories of information were just emerging. The modern American corporation was just being born. The concept of corporate strategy was yet to emerge.

During the next 75 years a dramatic change took place. An incredible technological revolution has created hardware and software opportunities of staggering proportions. Scientists, philosophers, and practitioners have begun to think about information as a separable concept. They have evolved theories and procedures for using it.

While research was producing new information technologies and theories, managers were creating new organizations. The practical efforts of men like Vail, Durant, Sloan, and Ford created a demand for information as a tool of organization. In response, a revolution in organizational structure took place, and new theories emerged to explain it. Concepts of business policy and of corporate strategy were created to inject the manager's willful guidance into the process.

During this 75 years a remarkable change also took place in the concept of information itself. At the outset it played an auxiliary role in business affairs. Information that was collected and processed was used primarily for stewardship purposes--to keep track of labor, capital, and other resources and to coordinate their use. But the role of information as an input to decision making became increasingly clear. Theories for effectively linking information with decision making were developed. With these, a subtle change took place in the concept of information itself. It ceased to be seen as primarily something that was embedded in other resources and came to be considered a resource in its own right. Information, it was discovered, can be acquired, manipulated, and allocated just as any other economic resource can. This realization gave information a strategic significance in organizations.

Today these three forces--technology, concepts of information, and organizational structure--are almost indistinguishable from one another. A commercial bank, for example, that intends to offer an adjustable-rate real estate mortgage service in a competitive marketplace inextricably ties its strategy to its concepts of data, management control, and financial environmental monitoring. It also commits itself to a complex of communications and data processing technology necessary to carry out the concepts. How the people involved relate to one another, both formally in terms of patterns of authority and responsibility and informally in terms of emotions and well-being, is also highly influenced by their chosen information systems design. In effect, strategy, structure, and information systems are one.

The unification of information with the strategies and structures to which it relates has turned information into a crucial resource. The special information an organization possesses, the concepts through which it interprets and relates information, and the manner in which it deploys information provide economic value to the organization in the same way its use of capital and labor do. Consequently, information systems planning is becoming an integral part of corporate strategic planning and vice versa. New opportunities are created for managers; new demands are placed on them.

This synthesis of information with strategy and structure, though clearly emergent, is relatively new. In the spring of 1974 the UCLA Graduate School of Management and McKinsey & Co. sponsored a conference on strategic planning for management information systems (MIS). Representatives from 20 leading firms attended and shared their experience and ideas on planning and information services. Later, Ephraim McLean and John Soden conducted follow-up studies on these firms and reported their results in <u>Strategic Planning for MIS</u>. The value of interweaving information systems strategy with corporate strategy was apparent to all participants, and all indicated that they were moving in that direction. Few, however, as of 1974 had achieved that goal. Much of the MIS planning reported was tactical, not strategic, although those executives involved in strategic planning seemed to be having an impact. McLean and Soden summarized: "In those organizations most advanced in [MIS] planning, the MIS planners have become an integral part of the management team of the organization; and in these companies MIS strategies have a major impact on, and a corresponding interrelationship with, the longer term business plans of the enterprise" (1977, p. 7). In these organizations, information technology and service planning primarily supported already-existing corporate strategic plans. They were reactive, not proactive. Information systems had not yet become a vanguard of strategy.

To merge information systems planning with strategic planning executives must have the ideas, methods, and tools of analysis required to think in an integrative way about information and strategy. In response to this need, a variety of new methods have recently been developed. Consultants, practitioners, and academics have all contributed and during the last few years have produced a series of promising approaches. The next 75 years will involve significant extensions, additions, elaborations, tests, and shaking out. But the seeds are planted now. The question is: Where will we go from here? In large measure, the answer will be a product of our own choice.

Bibliography

Chandler, Alfred D., Jr. Strategy and Structure. Cambridge, Mass.: MIT Press, 1962.

David, Edward E., Jr. "By 1990 All Industries Must Be High Tech." High Technology, Vol. 3, No. 4, April 1983, pp. 65-68.

Galbraith, Jay. Organization Design. Reading, Mass.: Addison-Wesley, 1977.

McLean, Ephraim R.; and Soden, John V. Strategic Planning for MIS. New York: John Wiley & Sons, 1977.

Selznick, Philip. "Foundations of the Theory of Organizations." American Sociological Review, Vol. 21, February 1948, pp. 25-26.

CURRENT RESEARCH ISSUES

Richard O. Mason

Reversing the Logic

The 1980s is a period in which no organization can afford to ignore its commitment to information systems and services, nor in many cases can it afford to subordinate them to any other business process. Throughout the history of organization information played a derivative role. It served primarily as the lubricant for administrative activity and was shaped by the laws and customs of business and by the necessity to maintain records of economic activity. From its very beginnings information technology and its use have focused on processing elemental routine business transactions. As a result, most managers have come to believe that the logical progression for information architecture is from transactions to managerial decision making and then to strategy.

Today this process can and should be reversed. Business strategy is the predominant concern. Information systems, then, can serve as the leading edge of a firm's strategy. For several companies today information systems have become a key part of their distinctive competitiveness in the marketplace. Information systems and services can also be planned to strengthen business decision making and, through the judicious avoidance of "red tape," not to hinder it. Finally, information systems and services can be planned so that their cost for performance on routine transactions is consistent with the strategic intent of the firm.

During the last few years, several new approaches have evolved for thinking about information systems as components of strategy. Some have proven successful in limited engagements. A few are conceptual delights, yet to be fully tested on the corporate battlefield. From these embryonic beginnings, however,

---

This paper has benefited from comments and material provided by James I. Cash, Jr., M. Victor Janulaitis, Vincent P. Barabba, Alan J. Rowe, John F. Rockart, Gerald Loev, Tomas Scurrah, and Ephraim R. McLean.

will emerge the methods of the future. This paper constitutes a progress report on the approaches found useful so far.

Information Systems as the Vanguard of Strategy

Information plays three roles in a firm's strategy:

1. Information is used to report on the exchange transactions of the business. In this role it performs the stewardship function of keeping track of "what things are where" and "who owes what to whom."

2. Information is used to guide business decision making. In this role it may inform the decision maker about how well the business and its components are functioning, what problems to attend to, and what alternatives to consider. The management sciences, and most recently the concepts of management information and decision support systems, have addressed this role.

3. Information is used as an integral part of the product or service the business offers its customers. In this special role information becomes--in the customers' eyes at least--indistinguishable from facilities, people, and commodities. Hence, it becomes part of the business's product/market planning. This is, perhaps, the most exciting role information plays, the one that has the tightest link with strategic planning, and the one about which we know the least.

It is in this third category that immense opportunities are open to businesses to make information systems the vanguard of their strategy. Thomas Peters and Robert Waterman (1982) call this getting "close to the customer" and count it as one of the keys to excellence for American business firms. Being close to the customer involves focusing on revenue generation, as opposed to cost reduction, and being obsessed with providing service and quality in distinctive packages.

One company that has used information systems effectively in this strategic vanguard role is American Hospital Supply Corporation (AHSC). Its strategy illustrates the approach. American Hospital Supply became an industry leader by devising a system that played all three information roles. It integrated information services with the product line to enhance the competitive distinctiveness of the company's offerings. It provided AHSC's management with information about orders and inventories so they could establish greater control over their business, rationalize their operations, and increase their productivity. And, furthermore, it provided data for financial and managerial accounting transactions. The story of what AHSC did and how it did it is revealing.

As a part of its strategic planning, AHSC surveyed its customers, principally purchasing agents in hospitals and clinics throughout the United States. It discovered that its current and potential customers faced difficult purchasing problems because of the diversity of their sources of supply. There was no single distributor of medical supplies that could meet the majority of a hospital's needs. As a result, AHSC embarked on a "full-line" product distribution strategy, the intent of which was to place "at the purchasers' fingertips" the capacity to order all the hospital supplies they needed. This solution is reminiscent of Sears, Roebuck's 1891 outreach to potential customers with a mail-order catalog, only AHSC did it electronically.

The AHSC system ensured effectiveness by placing a terminal in each hospital purchasing agent's office. The corporation's full catalog of nearly 30,000 items was available on the screen and could be accessed by a convenient menu-driven, key word system. Orders could be placed by merely sitting down at the terminal and inputting the relevant data. From that point on, AHSC's system took care of order entry, invoicing and billing, inventory control, and shipping--automatically and with a high degree of timeliness, responsiveness, and accuracy. Further, AHSC's automated purchasing system helped it meet a 24-hour delivery schedule. As a result, hospitals could reduce their inventory stock levels from an average of 75-90 days to about 30 days. Hospitals' purchasing costs went down, their inventory financing and control costs went down, and their cost for achieving these benefits appeared to be minimal. Consequently many hospital purchasing agents tended to order from AHSC even if a product was available at a lower cost from another vendor. Competitive bidding virtually stopped.

As AHSC's customers became more dependent on it, its business flourished. Since 1978, when it embarked on this strategy, AHSC's sales have grown at an approximate compounded rate of 17% per year. It enjoys pre-tax profit margins about four times the industry average and a market share of nearly 50%. Indeed, AHSC has been so successful that it has become the defendant in several lawsuits for restraint of trade.

Other companies have also used information services as a leading edge in their strategies. American Airlines with its Sabre reservation system, Avis's Wizard, Merrill Lynch's cash management system, and Citibank's international telecommunications system are prominent examples. The formula for success seems to be straightforward:

- Identify an unfulfilled customer need or want.

- Create a means by which information services can fill that need in a manner that enhances the level of services, improves the quality and reliability of the product, and distinguishes your offering from all your competitors' offerings.

- Bring the information systems and services to the marketplace as integral parts of the corporate product and market strategy.

When information systems and services are not the vanguard of strategy, they play an important supporting role. In these cases, business strategy determines the nature of information systems.

Strategy as the Primary Determinant of IS

Stakeholder Approaches

Stakeholders are parties outside and within an organization who are affected by the organization's activities or with whom the organization engages in conducting its business. Stakeholders, then, have a "stake" in the business and its activities. During the last few years several approaches have been designed to help firms develop effective strategies in the context of their stakeholder environments. Each of these approaches has implications for information services planning as well. Among the most popular methods is the competitive strategy approach taken by Michael Porter (1980).

Competitive Strategy. By applying concepts from the economics of industrial structure to problems of strategy, Porter has identified five basic stakeholder forces that affect the competitive position of a firm:

Customer power

Supplier power

Substitution--the possibility that other firms will provide products or services that can be substituted for yours

New entrants--the attractiveness of your industry to others and the magnitude of the barriers that preclude them from entering

Rivalry--the intensity of intraindustry competition

Information systems and services can be used to improve a firm's position with respect to each of these five forces.

In the next paper Warren McFarlan demonstrates a method by which Porter's concepts can be applied to information technology. The key to his approach is initially to assess the threat of each of the five forces to the firm (low to high) and then to attribute some amount of that threat to the impact of information technology. The resulting relationship is plotted on a two-dimensional map that serves as a temporal snapshot of the firm's competitive position and the role information systems and services play in it. The map becomes a planning tool for plotting new strategies and forecasting changes through time.

Strategic Assumption Surfacing and Testing. At Kodak and Xerox corporations, Ian Mitroff, Vincent Barabba, and I have engaged in several projects that used strategic assumption surfacing and testing (SAST) methods.[1] Their purpose was to create an information utility that would provide market intelligence (MAIN). Strategic assumption surfacing and testing is a participatory planning process that was used to generate

Answers to strategic questions

Assumptions underlying strategic options, including technical aspects (hardware and software), environmental forces, and interpersonal considerations within the organization

New strategic questions

Design criteria for decision support and other information systems

This output was used in turn to design MAIN, an ongoing activity that

Works with strategic management and their understanding of the marketplace reality to determine information requirements

Goes to the marketplace with the market research function to collect data

Provides the interface between market research and the organization's decision makers--largely product planners, market managers, brand managers, and others--so information can be summarized, stored, retrieved, and disseminated as needed

---

[1]The SAST approach, together with other dialectical planning methods, is treated at length in Mason and Mitroff (1981). An overview of the MAIN system is contained in Barabba (1980). An overview of both processes is given in Barabba (1983).

> Analyzes and interprets the organizational decision-making process so strategic management can evaluate it.

J. Phillip Samper, group vice president and general manager of Kodak's Photographic Marketing Group, summarized the intent of the SAST/MAIN effort in an internal memo:

> Our job is to insure, on a worldwide basis, that the information about the marketplace, about technology, about competition, about our performance--that all these are joined together to develop a scenario which allows us to position ourselves in the marketplace.
>
> I am convinced that the Kodak MArket INtelligence System (the MAIN system) can enhance these functions greatly with the availability of a worldwide data bank-- retrievable on demand--that ties business objectives to critical issues.

How are these results achieved? Philosophically, by applying the theories of teleological systems and knowledge of utilization to problems of strategic planning; in practice, by going through a systematic process. Here's how one firm proceeded.

A group of executives and planners met at a retreat and were assigned to working groups, each of which was to consider one of the key strategic options the business had identified. The working groups determined all the relevant stakeholders and then specified the assumptions that had to be made about each for a given strategic option to be successful. These assumptions were then evaluated according to their importance--how significant they were to the success of the option--and their certainty--how much evidence could be adduced to support their validity. The groups next debated their assumptions and ratings and then collectively identified a set of remaining issues. Important and relatively uncertain assumptions pinpointed targets for strategic information, that is, places where information could be used to reduce the uncertainty of the business. In our experience many of these critical assumptions refer to the marketplace and its dynamics. Hence, the MAIN system.

One basic premise of the MAIN system is that there is no limit to the amount of information that can be collected about markets and customers. Commensurately, there is no limit to the amount of money that can be spent on acquiring marketing information. This is the common situation Russell Ackoff alluded to in his classic, "Management Misinformation Systems" (1967). The solution is to focus the firm's information systems and services on a few high-payoff areas. The MAIN system does this by translating important, yet uncertain, strategic planning assumptions into critical market research questions. These questions are then prioritized, budgets are allocated according to priority, and a search is made for data that will answer the questions posed.

A second basic premise of the MAIN system is that information is not just a "thing in itself," rather it is part of a complex relationship among four key entities:

The marketplace, which provides signals about what customers need or say they need

The firm's market research function, which collects data, assesses their reliability and validity, analyzes them, and reports them to decision makers

Organizational decision makers, who determine what products and services the business is capable of presenting and willing to present to the marketplace and what the attendant economic terms will be

Strategic managers, who are responsible and accountable for the performance of the other three

The MAIN system is an information utility that coordinates the activities of these four parties. It contains market data, a library of past studies, a system bibliography, analytical software, graphic and portrayal software, communications software, user help--both automated and interpersonal--a support organization, and, of course, the requisite hardware. All these information resources are focused on the prioritized critical market research questions that were elicited during the SAST planning process.

Business Analysis Approaches

Stakeholder approaches tend to look outside the organization to identify opportunities for response. Business analysis approaches, on the other hand, begin with the people and characteristics of the business itself and seek ways of drawing on these to evolve new strategies. Each of the following eight business analysis methods tends to focus on a different principle of business.

Critical Success Factors. John Rockart and Christine Bullen at MIT have developed an approach for helping businesses identify information requirements by means of critical success factors (CSFs). (See Bullen and Rockart, 1981; Rockart, 1979, 1982; and Rockart and Treacy, 1982.) Their method builds on the principle that practicing managers know a lot about the ends they want to achieve and the means by which these may be obtained. Critical success factors aid the manager in the kind of ends-to-means analysis necessary to decompose broad strategic objectives into meaningful action steps. It is a short step, as Index Systems, Arthur Young, and other consulting firms have learned, from these CSFs to information systems project definition and selection and only another short step further to detailed specification of data elements and data base design. The concept has been used for at least three related purposes:

> Clarifying managerial focus--by highlighting similarities and differences among executive CSFs
>
> Developing top management information needs--by relating CSFs to specific data bases and items of decision support information.
>
> Setting information systems priorities--by exposing the gap between available and required information as it is related to the importance of the CSF. Used this way, CSFs in effect help establish the businesswide perspective and initial requirements definition necessary to apply other methods, such as IBM's business systems planning procedure.

The CSF procedure can be summarized as follows. An adviser holds interviews with the firm's executives to consider the question, What does it take to be successful in this business? The results are analyzed and restated as objectives for the executives to reconsider. After a few iterations in which the adviser feeds back the results to each executive for review, redefinition, and elaboration, the original list is pared down to the 7 to 10 most critical factors. At this point the adviser's attention is turned to generating measures of performance--scorecard data that will tell the executives how well they are mastering their CSFs.

With the CSFs and their appropriate measures identified, the next key question is, What does the manager need to know to take the actions necessary to improve the firm's performance with respect to its CSFs? This question, repeated at various levels of the business, can yield the basic data structure required to inform management. It thus has the advantage of focusing attention on the critical areas of the business; however, it should be used in conjunction with other methods to develop a comprehensive information systems design.

Advantages of the CSF approach are that it focuses on high-payoff, critical factors; it is relatively fast and inexpensive to administer; and it frequently reveals new insights to the executives involved. Its major disadvantages are that it is not comprehensive and that it results in a snapshot that can quickly be made obsolete by any major change in the business. To overcome some of these disadvantages, some consultants combine a business systems planning approach with the CSF method.

Business Systems Planning. In 1975 analysts at IBM developed a systematic approach for identifying computer-independent information requirements for any organization (see Business Systems Planning, 1975). This business systems planning approach is based on a conceptual framework that can be summarized as follows.

Organizations are composed of business processes, such as marketing, finance, and manufacturing, which make decisions and allocate resources. These processes take place within organizational units by means of a management system. Organizations serve as the sources of raw data to be stored in data bases. Elements and classes of data are drawn from the data base and used by information systems and applications. The resulting information is disseminated through a network to support the actions taken in the processes. The cycle is then repeated.

By systematically tracking this cycle throughout an organization and recording the results on forms and in matrices, an analyst can work all the way from business objectives and problems at the top down to identifiable classes of data. From this a general data classification scheme and data base approach can be developed. Finally, one can work back up from data to relate the results to systems, processes, and objectives. Because it is based on a general model, this approach is comprehensive, thorough, and somewhat stable in the face of organizational change. However, in application it tends to be more tactical than strategic and, unless carefully managed, it frequently gets mired in data classes and data bases and fails to achieve the full advantages of the top-down approach. Moreover, business systems planning is time consuming and costly. For these reasons, it is often used in conjunction with other strategic planning approaches, such as CSF.

Architecture Planning. A common complaint about the results of business systems planning is that they are quite difficult for many managers to understand. Their strength--comprehensiveness--becomes a weakness when they are used as a vehicle for communicating with high-level executives. A few corporations and consultants believe that understanding and credibility are the most important objectives. They argue that for information systems planning to be effective there must be mutual understanding between management information systems personnel on the one hand and top management and users on the other. The relationship should be one of trust and believability.

To achieve these objectives a three-component planning system has been developed: architecture charts, planning matrix, and project worksheet. All three components are as much communication devices as they are analytical tools.

The architecture planning approach is analogous to building construction. Just as a building architect will render a perspective drawing first, secure agreement on it, then proceed to more specification--elevation, structure, framing, electricity, plumbing, and so on--so too must the information systems architect proceed from broad business- and management-oriented perspectives down, step by step, to the details of construction. The starting point is the architecture chart.

Architecture charts lay out the basic structure of information as it pertains to the organization as a whole in a graphic and nontechnical format. They are designed to communicate how information systems affect a given business area to a business manager in 15 to 20 minutes. Graphic charts are used to depict the broad outlines of the relevant interfaces and reporting requirements such as, for example, the principal organizational relationships an information center might have. Functional charts reveal the logic of information as it relates to a specific business function. Flow graphics describe specific sequences of events and processes. Finally, technical charts, not intended for business managers, provide specific construction instructions.

Every major system is also documented by a planning matrix, which describes the system user, planning environment and assumptions, current system, work in process and planned, and projected short- and long-term needs for the system. The planning matrix is intended as a management tool to help the information systems executive and corporate executives make planning decisions.

Finally, detailed project worksheets are prepared for each current and planned project.

The architecture planning approach is currently being refined and tested at a few companies. Its principal advantage is that it proceeds from a broad systems perspective down through increasingly detailed subsystem specifications based on relevancy and understandability to the managers involved. It focuses on the processes of building a system and supervising its construction rather than on the detailed data elements and classes that are the objects of the system. As a result, this approach needs to be used with other approaches to develop a complete system.

Two Cultures. Executives at Index Systems believe that the critical success factors and business systems planning approaches may be premature unless some other things are taken care of first. They take these concerns a step further than did the proponents of architecture planning; the key question in their minds is whether the management philosophy of the information systems group is in alignment with the management philosophy of the firm. Some corporations shoot for market share, others for return on investment and control. Historically, most data processing and information systems groups have been in the control camp. So what happens when a firm shifts to a market orientation, as, say, American Hospital Supply did? Many people would argue that unless the information systems group's orientation shifted accordingly, there would be a misfit and problems would ensue.

Samuel Culbert and John McDonough (1980) refer to this matching of the values, interests, and skills of a group to the task requirements of the situation as alignment. An information systems group aligned with a market-oriented management would be characterized in theory by more aggressive leadership style, more emphasis on innovation, greater end user involvement, more applications that are "closer to the customer," more distributed data processing, more on-line memory, sloppier code, and generally less efficient operations than would a control-oriented group. Experience from a limited number of consulting engagements suggests that these propositions generally hold true; however, more extensive field research is needed to test them with greater rigor.

Product Portfolio and Life Cycle. Analysts at Nolan, Norton & Company are developing a methodology for linking corporate strategic planning with information systems planning (Gibson and Nolan, 1974; Nolan, 1979). The approach, still evolving and being tested at client firms, is comprehensive and detailed, but it pivots on the following key concepts:

1. From consideration of the products the firm offers, their places in the product life cycle, and their relative market shares, one can determine whether the primary support needs for each product are strategic, management control, or operational. The general proposition (and it is really a researchable hypothesis) is that early-life-cycle, high-market-share products tend to need strategic information support; early-life-cycle, low-share products tend to need operational support; later-life-cycle, high-share products tend to need management control support; and later-life-cycle, low-share products tend to need strategic support.

2. Similarly, the market needs for each product are identified and summarized into three categories--cost reduction, improved productivity, and product differentiation. Again, the presumption is that information systems should provide information consistent with these needs.

3. A third consideration is where the information systems activity lies in the Gibson and Nolan four-stage model: initiation (in which technology specification, systems creation, and original investment are crucial), expansion (in which learning and adaptation are crucial), control (in which rationalization and elaboration are crucial), or maturity (in which careful review of projects for continuance and the need for integration are crucial).

4. Finally, existing and proposed applications are reviewed and subsumed under a functional portfolio model. This model represents all key activities in the business and groups them together as operations, management control, or strategy.

The results of these analyses can then be used to answer broad questions: How do the product needs relate to the market needs? How do the stages of electronic data processing relate to the product needs? How do the product needs relate to the functional portfolio? How do the stages relate to the market needs? How do the market needs relate to the functional portfolio? How do the stages relate to the functional portfolio? Each of these questions can be answered in terms of costs, coverage, and systems support. The result is an overall evaluation of the application and information systems as they relate to the business's needs. Guidelines for budgets, improvements to existing systems, and opportunities for new systems emerge.

Industry Comparisons. As Marc Porat (1977) and others have argued, this is an information age. More people are involved in the production and dissemination of information, and companies are devoting more of their budgets to information services. Many firms spend 1-3% of total revenues on electronic data processing alone. Most draw heavily on the more than 500 available data bases and other commercial information services. But is this enough?

Robert Hayes, dean of the UCLA Graduate School of Library and Information Science, thinks not. He has produced some interesting econometric evidence to suggest that U.S. manufacturing industries are underinvesting in information (Hayes and Erickson, 1982). Using data from 51 industries, Hayes and Erickson applied log-linear regression analysis to a Cobb-Douglas model in which the industries' value added was assumed to be a function of its labor (L), capital (K), external purchases of information services (I), and other purchases (X). The model is then:

$$\text{Output Value Added} = A L^{a} K^{b} I^{c} X^{d}$$

where A is a constant and a, b, c, and d are coefficients. Econometric theory asserts that if an industry is operating in an optimal manner, then the marginal return from external purchases of information (I) and other services (X) should be zero. That is, the coefficients c and d should be zero if the industry is in equilibrium. If the coefficients are positive, the industry is not using enough external information resources; if the coefficients are negative, the industry is using too many of them. The result in applying this model to 1972 data was

$$\text{Output Value Added} = e^{1.504} L^{0.256} K^{0.415} I^{0.320} X^{0.014}$$

$$R^2 = 0.962$$

A relatively large positive coefficient for I ($c = 0.320$) indicates that manufacturing industry in general is purchasing fewer external information services than is optimal. The results suggest that manufacturing firms could improve their value added and, hence, their profits if they used more external information.

There are a few caveats to this conclusion. The data are

from aggregate U.S. government Bureau of Economic Analysis and census data and therefore suffer from the same measurement problems that all macroeconomic analyses of this type do. Porat's broad definition and classifications were used to determine the amount of information services purchased. Therefore, some services, such as legal, advertising, and engineering are included. Finally, the results apply only to the external purchase of information services and not to the heavy internal investments companies make in computers, telecommunications, and software. Nevertheless, the results pose a serious question: Is today's management sufficiently aware of the productive role information plays as an economic resource? They further question whether managers are allocating enough of their businesses' resources for acquisition of information.

Recognition of this management plight has led several consulting firms to develop analytical models that aid executives in evaluating their businesses' current position. The models vary and employ some rather complex reasoning, but the general train of their argument is fairly straightforward.

Information services are a contributing factor to the total value added of all industry. Moreover, their percentage contribution has been increasing during the past two decades or longer. The percentage contribution is greater in information processing and services and financial services industries than it is in manufacturing industries. As the potential for information services' contributions to total value added increases (2-3% per year has not been unusual), alert management will continue to maintain the ratio of its information services delivery capability (ISC) to the industry percentage of potential information systems contribution to total value added (VA). The ISC/VA ratio is a systematic measure that reflects the amount of information systems potential the firm is realizing.

If the ISC/VA ratio gets too large, compared with industry standards, the business may be too ambitious with respect to information services or, perhaps, too inefficient in the area. The exception to this interpretation is the firm that, as a conscious part of its strategy, wishes to "leap ahead" of its industry in the application of information services.

On the other hand, if the ISC/VA ratio is too low compared with industry standards, then the business may have slipped into a "sphere of vulnerability," in which information services capabilities have fallen behind their potential contribution to the firm's total value added. Unless a firm in this situation has offsetting advantages in its products, facilities, or personnel, its competitive position is likely to be eroding.

Although enormous measurement and calibration issues remain in applying the ISC/VA model with quantitative precision, it is nevertheless useful as a conceptual tool. As with all effective strategic planning methods, it focuses attention on good questions. It doesn't provide answers, but it stimulates useful inquiry. Furthermore, it has a strong intuitive appeal.

Consider, for example, a bank that in the late 1960s had automated demand deposits, proof and transit, and loans on a back-office batch processing system. These applications contributed a relatively large percentage to the total value added of the bank as a whole. However, during the last decade or so there have been dramatic improvements in computers, telecommunications, and software, such as automatic teller machines, on-line-teller terminals, interactive inquiry, and cash management systems. As a result, the potential contribution of information services to the bank's value added has risen significantly. That is, the denominator in the ISC/VA ratio has increased. The question the model poses is, Has the numerator gone up commensurately? Suppose the bank has the same back-office batch system. Even if it has upgraded its hardware significantly, it still may not have maintained its competitive advantage and its ability to secure that advantage for the future. A drop in the bank's ISC/VA ratio signals that it may be falling behind in achieving its potential.

Signals of possible over- or underinvestment in information services are warnings, but they do not point to targets of opportunity. As a result, Victor Janulaitis and I (1982) have attempted to take the model a step further. We suggest that a CEO undertake the following:

1. Make a list of the business's major information and communication functions.

2. For each of these functions, rate the company and its competitors on how dependent the business is on information systems technology and how mature it is in making effective use of state-of-the-art technology. A scale of, say, 1 to 10 will suffice.

3. Multiply the two ratings to yield an information systems "absorption" rate.

4. Compare the results. A firm that is behind in its industry in absorption rate may have some "catching up" to do. A firm that is ahead may be a technological innovator or it may have assumed too much risk.

Value-Added Approaches. Another approach is to consider the total chain of value added within a business and ask how improved information services can result in improved performance. A value-added approach recognizes that information may be an effective factor of production along with capital and labor at any point in the business's input-output processes. That is, information is used at each of the activities starting with raw materials acquisition; flowing through raw materials processing, manufacturing, and distribution; and finally reaching the customer. Just as strategists have studied the value-added chain to discover promising business opportunities, clever information analysts are studying it to reveal opportunities for profit improvement through information. The approach is straightforward but often quite insightful.

First, a full systems diagram of the industry is drawn showing the elemental inputs, the final outputs, and all the major processes by which inputs are converted into outputs. The business in question is identified as a subset of this larger map. For each component of the industry map, the questions asked are What is its function? What major decisions are made here? What are the risks involved? What are the constraints and problems? What role does information play for this component? and, ultimately, How can an improvement in information for this component lead to an improvement in the performance of the system as a whole from the standpoint of our business? That is, Can better information here lead to better profits? In several firms the answer has been "yes." New applications, such as vendor rating systems, production scheduling systems, or customer profiling systems have been identified and implemented to improve the firm's performance. In my experience the value-added approach often ends (as do the SAST and CSF approaches) in the firm concentrating on a strategic area similar to one of the nine driving forces identified by Benjamin Tregoe and John Zimmerman (1980). These are products offered, market needs, technology employed, production capability, method of sale, method of distribution, natural resources and raw materials, size/growth, and return/profit. Their categorization is not a substitute for the more detailed methods described below, but it serves as a valuable guideline for their application.

One common mistake, in my opinion, is to equate performing value-added analysis with simply moving closer to the customer. Certainly there have been some spectacular results achieved by doing this, as American Hospital Supply, American Airlines' Sabre, Avis's Wizard, and a host of financial cash management systems attest. Of course, this possibility should be explored. It is a mistake, however, to assume that a business is embedded in a single cause-and-effect chain from raw materials to end user. This long-link cause-and-effect chain is only one of the "macrostructures" through which value may be added.

Some years ago James Thompson (1967) identified three macrostructures, or "technological cores" as he called them, that are the underlying structure of a business. By means of a little logical analysis we can add a fourth. Because value is added by a transformation process, the key to understanding a business is to identify the dominant features of the transformation. A simple taxonomy based on the quantity of relationships between inputs and outputs can serve as a basic classification scheme. Figure 1 summarizes the model.

Long-link technologies are characterized by a series of single cause-and-effect chains, such as those on assembly lines (see Figure 2). Many manufacturing businesses basically follow this pattern because their predominant product flow is design → engineering → production → marketing → sales → service, or some similar sequence.

Figure 1. *Input-Output Matrix*

Outputs: → / Inputs: ↓	One Distinctive	Many Distinctive
One Distinctive	Long-Link Technology	Extensive Technology
Many Distinctive	Intensive Technology	Mediating Technology

Figure 2. *Long-Link Technology*

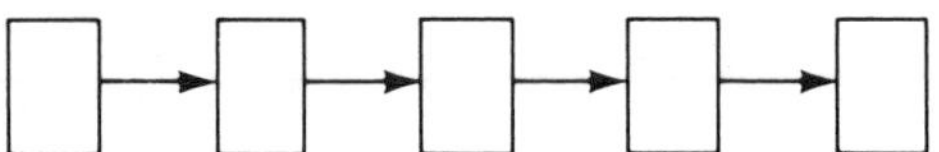

Information plays two key roles in a long-link technology. First, it is used to coordinate and to smooth the flow of activity from one stage to another. This is its overview function. Second, information can be used as a factor of production at any individual stage. For example, a firm can study the design process and determine how information systems technology can improve its performance in that area and, perhaps, how it might secure a competitive edge. Then it can consider the engineering process and so on. Because the percentage contribution of information systems technology to businesses' total value added has been rising in many industries, this sort of systematic examination of the business as a long-link technology is likely to uncover some strategic opportunities for application of information technology to the business. But used alone it may also miss opportunities that an examination from the point of view of other macrostructures would reveal.

Extensive technologies are characterized by one input converted into two or more distinctive outputs (see Figure 3). Examples are timber being converted into lumber or paper; grapes being converted into raisins, table grapes, or wine; and sheep being converted into mutton and wool. In the cases of timber and grapes, the firm can decide how to allocate its output with few constraints, whereas in sheep farming the conversion ratios are relatively fixed. Many industries, notably oil, fall somewhere between these two extremes. In the petroleum industry hydrocarbon bonding chemistry constrains the range of alternative outputs that can be produced. Within these limits, however, the chemistry is flexible enough to provide considerable options.

Information can play several important roles in extensive technology industries. First, it can be used to monitor the demand and price characteristics of each potential output area so the business can shift its emphasis among products. This is part of strategic product portfolio management. Second, a business can scan the technological environment for ways of increasing the range of outputs and the flexibility of shifting among them. The third information opportunity is as much a necessity as it is an option. Extensive technologies must deal with the joint cost problem. That is, they must arrive at a rational way of allocating the cost of inputs to the cost of each output. This is the only way they can establish profitability and determine whether or not they can economically shift emphasis from one product output to another.

Figure 3. *Extensive Technology*

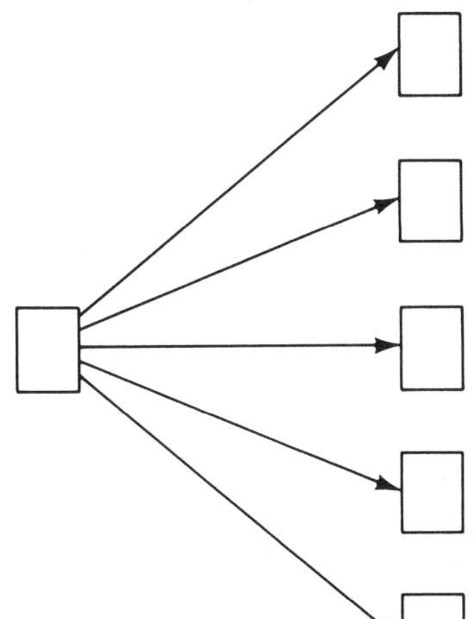

Intensive technologies are the mirror image of extensive technologies; they are characterized by a variety of inputs combined into a single output (see Figure 4). Construction projects and one-time events, such as rock concerts, are generally intensive. Scheduling systems such as program evaluation and review technique (PERT) and critical path method (CPM) provide valuable information for guiding the application of inputs to the output so that time/cost objectives can be met. Furthermore, waste can be avoided by identifying the limiting factors along the critical path.

The archetypes of intensive technologies, however, are case management or case processing systems. A case in this context is an individual business transaction that is opened, processed, and closed. Examples of case management systems include patients in a hospital, claimants in an insurance firm, and clients for a professional's services. As Stephen Rosenthal (1982) points out, case management systems have four principal phases: identification--in which new cases are searched for, received, screened, and either accepted for further processing or rejected; analysis--in which data are collected and interpreted about each case and the case is diagnosed, prioritized, and scheduled; response--in which the resources are actually applied to the case and an output such as a finding, verdict, or cured patient is reached; and resolution--in which the output exists in the system and the case is closed, although it may be monitored for performance and subsequent recidivism. Each of these phases requires information. All are good targets for the application of information services technology.

Figure 4. *Intensive Technology*

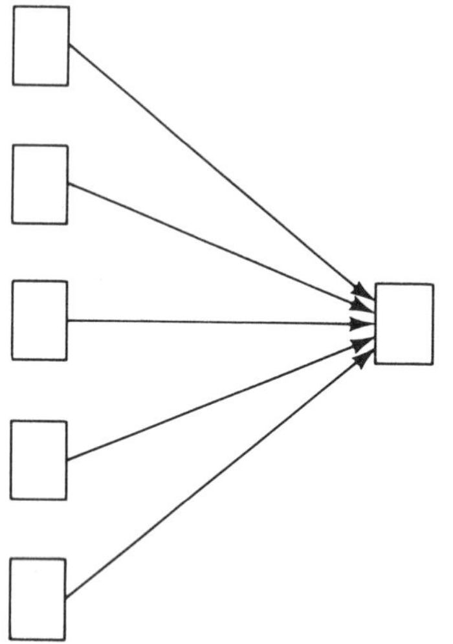

The response phase of case management is characterized by an information requirement that might be called the "recipe" problem. This is the need to decide on the proportions of each input to be applied to the output. It is especially important when there are alternative mixtures that produce a satisfactory output and the costs of inputs change with time. The hot dog industry is a case in point. Total demand tends to be rather constant, so strategic advantages generally come more from cost reduction than revenue maximization. Many blends satisfy Food and Drug Administration regulations for the composition of frankfurters, and at any given time one blend will minimize costs. Because swings in the cost of inputs can easily affect the cost of a blend by one to two cents per pound, one company I know monitors the price of its possible inputs carefully and uses a linear programming model to identify its lowest-cost blend. In one case, this resulted in a $0.0125 per pound savings on 4 million pounds of output, or $50,000 additional contribution to profit. For an industry with an annual consumption of over 1,700 million pounds of frankfurters, these small savings per pound can amount to total savings of $20 million or more per year.

Mediating technologies add value by matching diverse inputs with diverse outputs (see Figure 5). A mediating technology is somewhat like an intensive technology conjoined to an extensive technology. An example is a real estate brokerage firm that opens an input case for each property listing and an output case for each prospective buyer. Then it seeks to match a property to a buyer. Most brokerage systems are mediating technologies. Reservation systems such as American Airlines' Sabre and Avis's Wizard also fall into this category. Wizard, for example, permits an Avis customer anywhere in the United States to order a particular style car to be available in another city at a specified time. A complex telecommunications and computer system does the matching, informs Avis decision makers, and keeps track of accounting transactions once the entry is made. Both American and Avis achieved initial strategic advantages over their competitors by designing systems that facilitated their mediating activities. By improving their mediating function they provided better services to their customers and reduced their cost of performance.

Figure 5. *Mediating Technology*

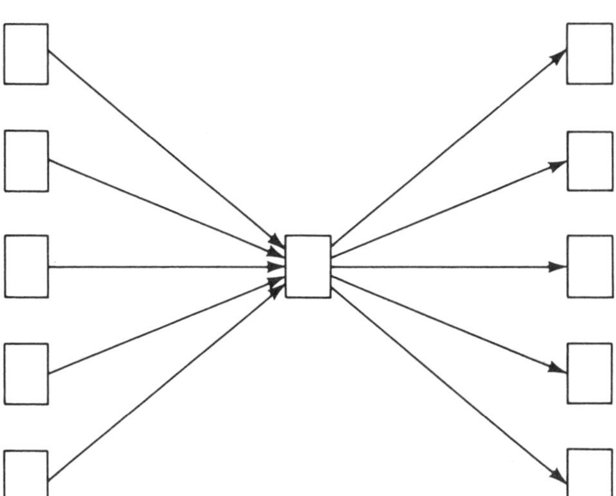

As financial intermediaries, banks and other financial institutions would seem to be classic mediating technologies. In my experience, however, they tend to bifurcate the process and deal with their deposits and sources of funds as an intensive technology and their loans and investments as an extensive technology. This is possible because money is fungible and because bank management uses indicators such as the loan-to-deposit ratio to equilibrate the flows of inputs and outputs. With the advent of cash management systems and other customer services, however, the bounds of this bifurcation are eroding. Today we find more financial institutions trying to manage a diverse customer base by matching customers to the combination of deposit, loan, and investment services they want. This also affords an opportunity to estimate one piece of information that has eluded bankers in the past, What is the profit or loss contribution of a customer?

Information is central in mediating technologies. It is used to identify and service input suppliers and output customers and to match them effectively and profitably. Any place within a business that a mediating technology macrostructure is found is a good candidate for the strategic application of information services technology. Moreover, creative applications can lead to competitive advantages.

Information Systems Risk Assessment. Every unique strategy entails risk. The central managerial question is whether the likelihood of securing benefits warrants the degree of risk undertaken. Warren McFarlan (1981) has pointed out that information systems projects require the strategic management of risk just as much as, say, new product release or any other business venture. Several factors intensify a firm's risk position: project size, in terms of dollar expense and resource commitments; newness of the technology; the firm's prior experience; ambiguity of the project and its proposed outcomes; and the degree of consensus among the parties. The controlling determinant of risk, however, is the project's centrality to the business's technological core. The more dependent the business is on the project to contribute to its total value added, the greater the risk. Consequently, an integral part of strategic planning must be an assessment of risk and return involved in undertaking or not undertaking an information services project. In a phrase, Is it a good bet?

We have seen in the preceding value-added discussions that a form of technological imperative is at work in most industries. Advances in information services technology are generally shifting the burden of risk to those who fail to take advantage of the technology. These lagging businesses tend to have a strategic deficiency that they must make up by exceptional performance in some other sphere.

On the other hand, companies like American Airlines, American Hospital Supply Corporation, and Avis undertook enormous risks by embarking on large information systems projects that employed relatively untested technology and for which the proposed outcome was relatively uncertain when they began. In each case the projects were central to the way the companies did business. The stakes were high, but so were the payoffs. By commitment and careful management, these companies made their projects succeed and in the process gained strategic advantages in their industries.

So we often find managers caught between the horns of the dilemma of change. If they don't make changes in their businesses, they incur the risks of obsolescence and impotence. If they make too many changes, they incur the risks of reckless instability and failure. Because these two components of risk go in opposite directions, an optimum amount of change exists somewhere between the extremes. Some point minimizes the firm's total risk. The trick is to find it.

Questionnaires, such as those suggested by McFarlan, are extremely valuable for assessing the intrinsic risk of a project. They are not intended, however, to assess strategic risk in payoffs won or lost. Here I have found the following simple application of decision theory helpful. At a minimum, it helps to focus on the right questions. Consider the action/outcome matrix in Figure 6.

Figure 6. Action/Outcome Matrix

Outcomes → / Action ↓	*Success (feasible)*	*Failure (infeasible)*
Implement IS Project	A= Payoffs in strategic advantage, cost savings, market share, etc.	B= Losses in money, time, prestige, etc.
Abandon IS Project	C= Loss of competitive position, cost of catching up, lost sales, lost profits, etc.	D= Modest cost of search, review of project, etc.

The risk, $\underline{r}$, in this model, is the probability of failure. It may be obtained by administering McFarlan's risk assessment procedures or by a creative application of Rockart's CSF method. Decision theory prescribes that a project should be undertaken whenever the following condition holds:

$$\underline{r} \leq \frac{(\underline{A} - \underline{C})}{(\underline{A} - \underline{C}) + (\underline{D} - \underline{B})}$$

Substantial measurement problems must be overcome to use this model formally. However, I have worked with executives who have found it insightful to try. First we make a qualitative list of the factors pertaining to each box. Then we assign each box some kind of overall utility score. The calculations are done and compared with the McFarlan risk score. Finally, the results are discussed. The discussion and the assumptions it reveals are most beneficial.

On the basis of secondhand reports, I assume that had the executives of American Hospital Supply Corporation, American Airlines, or Avis applied this model, their A box utility would have been very high. On the other hand, I know of one bank that delayed its aggressive movement into automatic teller machines because, in effect, it thought its C score was relatively low. Its strategy was to let other banks incur the costs of pioneering. The bank planned to monitor its competitors' progress carefully. Then it would move in as soon as its experience showed that the risk was reduced to acceptable levels and before the cost of catching up was too high.

Finally, in assessing risk, an information services project should be considered as a social change problem, with all the attendant issues associated with "unfreezing," "changing," and "refreezing" the business that Kurt Lewin identified. Information services managers need to look at the supporting and resisting forces surrounding the change and evaluate the social resources they have to cope with these forces.

When assessing social change possibilities, I have found the following principles useful:

1. Select the easiest possible relevant information service change within the organization. This can be estimated by evaluating the ease with which the project can be introduced, the willingness of people to accept it, and its degree of similarity to other functions performed by the business.

2. Select an application target that is sufficiently independent from the rest of the business to be shielded from outside pressures. A project must be protected and nurtured until it is successfully under way and has gained some robustness of its own.

3. Begin the change so that extension and expansion to other parts of the business are possible. The point is

to create a social chain reaction that accumulates support for the project as it grows.

These three principles often give conflicting advice, so it is important to balance them. Attention to them, however, can help direct information systems implementation strategy.

Future Challenges

For most of the past 75 years, information technology and systems have been applied to the routine transactions of businesses. Operational needs have been the primary focus of electronic data processing and management information systems planning. During the last decade, however, questions of strategic compatibility have also been asked. Is the information systems plan consistent with the corporate strategy? Does the allocation of information systems technology and services adequately support the priority products, markets, and programs of the business? Most of the methods reviewed in this paper seek to respond to these questions.

There is still another question to be asked. How can information become a strategic resource? This is a question only an information age can envision, a question to which only an information age can respond. During the next 75 years leaders, managers, researchers, and educators will grapple with this question. Those who find answers will benefit. Those who do not will most likely suffer.

The concepts, methods, and approaches summarized in this paper are only a beginning. There are great challenges ahead for managers who seek to prosper in the information age. Equally great challenges await researchers who wish to evolve and test theories for integrating information systems and corporate strategy.

Bibliography

Ackoff, Russell L. "Management Misinformation Systems." Management Science, Vol. 14, 1967, B-147-B-156.

Barabba, Vincent P. "The Future Role of Information in American Life." In Reflections of America, Norman Cousins, ed. Washington, D.C.: U.S. Department of Commerce, Bureau of the Census, December 1980, pp. 193-202.

_______. "Steel Axes for Stone Age Men." Paper presented at Harvard Business School 75th Anniversary Celebration Marketing Colloquium. July 27-29, 1983.

Bullen, Christine V.; and Rockart, John F. "A Primer on Critical Success Factors." MIT, Sloan School of Management, Center for Information Systems Research. Working Paper No. 69. June 1981.

Business Systems Planning: Information Systems Planning Guide. White Plains, N.Y.: IBM, 1975; revised 1978 and 1981.

Cash, James I., Jr.; McFarlan, F. Warren; and McKenney, James L. Corporate Information Systems Management Text and Cases. Homewood, Ill.: Richard D. Irwin, 1983.

Culbert, Samuel A.; and McDonough, John J. The Invisible War. New York: John Wiley & Sons, 1980.

Gibson, Cyrus F.; and Nolan, Richard L. "Managing the Four Stages of EDP Growth." Harvard Business Review, January-February 1974, pp. 76-88.

Hayes, Robert M.; and Erickson, Timothy. "Added Value as a Function of Purchases of Information Services." UCLA, Graduate School of Library and Information Science. Working Paper. March 1982.

Janulaitis, M. Victor; and Mason, Richard O. "Gaining Competitive Advantage--A CEO's Perspective," Malibu, Calif.: Positive Support Review, 1982.

Kriebel, Charles H. "The Strategic Dimension of Computer Systems Planning." Long-Range Planning, September 1968, pp. 7-12.

Mason, Richard O.; and Mitroff, Ian I. Challenging Strategic Planning Assumptions. New York: John Wiley & Sons, 1981.

Mason, Richard O.; and Swanson, E. Burton. Measurement for Management Decision. Reading, Mass.: Addison-Wesley, 1981.

McFarlan, F. Warren. "Portfolio Approach to Information Systems." Harvard Business Review, September-October 1981, pp. 142-150.

McFarlan, F. Warren; Nolan, Richard L.; and Norton, David P. Information Systems Administration. New York: Holt, Rinehart and Winston, 1973.

Nolan, Richard L. "Managing the Crisis in Data Processing." Harvard Business Review, March-April 1979, pp. 115-126.

Peters, Thomas J.; and Waterman, Robert H., Jr. In Search of Excellence: Lessons from America's Best-Run Companies. New York: Harper & Row, 1982.

Porat, Marc. The Information Economy. Washington, D.C.: U.S. Department of Commerce, 1977.

Porter, Michael E. Competitive Strategy: Techniques for Analyzing Industries and Competition. New York: Free Press, 1980.

Rockart, John F. "Chief Executives Define Their Own Data Needs." Harvard Business Review, March-April 1979, pp. 81-92.

________. "The Changing Role of the Information Systems Executive: A Critical Success Factors Perspective." Sloan Management Review, Vol. 24, No. 1, Fall 1982, p. 3.

Rockart, John F.; and Treacy, Michael E. "The CEO Goes On-Line." Harvard Business Review, January-February 1982, pp. 82-89.

Rosenthal, Stephen R. Managing Government Operations. Glenview, Ill.: Scott, Foresman, 1982.

Rowe, Alan J.; Mason, Richard O.; and Dickel, Karl. Strategic Management and Business Policy. Reading, Mass.: Addison-Wesley, 1982.

Synnott, William R.; and Gruber, William H. Information Resource Management--Opportunities and Strategies for the 1980s. New York: John Wiley & Sons, 1981.

Thompson, James D. Organization in Action. New York: McGraw-Hill, 1967.

Tregoe, Benjamin; and Zimmerman, John W. Top Management Strategy. New York: Simon & Schuster, 1980.

DISCUSSION: MASON PAPER

The discussion of Richard Mason's paper began with an extensive examination of two financial organizations represented in the group. It was generally agreed that the need for information systems (IS)-corporate strategy links in both was relatively obvious, and the representatives noted that in fact they did exist. Both representatives reported fairly formalized planning processes, in which IS planning played a major role in corporate planning because their businesses were so intrinsically involved with IS. Both said, however, that recognition of this "fact of life" had been slow to come.

Then representatives from three manufacturing organizations described their situations. In one case a key corporate objective was to improve operational and administrative productivity; although it had not directly participated in the selection of this objective, the IS area was perceived to have a specific role in its achievement. The second setting, a highly decentralized conglomerate, had highly decentralized objectives and planning, but IS played a role in facilitating measurement. In the third, planning was the responsibility of line and staff management (not of people with the title of planner), and all made "fuzzy" plans that seemed to work together because of the corporate style. The IS area was involved in this process. In all three cases IS seemed to be given the overall tasks of perceiving the potential impact of IS technology and "bringing to the table" suggestions whose adoption depended on how much the confidence of other managers was secured.

Finally, two representatives from technology companies spoke. In one case a formal planning process, based on the group-division hierarchy, had been put in place over the past three years and was beginning to produce meaningful strategic plans. The representative noted that this process had stimulated a realization of interdependency among units and generated much more interaction and consultation, including some IS-corporate strategy linkage. ("Everybody ran off and said, 'Oh, good, we can do our own thing,' and then they said, 'Oops, we don't know how.'") In the other case IS technology was being used to facilitate management interaction ("network the corporation"), which indirectly led to greater strategic linkage.

Despite these instances, participants felt that many companies carry out their planning functions without considering the potential linkage of IS and corporate strategy. Examples were cited, however, of top management now asking IS managers about linkage possibilities. An initial motivation for change--operational crisis, new CEO, or competitive action--as opposed to business as usual, seems to be a prerequisite. The group noted that in many cases IS managers seem to get involved with corporate planning by accident, but after getting there they make proactive contributions.

One factor influencing linkage that the group considered researchable was the effect of organizational structure on the "flow and directionality" of strategy (does it come from the top down or bottom up, and what is the impact of direction on linkage?).

Time horizon was also felt to be an important area for research. Is it easier for IS planning to link with corporate strategy where it looks at only a couple of years, or is it more feasible to consider a ten-year horizon? The contents and contribution of the IS planning process were felt to be quite different for each. In either case it takes time to develop an effective linkage, even under favorable circumstances.

The group also discussed how an organization decides to be a prime innovator in IS technology--for whom the payoff might be big, but risk of loss is also great--and how the IS-corporate strategy link might relate to this decision. Citicorp's introduction of automatic teller machines was cited as a case in which enormous resources were invested while other banks watched closely and engaged in "cautious experimentation." American Hospital Supply's success in a high-risk venture was seen as an impetus to its cautious competitors to consider strategic linkage as a means of catching up and ensuring that they didn't get caught short again.

The notion was advanced that the role of IS strategy is twofold--linking to and making sure IS supports existing corporate strategy, and helping top managers develop strategy and realize that IS technology may be important in the selection of a corporation's strategic objectives. The group considered research on this second role especially fruitful because it "flies in the face of business school teaching" and traditional conceptions of strategic planning.

Another suggested topic for research was understanding the many dimensions of IS's role in "educating line management about technical possibilities." Better ways for IS and senior management to be gotten "up to speed" about the potential impacts of IS technology are important to identify.

Various degrees of formality in planning processes were considered and speculations advanced about what they meant for linkage. In some cases general planning is so formalized that it gets in the way of strategic linkage and can choke off the flow of innovative ideas. In others the group felt that informality fosters a lack of linkage between senior management and the people doing the planning and allows key items to drop through the cracks. Participants disagreed about whether planning is carried on informally where formal activity is absent. In all cases they felt that mechanisms for better translating how IS can support primary strategic objectives must be found.

It was also suggested that the "information intensity" in organizations may be a key determinant of how aggressively IS-corporate strategy linkage should be pursued. If information processing has not been built into the corporate "language system," it is seen as so much technology, to be contained in the budgeting process, and the linkage is more difficult. It was noted that Michael Porter's book Competitive Strategy exhibits a language system that has great credibility with management, but that it gives "not even a peripheral reference to IS."

Some in the group argued that to remedy this gap practitioners must develop and deal with a few simple notions. Carl Reynolds's concept of "a business within a business" (see his paper in Part III) was advanced as one. But some felt this notion obscured rather than explained strategic linkage.

Although linkage is frequently discussed as a means to generate highly sophisticated models, simulations, and the like, its result is often much simpler. For example, putting a terminal in a purchasing agent's office to permit development of an interorganizational system may have great impact. The question is how to focus strategic thinking on high-leverage applications as opposed to elegant but perhaps irrelevant ones.

Finally, the group considered the difficulties of IS-corporate strategy linkage, given the complex and often unstated nature of what is wanted. Good planning requires knowing both the technology and the subtleties of the business. A formal strategy of remaining loose, to be able to acquire and divest without being hamstrung by network data structures, was cited as an example. In another setting actual corporate plans were kept under wraps because the strategy was to get rid of a division on the most attractive terms possible. Part of the resulting misdirection involved installing a large and expensive new IS for that division. Given the satisfactory price ultimately obtained, the corporation felt that the investment was appropriate, but this type of issue endlessly complicates research.

Many participants were frustrated with the "inertia built into corporate ways of doing things," including approaching IS. They observed that planning often takes place either in a crisis situation or when an excess of resources must be put to use. All too often management fails to pay sufficient attention to the real or possible uses of the information IS technology produces.

CURRENT RESEARCH ISSUES: AN ALTERNATIVE PERSPECTIVE

F. Warren McFarlan

The subject of linking information systems (IS) strategy to corporate strategy is not new. Starting with Harold J. Leavitt and Thomas L. Whisler's 1958 article, there has been great interest in the impact of IS technology on corporate strategy and structure. From the late 1960s through the 1970s, work by Sherman Blumenthal (1969), Charles Kriebel (1968), Warren McFarlan (1971), William King and David I. Cleland (1975), and Ephraim McLean and John Soden (1977), as well as IBM's business systems planning process (1975), emphasized the importance of the link between IS and corporate strategy and prescribed organizational procedures for its implementation. Almost universally, however, this work has been done by IS professors and professionals reaching toward general management and corporate planning rather than general managers and corporate planners reaching toward IS.

Given the authors' backgrounds, it is not surprising that much of this work was built on foundations of general management theory (Fayol, 1950), rational man theory (March and Simon, 1958), rather structured accounting and management science notions, and idealized views of corporate planning processes (Koontz, O'Donnell, and Weihrich, 1980). Further, it assumed that information systems were of critical importance to all firms and that major investments and benefits would automatically follow if senior management could only understand this importance. But without the perspectives of corporate strategy formulation, organizational behavior, and general management, this work dealt inadequately or not at all with fundamental related items, such as corporate culture, organizational learning, and the relative potential strategic impact of the technology.

On the other hand, research on corporate planning and strategy has been done largely by individuals with only a cursory understanding of information technology, its issues, and their impact on the organization. Consequently, a significant gap has opened. Gaining insight into how to close the gap represents a major research opportunity for the 1980s. But this work will not be easy; many structural and attitudinal barriers stand in the way.

Major Strategic Changes

In the past decade many products and processes have been developed that have fundamentally increased the potential strategic relevance of IS technology to organizations and heightened the importance of the link between IS and corporate strategy. The following paragraphs enumerate the six most important changes.

Technological Developments and Decreasing Costs

New developments in information technology have made available an array of potential products, services, and channels of product distribution that were previously either technically impossible or economically prohibitive. In the early 1970s the computer was primary, but a much broader set of technologies now exist and can be interconnected in local and extended networks; they include data processing, teleprocessing (voice and data), office automation, and stand alone microcomputers. New technological capabilities and significant cost decreases, which are expected to continue, permit businesses to gain new economies and offer radically different services.

Strategic IS Applications

Many organizations have built a base of applications and applications development expertise that allows more complex and potentially strategic IS applications. They have evolved from the caterpillar and cocoon stage of data processing, with its transaction-oriented systems and conversion of increasing numbers of data elements (often badly done), through electronic format toward the butterfly stage of IS as a competitive weapon.

This evolution can only improve communication between IS and general management. Information in the abstract has always been a curious intangible for general managers, who are attracted to the notion of improving decisions, but find it difficult or impossible to identify a specific benefit with provision of particular types of information. However, as the technology has increasingly been used in applications such as data base access, airline reservations systems, and customer sales reports, to which a specific market value is attached, managers have become able to conceive of and plan for information as a discrete end product with tangible worth.

Corporate Strategy Frameworks

During the past decade many new ways of thinking about corporate planning and strategy formulation have been developed. In the late 1960s and 1970s, the Boston Consulting Group's relatively simple conceptual grid on market growth and market share was widely accepted and utilized. In the early 1980s more complex value-added (Cash, Howe, and McLaughlin, 1983) and microeconomics-based (Porter, 1980) competitive strategy frameworks are making important contributions to strategy formulation and are proving more tractable for understanding and shaping the potential impact of IS technology. In many ways the field of corporate planning is as dynamic as that of IS technology, further complicating the pursuit of linkage.

Planning Processes and Organizational Structure

Research over the past decade has substantially demonstrated the importance of corporate culture (Pascale and Athos, 1981) and management style (Peters and Waterman, 1982) in developing appropriate planning processes and organizational structures. To date, the findings of this work, although clearly relevant, have not been systematically applied to IS strategy formulation.

IS Embedment in Organizations

New technology is dynamic, but in many organizations IS possibilities are a function of IS history. Instead of supporting new systems development, a majority of IS expenditures today go into systems maintenance and major rehabilitation of aged systems, which were developed in a different technology and often for different economic reasons. This trend has intensified the need for an effective link between IS strategy and corporate strategy to get the optimum payoff from very limited staff resources for new developments. As more systems are being purchased than made, a long-term view is also essential to build relevant skills in the organization.

Further, IS technology is not of equal strategic importance to all organizations or even to an individual organization at various points in time (McFarlan, McKenney, and Pyburn, 1983). These recognitions substantially increase the already complex task of developing an appropriate linkage between IS and corporate strategy for any particular setting. For example, the tight, sustained dialogue between IS and the general management group of a brokerage firm may be overkill in some forms of process manufacturing industry.

Contingency Theory

Finally, contingency theory concepts have exploded into a whole array of management environments (Kimberly and Miles, 1980). They have introduced far more useful albeit more complex prescriptions of managerial action, which are only beginning to be applied to IS-corporate strategy linkage.

Research Issues

A number of major changes have combined to make the area of IS strategy and corporate strategy linkage important and complex in the 1980s. This is a particularly rich, multifaceted field of research that will require different studies by individuals from many disciplines building on one another over time.

This section outlines five broad avenues along which research needs to be done. They are meant to be suggestive and not to be totally inclusive. Each avenue poses very broad research agendas. All assume a research methodology that relies heavily on experienced field investigators collecting data through in-depth patterned interviews in a limited number of field sites. These methodologies respond to the issues raised by J. P. Campbell (1970) when the complexity of the phenomena being examined and the preliminary state of the research make laboratory experiments or questionnaires inappropriate.

Use of IS Technology in Competitive Strategy

Systematic collection of data in different industry settings is needed to understand better how IS technology is being used as a competitive weapon and to gain insight into how this use can be better planned. In many cases we have found evidence that the competitive advantage, although real, resulted more from good luck than from foresight.

In the early years of IS technology, its competitive advantage was in two areas. It could reduce costs through staff reduction, future expense growth avoidance, tighter inventory controls, and so on (Davis, 1967) or it could provide better information for decision making (when assessing the actual value added was difficult and at best highly subjective). Today potential IS contributions to competitive strategy are significantly more diverse.

Our research has yielded a preliminary list of six questions with which a company can assess whether IS technology might significantly affect its competitive strategy. Though they include cost and quality of information issues, these questions provide a broader context for planning. They apply Michael Porter's framework of industrial competitive strategy to information technology. Additional organized field data would allow these questions to be expanded into subquestions that would give further insight into the link between IS and corporate strategy.

Can IS Technology Create Defensible Entry Barriers? Can the technology be used to gain and protect market share successfully? The word *protect* is particularly important; often an advantage can be momentarily seized but others can quickly copy it and negate the advantage.

An example of IS technology being used as a defensible entry barrier is American Hospital Supply's (AHSC's) installation of computer terminals in hospital purchasing departments. This network made it much easier for the hospitals to submit rush orders and reduce inventory, so many more orders were made to AHSC. As a result, a number of its competitors experienced significant drops in sales of major product groups. To counter the AHSC network, competitors offered hospitals their own terminals, but the hospitals refused them as unnecessary duplication and complication. In short, AHSC created a new electronic channel of delivery of great value to the end users, preempted it, and locked competitors out.

A second example is the Merrill Lynch Cash Management Account. Because the account requires complex software, which is difficult for competitors to reproduce, Merrill Lynch has gained a built-in edge. As other funds have developed similar software, Merrill Lynch has added features that expand the Cash Management Account's appeal and maintain its competitive edge.

Can IS Technology Strengthen Customer Relationships? Can IS technology be used to tie customers more closely to a supplier in subtle ways, so that the penalties of moving to another supplier become more severe? Can the technology be used to increase customer switching costs? For instance, in today's technology customers using a home banking system have to encode the names and addresses of all their monthly creditors for storage in the bank's computer. The effort required to do the coding and learn to operate the bank's computer creates an investment that complicates the decision to shift from one bank to another.

In the same vein, can the technology be used to generate new features that are important to customers? For example, automatic bill paying by home banking systems created a product where none existed before.

An example of using IS to bind customers more closely to suppliers by means of a new feature is a major distributor of magazines to newsstands. In a business with an essentially undifferentiated product where the major competitive weapon was price, this distributor combined an inventory management system with the basic magazine delivery service. By using data on weekly shipments to and returns from each newsstand, the distributor calculated a profit per square foot for each magazine and recommended changes in the mix of magazines to optimize each stand's profitability. This information was of great value to the stands. The distributor differentiated itself from its competition and was able to increase its margins and thus its profits substantially.

Can IS Technology Change Intraindustry Competitive Balance? Does IS technology offer the potential to change the industry economies of scale or other factors that dramatically affect the relative strength of the participants? For example, the complexity of software needed to run a demand deposit accounting system makes it nearly as expensive for a medium-sized bank to develop as for a large money center bank. The large bank with its substantial depositor base continues to add features, making its product more attractive to its customers and making it more difficult for smaller competitors to follow. The competitive response by smaller companies has resulted in a thriving software industry to develop general-purpose software for regional banks. By submerging their individuality, these banks can gain access to important and otherwise unavailable product features and maintain the competitive balance.

A second example is the three major U.S. airlines (American, TWA, and United) that sell fully integrated reservation systems to travel agencies. Each system handles reservations for all airlines, but the flights of the airline that has provided the system are always listed first. The influence of these reservation systems on competition became an issue when Braniff Airlines alleged that the warnings about its potential financial instability that American Airlines had included under each Braniff flight listing in its computer had significantly contributed to Braniff's bankruptcy. Braniff judged that the warnings drastically reduced its passenger loads and disrupted its cash flow by leading travel agents to write tickets for Braniff flights on the ticket stock of other airlines, who initially received payment and, in due course, forwarded the money to Braniff.

Can IS Technology Be Used to Change a Firm's Basic Competitive Strategy? Can IS technology provide such dramatic shocks to a firm's cost structure or to its product offerings that its very base of competitive strength is altered?

For example, the magazine distributor described previously changed its competitive strategy from low-cost production to product differentiation and thus gained significantly higher margins and profits. Other examples are the hotel reservation services that have expanded into tour arrangement, car rental, and air travel reservations, thereby becoming brokers (with appropriate fee income) instead of adjuncts to a hotel's basic operations.

Can IS Technology Be Used to Change the Balance of Power in Supplier Relationships? Can the technology be used to permit a firm to manage its supplier relationships better, driving cost down while speeding up essential service?

One manufacturing firm, by having on-line access to its key suppliers' order entry systems, has been able to reduce substantially its raw material and spare parts inventory. It can expedite rush orders as needed, eliminate significant amounts of paperwork, and cut the staff of inventory managers. Access to multiple supplier systems has also permitted the firm to identify the current low-cost supplier more rapidly.

William Abernathy's (1983) analysis of Japanese manufacturing management indicates that this strategy is one of their most significant means of reducing cost.

Can IS Technology Initiate New Products or Substitutes for Existing Products? Can the technology open up new markets with products not previously possible? Can it supersede existing products with more efficient alternatives?

Econometric data base services have become available on a cost-effective basis not only to corporations but to consumers who own personal computers and have satisfactory credit ratings.

This new market segment can now receive useful but hitherto unavailable data.

One potential product substitute with great promise is videoconferencing. It would allow executives to cut back on air travel while preserving essential communication in their firms.

Influence of the Competitive Environment

Recent work has suggested that organizational structure, management control, selection of distribution channels, and so on are functions of a firm's competitive environment. Our research further suggests that its competitive environment significantly influences how a firm should investigate whether IS can make a major strategic contribution.

When cost minimization is critical, IS creates strategic advantage if it can

Significantly cut or defer buildup of production and clerical staff

Measurably increase utilization of plant or reduce unscheduled machine downtime

Substantially decrease inventory level without affecting customer service or more efficiently manage accounts receivable

Improve material usage through reduction of scrap by better designs and other means

Provide new service, product, or quality features that will change the basis of competition to product differentiation

Keep cost and investment differences from competitors low enough that competition can take place on other bases

Depending on a firm's position in its industry, these questions may be addressed either to gain competitive advantage or to maintain parity.

When product differentiation is the basis for competition, IS offers a major competitive strategic advantage if it can

Substantially reduce product development lead time

Significantly improve product customization or service levels

Measurably speed rush order deliveries or enhance ability to confirm order or shipment status

Open new, more consumer-oriented electronic distribution channels to customers

Considerably reduce costs to convert the basis of competition to low cost

Add perceived quality to differentiate a product from the rest of the market offerings, for instance, through computer-aided design or production monitoring

As before, these questions may be addressed either from an offensive perspective or from a more reactive posture.

The contributions of IS technology to corporate strategy when competition is based on price are very different from the advantages it can offer for product differentiation. Deeper understanding of different generic competitive environments and their implications for the strategic contributions IS can make is a critical research avenue. Effect of Corporate Style and Culture

Much of the recent research in areas such as management control and transfer pricing has focused on the impact of corporate style and culture (Sathe, 1983). This research has led to sharp revisions in thinking about good management practice. To date this analysis has been only sparingly applied to IS planning. Philip Pyburn (1981) noted in his work at two multidivision companies that effective IS planning is influenced in the following ways:

Business Planning Formality: Companies in which business planning is formal regard IS planning as more effective when it is done formally. Companies in which business planning is informal find the key to success is good informal interpersonal relations.

Business Complexity and Volatility: In highly complex and volatile businesses, effective interpersonal dialogue is vital to good IS planning. In less volatile environments a formal planning system produces adequate results.

Status of IS Director: Where the IS director's status is high in the business unit, good interpersonal dialogue is the most productive IS planning device. Where the IS director's status is low, the formal process is essential.

IS Applications Portfolio Size and Complexity: In environments where the applications portfolio is large and complex, formal planning becomes crucial. In environments where the portfolio is small and straightforward, more informal procedures are appropriate.

Proximity of IS to Corporate Headquarters: When the senior managers of IS are geographically close to corporate headquarters, informal interpersonal processes may suffice. When the IS unit is far from headquarters, formal planning processes become vital.

Senior Management Culture: In companies where the basic management culture is formal, formal IS planning processes become necessary. In companies where the basic management culture is informal, interpersonal communication is critical to good IS planning.

Pyburn's work has merely touched the tip of a large iceberg that requires substantially deeper investigation. Research on strategic planning for IS as a major management system has not included the same broad general management reach investigative flavor as has research in fields such as corporate management control and corporate strategic planning.

Organizational Learning

The fourth major area of research concerns the differences between planning new applications for new technologies and planning new applications for old technologies. A hidden assumption of the early work on IS planning was that shortly after the announcement of a new IS technology, combined hard thinking and intense discussion by members of the IS organization and key users would identify its major implications for the firm and accurately assess their overall impact. Unfortunately, the research evidence over the past several decades in organizational learning and more recently in information services has suggested that this is an unsupportable notion. In fact, periods of experimentation as long as three to five years from the introduction of a technology to understanding of its full implications are not unknown. McFarlan, McKenney, and Pyburn noted in 1983 that an information technology appeared to pass through four phases, each with a different role of planning (see Table 1).

A critical unanswered question is how to "manage" this learning process and develop an ordered diffusion of relevant technology throughout an organization.

Information Systems as Products

Implicitly, most of the research work and thinking in the field of IS has viewed the technology's use as an internal information support tool. In many settings, however, IS technology is also being used to deliver concrete, independently priced products to customers. The implications of these two contrasting uses have not been explored. Preliminary research at large companies that are both selling IS products (such as data base services and published reports) and using IS for internal control and operations suggests that the management structures and strategies needed for these two uses are quite different. Substantial field-based research is necessary to delineate more fully these differences and what they mean for management.

Obstacles to Research

Execution of these five avenues of research is not going to be easy. Four significant structural and attitudinal barriers exist.

Table 1

Role of IS Planning in Phases of Information Technology

Phase 1 - To identify the existence of a promising new technology

- To invest in pilot projects to gain insight into the problems of using the new technology and acquire some skills in applying it

- To gain broad understanding of potential applications of the new technology

Valid long-term insights on the technology's potential for the firm are very difficult to gain at this time.

Phase 2 - To communicate widely to appropriate clusters of potential users about the existence of the technology and what it might mean to them

- To encourage establishment of user-oriented pilot projects to learn about the technology's real applications and the practical difficulties of its implementation

The broad view of the technology's ultimate impact will be quite clouded in this phase.

Phase 3 - To get the detailed controls for the technology in place and ensure that new applications are carefully thought through

- To develop a detailed and realistic view of the future

- To ensure that money is not invested in poorly conceived endeavors

Insights into the technology's implications and benefits become quite crisp in this phase.

Phase 4 - To ensure that known technologies are appropriately applied to new opportunities and changed business circumstances as they develop

- To permit long-term acquisition of staff and technology to support these applications

The ultimate applications and benefits of the technology are quite clear at this point.

The Two-Culture Problem

The first of these barriers stems from the background of the majority of IS researchers, who came into the field because of their interest and proficiency in managing data processing technology. They bring understanding of how to develop transaction and decision support applications and how to structure data files, insights on new developments in IS technology and their economics, and comfort with the technology. These assets are absolutely essential to the research agenda proposed here, but they are not sufficient.

This work draws heavily on research in business policy/competitive strategy, organizational behavior and learning, and the management of technology, broadly defined. Unfortunately, researchers in these fields lack the technical skills and insights to investigate IS problems and often lack an appreciation for, or even an awareness of, these skills. Our doctoral programs, through which the next generation of scholars and researchers is now passing, still tend to be isolated. The IS programs unwittingly stress technology and narrowness, while programs in other fields tend to ignore the existence of IS issues.

In a real way, the two-culture problem between IS professionals and general management in the corporate world is mirrored in the universities. Not infrequently, companies have resolved this dilemma by moving general managers into positions where they can provide leadership to the IS function and appropriate direction to the IS managers. Universities, however, have not generally made such moves. Until there is significant merging of individuals with different backgrounds on each side of this barrier, research is likely to be mechanistic and distressingly slim in its managerial insight.

Academic Research Biases

The second barrier stems from the type of research being done. This problem is, of course, not limited to the information systems field, but affects all areas of business research. Universities prize highly quantitative and elegantly structured studies of rather small problems more than qualitative investigations of very complex, messy problems. All the research suggested in this paper is clearly of the second type. Field-based research projects, which are by nature less yielding of hard conclusions, are viewed with considerable suspicion. Further, much of this research is multiyear and often multiperson; it requires a long gestation period. The relentless race toward tenure in many institutions systematically discourages younger faculty members from undertaking these fundamental, but far more risky research efforts. To counteract this, several institutions represented at this colloquium are organizing longitudinal research projects.

Requirements of Longitudinal Research

Third, the type of research we are suggesting is expensive and requires sustained cooperation from both the business firms and the faculty members involved over several years. Extended in-depth investigations in several organizations are necessary to tease out insights. The model for these projects is Joseph Bower's (1970) research on the resource allocation process; he devoted nearly a year to working intimately inside one large organization. Significant understandings may be won from such efforts, but, unfortunately, they will not be statistically verifiable. The risks of this kind of approach are obvious, and it is hardly surprising that the quick-hit "mail 400 questionnaires" procedure is seen as more desirable.

The issue is complicated by the fact that corporate strategy is multifaceted and evolves over time. Further, strategy is exceedingly complex, and there is a substantial possibility that a researcher will reach an incorrect conclusion about it.

Rate of Technological Change

Finally, because of the dynamic technology of the IS field, research is always moving against a shifting target. A research project painfully executed over two to three years may produce findings about the use of a technology that is no longer of commercial interest. Avoiding this pitfall requires hypotheses and research questions rooted in broad behavioral and systems parameters. This, however, is the easiest of the four research barriers to counter.

The research issues in IS strategy and corporate strategy are fundamental. They offer a major opportunity to make a significant impact on industrial practice. Barriers to rapid progress exist, but they should not detract from serious efforts to address these important research avenues.

Bibliography

Abernathy, William. Industrial Renaissance: Producing a Competitive Future in America. New York: Basic Books, 1983.

Blumenthal, Sherman C. MIS: A Framework for Planning and Development. Englewood Cliffs, N.J.: Prentice-Hall, 1969.

Bower, Joseph L. "Managing the Resource Allocation Process: A Study of Corporate Planning." Harvard Business School, Division of Research, 1970.

Campbell, J. P. Managerial Behavior, Performance, and Effectiveness. New York: McGraw-Hill, 1970.

Cash, James I.; Howe, Robert; and McLaughlin, Michael. "The Impact of Computers and Communications in the 1980s." Unpublished Harvard Business School Working Paper, 1983.

Davis, Gordon B. Managing the DP Function. New York: McGraw-Hill, 1967.

Fayol, Henri. "Administration industrielle et general." Paris: Duned, 1950; first published 1916.

IBM Corporation. Business Systems Planning: Information Systems Planning Guide. Application Manual GE 20-0527-1, August 1975.

Kimberly, J. R.; and Miles, Robert. The Organizational Life Cycle: Issues in the Creation, Transformation, and Decline of Organizations. San Francisco: Jossey-Bass, 1980.

King, William R.; and Cleland, David I. "A New Method for Strategic Systems Planning." Business Horizons, August 1975.

Koontz, Harold; O'Donnell, Cyril; and Wihrich, Heinz. Principles of Management, 7th ed. New York: McGraw-Hill, 1980.

Kriebel, Charles H. "The Strategic Dimensions of Computer Systems Planning." Long-Range Planning, September 1968.

McFarlan, F. Warren. "Problems in Planning the Information System." Harvard Business Review, May-June 1971.

McFarlan, F. Warren; McKenney, James L.; and Pyburn, Philip. "Information Archipelago: Charting the Course." Harvard Business Review, January-February 1983.

McLean, Ephraim; and Soden, John V. Strategic Planning for MIS. New York: John Wiley & Sons, 1977.

March, James G.; and Simon, Herbert A. Organizations. New York: John Wiley & Sons, 1958.

Pascale, R. T.; and Athos, A. G. The Art of Japanese Management. New York: Simon & Schuster, 1981.

Peters, Thomas J.; and Waterman, Robert H., Jr. In Search of Excellence: Lessons from America's Best-Run Companies. New York: Harper & Row, 1982.

Porter, Michael. Competitive Strategy: Techniques for Analyzing Industries and Competition. New York: Free Press, 1980.

Pyburn, Philip. "Information Systems Planning: A Contingency Perspective." Unpublished doctoral dissertation, Harvard Business School, 1981.

Sathe, Vijay. "Managerial Action and Corporate Culture." Unpublished manuscript, Harvard Business School, 1983.

Whisler, Thomas L.; and Leavitt, Harold J. "Management in the 1980s." Harvard Business Review, November-December 1958.

DISCUSSION: MCFARLAN PAPER

The discussion of Warren McFarlan's paper was heavily dominated by practitioners (in contrast to some of the earlier sessions, where the academicians held sway). In their opening comments, the practitioners present suggested that organizations vary widely in their degree of strategic linkage, but a "one-way linkage"--in which strategic business issues are used to frame questions about "how the IS [information systems] technology can help"--often emerges first. In some cases senior management had approached IS department management; in other instances IS managers had made presentations to senior managers. It was noted that this linkage is happening in the manufacturing and transportation industries as well as in financial services, where it is better known. Manufacturers and transportation firms have begun to perceive that IS can give them a competitive edge, not just through greater efficiency but through effectiveness. The executives noted some of the natural problems in being "the first kid on the block," but they acknowledged that a right guess may give the "kid" a preemptive advantage.

Six corporate representatives then talked about the current situations in their own firms. Of these, five described formal planning activities that included IS, most often in a one-way linkage. The sixth representative, from a corporation that is largely a government contractor, noted that the firm considers the Department of Defense its planning surrogate.

A university representative offered the opinion that linkage in educational institutions should be considered in two ways. First, concentrating on IS technology in teaching or research can have payoffs; such an approach in a new field might allow a very strong department to emerge in an otherwise average institution, enhancing the university's overall competitive posture. Second, universities can use IS to assist their strategic planning for products and resources; for instance, by tracking student programs.

In summarizing this part of the discussion, the participants noted that the corporate examples presented might have been biased toward more linkage than the norm, because organizations with greater IS strategic activity were more likely to have been invited to the colloquium.

The use of IS as a competitive tool generated the most interest among both academicians and practitioners in the discussion. It was suggested that the starting point for analysis could be the phrase <u>competitive advantage</u>, which could then be broken down by how IS technology can help achieve the advantage--through being a low-cost producer or through creating a value-added product. Use of IS to hook in customers with value-added service (what one participant dubbed "electronic heroin") was noted as an example of IS in competitive strategy.

The Holiday Inn room reservation system illustrates the potential for competitive use of "information analysis" employing IS already in place to analyze customer data and the like. Further examples are insurance companies that are varying their product lines and changing policy provisions in response to competitive pressures.

To the extent that universities are using IS technology for more than "short-term product information," they offer another interesting case in point. It was claimed that Carnegie-Mellon's announced plans to make personal computing available to students were intended to achieve a true visible competitive edge, in contrast to the plans of another university, which "hadn't developed the infrastructure."

Regarding McFarlan's dichotomy between low-cost production and product differentiation (an aspect of the influence of the competitive environment on IS strategy), the group suggested that the different classes of opportunities available to "hard product" companies and "financial services" organizations should be considered. They noted that most examples cited in the paper were financial service organizations. Why, in the face of the cases already known, more organizations do not understand the strategic potential of IS came up repeatedly. This was seen to be a relevant and researchable question.

Turning to the use of IS technology as products, the group noted that automatic teller machines in the banking industry could be considered examples. They also observed that many organizations seem to be trying to develop and market information services as products unrelated to their basic businesses. This is not like "the old days when everybody had a little extra information capacity so they thought they'd sell it," but, despite the effort, only limited success with the approach was noted.

With regard to the effect of corporate style and culture on IS strategy, participants discussed the resistance of "old-line" personnel to IS innovation. (Equally intriguing is the resistance of IS personnel to a change in role.) Many seemed to think this was one of the principal barriers to effective linkage. It was suggested that the cultural change that transpires "between saying, 'My God, we don't want that,' and 'My God, how can we get more of that?'" be investigated. Participants also noted that innovation does not come out of "large, committeelike structures," although this often seems to be expected.

The discussion of remedies for resistance to innovation spilled over into the subject of organizational learning. The group noted that a selling job is often necessary to raise the consciousness of management and staff at all levels regarding new technologies. They also acknowledged that there is a growing recognition of the lags associated with "time to market" within IS organizations. The relative ease or difficulty with which linkage issues can be communicated to CEOs and other top managers, including IS managers themselves, was also discussed. The fact that not only general managers but many IS managers themselves in the past have considered IS management to be in the "support quadrant" was seen as a barrier to developing the linkage. It was also recognized that this role perception depends somewhat on the industry.

Overall, there was favorable reaction to McFarlan's research avenues as a basis for classification. "Structural questions that can facilitate linkage," such as moving the IS director out of the traditional reporting relationship to the controller and creating a director of technology position that encompasses more than IS, were mentioned as ways to help companies move forward. Another important use of the IS function, perhaps a sixth research avenue, was ways "to better understand the plans and current actions of the contenders" in a competitive market. The charges brought by Frontier Airlines against United Airlines were cited as an example.

The concept of range of linkage--from tightly to loosely coupled--was considered in terms of overall corporate success. Among the organizations represented, the group noted that tight coupling appeared to have led to more success stories. This is a highly complex problem, but it was felt to be worthy of more serious investigation.

The discussion then broadened to include themes that can be characterized by catchwords. On the topic of "proactive versus reactive," an analogy was made to psychiatric treatment, in which patients have to know that they need help before it can be effective. But it was also pointed out that, in today's fast-moving technological environment, it may be difficult or impossible to play "catch-up ball"; reactive may be too late.

A practical question--and one that participants felt should be researched--is "In the absence of a clear and present threat, but in the presence of a potential one, how do you make it real enough to wake people up?"

A subject of considerable discussion was whether strategic linking had occurred by accident or by design in the various cases where IS has most profoundly affected firms' operations. Although opinions differed about how conscious airlines had been of the competitive opportunities in their reservation systems, there were graphic depictions of how these opportunities were being used. Major airlines feel because they put up the money to develop the systems, they are entitled to the competitive advantage the systems afford. Another case "that always comes to mind" is American Hospital Supply. The opinion was advanced that a system basically designed to correct an internal inventory problem became by serendipity a customer service. In the photofinishing business retailers were given access to a network initially set up for internal management of the photo- development process; this move also met with great commercial success.

In this vein, an MIT case study of six firms was cited to support the notion that planning was not rational but opportunistic, that of the "interesting things" done in the firms studied, not one was the result of planning or had been advanced by the IS department. Rather, "there was somebody with an idea who seized an opportunity and moved right in." General Electric's "factory of the future" for the upper end of its product line was mentioned as an example. The Japanese were noted as successful incrementalists, who "listen carefully," rather than as "grand strategists." This subject was felt to be worthy of significant additional investigation.

Finally, other observations on existing research and research opportunities were scattered throughout the discussion. For example, work from MIT on the diffusion of innovation, though not done specifically in the context of IS, gives insights relevant to organizational learning about IS. On a grander scale, it was suggested that researchers study how IS technology "can enable small businesses to be extraordinarily effective versus large businesses by allowing the large firms' economies of scale to be offset by opportunities for forming consortia and using networks."

CONCLUSION TO PART IV

Robert L. Ashenhurst

As the preceding papers and discussions indicate, there was a broad consensus concerning the fundamental importance of the work to be done on linking information systems (IS) and corporate strategy. The combination of today's very different technology economics; development of new, effective paradigms in other management disciplines potentially relevant to this field; and the increasing number of competitive successes with IS have given impetus to these investigations. There are many more issues to examine than there are human resources to implement these investigations. The following paragraphs synthesize the general colloquium consensus on the relative importance of these issues.

Research Methods

Most participants agreed that the research methodology most appropriate for investigating this area at present is development of in-depth field-based observations over a long period of time (longitudinal field research). This work was felt most likely to generate materials that, in addition to providing better insights for practicing managers, could lead to

1. More insightful hypothesis generation for later investigation
2. More comprehensive models
3. Development of organizing taxonomies

The field is too new, unstructured, and ill-defined at present to permit effective use of more formal data collection methods or refined applications of statistical methodologies. As better organizing structures evolve, knowledge can be built in a more defined and systematic fashion.

Overall Issues

The discussion revealed a series of quite general research questions that deal with the field as a whole. Some of these are

1. What are the key determinants for a successful strategic

IS application? How can a firm best approach finding these applications?

2. How can a firm assess whether there are potentially strategic IS applications in its industry? How should a firm think about the desirability of industry standards?

3. What factors can be managed to ensure a creative (as opposed to mechanical) interchange between IS and corporate strategy?

4. Why has strategic linkage been so imperfectly examined? What can be done on a national or industry basis to stimulate greater urgency about examining this issue?

Although the group felt these questions captured the breadth of their research interest, they recognized that such broad issues defy easy investigation. Consequently, narrower questions, which would be somewhat easier to examine, were also posed. The group hoped that addressing these questions would develop insights for approaching the broader ones.

Communications

It was asserted that one of the barriers to better linkage is the very different language systems used in the IS and general management worlds. (This is also called the two-culture problem.) This situation makes communication between the two groups quite difficult and increases the possibility of misunderstanding. Participants' concern about this issue translated itself into the following questions:

1. What can facilitate better IS managers' communication of their problems and opportunities to general management? Are the answers in a new language system, different and perhaps better training for IS managers, different general management training, or some other approach? If a new language system is the solution, what is it, and how can it be developed?

2. What organizational structure and management processes appear to improve communication in different settings?

3. What are the barriers to assimilation of IS managers into the top management team? What approaches help overcome these barriers?

4. To improve communication many firms are appointing general managers to oversee IS departments. How effectively can general managers perform as heads of IS

functions? What must be done to make them successful?

5. How can IS managers who have come up through the technical ranks make the transition from technical specialists to corporate planners? What hurdles must they overcome? To what extent do IS managers really want this strategic linkage?

Corporate Strategic Planning Process

The structure and type of strategic planning process in a firm were felt to have a real impact on the most effective kinds of linkages between IS and overall strategy. Participants noted that significant general research has occurred on the effectiveness of different types of corporate planning approaches and structures. Very little of this, however, has dealt with IS-related issues. The following research questions emerged on this topic:

1. What is the impact of the formality of corporate planning on the nature and type of successful IS linkage?

2. How can an IS manager best evolve the linkage in an environment where corporate strategies are deliberately not articulated?

3. In some firms, for reasons of confidentiality, corporate strategies are very closely held. What approaches for effective linkage can work effectively in such situations?

4. To what extent have the significant strategic IS already implemented resulted from careful planning and linkage? To what extent have they come from simply being lucky and in the right place at the right time? Is there any compelling evidence that good linkage really helps?

5. What can an IS manager do to assure that the IS function is appropriately supporting the firm, and that no big bets are being missed?

Creativity

A crucial prerequisite for successful strategic IS application is improving the odds that creative ideas for IS technology uses will be generated. Although many ideas lose their impact because of execution problems, without the ideas in the first place, failure is ensured. The topics of creativity and entrepreneurship are very broad and provide insights far beyond the arena of IS.

Likewise, research on this subject in other settings could provide insights relevant to IS.

1. What are the recognizable patterns of where good ideas come from in different settings? Are ideas a result of proactive IS management? Do knowledgeable users help? Can senior management make a contribution? Are there generalizable factors that can be identified, or is it primarily happenstance?

2. What steps can be taken to shake up an organization and encourage staff to think more imaginatively about strategic uses of IS technology?

3. How can a firm optimize identification of new technologies for potential strategic use? How can it better project "good bets" for IS strategic innovation?

Risk-Benefit Assessment

The group extensively discussed the observation that many of the strategic IS applications presented at the colloquium appear to have very high risks compared with their potential benefits. What techniques can be used to encourage a broader and more comprehensive assessment of these risks and benefits? Researchable questions that emerged from this discussion were

1. Are there different patterns across industry groups of risk taking related to IS technology and its use as a strategic competitive weapon? How did these differences arise? Are they appropriate?

2. What preconditions should encourage a firm to take risks in this area and be a preemptive pioneer? What are the preconditions that should encourage a firm to take a more conservative, reactive posture?

3. In different settings what can be done to ensure that the strategic risk-benefit trade-offs are appropriately raised for evaluation?

Industry or Business Characteristics

Business or industry characteristics that might influence the potential strategic impact of IS technology were felt to be an important area of investigation. Participants generally accepted the fact that this technology must be very close to the hearts of firms in the financial sector but of less burning significance to, for example, public utilities. This, however, was a relatively intuitive assessment and was felt worthy of considerably more research. The following questions were raised:

1. What is the effect of a business's information intensity on the best way for it to approach IS-corporate strategy linkage?

2. What is the full taxonomy of how IS technology can be used for competitive advantage? Examples discussed included leveraging operational productivity, remarketing captured data, creating market access barriers, gaining customer commitment by increasing switching costs, developing new products, and gaining insight into the actions and plans of competitors. This was recognized, however, as a preliminary and very superficial list. Both a broader taxonomy and an understanding of how it would vary by industry were felt to be of great importance.

3. Are there important differences between service industries and manufacturing industries in thinking about the use of IS technology?

4. Are there industry differences in planning, budgeting, and other resource allocation processes that affect the strategic use of IS technology? Are these differences appropriate? Are they related to an industry's cost structure or to some other phenomena?

Organizational Issues

The final major topic in this area harkened back to the earlier colloquium discussion on the impact of organizational climate and culture on achieving IS-corporate strategy linkage. Questions raised in this context included the following:

1. How can different corporate cultures and climates be modified from resistance to acceptance of appropriate examination of IS technology's potential contribution to strategic and competitive success?

2. What are the sources of corporate inertia or resistance to consideration of strategic applications? Examples include the line organization view, "old-boy" networks, government regulation, and the attitude that "we have always done it that way." What approaches are there for dealing effectively with these sources of resistance?

3. How can a firm assess its organizational readiness for moving ahead to strategic application? How can it facilitate diffusion of readiness to examine IS-corporate strategy linkage?

PART V

BUSINESS SCHOOL RESEARCH STRATEGIES

INTRODUCTION TO PART V

James L. McKenney

Research strategies for specific fields in business schools are a new development. A few faculty groups began to define strategies in the late 1970s to provide bases for cooperation with business research sponsors and to articulate their roles for school administrators so they could grow to meet student demand. These evolving efforts in information systems (IS) were discussed at the 1982 spring meeting of a loose coalition of IS faculty who gather periodically to share research notions and plan the annual Conference on Information Systems (CIS). Sponsored by the Society for Management Information Systems and the Institute of Management Sciences, this planning committee has grown from 15 to about 50 academicians, representing 33 schools.

Increasing numbers of students, accelerated business recruiting of doctoral students, and promotion difficulties are putting enormous pressures on the modest number of researchers in IS. The schools represented on the CIS planning committee agreed that a compilation of research strategy statements would both more legitimately define IS research and improve research efforts under current conditions by facilitating coordination. Intentions did not produce many statements, but the steering committee for this colloquium felt that a wide range of schools had implicit strategies if not explicit programs and that a request for strategy statements would generate a useful indication of the state of the art of IS research. About 25 schools were asked for strategy statements; the 12 submitted represent a broad sample of public and private as well as large and small institutions.

This sample includes about 25% of the schools in the United States and Canada that have research programs represented by papers in *Computer and Information Systems* or *MIS Quarterly*. The faculties and doctoral students of these schools wrote about 60% of the IS-related articles in *Communications of the Association for Computing Machinery*, *Harvard Business Review*, *Management Sciences*, *MIS Quarterly*, and *Sloan Management Review*. The sample includes 108 faculty members, 40 of whom are tenured. In 1983-84 these 12 schools enrolled 180 doctoral students in IS. If we broaden the sample to include all 23 schools represented at this colloquium, the proportion of published research output accounted for increases to 85%. If we add the 11 schools represented on the CIS planning committee but not at this colloquium, 95% of the research output and a total of 220 faculty are represented. These are modest numbers for a field concerned with managing a complex technology that is growing 25% per year.

The original strategy statements submitted reflected a wonderful heterogeneity of ideas about what constitutes a research strategy. Our request was relatively broad and encouraged variety; our objective was to include a wide spectrum. After the colloquium a statement format was developed and the statements were revised and then edited for common style. In their statements several schools delineate the implicit strategies that have been understood rationales for their activities. An equal number simply outline their faculties' and doctoral students' current work. All the statements reflect the ongoing traditions of their institutions.

Table 1 is a thematic analysis of the strategy statements. It represents the breadth of the IS field as well as schools' divergent approaches to it. Each school's strategy is based on its faculty's and doctoral students' interests and present work. The University of Arizona, Harvard, MIT, the University of Minnesota, and New York University consciously chose to focus on a few topics and build coordinated programs. In Gordon Davis's words, their strategies "reflect each institution's comparative advantage." All the schools employ eclectic methodologies, including experimental labs, simulation models, and field cases. A few--Arizona, MIT, and Purdue--do substantial research on hardware, but most do not. The significant majority focus on management of the IS resource and the impact of IS on organizations.

Table 1. *Information Systems Research Themes*

Research Theme	*Arizona*	*UCLA*	*CMU*	*CWRU*	*HBS*	*MIT*	*Michigan*	*Minnesota*	*NYU*	*Pennsylvania*	*Pittsburgh*	*Purdue*
Cost-benefit analysis	x	x	x	x						x		
Data bases, systems, software design	x	x	x	x		x	x	x	x	x	x	x
Data management, information resource management	x		x	x			x					
Decision support systems, decision theory	x	x	x	x		x	x			x	x	x
End user computing		x		x	x	x				x		
Expert systems, artificial intelligence		x	x				x	x	x	x	x	x
Human-computer interface					x		x	x		x		x
Impact		x	x		x	x	x	x	x		x	
Implementation				x	x	x		x	x	x	x	
Information requirements analysis		x		x			x	x				
Interorganizational systems	x											
Management of and planning for IS	x	x	x	x	x	x	x	x				
Organizational design								x				
Strategic use of IS	x				x					x		
Technology transfer	x				x							

UNIVERSITY OF ARIZONA
COLLEGE OF BUSINESS AND PUBLIC ADMINISTRATION

Jay F. Nunamaker
Benn Konsynski

The University

During the past ten years the University of Arizona has fostered an environment of strong research programs. The 200% growth in its research and development spending from 1975 to 1983 is nearly twice the national average. Among the nation's public research universities, Arizona was ranked second in support from the private sector in 1983.

The University of Arizona has emphasized programs in the physical sciences. Signals from the administration have been very clear--build a strong research program and stress doctoral education. Within this climate, the departments of computer science and management information systems were founded.

The Management Information Systems Department

The Department of Management Information Systems (MIS) was founded in 1974 as an adjunct to the Department of Accounting; it became a separate department in 1976. The long-range strategy of the department chair, Jay F. Nunamaker, was to develop three major areas, which embrace much of the MIS field: information systems (IS), decision sciences, and policy. Initial departmental strengths were in the IS area which had a technical and design orientation. A dominant theme in the department is that design is the key to MIS. Financially supported research areas have emphasized rigorous technical IS design and application.

The MIS Department consists of 17 faculty members, including full-time professors Seymour Goodman, Benn Konsynski, Averill Law, Roy Marsten, Richard Mason, and Jay Nunamaker. Two professional computer staff and 38 teaching assistants supported by university funding round out the department. The number of research positions is a function of the amount of grant support. The MIS Department has 825 undergraduate majors, 125 master's candidates in MIS, 40 M.B.A. students with majors in MIS, and 30 Ph.D. students. Its total operating budget exceeds $1.7 million.

The MIS Department has thrived as a result of support from the university's executive vice president; the vice president for planning and budgeting; former dean of the College of Business and Public Administration Rene Manes; and the current dean, Kenneth R. Smith. Without their backing, it would have been impossible for the department to grow.

Continued internal support from university administrators depended on development of a strategy to establish the credibility of MIS. The faculty pursued grants for technically oriented projects from the National Science Foundation, Army Communications Command, Army Computer Systems Command, Office of Naval Research, Electrical Power Research Institute, Digital Equipment Corporation, IBM, and NCR. The department received six National Science Foundation grants between 1976 and 1983.

A turning point in terms of research productivity and faculty and graduate student recruiting was the acquisition of dedicated computer systems for the MIS Department. The data laboratory and MIS Inc. further enhance the research and educational environment.

The Data Laboratory

The data laboratory at the university was developed to provide a real-world environment for testing software, tools, and techniques. It combines three methodologies: the case study, quantitative, and hands-on approaches.

The data laboratory is used to test procedures for collecting and organizing information in the IS design effort. A data base of specification requirements is utilized, along with a query facility, to simulate behavioral and technical problems that systems analysts encounter. Specially created case studies permit systems design by various methodologies. The laboratory thus allows researchers to explore and compare alternatives. It also allows researchers to formalize the duties of the analyst and examine the differing roles of the user, the analyst, and the programmer. Evaluating different team organizations and role-playing are important parts of the laboratory environment. Finally, the data laboratory illustrates how computer-aided tools can be used in the systems analysis process and allows researchers to develop new computer-aided tools and techniques.

The data laboratory took a major step forward in 1983 with the aid of a $2 million grant from NCR. About 200 NCR personal computers are being formed into a campus network. Five laboratory sites have been established to make computer services broadly available for MIS students. In this environment students are exposed to a wide variety of computer and IS concepts. The new laboratories also have added significantly to the research program at Arizona. Faculty and graduate students currently have research projects under way on networking, information flow, languages, computer-aided instruction, computer-managed instruction, electronic mail, and many other areas that take advantage of the new facilities. Executive training programs are also being developed. A $1 million grant from Digital was used to add to the research computer facilities in the MIS Department and to support the data laboratory.

MIS Inc.

The MIS research program has carried the data laboratory concept one step further with MIS Inc., a simulation of a systems development environment. Students participate as managers, analysts, programmers, and support staff to learn software development and its management. This experiment was first run on a large scale in the spring of 1981; it continued in a different form in the fall of 1982. Students assume responsibility for the entire project activity, which serves as a test situation for examining the management and practice of systems development.

The task in MIS Inc. is to define, design, and implement a large-scale software project. The project involves more than 180 students from three courses each semester: an undergraduate course in IS design and implementation, a graduate course in computer-aided IS analysis and design, and a graduate course in behavioral and economic aspects of IS. The undergraduate students form the programming teams and the systems support staff, the graduate analysis and design students constitute the team and group managers, and the graduate behavioral and economic aspects students form the evaluation teams and assume other administrative responsibilities.

Research Activities

Research activities in the MIS Department emphasize formalizing the processes of analyzing, designing, building, and operating (using) management information systems. Other research concerns are improvement of MIS operations by increased application of quantitative techniques, use of the computer itself in the design process, and development of students' administrative skills for management and operation of computer facilities and resources.

Research in the department integrates a variety of topics in related fields: (1) an IS focus on systems analysis and design methodology, data base management, data communications networks, decision support systems, and office automation; (2) decision sciences, particularly large-scale optimization problems, scheduling, and simulation; and (3) management policy in IS, including issues of centralization versus decentralization, cost allocation and pricing, and management of computing facilities.

The MIS Department has several active research programs that encompass many individual research efforts.

IS Development Support

Integration of the organizational strategic and IS strategic planning activities

Development of languages and analyzers for requirements specification and analysis

Computer-aided procedures for logical design support

Computer-aided techniques for physical design and implementation

Computing Facilities Management

Classification of manpower skills and needs for MIS support

Cost allocation and pricing of computer services

Development of an audit language for internal control evaluation

Information Resource Management

Logical data base design support

Performance evaluation of alternative data base organizations

Data management in distributed data base environments

Global schema design in heterogeneous data base environments

Decision Support

Profit maximization techniques in transport environments

Dialogue management alternatives in decision support system implementation

Model management techniques

Exploration of new forms of information presentation (for example, FACES)

Technology Transfer

Computer-related technology transfer and Soviet energy industries

Value conflicts and policy choices in U.S. computer export control

Integration of the Specialty Equipment Manufacturers Association computer industries

Acceleration of technology transfer in domestic industries

Interorganizational Systems

Identification and motivation of interorganizational sharing opportunities

Cost and revenue allocation in interorganizational systems

Interorganizational systems as major competitive strategic alternatives

The following brief explanations represent some of the activities that might emerge under the first research program--a workbench environment for IS development support:

Logical Data Design. The logical data design (LDD) project explores the use of color graphics to specify individual logical data views by means of bubble charts. It allows interactive specification of views on a potentially huge space, zooming in-out, and windowing. To demonstrate the capability to interface automatically with logical design tools, an automatic encoding is available for interfacing with the Data Designer design tool, which performs view integration activities.

Front-End Planning System. After significant review of our past research efforts on the ISDOS project, we are building support to integrate the organizational strategic planning activity with IS strategic planning and logical design. This tool incorporates many of the elements of BSP, BIAIT, BICS, BASE, Information Engineering, SAST, ISDOS, (PSL/PSA), and other techniques under the PLEXSYS framework.

Data Flow Diagram and Entity-Relationship Diagram Charter. We are developing a tool to assist in the graphic specification of special charts for requirements and systems documentation. An icon builder is used to construct a library of icons for one or several charting techniques, such as data flow diagrams, entity-relationship charts, document information, and material flow charts. The tool is not intended to be merely a passive editor; its information can be used by analysis, transform, and other design tools.

Computer-aided Process Organization. Computer-aided process organization (CAPO) analyzes interprocess relationships and derives appropriate process groupings into functional modules. Factors such as transport volume, information hiding, control transfer, and coupling and cohesion are used in multidimensional analysis techniques for module specification.

Financial Analysis Critical Evaluation System. The financial analysis critical evaluation system (FACES) addresses multidimensional display of financial information for comparisons and threshold alerting. This approach is emerging as a new means of business information presentation. It has on-line color, multipresentation support.

Data Dictionaries and Metaprocessors. We have been working on extensive review of current and planned data dictionary systems, metaprocessors, and extensible forms. We are interested in adding value to existing designs of such systems and have software development under way for implementation of intelligent support tools.

OFFIS Analyzer and OFFICE Design Tools. The OFFIS system was an initial prototype for an office system design support tool. The OFFICE system defines and profiles role/work station activities statistically for interface with office simulation software (using SAINT).

TOKEN. The TOKEN system is a discrete event simulator for token ring architectures in local network environments. It can be extended to simulate Carrier Sense Multiple Access/Collision Detect (CSMA/CD)-type protocols. The profiles are office oriented and the interface is designed for interactive simulation.

UNIVERSITY OF CALIFORNIA, LOS ANGELES
GRADUATE SCHOOL OF MANAGEMENT

Ephraim R. McLean
E. Burton Swanson

The University and Its Setting

Located in the largest city in California and the second largest in the United States, the University of California, Los Angeles (UCLA), was first established as the "southern branch" of the University of California's Berkeley campus in 1919. Originally a tiny two-year college in downtown Los Angeles, UCLA rapidly outgrew those facilities and moved to a new campus in Westwood in 1929. Today it is the largest of the nine University of California campuses, with 22,000 undergraduates and nearly 12,000 graduate students. In addition to the Colleges of Letters and Sciences and of Fine Arts, the graduate professional schools include architecture, dentistry, education, engineering, law, library science, management, medicine, nursing, public health, and social welfare. In a recent ranking of research universities by the Associated Research Councils, UCLA was placed second among all public universities (after the University of California, Berkeley) and fifth overall in the nation.

The School

The Graduate School of Management was established in 1935 and now offers both master's and doctoral degrees in 11 major subject areas. The master's program, leading to the M.B.A. degree, is a two-year full-time program with about 800 students. In addition, there are approximately 100 students in two special M.B.A. programs for executives and middle managers who are working full time. There are currently about 150 students studying for the Ph.D. degree. The school has 94 permanent faculty members, with an additional 30 to 40 visitors, adjuncts, and lecturers.

The Computers and Information Systems Area

Although computer-related courses have been offered in the School of Management since the early 1950s, the Computers and

Information Systems (C&IS) area was formally established in 1970. There are now six full-time faculty in the area: Jason L. Frand, Martin Greenberger, Bennet P. Lientz, Ephraim R. McLean, Clay Sprowls, and E. Burton Swanson. The area offers 16 courses in information systems. Typically, an M.B.A. student chooses 8 of these courses to concentrate in C&IS. Recently, a joint program has been established with the UCLA Computer Science Department, leading to both an M.B.A. in information systems (IS) and an M.S. in computer science at the end of three years of study.

Research and doctoral education is of particular importance to the C&IS faculty. Eighteen students have received doctorates in IS in the past ten years; 16 of them hold faculty appointments at universities throughout the world. Nineteen students are currently pursuing C&IS doctoral degrees, making this program the largest doctoral area in the school.

The C&IS Research Program

The C&IS Research Program, established in 1977, was organized to provide a formal structure and focus for C&IS research activities in the school. Professor McLean was named the first director and continues to hold that position. The program has a professional staff of two and a half people and employs a number of doctoral students as research assistants. It also maintains a special library of publications in the field; sponsors a biweekly colloquium series that highlights both advanced academic research and innovative professional developments; publishes a quarterly newsletter, CHANNEL, which is distributed to over 1,000 academics and professionals worldwide; and provides for faculty and student travel to conferences and meetings. Finally, the program has acquired microcomputers and word processing equipment for the C&IS area.

A vital aspect of the C&IS Research Program is its links with the professional community. If metropolitan Los Angeles were considered as a separate country, it would have the fourteenth largest gross national product in the world. This concentration of business and industry provides a firm base for academic-professional activities, to the benefit of both communities.

The C&IS Associates Program was established in 1977 to bring together senior managers and computer professionals who are involved, either wholly or partially, in the information services function of their organizations. Representatives from nearly 30 national firms provide an important base of financial support for C&IS Research Program activities. Additionally, they are a vital source of professional advice and counsel, reinforcing the applied aspects of much C&IS research and frequently providing field sites for dissertation research studies. Together, the C&IS Research Program and the C&IS Associates Program form a strong bond between theory and practice, between the academician and the professional.

Research Strategy

The field of IS considers the use of information by individuals and organizations and the management of the systems and organizations that supply this information. Research activities in this field at UCLA reflect this dual orientation. The C&IS area follows an eclectic approach to specific research pursuits. No one topic or research domain dominates; individual faculty, doctoral students, and visiting scholars are free to choose according to their personal inclinations and available opportunities. Collective efforts among faculty and doctoral students are also encouraged.

A key strategy has been to employ multiple reference disciplines in undertaking research projects. This is accomplished by building intellectual and organizational bridges to other disciplines in the school. Recent dissertations in C&IS have been based in microeconomic theory, management science, organization theory, and other related areas. This strategy relies heavily on the strengths of the areas to which the bridges are built. At UCLA the quality of the Graduate School of Management and the university as a whole offers a rich set of options. In addition, the relatively independent position of the C&IS area, which is not a subgroup of any other area in the school, means that no one discipline can claim to be *the* reference discipline or source of research paradigms for C&IS.

Research Activities

The following is a sample of some topics presently being investigated at UCLA. It illustrates that no one theme or research paradigm dominates these research efforts. They are as diverse as the information systems field itself and reflect both applied and theoretical aspects.

Managing the IS Function

Planning. A continuation of the early planning study that led to the book *Strategic Planning for MIS* (1977). A number of competing planning methodologies are being investigated and their potential contributions to the emerging "information architectures" are being evaluated (McLean).

Application Software Maintenance. A follow-up to the 1977 survey of approximately 500 data processing organizations, which was published in the book *Application Software Maintenance*. The current focus is on comparative maintenance environments, management strategies, organizational design, task definition and assignment, work techniques, and policies for coordination and control (Lientz and Swanson).

Data Base Management Systems. An exploration of the characteristics and comparative advantages of the commercially available data base management systems, with emphasis on microcomputer-based systems (Sprowls).

Management of Computer Networks. A theoretical and empirical investigation of the configuration and use of computer networks for management purposes. This multiyear study is funded by the Office of Naval Research (Lientz).

Use of Budgeting and Chargeback Systems. An identification and testing of several variables that may explain managers' willingness to participate in preparing and using data processing budgets (François Bergeron[*]).

Information Systems Requirements Analysis

The Analyst-User Interface. The development of an analyst-user interaction process based on the learning theory of Chris Argyris and Donald Schon, with application to the problems of information requirements analysis. This process is being tested in a specially designed course for professional analysts and users (Gail Salaway*).

Entity-Relational Models. Extension of the entity-relational approach, pioneered by Peter Chen, to the problems of applications development and specification of data base requirements (Peter Chen, Il Choo Chung,* and Dennis Perry*).

Computer-based Development Aids. The use of computer-based development tools, in particular the Problem Statement Language/Problem Statement Analyzer (PSL/PSA) and the System Encyclopedia Manager (SEM) from ISDOS, Inc., as aids in systems development (Sprowls).

Information Systems Utilization. A long-term study directed toward development of a theory of IS utilization. A descriptive model of individual information channel disposition and use is proposed as a basis for the theory. Data on utilization of ten management reports in four organizations (incorporating a total of nearly 200 individual users) have been gathered and analyzed (Swanson).

Emerging Environments for IS

Decision Support Systems. A continuing investigation, begun in 1976, of the special characteristics of decision support or management support systems. The potential contribution of the interactive programming language APL is also being studied within this area (McLean).

Expert Systems. A prototype system, to be tested empirically, designed to support IS requirements generation using

---

*C&IS doctoral students

the principles of expert systems and knowledge engineering (Elie Harel[*]).

End User Applications Development. A general investigation of the use of end user-oriented software tools. In particular, a recent study explored the relative productivity gains of using nonprocedural fourth-generation languages for applications development and report generation. Six applications were studied using matched pairs; the study indicates that nonprocedural approaches offer significant advantages (McLean and Harel*).

The Decision Process. A model of the management decision process in terms of microeconomic production theory. Productivity of an IS as a factor of decision and firm production is being assessed by applying the model to material requirements planning with data from 62 firms (Randolph Cooper*).

Office Automation. An inquiry into the emerging problems of office automation and the interrelated aspects of documentation, communication, and decision making. The first phase of the study is aimed at understanding the key dimensions of the office environment and the potential contributions of technology. Later phases will look at implementation strategies (Frand and McLean).

Areas of Application for IS

The Newspaper Industry. An empirical study of trends in the automation of newspaper organizations, from the back end (production) to the front end (news editing), with an assessment of the impacts on the form, content, and style of information distributed, as well as on power structures and role relationships. Also, the situations in Japan and the United States are compared. A companion study focuses on electronic publishing and videotext technologies (Greenberger).

Financial Institutions. An ongoing study of the use of computer technology in banks and insurance companies, with a particular focus on distributed and end user-oriented applications (Lientz and McLean).

Small Business Computer Systems. A recently completed survey of nearly 100 small businesses, in which an IS success model involving nine factors was tested. Chief executive knowledge of computers was found to be one of the key variables (William Delone*).

Energy Policy. A multiyear investigation of the use of analysis and computer modeling in the debates, political skirmishes, and policy formulations that took place during the 1970s over energy policy in the United States. This research was published in 1983 in the book Caught Unawares: The Energy Decade in Retrospect (Greenberger).

---

*C&IS doctoral students

CARNEGIE-MELLON UNIVERSITY
GRADUATE SCHOOL OF INDUSTRIAL ADMINISTRATION

Charles H. Kriebel

The University and the School

Carnegie Tech was founded essentially as an engineering school. This tradition has had a strong influence in shaping the character of the Graduate School of Industrial Administration. The graduate program's original curriculum departed from the institutional approach to management education to stress problem-solving capabilities, technical skills, and underlying disciplines, such as economics, mathematics, and psychology.

Since its establishment in 1949, the school has been an innovator in management education and research. It operates with a relatively small and cohesive body of faculty and students to maintain the highest quality in its programs. The commitment is to excellence and innovation rather than volume as the means to achieve impact. The research history of the school can be characterized as interdisciplinary, with emphasis on the analytical approach to problem solving in "the sciences of the artificial," in other words, understanding and creating human artifacts. Today faculty and doctoral students are actively engaged in research in management, economics, operations research, behavioral science, political economy, and information systems (IS).

The Information Systems Area

In 1965 the Computer Science Department at Carnegie-Mellon was established as an organizational entity separate from the Graduate School of Industrial Administration under the leadership of Alan Perlis. Shortly thereafter the doctoral program at the school was revised and a within-the-school major in IS installed. Joint research with the Computer Science Department has continued since that time; however, the research focus of the two groups is distinct. The doctoral program in systems sciences at the Graduate School of Industrial Administration is directed toward analysis and design of complex systems and communications, information processing, and decision making within them. Typically, but not exclusively, the operating environment of these systems is the firm.

Current faculty with research interests in the IS area include Mark Fox, Eric Johnson, Charles Kriebel, Steven Miller, Thomas Morton, and Gerald Thompson. In addition, university professors Allen Newell and Herbert Simon continue to work with doctoral students in the systems sciences.

Faculty are largely independent in their choice of research topics. Although each faculty member has a professional area identification, there are no departments in the school. Consequently, joint research is often across areas and is usually addressed to specific problems. Faculty work closely with doctoral students, and joint research is strongly encouraged. Upon entering the program each doctoral student is assigned two faculty advisers, one of whom need not be in the student's designated major area. Similarly, a student's dissertation committee may include members from different areas or from other departments of the university. For IS students these are often faculty from computer science, social science, or psychology. At present there are eight doctoral students majoring in IS distributed over a time frame of roughly four years.

Research Background

One antecedent of IS research at the school was the early work by Allen Newell, Herbert Simon, and others on problem-solving processes and cognitive psychology. Two outgrowths of these efforts were the information processing system (IPS) model of organizations and the field of artificial intelligence. Abraham Charnes, William Cooper, Gerald Thompson, and others at the school pioneered research on mathematical programming methods and their application in systems. In the computational area this work led to heuristic programming. Another outcome, in management control, was Yuji Ijiri's seminal reformulation of the traditional accounting model of IS into an explicit mathematical representation.

Perhaps the best illustration of interdisciplinary research at the school is the behavioral theory of the firm, a more descriptive paradigm than the conventional model in economics, developed by Richard Cyert and James March. The ramifications of this theory were investigated in Oliver Williamson's formal analysis and in Charles Bonini's thesis on a simulation of information and decision systems in the firm.

Research Strategy

The fundamental goal of the Graduate School of Industrial Administration is to make intellectual contributions of the highest academic quality to solving problems of management and problems in the managerial environment.[1] The school's statement of research goals expresses preference along three dimensions: substance, method, and quality.

Substance: The Management Orientation

The school's activities are focused on a common field of inquiry: management and the managerial environment. This encompasses the economic, legal, political, technological, psychological, and sociological environment of management as well as the analytical methods relevant to management.

Method: The Problem-solving Orientation

The school's activities are oriented toward solving problems by means of systematic analysis. This is consistent with the interdisciplinary approach, because knowledge and methods of various disciplines must often be integrated to solve a specific problem. In addition, the problem-solving orientation implies the need to make theories consistent with empirical phenomena and relevant to managerial problems.

Quality: The Academic Quality Orientation

The school's activities are oriented toward areas where contributions of the highest academic quality can be made. Unlike consulting activities, which may solve particular problems, academic activities develop principles, frameworks, and theories by which current and future problems may be solved effectively. This is essentially what is involved in scientific inquiries, and the academic quality of problem-solving activities critically depends on the depth of such inquiries.

Research Activities

Historically, faculty independence and the size of the school have mitigated against establishing organized and explicit strategies for research, except for the preceding statement of goals. Nonetheless, over time specific research projects have existed, and one can also identify research themes and problem areas being addressed. Several of these are mentioned below to illustrate ongoing research activities.

Evaluation and Economics of IS

How can the evaluation process be improved? Can a theoretical framework for the process be formulated? Researchers are currently developing such a framework by expanding on methods and results from the information economics and statistical

---

[1] This section is adapted from "The Goals of GSIA," March 1976.

decision theory fields. Modeling and measuring the impact of information on an organization and a worker are also relevant to this area.

Computer-based Decision Support Systems

Part of our research on decision support systems is investigating how the strengths of experts can be used in conjunction with computers. Other research in this area concerns how management can employ expert systems to aid strategy formulation and development.

Production Scheduling Systems

The purpose of our research on production scheduling systems is to study the theory and implementation of scheduling rules in order to develop an intelligent scheduling information system. This work is being conducted jointly with the Robotics Institute at Carnegie-Mellon.

Administration of IS Resources

Are the resources allocated for information systems and services being utilized effectively? How would one know? Research on this topic is proceeding on several dimensions. A continuing survey of the management information systems and telecommunications activities of major business firms is identifying leading-edge practitioners. An extensive review of the empirical research in the area is under way to pinpoint the major research findings as compared with the "conventional wisdom." Researchers are also investigating project development strategies and their relations to project risks, planning, and control.

A variety of other activities at the Graduate School of Industrial Administration and elsewhere on campus concern IS research. For example, a committee was established last year for research on the social and organizational aspects of computing environments. This was an outgrowth of the large-scale joint Carnegie-Mellon-IBM effort to develop a universitywide network of powerful personal computers and associated software.

CASE WESTERN RESERVE UNIVERSITY
WEATHERHEAD SCHOOL OF MANAGEMENT

Martin L. Bariff
Miles H. Kennedy

The University

Case Western Reserve University is a nationally recognized independent university located in Cleveland, Ohio, about four miles east of the downtown area. Established in 1967 by the federation of Case Institute of Technology (founded in 1880) and Western Reserve University (founded in 1826), Case Western Reserve is composed of an institute of science and technology, a liberal arts college, a school of graduate studies, and seven professional schools.

The university enrolls about 8,800 students, about 5,000 of whom are seeking graduate or professional degrees. The university offers courses in more than 60 academic and research fields and increasing numbers of interdisciplinary combinations and stresses quality in its students, faculty, and programs. Seven of its faculty and alumni have been awarded Nobel Prizes, and many others are nationally recognized for their work.

The School

The Weatherhead School of Management has rapidly developed in importance as a center for management education and research. The first M.B.A. earned in Cleveland was awarded by the graduate school in 1930. The present school was formed in 1967 through a merger of the School of Western Reserve University and the Division of Organizational Sciences of Case Institute of Technology. Each of these units was formed in 1947. In 1958 the School of Business was accredited at the graduate and undergraduate levels by the American Assembly of Collegiate Schools of Business. In the late 1950s and early 1960s, the Division of Organizational Sciences originated the first doctoral programs in the nation to specialize in operations research and organizational behavior. On April 21, 1980, the School of Management was formally dedicated as the Weatherhead School of Management, to honor a family long noted for its tradition of entrepreneurship, innovativeness, and business development.

The Weatherhead School currently enrolls 950 students in programs at the master's and doctoral levels and 200 students in undergraduate programs in business and accounting. From 1977 through 1982 enrollment in the school increased 100%.

The faculty of the Weatherhead School, which numbers 52, continues to grow steadily in quality. Ninety percent of the faculty has been hired since 1967. This includes a new faculty in management information systems; expanded marketing, accounting, and finance faculties; new divisions of industrial relations, business policy, and operations management; and increasing strength in organizational behavior and operations research. Faculty members are on the editorial boards of numerous journals, and the Weatherhead School is home for the Journal of Industrial Marketing Management.

The Management Information-Decision Systems Research Program

The Management Information-Decision Systems (MIDS) program was established during the late 1960s by Miles Kennedy. At present the MIDS group, a division of the Managerial Studies Department, includes five faculty (Alan F. Dowling, Jr.; Tor Guimaraes; Miles H. Kennedy; A. Michenzi; and J. Parameswaran), four Ph.D. students, and five advanced M.B.A. graduate assistants. Approximately 15% of M.B.A. students select MIDS as their major area. The size of the management school faculty encourages research collaboration with colleagues in other areas, for instance, accounting, marketing, operations research, and organizational behavior. Within the university the MIDS group has cosponsored research workshops and served on Ph.D. dissertation committees with the biometry, computer engineering and science, library science, and psychology departments.

The Weatherhead School graduate programs include M.B.A., executive M.B.A., Ph.D., and various M.S. degrees. In both M.B.A. programs, an end user-oriented course is required. A student majoring in MIDS typically enrolls in five to six additional electives. Many students with concentrations in MIDS-related areas choose one to two MIDS application-oriented electives. A management information systems certificate program provides post-master's degree study to integrate information systems (IS) management and technology with related functional areas. The MIDS faculty teach two required IS courses for undergraduates in the Case management science and Western Reserve management and accounting programs. During the academic year they also participate in the continuing education programs of the Center for Management Development and Research.

Research Strategy

Although a research program changes with modifications in faculty composition, the MIDS strategy reflects the Weatherhead

School's emphasis on application-oriented, theory-based research. Whether by direct deductive hypothesis testing or by initial descriptive field research leading to model building and subsequent hypothesis testing, our research objective is to improve our understanding of the management and use of IS in organizations. Drawing on theories and past research of reference disciplines--for instance, computer science, economics, management science, and social sciences--research findings can build toward a cumulative knowledge. Thus, policy insights and recommendations from much MIDS research can contribute to both the research and practitioner communities.

Research Activities

The MIDS research focus is twofold: management of an organization's information resources (including both the IS function and end user computing), and design and implementation of decision systems (including both embedded automated models and decision aiding/artificial intelligence support).

Over the years six MIDS research themes have developed: management of information resources, decision support systems, information requirements analysis, implementation of IS, data management, and control and auditability.

Management of Information Resources

Tor Guimaraes studied the management of information centers and/or personal computers in 21 organizations. Overall, senior management and IS executives were satisfied with both strategies. The study identified specific benefits and problems and made recommendations. Guimaraes also examined applications program development and maintenance processes in 48 organizations to determine major influences on maintenance costs.

Steven Schindler studied large-scale computer systems conversion projects in eight organizations to analyze the management issues related to various technological approaches to conversion. His case studies focused on hardware and operating systems conversions.

Guimaraes and David Kolb are studying the relationship between senior corporate management and the chief information officer.

Decision Support Systems

During the past ten years, Miles Kennedy and colleagues have developed and enhanced STRATAGEM, a computer-based planning tool. It is one of the first modeling systems to process simultaneous equations. Researchers and students have built more than 100 models with STRATAGEM; they include nursing personnel demand projection, alternative depreciation policies, cable television franchise analysis, and plant expansion planning. Current research plans include two enhancements: a "how come" facility to augment traditional "what if" capabilities, and a flexible and fully automated heuristic optimization facility. We hope research on the latter will demonstrate that decision makers can comfortably validate model logic and structure by inspecting the optimal conclusions these imply.

Kenneth Kutina designed a computer-based model using DYNAMO for analyzing operations of a medical school. The Medical Center Model (MCM) is recognized nationally as a standard methodology for medical school planning.

Brian Dos Santos, using undergraduate students in a laboratory experiment, found that both structured model usage and display of differences from base case rather than final values significantly improve problem finding and prioritization capabilities with a decision support system.

Information Requirements Analysis

Miles Kennedy and Sitikantha Mahaptra developed a methodology, DEFINEPAC, which used both direct and indirect procedures to elicit user requirements. Fieldwork has indicated that DEFINEPAC generates more complete requirements specifications than other traditional methods.

Martin Bariff proposed an information requirements analysis process model; he evaluated past research on requirements methodologies and suggested selection guidelines. His study of 32 organizations indicated that 12 used commercial methods, 13 used self-developed methods, and 7 had no formal methods for developing user requirements. In 10 organizations an information analyst position existed; each of these organizations had one to nine such professionals.

In an experiment using M.B.A. students, Bariff found that a pictorial problem representation (a table or decision tree) significantly reduces the isolation effect bias in evaluating probabilistic choice scenarios.

Luiz Pizani is evaluating 15 information requirements analysis methodologies to identify common and unique processes and data flows. This is a first step toward automation of the selection process given task, individual, and organizational factors.

Jeffrey Hoffer and Miles Kennedy developed a methodology for allocating batch and sequential decision-making needs to type of computer system support.

Implementation of IS

Alan Dowling developed, tested, and implemented a measure to determine the level of success a system achieves. In a related current project, he has developed the expectation curve, which traces the net system adoption outcome expectation of people in the adopting organization. The amplitude of the curve is being measured in 80 organizations throughout the adoption process. Another Dowling project addresses identification of key factors affecting the success of an adoption in the hospital industry.

Lynn Markus, in four case studies, identified political factors that either inhibit or facilitate adoption of IS technology.

Dowling studied the sabotage activities by potential users in one organization. He estimated the incidence (45% at a 95% confidence level) and variety (primarily five types of covert activity) of systems sabotage in American acute-care hospitals.

Data Management

Jeffrey Hoffer performed an analytical simulation of different combinations of joint indices to evaluate performance on secondary indexing. He further developed an optimization model for this choice process. Hoffer and Jon Clark formulated a methodology for calculating parameter values used in requirements specification for data base design.

Tor Guimaraes examined the cost effectiveness of host language data base management systems in relation to a reduction of applications development costs. The findings indicated that careful management of the systems must occur to achieve cost reductions. A current study by Guimaraes will determine organizational issues related to successful introduction of a data administration function.

Control and Auditability

Martin Bariff, in studying 27 electronic data processing auditors, found that those with primarily general audit, as opposed to data processing, backgrounds significantly underestimate the importance of general controls for internal data processing control evaluation. Both interrater and intrarater reliabilities were high. In a study of task, motivational, and organizational influences on internal data processing auditor job satisfaction, organizational commitment, and turnover, Bariff found that perceived task structure and promotion possibilities are key determinants.

HARVARD UNIVERSITY GRADUATE SCHOOL OF BUSINESS ADMINISTRATION

James L. McKenney

The University and the School

Harvard College, founded in 1636 in Cambridge, Massachusetts, has grown to be one of the largest graduate universities in the world. With 11 graduate schools and two colleges, located in Boston as well as Cambridge, the university operates in a very decentralized manner. Each graduate school sets its own goals and manages its own financing. The Harvard Business School, founded in 1908, is the second largest graduate school, after the Graduate School of Arts and Sciences. It has a faculty of 180 and about 2,000 students. It is a self-contained campus with classrooms, dormitories, libraries, computer center, and recreational functions on the Boston side of the Charles River.

The Information Resource Research Program

Information resource research is one of 14 topics in the Harvard Business School research program, which has been part of the school since 1922. Funded primarily by corporate gifts and alumni donations, research activity is an integral part of faculty responsibilities.

The information resource (IR) program includes six faculty and four doctoral students. Faculty members are Warren McFarlan, James McKenney, James Cash, Gregory Parsons, Leslie Porter, and Michael Vitale. The program is a subgroup of the Control Area in the school. Faculty teach during the academic year in the doctoral program and in either the executive or the M.B.A. program. A typical faculty assignment includes at least 40% research/course development over five years. Material on IR in the required M.B.A. curriculum is embedded in several first-year courses as well as in the business game. There is one IR elective in the fall of the second year and three, including a field research course, in the spring.

Two full-time, 14-week executive programs with enrollments of 130 and 160 are held concurrently each fall and spring. In recent years IR faculty have taught in these programs to experiment with merging new IR ideas into the required curricula.

In addition, several 2- to 3-week programs convene throughout the calendar year. One of these, Managing the Information Services Resource, is organized and conducted by the IR faculty. This program, which started in 1964 as a three-day update session, has evolved into a 2-week course for senior IR managers and other interested senior general managers. Alumni from the program have been an invaluable source of research issues and case study sites.

Research Background

Research on the management of electronic information processing started at the Harvard Business School in 1954. Since then 37 D.B.A. theses have contributed to the IR research program. Robert Anthony organized and supervised seven research projects on automatic data processing systems; they developed two main themes--planning and control issues and impact of the new systems on the organization. Anthony continued the planning research until 1962, and Paul Lawrence coordinated research on organizational impacts. John Dearden and Warren McFarlan extended these focuses in the 1960s; doctoral theses during this time included David Norton's work on centralized planning and Charles Doryland's planning model for information systems. James McKenney initiated a business simulation research project in 1961 as a managerial information design laboratory. This effort was continued by Michael Scott Morton, Brandt Allen, Peter Keen, and Louis Gutentag, to name a few.

In 1968 Richard Nolan and Neil Churchill joined the group and developed a new topic--managing the data processing function. Robert Lord's study of planning and control systems and Robert Goldstein's work on the cost of privacy contributed to this effort. In 1974 McKenney started a longitudinal study to define and model the impact of information systems on management work, which he called "organizational learning." Edward Cale's work on implementing standard computer base systems, Lee Gremillion's study of managing the organizational learning process, and Kathleen Curley's analysis of word processing's impact developed this theme. With the arrival of James Cash in 1976, the focus shifted from control to software issues.

Since 1978 we have been formulating the research strategy described below. Phillip Pyburn's study "Information Systems Planning: A Contingency Perspective," Richard Linowes's analysis of strategy structure and information systems, and McFarlan and McKenney's book Corporate Information Systems are the products of this effort.

Research Strategy

The objective of the IR research program is to develop substantive concepts that will aid senior executives in managing information resources. This effort focuses on timely issues to generate useful information for managers and systems scholars as well as practitioners.

Research Activities

Our research objective is operationally divided into four themes, which are the basis for a series of longitudinal field studies.

1. The strategic role of IR--linking IR programs to business programs (McFarlan and Parsons)

2. The value-added concept--exploiting IR technology as a competitive force for a firm and planning its use (Cash)

3. The assimilation management project--management of the integration of IR technology to sustain a humane and productive organization (McKenney and Vitale)

4. End user support systems--creation of a basis for managing the introduction and evolution of end user support systems (Porter)

The Strategic Role of IR

Study of the strategic role of IR involves investigating IR and associated technology as a competitive resource with the potential to give firms a significant strategic advantage in the marketplace. This study is exploring the major exogenous factors that determine the strategic value or potential of IR and establishing guidelines for management practices that link IR to business objectives and needs.

Not all firms studied have significant competitive opportunities for IR. However, many are in competitive environments where IR currently has, or will soon have, a major competitive impact. The exogenous factors being analyzed are industry variables (IR has more strategic potential in some industries than others), technology variables (the technology currently available is more cost effective and more obviously applied to some tasks and functions than others), and organizational variables (some organizations are more effective at IR technology assimilation and use than others).

The study of industry and competition draws heavily on the works of Alfred Chandler and Michael Porter. A longitudinal multiindustry project has been developed to investigate the effects of these variables in the financial services (12 firms), transportation (8 firms), and manufacturing (8 firms) sectors.

There has been a parallel study of management practices, or IR strategies, that have guided IR into and within each firm. The evolution of these strategies and their effectiveness in meeting the firm's IR needs are also major concerns of this study. Components of IR strategies are planning processes, organizational structures, leadership styles, IR allocations, and performance monitoring. Currently, qualitative evaluations of effectiveness are being developed, and follow-up studies to refine these evaluations are planned.

The Value-added Concept

The value-added concept is a framework for analyzing the penetration of IR technology into an organization's product and service flow and determining possibilities for exploiting new technologies in areas of highest value to the organization. The concept is being used to link the strategic role of IR with approaches to managing assimilation of IR technology. This effort describes four aspects of the way a firm competes that IR will significantly affect: cost effectiveness of operations, restructured access to markets, differentiation in products and services, and new industry boundaries.

An important piece of this project is an evolving set of criteria to guide IR development policies. In summary, they ask whether a given firm appears to be using newer IR technology in established low-value-added applications or whether it is exploiting the new functionality for higher-value-added uses. For example, rewriting an adequate batch accounting system with on-line data base technology may be a low-value-added application.

This framework is also being applied at an industry level to describe the nature of structural change and how IR technology contributes to it.

The Assimilation Management Project

The assimilation management project has focused on three issues essential to effective management of the diffusion of technology: a useful taxonomy of IR services, the organizational impact of electronic mail, and the process of organizational learning in assimilation of office automation.

The taxonomy of IR services is part of an ongoing effort to build a framework and establish a sensible set of terms to describe the evolving technology. The operational focus is testing the relevance of group and communications concepts to organizations using electronic mail for managerial communications. We have constructed a management model based on the work of Richard Pascale, Anthony Athos, and Thomas Peters which assumes that the assimilation of technology is a function of the culture plus individual style and skills. The structure of analysis is drawn from Karl Weick's causality chains with a bit of

Victor Vroom's notion of leadership style.

We hope to trace the life and death of a large set of electronic mail groups. Our initial sites are three large companies that have relied on electronic mail to manage product development for several years. We are gathering information on electronic mail use by two management groups in each company. At present we are developing measurements for electronic mail behavior and refining our analytical procedures. We intend to expand the study to three financial services firms.

The organizational learning study is in the data-gathering stage. Its focus is on the leader-manager and the role of technical support in introduction of a professional support system into an organization. We are particularly focusing on intellectual learning and facilitating cultures. Some organizations seem to gain momentum and be open to new processes; others seem to start all over with each new effort.

End User Support Systems

The end user support study has concentrated on how organizations are responding to mounting user pressures for more direct access to IR. To anticipate the growth of personal computing, the study first looked at the underlying structural changes in the user, organization, and corporate environments that are responsible for this increase in demand. In the organizations we visited, personal computing appeared to be in the middle of the introduction phase and rapidly moving toward the contagion phase. Because of the potentially large investment firms are making in personal computing and the impact personal computing will have on information flows within organizations, it is extremely important to conduct research on how this introduction and growth can best be managed given each firm's organizational constraints.

In 1982 we started a longitudinal study in three manufacturing firms that have taken distinctly different approaches to supporting end user computing. The study initially focused on the effectiveness of the introduction of personal computing, with particular emphasis on determining the types of controls appropriate for use of this new technology. They have to balance between controlling the spread of a potentially expensive novelty and encouraging innovative use and organizational learning.

In 1983 two new firms were added to the study, and all have agreed to participate for the next three years. In each firm the users of personal computing will be identified and their individual progress tracked over three years. This study will determine how use of the technology changes over time, how corporations benefit from its use, and how corporate policies stimulate or hinder its growth.

We expect that in some environments the impact of personal computing will be limited to automating clerical functions; in other settings it will rapidly become the managers' and professionals' support tool anticipated in so much of the literature. If we believe that the payoff of personal computing is in supporting the manager, then it is important to identify the corporate factors that encourage this. By monitoring several firms, each with several hundred users, it should be possible to identify the most productive policies and practices.

Research Methodology

Our research process starts with a "scoping" stage, followed by an inductive analysis and then a multifirm study. As do most methodologies, ours begins by coupling a review of published research with field data from a few test sites. A crude model of likely exogenous factors as well as controllable forces is then developed. This model is tested in an in-depth analysis of two or three field sites, which yields case studies. The resulting revised model is then tested in a multifirm study, in which data are often gathered by structured interviews or questionnaires.

Where possible our research strategy is to develop a theme, such as systems planning, and organize several pertinent doctoral theses that build on one another. Concurrently, a course module is developed for the summer Managing the Information Services Resource course on the topic. Recently we have organized studies around "industries"--such as financial services or transportation--and we are attempting to examine several themes simultaneously through joint efforts. We intend to conduct more longitudinal studies.

This cooperative effort is bringing in more useful, multipurpose information, but it is far from a refined approach. The in-depth case studies often provide insights for models other than the one being tested. The firm then becomes a much more productive interview or questionnaire setting or the site for a follow-up case study on another theme. For example, our present study of financial services has involved about 18 case studies and three different questionnaires. The cases mainly provide data for the theme of linking information systems to strategic planning, but they also contain data on technology transfer, office automation, and organizational learning.

MASSACHUSETTS INSTITUTE OF TECHNOLOGY
SLOAN SCHOOL OF MANAGEMENT

John F. Rockart

Research in information systems (IS) at the Sloan School has been, and continues to be, heavily influenced by five factors: integration of the school into its parent institution, the Massachusetts Institute of Technology (MIT); the orientation of the Sloan School; location of the Information Systems Group within the Management Science Group; the particular faculty mix in IS: and the presence of the Center for Information Systems Research.

The Institute

The institute is committed to both aspects of technology--science and engineering. In addition to its fundamental emphasis on basic research, MIT has long devoted energies to solving some of the nation's and world's major problems. Each school in MIT is an integral part of the university, which has few boundaries. For instance, students have little difficulty cross-registering among schools. Thus, a "one university" ethos centering on a scientific perspective and approach underlies almost all that is done throughout MIT.

The School

As opposed to many case-oriented schools, the Sloan School from its inception has been based on teaching the fundamental disciplines underlying management. Research to extend the frontiers of fundamental disciplinary knowledge is strongly encouraged. Much emphasis is placed on research progress in hard disciplines, such as operations research, and some of the softer sciences, such as those connected with human behavior. Interdisciplinary research is desired but is often seen as more difficult to evaluate.

The Information Systems Group

For the past decade the Information Systems Group at Sloan has been one of a half-dozen components of the Management Science Group. The Management Science Group itself is somewhat eclectic, housing faculty with backgrounds ranging from operations research to organizational behavior and including some whose fundamental discipline is economics. The group teaches and researches in areas including marketing, operations management, planning and control, and IS. A variety of disciplinary approaches is necessary to perform effective research in these areas.

Information Systems Group Faculty

The IS Group includes a wide variety of disciplines and training--ranging from electrical engineering to organizational behavior. Eight Sloan School faculty are full-time members of the group: John J. Donovan, John C. Henderson, Stuart E. Madnick, Thomas W. Malone, Jeffrey A. Meldman, John F. Rockart, Michael S. Scott Morton, and Michael E. Treacy. In an atmosphere in which each person is attempting to maximize the output of his or her research stream, and thus his or her reputation, development of more than an "umbrella" of basic directions for research is neither possible nor desirable. Those on the tenure track must carve out their own niches, perhaps influenced by senior faculty, but certainly not diverted by them.

The Center for Information Systems Research

The Center for Information Systems Research (CISR) began in 1974. It was established to "work on major problem-centered research issues of interest to both faculty and practitioners in the field." At approximately the same time, several other centers were established in the Sloan School in response to both the MIT tradition of problem-based, application-driven research and a felt need at Sloan to establish better links with industry.

Four major objectives were established for CISR: (1) to perform high-quality research that is relevant and useful to practicing managers in the IS field; (2) to increase contact with managers in the IS function in industry and nonprofit organizations to ensure the relevance of the research; (3) to provide students at all levels with increased opportunities for real-world involvement; and (4) to expand financial support for research on IS at Sloan.

A major mechanism to carry out these objectives was a group of sponsors, who would provide both funding and--equally important--advice on research areas they believe should be pursued. Funding was to come solely from the IS area budget, not the corporate gifts department, of the sponsor organization. This was to ensure CISR's continuing interaction with the IS personnel in each organization. The number of CISR sponsors increased steadily from 2 in 1974 to 22 in 1979. It has been held at this level to allow effective continuing interaction.

Today almost all faculty members of the IS Group devote at least half their time to research, many as a result of CISR funding, which allows them to "buy out" time from teaching. Research at CISR is also carried on by two full-time research associates (usually with master's degrees in management and some years of field experience in the IS area) and graduate students. An administrative staff organizes seminars, performs financial management, and supports the research staff.

The center, directed by John Rockart, reports to the dean of the Sloan School and to the head of the Management Science Group in a matrix fashion. A steering committee composed of Rockart, the assistant director, and three IS faculty members provides policy direction.

A primary source of CISR research funding is the sponsors, who contribute approximately $600,000 per year. A second major source is the traditional large research grant or contract mechanism, which in an average year provides $200,000-$300,000 to various IS faculty members.

Research Strategy

A review of the IS research "strategy" at Sloan for the past two decades suggests strongly that faculty composition has primarily determined the research agenda. The streams of activity are very much sums of the individual research strategies of the faculty members who have been at Sloan for most of the past 10 to 15 years. In this sense we have no overall research strategy. However, the other background factors at Sloan have played a part in selecting faculty and in directing them toward particular lines of endeavor.

Research Activities

The research agenda, as noted in Table 1, has centered in the past on three major categories of work: IS technological delivery platform, "enabling concepts" to further the managerial application of the technology, and management of the IS function. In the past year a fourth major research stream has emerged--organizational and managerial impacts of the new technology.

The Technological Delivery Platform

In the area of the technological delivery platform, John Donovan, Stuart Madnick, and Hoo-min Toong have done significant work over the past decade on some aspects of hardware design, but have placed most emphasis on systems software and data base design. All three have their Ph.D.'s in engineering. The research methodology in this area is thus heavily oriented toward the engineering paradigm of "build it, test it experimentally, and report the results." Much early work was performed on the effectiveness of relational data base systems. In like manner, Sloan faculty made significant contributions to the literature on the use of virtual machines. Much of our continuing work is related to design, efficiency, and effectiveness of computer systems in an era when multiple processors will be either connected within a single machine or networked.

Table 1. *Research Portfolio*

	Historical		*New Area*
Technological Delivery Platform	*Enabling Concepts*	*Management of the IS Function*	*Organizational and Managerial Impacts*
Hardware	Decision Support Systems	Centralization versus Decentralization	Organizational Impacts of the Technology
Operating Systems	Executive Support Systems	Human Resources Management	Technology Driving Strategy
Data Base Issues	Critical Success Factors	Management of End User Computing	Technology and Culture Change
	Office Systems	Corporate IS Structure	Technology-induced Change in Organizational Processes, Roles, and Structure

Enabling Concepts

"Enabling concepts" for the use of IS in organizations are frameworks and processes that help managers understand and effectively employ the technology. This is the area in which the managerial-behavioral side of our IS faculty has primarily focused. One of the most striking, and one of the earliest, outputs of this research area was Michael Scott Morton's pioneering work on decision support systems. Much effort has gone into decision support systems concepts and implementation and the lessons learned from these implementations over the past decade. Scott Morton's early book was followed by the seminal Andrew Gorry and Scott Morton paper. Later the works of Peter Keen and Scott Morton's students (Thomas Gerrity, Steven Alter, and Michael Ginzberg, among others) provided further conceptual understanding of the field and insights into the processes necessary for effective implementation of decision support systems. This will continue to be a primary area of effort at Sloan.

Research in "support systems" has come to include executive support systems (John Rockart and Michael Treacy), which differ dramatically from decision-centered decision support systems. Most recently, work in the area of support systems has taken yet a further tack. We are now considering expert systems as support systems. We believe this view, which differs distinctly from traditional artificial intelligence, provides a promising field for research.

A second major example of enabling concepts is work on critical success factors. Case-based insights into this technique were originally designed to help managers think about the information they individually needed. New concepts and processes, derived from field research into use of critical success factors analysis by consulting companies, have been developed in IS planning, focus for top management teams, and corporatewide reporting systems. Recently, Treacy has contributed to the theoretical underpinnings of the concept and extended it in an empirical study.

Similarly, Christine Bullen is working to improve understanding of the impact of office systems. Her efforts have been reported in the IBM Systems Journal.

Management of the IS Function

In part through the influence of CISR's sponsors, there has been a strong pragmatic streak in Sloan IS research. We have been concerned with developing concepts, frameworks, and processes to aid management of the IS function. In this area, much attention has been placed on IS centralization and decentralization (Rockart and Bullen). Robert Alloway and Judith Quillard carried out a major study of end user needs and their managerial implications. A study by Thomas Barocci focused on IS human resource planning. The role of the chief information officer and the organization structure and processes that corporate IS staff utilize are also subjects of recent work. Another major focus in this area has been the management of end user computing. A prescription has emerged from field interviews with 200 time-sharing end users, 83 personal computer users, and 80 IS managers associated with end user computing.

As the technology continues to evolve, the managerial process for IS will have to change. Issues such as managing data and managing networks are becoming critical and will provide a wealth of research opportunities. We plan to maintain a research presence in this field; the focuses of our work will continue to emerge as the field develops.

Organizational and Managerial Impacts

As a result of our previous research efforts, and through contact with our sponsors, we have become convinced that almost all aspects of how corporations are managed are undergoing major technology-induced change. The focus of our current research in this area is on understanding the complexion and magnitude of the changes coming in the next decade.

Significant changes, some overt, some subtle, are occurring even today in the way organizations function. The composition and size of staff groups are changing--in part as a result of the new technological capabilities. How work is performed by everyone in the corporation (executives, staff, secretaries, line managers) is being affected. Communication-engendered new communities are springing up in many organizations. If we believe with Jay Galbraith that communication is an important factor in structuring organizations, then even organizational structures may be expected to change. Perhaps most important, new computer communication-based capabilities are driving changes in corporate strategy.

In sum, evidence is appearing from this era of information-communications applications that Leavitt and Whisler's predictions in their classic 1958 article "Management in the 1980s" will most likely be fulfilled. We expect that the computer-based revolution will have as profound an effect on the structure, processes, and roles of major corporations as the first Industrial Revolution did.

Our work in this area began in 1983. Research on the technology-strategy link is under way. Ed Schein (of the Organizational Behavior Group at Sloan) is interested in the impact of technology on corporate culture. Eliot Levinson, Michael Treacy, and John Rockart have initiated research concerning technology's effect on roles and processes of the organization. We expect to be joined by others on the Sloan faculty in this area of research.

Research Methodology

It is clear that at Sloan no single research method predominates. Rather, we use the "appropriate rigor" for a particular piece of research. Depending on the maturity of the research field and the style of the researcher, a method must be chosen from what we see as a rough research progression model. An entirely new research topic starts with the researcher's "rough model" or "concept." Initial cases are used to validate the model's appropriateness and flesh out the researcher's understanding of the field. The result of the cases is a richer, improved model ready for testing in one of several ways: structured data gathering, field data gathering, field experiments, or laboratory work.

Most of our research on the technological delivery platform employs laboratory-based building and testing of systems. Most of the work on enabling concepts starts with a rough model and continues through the development of improved models, which are usually further refined by field data gathering, field experiments, or laboratory work.

Research on the management of IS most often progresses very quickly from conceptual model to field data gathering, which, in this area, is the predominant method. Thousands of field experiments are being run today in this area, so we feel no need to create our own laboratory situations. Finally, in technology impacts, we are now concentrating on development of rough models and a series of initial cases.

UNIVERSITY OF MICHIGAN
GRADUATE SCHOOL OF BUSINESS ADMINISTRATION

Dennis G. Severance

The University and Its Setting

The University of Michigan was founded in 1817 and was the first public university in the nation. In 1837 the school moved from Detroit to Ann Arbor, a new, small town with a population of 2,000. Today the university is composed of 17 schools and colleges; about half of Ann Arbor's population of 100,000 is related to the university in some way. Approximately two-thirds of the 38,000 students on the Ann Arbor campus are undergraduates.

The School

The Graduate School of Business Administration was founded in 1924, with nine professors, six lecturers, and 22 students. The school grew rapidly, and today its 19,000 alumni are among the leaders of business in this country and around the world. Nearly 7,000 managers attend our executive programs annually. More than 400 M.B.A. degrees and almost 300 B.B.A. degrees are granted each year. Approximately 100 Ph.D. students are currently in residence.

Our courses in business have changed much over the years, constantly delving into new areas of application and research. But one element of the school's character has remained constant: its steadfast dedication to excellence in education. In the words of Dean Gilbert R. Whitaker, Jr., "Our teaching programs are strengthened and enhanced by a faculty who are actively engaged not only in the transmission of current knowledge, but also in the discovery of new knowledge and its application to a broad range of national and international concerns."

The Computer and Information Systems Group and Its Strategy

The first courses in computing were offered in the Business School in 1965. Since that time the objectives of the school's computer and information systems activities have been to provide a high-quality curriculum for students at all levels and to maintain a significant and productive research program. Today there is a separate Computer and Information Systems (CIS) group with nine full-time faculty: David C. Blair, Randolph B. Cooper, James P. Fry, Manfred Kochen, Marilyn Mantei, Alan G. Merten, Judith Reitman Olson, Thomas J. Schriber, and Dennis G. Severance.

We believe that the keys to our success in the CIS area have been the following:

1. A "critical mass" of faculty members, highly skilled in both research and teaching

2. Various ongoing research programs that produce significant contributions to journals and conference proceedings

3. Programs and courses for all degree levels and for executive education programs

4. Adequate computer resources for students and faculty, including terminals, special computers, software, and support staff

5. Strong relationships with faculty in other programs at the University of Michigan, faculty from other universities, and local and national business communities.

We strive to tie our activities closely to both the university and business communities. We have established relationships with other groups engaged in computer-related activities at the University of Michigan through joint appointments, cross-listed courses, Ph.D. student support, and committees. Our faculty is active in field research, executive education programs, and business consulting. Our efforts in the future will include further involvement with the local business community and with other Business School faculty.

Our curriculum and programs have expanded significantly since 1965. All M.B.A. and B.B.A. candidates are now required to take a course in information systems and eight additional M.B.A. and Ph.D. courses are available in the CIS area. We are currently working with several non-CIS faculty members to integrate computer and information systems assignments in the Business School's functional area courses.

Our computer facilities support both the teaching and research programs of the school. We currently have access to the time-sharing facilities of the university via 36 terminals. We also have in-house minicomputers and microcomputers. A new and significantly expanded computing facility for the Business School is currently under construction and will open in September, 1984.

The Information Systems Research Group

The Information Systems Research Group, through external research grants and support from the Business School, provides access to research facilities, liaison with students from throughout the university, contacts with funding sources, and clerical support. The group is staffed by a balance of experienced researchers--faculty from the Business School and the College of Engineering and associate faculty members from the School of Library Science and the Mental Health Research Institute. In addition, it has approximately 20 exceptional graduate students from a variety of disciplines. External developmental grants to the CIS program allow faculty members to reduce their teaching loads and spend additional time on research activities.

Research Activities

The current CIS faculty group includes professors with backgrounds and interests in the following areas: management of the information resource, decision support systems, data management, information science, analysis and design methodologies, document and text processing, human interface with information technology, senior management control of computer-based systems, and computer-based modeling. In addition to these, areas of interest for future faculty members are likely to include organizational impact of information technology, telecommunications systems, and office automation.

The CIS group is currently expanding the depth and scope of its research activities. Faculty and research staff have already established national reputations in computer-based simulation modeling, data management, information systems control, and information science. In addition, we are developing research programs on the impact of information technology on people and organizations and extending our data management research efforts to include text and document management. We are also pursuing joint research with faculty from other business functional areas, such as organizational behavior, marketing, accounting, and finance.

Research Activities in the Ph.D. Program

Ten students are currently enrolled in our Ph.D. program in CIS. The program's major objective is development of sound research skills in business information systems. These skills include the ability to conceptualize and understand the nature of information systems; their design, development, and evolution; their impact on individuals and organizations; and strategies for their successful implementation.

Our Ph.D. students are expected to pursue one of two avenues of research. The first is to work within the information systems field developing tools and methodologies. Examples include creation and evaluation of software tools to assist data base designers in selecting efficient computer storage structures or development of cognitive processing models to guide systems designers in analyzing and building useful decision support systems. Alternatively, students can apply existing technology in creative ways to support other business disciplines--for example, design and development of effective computerized systems to improve management performance in functional areas such as marketing, finance, or production.

Our program reflects the university's long tradition of interdisciplinary research. Students can investigate information-related problems of other business areas or can work toward synthesizing concepts and ideas from computer science, computer engineering, industrial engineering, and psychology in novel ways relevant to business information systems.

The Ph.D. program is currently divided into three research areas: development of software methodologies and tools for use in the analysis and design of information systems; study of the interaction of information systems with individuals and organizations; and analysis and development of methods for storing, processing, and presenting information. The first area is exemplified by our Information Systems Research Group's current efforts to build a data base administrator's "design workbench." An example of the second area is the study of communication problems between information systems clients and systems designers. The development of modeling systems, decision support aids, or new ways of representing information exemplifies the third area.

UNIVERSITY OF MINNESOTA SCHOOL OF MANAGEMENT

Gordon B. Davis

The University of Minnesota's management information systems (MIS) program and research strategy were developed in an environment consisting of the university, the School of Management, and the business community in the Minneapolis-St. Paul metropolitan area. Work on MIS occurs in the school's MIS academic area and the Management Information Systems Research Center.

The University and Its Setting

The University of Minnesota was founded in 1862 as a land grant institution. It has five campuses, but the main campus, which includes the School of Management, is in Minneapolis and serves 47,383 students. The school is less than two miles from the center of Minneapolis and about ten miles from the center of St. Paul. Business in the Twin Cities area tends to be oriented to technology and knowledge-based activities rather than industrial processes or assembly lines. There is a strong computer industry component, with Control Data, major Univac facilities, and Cray, among others. The Twin Cities are headquarters for 3M, Honeywell, IDS, Pillsbury, General Mills, Cargill, and other large, well-known companies. Businesses are receptive to research and have strong local ties to the University of Minnesota.

The School

The School of Management offers an undergraduate degree in business, an M.B.A., an evening M.B.A., an M.A. in industrial relations, and a Ph.D. Graduate students may choose MIS as a major or concentration; there is no major for undergraduates. The school participates in a large evening extension division and has its own executive development program. It has made strategic decisions during the last five years to emphasize the M.B.A. and Ph.D. degrees and deemphasize the undergraduate program. The MIS area of concentration in the M.B.A. programs requires six MIS courses.

The first Ph.D.'s in MIS from Minnesota graduated in 1971. From 1971 to 1983 there have been 29 doctorates in business administration with MIS as their field. A number of students in other disciplines have taken MIS as a related field. The faculty in MIS recently decided to regularize the input of candidates to achieve a steady average output of five doctorates in MIS per year. The objective of the Ph.D. in MIS is to produce MIS scholars and researchers rather than consultants.

There are about 100 full-time faculty in the School of Management; 9 of these are MIS faculty: Gordon B. Davis, Gerardine L. DeSanctis, Gary W. Dickson, Gordon C. Everest, Thomas R. Hoffmann, John A. Lehman, Salvatore T. March, J. David Naumann, and James C. Wetherbe. Faculty members may cross area boundaries, and non-MIS faculty have helped develop the area and are active in current MIS activities.

The MIS Area

In 1968 three faculty members (Davis, Dickson, and Hoffmann) organized the MIS area; all three are still at Minnesota and still active in MIS. Management information systems was made an area within the Management Sciences Department. Departments in the School of Management are administrative conveniences, and a home was required for MIS. Its departmental location in management sciences added to a decision-making and modeling orientation; it also provided support for data-based research.

The area organizers enlisted a number of faculty members in other departments to participate in MIS teaching and research. During the first five years almost all the management sciences faculty taught the basic MIS course. Qualified personnel from local companies also assisted in teaching. Among the early MIS researchers were management science professors whose areas are not primarily MIS. For example, Carl Adams and Roger Schroeder did significant MIS research, and Norman Chervany was involved in the Minnesota MIS experiments. The MIS faculty have been major contributors to curriculum development in MIS and have written 22 textbooks for the field.

The Management Information Systems Research Center

The Management Information Systems Research Center (MISRC) was organized in 1968 to encourage research and provide continuing interaction with information systems practitioners. Gordon Davis was director for ten of the first twelve years, and Gary Dickson was director for two years. James Wetherbe has been director since 1980. The MISRC has received almost all its regular support from companies, which make yearly contributions as "associates" of the center. The center offers about 15 associate events per year featuring Minnesota faculty, outside speakers, and associates. It sponsors special interest groups of associates (and faculty and students) on topics of interest to associates, provides contacts for students doing research, and aids associate companies in contacts with students. The center publishes a working paper series in MIS and cosponsors the MIS Quarterly (with the Society for Information Management). It also provides some small research grants and administrative support for faculty with grants from other sources. Although initial associate contributions helped purchase computer resources for the MIS area, subsequent policy has been to use MISRC funds on support activities rather than computer equipment.

Associates of the center provide field sites for studies; they also suggest problems for research. Each year a planning exercise with the faculty and associates identifies key strategic thrusts for associate programs and research. The 1982-83 topics were MIS management, MIS planning, systems development, data base, distributed data processing, decision support systems, and organizational and behavioral issues of MIS.

Research Strategy

The type of research at Minnesota follows naturally from our view of the MIS area, which was formulated when the area and the research center were established. Gordon Davis articulated this view in a widely used 1974 definition: "A management information system . . . is an integrated, man/machine system for providing information to support the operations, management, and decision-making functions in an organization. The system utilizes computer hardware and software, manual procedures, management and decision models, and a data base."

This definition encompasses operational as well as decision support systems; the Minnesota faculty has included both in its domain from the beginning. Our view of MIS suggests the need for research on use of information for organizational functions, identification of information requirements, and design features of information-based support systems.

The identification of the MIS human-machine system focuses attention on the interface required. It suggests research on how best to present information, how to design computer systems to interact with humans, and how to design information systems to fit into the social fabric of organizations.

The information system as a support system should conform to the goals, culture, and organizational design of the host organization. This introduces the need for research on information systems planning and information systems organizational design. The information systems plan is implemented through applications using development methodologies and tools. This process causes organizational change and suggests the need for research in development and implementation processes and procedures.

The data base concept is consistent with our view of information as an organizational resource. This suggests research in data modeling and analytical models for translating logical data bases into efficient physical data bases.

This broad view of MIS defines the domain in which the Minnesota faculty and doctoral students have done research on topics such as the following:

1. Behavioral/experimental research on users, user interface, and use processes

2. Information requirements determination

3. Management of MIS, including planning

4. Applications development, including software engineering

5. Organizational and motivational issues

6. Data bases, especially tools and algorithms for selecting data structures

Current faculty and student research continues past emphases and includes increased activity in data modeling, expert systems, and computer graphics for the user interface.

Research Activities

The research methodology used in the Minnesota MIS dissertations reflects our implicit strategy of data-based, experimental, or field research. Forty-five percent of the dissertations were laboratory experiments, 38% were field studies or surveys, and 17% were simulations or models; all were data based.

The Minnesota faculty is somewhat nondirective in topic selection by doctoral students; however, we discourage topics for which there is inadequate faculty support. The faculty does not permit single case studies, systems development projects, or descriptions of systems, but comparative case studies are allowed. Insofar as possible, business personnel are elicited as experimental subjects for laboratory experiments.

The Minnesota Experiments

The eight doctoral dissertations labeled the "Minnesota experiments" (Norman Chervany, Gary Dickson, and James Senn, 1977) were laboratory experiments using classic methods for research in MIS. They were cumulative in their results and provided a base for many further studies by scholars elsewhere. The experiments focused on presentation of information and the effects of alternative presentations. A current research project on computer graphics is a continuation of this research.

Field Surveys

The close relationship of the MISRC and the information systems executives in the Twin Cities area has provided opportunities for field surveys of practice. In general, these have not reported on practice, but instead have tested various theories about practice. An example is a field survey of information systems practice to test a contingency theory.

Frameworks and Theories

Minnesota faculty members have developed a number of significant frameworks and theories. One of the first was the Gary Dickson's framework for information systems (1968). Gordon Davis's book Management Information Systems: Conceptual Foundations, Structure, and Development (1974) represents a comprehensive conceptual framework for MIS and a description of basic concepts underlying the design, development, and use of the systems. The Blake Ives, Scott Hamilton, and Gordon Davis research framework (1980) provides a taxonomy for research in the field. Gordon Everest has provided a framework and taxonomy for the data base area (1984). The James Wetherbe, Gordon Davis, and Brent Bowman three-stage model of MIS planning helps managers organize planning activities and select techniques or methods (1981).

Consistent with our tie to organizational behavior, a frequent Minnesota approach has been to formulate and test contingency theories. Examples are the David Naumann, Gordon Davis, and James McKeen contingency theory for selection of an applications development control strategy (1980), Gordon Davis's work on a contingency theory for information requirements analysis (1980), and Margrethe Olson's dissertation on MIS organization (1978). Field research has tested the contingency theories. A recent example is testing of the applications development strategy by David Naumann, James Wetherbe, and Milton Jenkins (1983).

Data Modeling and Data Base Design Tools

Some of the MIS faculty have been developing heuristics and design tools for data structures and data bases. The work of Dennis Severance, Salvatore March, and John Carlis illustrates this stream of research.

The Expertise Studies

The design of information support systems for various organizational functions is expected increasingly to incorporate expertise. The identification of expertise and the design of systems to perform like experts requires significant research. The typical research method is protocol analysis. Although there have not been enough Minnesota MIS studies in expertise to warrant a series label, one on systems analyst expertise and one in accounting/MIS on auditor expertise, with implications for information systems design, have been completed. Dissertations are in progress on data base design reasoning and strategic planning expertise.

NEW YORK UNIVERSITY
GRADUATE SCHOOL OF BUSINESS ADMINISTRATION

edited by Henry C. Lucas, Jr.

Background

The information systems (IS) strategy at New York University (NYU) is to conduct high-quality research and to make a significant impact on the curriculum of the Schools of Business. The Computer Applications and Information Systems Area is a separate academic department. Research efforts are coordinated through the Center for Research on Information Systems.

The University and Its Setting

New York University was found in 1831 and is one of the largest private universities in the United States. The undergraduate College of Business and Public Administration is located on the main NYU campus at Washington Square in New York City. The Graduate School of Business Administration is located in lower Manhattan near Wall Street.

New York City is the center of business and financial activities in the United States. Most companies' New York locations are extensively involved in information processing and services. The CAIS Area attempts to maintain close ties with the business community, and a number of firms are formally affiliated with our research center.

The Schools

The Schools of Business offer full-time degree programs and are unique in bringing the same high-quality programs to part-time students. There are about 180 full-time faculty in the schools. The Computer Applications and Information Systems (CAIS) Area currently has 14 full-time, tenure-track faculty members and 2 non-tenure-track faculty. Its teaching program includes bachelor's, master's, and Ph.D. degree programs. The schools also require an IS course for all nonmajors. At the undergraduate level it consists of about 70% hands-on computer work and 30% IS material. At the M.B.A. level the opposite percentages apply and the hands-on work is primarily with personal computers.

The Center for Research on Information Systems

Faculty members at the Center for Research on Information Systems are Gad Ariav, Jack Baroudi, James Clifford, Albert Croker, Vasant Dhar, Michael J. Ginzberg, Matthias Jarke, Kenneth C. Laudon, Henry C. Lucas, Jr., Margrethe H. Olson, Walter Reitman, Edward A. Stohr, Jon A. Turner, Myron Uretsky, Yannis Vassiliou, and Norman White. A common theme in all the research at the center is the implications of its results for management. Researchers attempt to draw conclusions from their work that will help managers improve the effectiveness of information processing and feel comfortable with their role. Through seminars, teaching programs, and publications aimed at managers, faculty members present key issues and recommendations in areas ranging from planning and control for information processing to systems analysis and design.

Research Strategy

Given the broad nature of the IS field and the presence of diverse areas of expertise, a natural strategy for the Center for Research on Information Systems is multidisciplinary research at the leading edge of information processing. Both the variety of faculty interests and the nature of the field make our applied research projects multidisciplinary.

Research Activities

The Center for Research on Information Systems has based its research program on three underlying disciplines:

Behavioral Science--including how organizations are structured and managed; the flow of information; individual perceptions; decision making and the behavior of individuals, groups, and organizations; and the use of information and systems.

Computer Science--especially data base design and formal systems for describing and representing knowledge, issues in the design and performance of hardware and software combinations, and development and integration of different aspects of technology.

Applied Mathematics--including approaches to optimization of decision problems, particularly those supported by computer-based applications, and optimization of aspects of IS and systems development.

The center has further focused its applied research projects in four areas: data bases, artificial intelligence and expert systems, implementation, and impact. Table 1 shows the relationship between our underlying disciplines and these research areas.

Table 1. *Applied Research and Underlying Disciplines*

Applied Research	*Behavioral Science*	*Computer Science*	*Applied Mathematics*
Data bases		X	X
Artificial Intelligence and Expert Systems	X	X	X
Implementation	X	X	
Impact	X	X	

Data Bases

The study of data base systems and their technology represents a point of intersection between the IS field and the traditional discipline of computer science. Data base applications may be found in operating systems, query processing, decision support, and artificial intelligence. Data base research provides guidelines for representing the required data in each of these areas.

1. A major objective of our expert system project is to explore the combined use of a data base management system and an expert system for a business application. The large body of facts usually required in business applications can be made available to the expert system through a commercial data base management system. In addition, the data base system itself can be used more intelligently and operated more efficiently if enhanced with expert systems technology.

We are also investigating the technical and theoretical problems of successful cooperation between data base and expert systems. A large relational data base system and a mathematical logic approach to expert systems are the research tools. The inherent similarities between the relational data base system and a mathematical logic approach to expert systems are the research tools. The inherent similarities between the relational model of data and and predicate logic should ease the task of coupling systems with substantial differences in basic philosophy and orientation.

2. The Advanced Language Project, currently in its final stages, is a multidisciplinary study comparing and contrasting a restricted natural query language with a structured language for retrieval from data bases. Researchers developed a data base application for alumni records in the business school, which became the focus of field and laboratory studies to evaluate the

two query languages, both of which process retrievals against the same relational data base system. The project draws on expertise in computer science, systems analysis and design, data base technology, and experimental and field research.

3. Once research effort is investigating techniques for organizing data to reflect their semantics accurately, that is, to specify the meanings of individual data items and the relationships among them.

A related project is considering how to maximize the number of users who can simultaneously and safely access the same data base; users must not interact with one another to produce incorrect results. This area of research, know as concurrency theory, has applications with both centralized and distributed data bases. By basing concurrency control techniques on the semantics of the data, it should be possible to increase the number of concurrent users of a data base.

4. The sense of time plays a central role in many management functions, yet it is rarely reflected in ways computer-based IS view these activities. A number of faculty members at the center are working to develop a basis for the explicit treatment of time in computerized IS and designing tools that address the unique temporal needs of these applications.

The effort is currently aimed at extending the generalized data base management systems that will support automatic generation of three-dimensional "data landscapes." The imaginary depth of the pictorial output corresponds to the time dimension, and retrieved events that happened earlier are shown further "inside." This project involves new options in interfacing with data bases and novel concepts for human-machine interaction, such as direct manipulation interfaces.

Artificial Intelligence and Expert Systems

Artificial intelligence techniques offer promise in three areas: expert or rule-based systems, natural languages, and expansion of decision support systems.

The center is currently engaged in a major project on expert systems, which consists of two parts: the interface of a large data base management system and an artificial intelligence language, and the development of a prototype business application. As described above under "Data Bases," various strategies for coupling the data base to the artificial intelligence language are under study. The completed interface will provide a tool for building expert systems.

We are currently evaluating the business application, but the leading candidate is a system for custom-tailoring life insurance policies. It would be prohibitively expensive to develop an individual policy for each customer using existing underwriting and actuarial personnel. However, an expert system that captured the knowledge of these professionals could develop unique policies. Such a system would need access to a large amount of data on individuals and insurance products as well as computational capabilities for actuarial analyses.

Implementation

Implementation research attempts to determine what factors and approaches are most likely to lead to successful systems. How should the analyst work with the user? What is the role of senior management in planning and controlling information processing?

1. A project is under way to develop a general model of system implementation and test it in a specific setting. We are attempting to synthesize the findings of a decade of research on implementation of IS and management science models into a unified model applicable to a wide range of systems and settings.

The system in the study supports the decisions of product planners, who have access to extensive company-maintained data bases and can create private files for analysis. There are some 600 users, though probably ten times that number could benefit from the system. An extension of the present study will focus on nonusers, to determine why they have not adopted the system.

2. Another center project is testing a model of the implementation process for software packages. The packages handle job accounting for small manufacturing firms and production planning for large firms. Our results should provide a better understanding of the implementation of this kind of software and guidelines for organizations contemplating its acquisition.

Impact

Managers and the information processing industry need to understand the impact of computers. The impact of forced use of a system is of great interest; it is also important to encourage use of voluntary computer applications. Related to impact research is the study of management control over information processing. How do firms take advantage of technology to gain a competitive edge? How should senior management evaluate information processing?

1. One area of our research is attempting to determine how jobs are changed when computer systems are used. The first question is whether extent of computer usage causes systematic differences among workers' jobs. The next issue is understanding how jobs are changed. A microtask model that relates performance and work life quality to the task environment of workers and to the form and degree of application system use explains changes in job content.

The first study of some 1,500 mortgage loan servicing workers in 800 mutual savings banks indicated that workers using computer systems more intensely have poorer jobs than workers using computers less. Job quality is related to the characteristics of the system. A second study of some 650 claims processing clerks in 30 Social Security offices showed an interrelationship between task and the application system.

A theory of software ergonomics has been developed to provide the conceptual basis for understanding how computer applications affect the task content of work. The model shows relationships between factors in systems design and their likely consequences. It leads to identification of strategies for division of labor between a computer application and its operators.

2. Computer equipment and communications capabilities make it possible to design new work environments. Another study seeks to evaluate the impact of work at home. What are its likely consequences for the employer and for the employee? How does an organization supervise and manage large numbers of individuals who infrequently come to a central location? The technology should make it possible to increase productivity and include a new skilled group of workers in the economy. The challenge is to create appropriate management techniques for organizing remote work.

The CAIS Area at NYU has assembled a faculty with diverse interests and expertise. The nature of the field allows members of this group to cooperate on various specific applied research projects relevant to today's organization. We hope, through this multidisciplinary approach to IS research, to make a major contribution to the state of the art.

UNIVERSITY OF PENNSYLVANIA
WHARTON SCHOOL

James C. Emery

The University

The University of Pennsylvania is a large private institution located in Philadelphia. It has a student body of over 22,000 and a faculty consisting of nearly 1,750 fully affiliated and 1,900 associated members. It offers a broad range of undergraduate, graduate, and professional educational programs and carries out one of the largest research programs of any university in the United States.

The School

The Wharton School was established in 1881; it was the first business school in the world. It enrolls about 2,200 undergraduate, 1,450 M.B.A., and 400 Ph.D. students. It has a very active research program and obtains more external research funding than any other business school. Its undergraduate program is generally regarded as the best of its kind, and its professional and graduate programs are ranked among the top handful in the country.

The Decision Sciences Department

In recognition of the growing importance of sophisticated information systems, the Decision Sciences Department was founded at the Wharton School in 1974. We felt that the field had progressed to the point that it could flourish as a separate academic department.

As viewed at Wharton, decision sciences consists of three underlying disciplines: information systems, quantitative methods, and decision analysis. Combining these disciplines into a single department would permit the close coordination and mutual support that will be increasingly necessary to develop comprehensive information systems to serve the decision-oriented as well as transaction-oriented functions of organizations.

Information systems deals with the physical means of processing information. It includes both transaction processing systems and decision support systems. Organizations' telecommunications infrastructures are also increasingly important parts of the field. Although the functional capabilities of computer hardware and systems software are not ignored, applications software is the dominant technical concern in our department. Other less technical issues also receive considerable attention; among these are the organizational, behavioral, and economic aspects of information system development in an organization.

Quantitative models play an important role in advanced information systems; therefore our department concerns itself with the mathematical methodologies involved in their development. Optimization models--with much attention to linear programming--are a principal focus. Simulation techniques and heuristic ("rules of thumb") methods to overcome the limitations of optimization models are also considered.

Most of the important problems organizations face involve a variety of goals that must be dealt with simultaneously. Public bodies must satisfy broad constituencies with multiple conflicting objectives; profit-making firms must consider not only short-term gain but also long-term growth, employee and customer satisfaction, and the social and economic environment in which their enterprises exist. Decision analysis considers the methodologies used to deal with these complex decision processes.

The Decision Sciences Department currently has a full-time faculty of 15, divided fairly evenly among full, associate, and assistant professors. The faculty consists of Stephanie Barrett, Colin Camerer, Michael Chang, Eric Clemons, Morris Cohen, James Emery, Marshall Fisher, John Hershey, E. Gerald Hurst, Paul Kleindorfer, Howard Kunreuther, James Laing, Lewis Miller, David Ness, and Ari Vepsalainen. Six other associated faculty--lecturers and visiting and adjunct professors--also contribute to its academic programs. The department offers undergraduate, M.B.A., and Ph.D. programs. There are currently 75 undergraduate majors, 35 M.B.A. majors, and 40 Ph.D. students in decision sciences.

Research Activities

The Decision Sciences Department is heavily committed to an active research program. A broad spectrum of research topics, reflecting the wide range of disciplinary interests in the department, has been investigated. The department currently receives over $500,000 of research support per year; in addition, considerable research is supported through general departmental funds. A representative list of current and recent research topics follows.

1. The Role of the Multifunctional Work Station in Support of Managerial, Professional, and Office Personnel--Among the issues considered are integration of functions, linking of heterogeneous equipment through a telecommunications network, and the behavioral effects of office automation.

2. Determination of Organizational Telecommunications Strategies--The design and implementation of an organization's network infrastructure is a crucial strategic issue. The network should provide a means to interconnect large and small computers, data bases, and specialized resources--not only within the organization's boundaries, but also with its customers, suppliers, government agencies, and others.

3. Design of the Human Interface in a Decision Support System--In a person-machine system, an effective link between the human decision maker and the computer system is critical. We must still learn a great deal about what constitutes an effective interface. Graphic display--including the use of icons to represent actions and entities--will almost certainly play an important role. Voice inputs and outputs are likely to provide a useful supplement to visual and tactile interfaces.

4. Expert Systems as Components of Decision Support Systems--As we seek ways to extend the usefulness of decision support systems, we will be constructing increasingly sophisticated decision procedures. Artificial intelligence techniques appear to offer an attractive approach for dealing with such complex problems as job shop scheduling and insurance claim processing.

5. Use of Fourth-Generation Implementation Tools--Development of applications software is perhaps the most serious barrier to the more rapid and effective implementation of advanced information systems. The conventional approach to systems design, in which complex systems are laboriously custom-tailored in a detailed procedural language, has created a tremendous bottleneck. Powerful nonprocedural tools, which show great promise in alleviating much of the time, cost, and inflexibility associated with that approach, are now being developed. They are likely to have a profound effect on the implementation and management of systems.

6. Representation of the Time Variable in Data Structures--The time dimension is a universal element in real-world events. An effective information system should permit a decision maker to reconstruct events at a specified moment in time to analyze decisions made on the basis of the information available at that time. Representing time in a way that permits such reconstruction presents a great technical challenge.

7. Optimum Vehicle Scheduling--The efficiency with which vehicle deliveries are scheduled has enormous economic consequences. In a number of industries, such deliveries constitute one of the largest components of cost. The size and complexity of the problem call for sophisticated mathematical and heuristic techniques.

8. Model Management Systems to Support Policy Analysis--Policy studies tend to be carried out by teams of analysts who develop a range of models that must eventually be integrated. Furthermore, these models undergo frequent revision

as learning takes place. Our research is developing methodologies and tools to facilitate working with computer models in such processes.

9. Operations Management of Temporarily Overloaded Queues-- Balancing the cost of providing capacity against the cost of waiting for service is one of the most difficult and important operational problems of management. Special cases are systems whose peak loads significantly exceed average demands. We are developing models to be used within a complex decision support system for scheduling aircraft transportation.

10. Flexible Manufacturing Systems--Recent development of robots, sophisticated materials-handling equipment, and more flexible production tools raises many fundamental issues for manufacturing firms. Basic strategies regarding matters such as product selection, delivery objectives, and pricing policies must be examined in light of the opportunities offered by new manufacturing technology.

11. Design of Logistics Systems--The design of a multilevel inventory system is an exceedingly complex problem with very large stakes. Investment in inventories, transportation and storage costs, and the level of service provided to customers all depend on the quality of stocking and ordering policies. This research aims to develop more effective ways to make these policy decisions.

12. Decision Making with Coalitions--In some situations decision-making authority is diffused among a number of coalitions having different objectives and points of view. Various legal and social barriers may restrict communication among members of these coalitions. Our purpose is to understand better the complex issues involved in such decision processes and to develop more effective strategies for dealing with them.

UNIVERSITY OF PITTSBURGH
GRADUATE SCHOOL OF BUSINESS

William R. King

The information systems (IS) program at the University of Pittsburgh has developed primarily in the Graduate School of Business. Other IS-related programs exist in the Graduate School of Library and Information Science and the Schools of Engineering and Health-related Professions at the university.

The University and Its Setting

The University of Pittsburgh is the largest educational institution in the region; it enrolled about 29,000 students in 1983. Its state-related character distinguishes it from both public and private institutions of higher learning. The school has a dual mission as well as two resource bases. The Graduate School of Business is housed in a new building on the university's main campus, about two miles from the "Golden Triangle," Pittsburgh's central business district. Pittsburgh is the third largest corporate-headquarters city in the nation; the proximity of sixteen Fortune 500 corporation headquarters and dozens of other large corporate facilities and financial institutions make the university a very desirable location for business research, education, and consulting.

The School

The Graduate School of Business, a long-established professional school within the university, offers the M.B.A. degree in three separate programs--full time, evening part time, and executive. The school has offered the Ph.D. in business since the 1930s. It also currently services undergraduate courses in a dual-major option in the School of Arts and Sciences; the University of Pittsburgh has not offered an undergraduate degree in business for about 25 years. Extensive executive development course offerings complement the School of Business's graduate degree programs.

The Information Systems Area

The information systems area was formalized in the Graduate School of Business by a working group of faculty in the late

1960s. Before that various faculty members had worked in the field more or less independently. The interest level was high and participation was extensive; faculty members with primary expertise in accounting, economics, behavioral science, and operations research, as well as those in computer systems, were involved. The area's current faculty members are Jacob G. Birnberg, John H. Grant, William R. King, Albert Lederer, Walter P. McGhee, Harry E. Pople, Jr., Dennis P. Slevin, Pandu R. Tadikamalla, and James T. C. Teng.

As a result of this interest and a concurrent redesign of the Ph.D. program, a top-down strategy to infuse the IS area into the school was adopted. An IS major for the Ph.D. program was developed and immediately began to attract high-quality students, who contributed to faculty research activities. Because Ph.D. students are supported solely as research assistants rather than teaching assistants in the School, this was both a costly and a highly effective strategy. The research output in IS and related areas increased dramatically beginning in the early 1970s, and a continuing flow of IS researchers has gone from our Ph.D. program to faculty positions at other universities and senior positions in industry.

The IS area began to be substantially strengthened in the M.B.A. program in the mid-1970s. The Graduate School of Business has developed its own microcomputer laboratory to complement the university's mainframe access. Course work utilizing both the mainframe and microcomputers is required of all M.B.A. students. Required computer work is also widespread in M.B.A. courses in statistics, accounting, finance, operations management, and other areas.

Thus, about 15 years after the beginning of formal activities in the IS area, the School has achieved considerable integration of the field into its principal graduate degree programs, continuous research funding, identification as one of a few schools that consistently produce high-quality Ph.D.'s in the field, and international visibility through major research conferences on implementation and the designation of a faculty member as senior editor of the field's major journal, the *MIS Quarterly*.

Research Strategy

Our current research objectives focus on the area in which faculty and students have knowledge and comparative advantage: the organization-IS interface. Joint faculty-student research enhances both the state of knowledge and the researchers' rate of learning. Some of our research is supported by the school from undesignated contributions, some by private industry, and some by the federal government. This diversity reflects both our plan and the current funding environment.

Research Activities

We are currently pursuing our research objectives along three primary related lines: information as an organizational resource, implementation of IS, and innovative decision support systems.

Information as an Organizational Resource

Research on information as an organizational resource, primarily under the guidance of William R. King, seeks to view information and IS in terms of their role in the organization. In contrast to much past research on IS, this stream does not view computer systems as an innovation whose impact on the organization need be of greatest concern. Rather, it sees them as integral elements of the organization's makeup, which must be effectively managed to aid in the accomplishment of organizational objectives.

A data base is being established to support this research stream. The project will collect data from a variety of firms on a continuing basis to permit longitudinal analyses. Student dissertation research is already under way, using the initial data from this project.

Implementation of IS

The program of research on implementation of IS, under the guidance of Dennis P. Slevin, has focused on the issues relating to successful implementation of models and systems in organizations. Much of the exploding body of research in the implementation area in the 1970s was related to two major research conferences held at the University of Pittsburgh.

This program continues to accumulate data from a wide variety of sources for further development of an implementation profile. This instrument defines crucial dimensions of implementation success and provides a vehicle for collecting normative data on successful and unsuccessful projects. So far norms have been collected for success and failure scores on over 140 projects.

Innovative Decision Support Systems

Research on decision support systems, guided primarily by Harry E. Pople, Jr., relates to the development of innovative systems to support decision making.

The CADUCEUS (originally INTERNIST) project, funded by the National Institutes of Health, has been under way since 1974; funding for an earlier system was obtained in 1972. The system has as its basis the development of models of clinical decision making in internal medicine. This study has led to what are generally recognized to be the most comprehensive, most successful computer-based diagnostic programs in existence. In recent years various researchers have been investigating the applicability of such models of diagnostic reasoning in a variety of management decision contexts. Systems have also been developed by other faculty on a prototype basis to support strategic decision making in competitive contexts.

The Institute for Audit Decision Support has recently been established to facilitate application of artificial intelligence to the design and implementation of a knowledge-based decision support system for auditors. Such a system will aid in all phases of an audit: initial audit planning, risk analysis, collection and evaluation of audit evidence, and expression of an opinion.

PURDUE UNIVERSITY
KRANNERT GRADUATE SCHOOL OF MANAGEMENT

Andrew B. Whinston

The University and Its Setting

Purdue University is a major state-supported institution in the Midwest with a strong orientation to science and engineering. At the graduate level Purdue has a commitment to professional education and basic research in many areas, with particular distinction in engineering. The university is fundamentally concerned about its contribution to the economy of the state and the nation.

Indiana, as other midwestern states, has relied on a traditional economic base of agriculture and smokestack industries. Major problems confronting these industries and the recent recession have led to efforts at diversification into high-technology industries. Both the state government and Purdue administration are exploring ways to facilitate the creation of new enterprises to contribute to the growth of a high-technology business center.

The School

The goals of the Krannert School of Management reflect those of Purdue. Emphasis is on teaching, research, and service. Topics in management information systems (MIS) constitute an important part of the curriculum at all levels: undergraduate, master's, and doctoral. At the undergraduate level the Krannert School has a concentration in MIS that currently enrolls about 800 students. This provides understanding of the role and potential of computer technology in assisting the management function. An MIS specialization at the master's level permits students with undergraduate degrees in science and engineering to pursue training in management with special emphasis on information systems. Graduates of these programs have positions in areas including consulting, computing center administration, systems development, marketing, and electronic data processing auditing.

Each year approximately four students are admitted to the doctoral program in MIS. Typically, they have the equivalent of a master's degree in computer science. Their course work involves fundamental management areas, such as accounting, finance, quantitative methods, and economics. In addition, advanced courses related to their interests are taken from a variety of Purdue's schools and departments, including management, engineering, computer science, linguistics, and psychology. The majority of Ph.D. degree recipients have joined the management/business school faculties of numerous universities, including Purdue, Harvard, the University of Illinois (at Champaign), New Mexico State, Northwestern, Notre Dame, Ohio State, the University of Rochester, the University of Florida, and the University of Wisconsin.

The Management Information Research Center

The Management Information Research Center (MIRC) within the Krannert School fosters a wide range of basic and applied research in the MIS field. This research is conducted by Krannert faculty who specialize in MIS and by MIS doctoral students under faculty guidance. Doctoral students receive financial support from MIRC. The center's research work has been funded by contributions from the computer industry (for instance, from IBM) and by grants from various agencies, including the National Science Foundation, the Army Research Office, and the Office of Water Research and Technology.

The director of MIRC is Andrew B. Whinston. Other Krannert faculty who participate heavily in the center include Robert H. Bonczek, Clyde W. Holsapple, and Robert Minch.

Results of MIRC research are presented in a variety of forums, including scholarly journals, books, national and international conferences, and the Krannert Institute Papers. Principal areas of research have included data base management, language processing, office automation, decision support systems, and the impacts of these on various functional areas of management. Specific research topics are selected by the faculty and doctoral students. For the most part, MIRC research work has a technical, rather than behavioral, orientation.

Research Strategy

Research activities at Krannert are geared toward facilitating current trends, which are radically shifting the potential supply and demand for computer resources to end users. Table 1 outlines categories of study on human-computer decision making. Each can be examined from a theoretical or applied angle and explored in terms of tools or the results of using those tools.

The results of a successful research strategy will enhance human capabilities, allowing individual or group interaction with a computer to improve human activities or decisions. The starting points for research should be the special cases of individual decision making and computer processing in a noninteractive environment. Most contemporary computer processing is

Table 1. *Human-Computer Decision Making*

	No Human	*Single User*	*Group*	*Organization*
No Computer		Decision Theory Management Science Psychology	Social Choice Theory	Organization Theory
One Computer	Computer Science Batch Processing Artificial Intelligence	Decision Support System	Automated Consensus	Centralized Data Processing
Computer Network	Distributed Processing Processing	DSS with More Extensive Computer Support	Office Automation	Computer-augmented Cooperative Problem-solving Systems

noninteractive, executing a program based on a fixed set of procedures, steps, or enhancements provided by artificial intelligence approaches.

The first step beyond these two cases is into the realm of human-computer interactive systems. The framework for decision support systems has been oriented to an individual having a productive interaction with a computer system. Many issues still remain to be resolved. However, the principal need is for a better understanding of the human decision process in a computer-assisted environment. We must learn how to engineer more effective decision support systems. Related issues are tools to build such systems that facilitate cost-effective software development.

A good deal of the current research in decision support systems is focused on how to design systems that are responsive to area needs. The methodology is based on testing a hypothesis, which is generally derived from a case study of one or several organizations, against empirical data. Research by this approach is limited to providing guidelines for systems that operate in relative isolation. Results applicable to organizational environments must await a theory that explains cooperative computer-augmented problem solving.

Research Activities

Decision Support Systems

Research on MIS at Krannert started around 1968 with the arrival of Jay Nunamaker. His initial work, in collaboration with

Andrew Whinston, was on the integration of models and data bases to support the decision-making process in analyzing water pollution problems. Application of these ideas to specific pollution problems in Indiana was carried out in the early 1970s. This research led to what are now referred to as decision support systems. In their thesis research at Purdue, Robert Bonczek and Clyde Holsapple extended and developed many new concepts in this area. Their work was summarized in the book Foundations of Decision Support Systems (1981).

Data Base Management Systems Software

An important component of decision support systems is knowledge management through data base management systems software. Research by former students Robert Bonczek, Clyde Holsapple, and Michael Gagle, in collaboration with Andrew Whinston, extended some of the earlier approaches to this problem, including many-to-many relationships, query and mapping languages, and various restructuring and performance capabilities. Some of these ideas were later implemented in commercial systems developed by Micro Data Base Systems.

Accounting Information Systems

Work on accounting IS began in the early 1970s with joint research by Claude Colantoni, Rene Manes, Arthur Lieberman, and Andrew Whinston to explore what form accounting systems could take in a computer environment. Proposals revolved around a variety of data base techniques. James Cash, in his thesis, explored the implications of auditing in an integrated office of the future with a language called TICOM. Several doctoral students, including James Gerlach and R. Preston McAfee, pursued this work to develop TICOM II. A forthcoming book by Andrew Bailey, James Gerlach, and Andrew Whinston summarizes this area of research. Gregory Parsons's dissertation studied the development of semantics and syntax of accounting so that an accounting information system could support requests stated in natural English.

The Factory of the Future

Developments in computer hardware and software make it possible to rethink the way manufacturing takes place. In the "factory of the future" computers will be able to create flexible manufacturing systems capable of integrating efficient standard machine tools into configurations to produce limited quantities of a greater variety of products over a short duration.

Research efforts have focused on developing advanced information systems to manage the flexible manufacturing systems. Artificial intelligence techniques based on mechanized deductive reasoning could handle conflict resolution, sequencing, and resource allocation problems. The language of first-order logic, modified to reflect the concept of time and permit reasoning about changes through time, was used to model the manufacturing environment. Representation and control techniques for a manufacturing system were outlined. More recent research has worked to integrate the manufacturing and office models and analyze the entire organization structure.

CONCLUSION TO PART V

JAMES L. McKENNEY

Several themes recurred in the discussions of research strategy; they can be organized under three topics: programmatic issues of business school research, critique of the research agendas, and information system (IS) management in the 1980s and its implications for research.

Programmatic Issues

To the surprise of many managers at the colloquium, business school research--particularly in emerging fields such as IS--is an entrepreneurial activity with few bounds on subject and many resource limitations. All the successful IS research programs grew from one or two individuals' efforts to forge an intellectual niche and develop the resources necessary to grow. Growth is often measured by publication of useful or significant concepts, that is, intellectual capital formation. Able individuals must be recruited and guided through the promotion process, which requires funding for faculty members' research time and for research expenses. Faculty must be released from teaching requirements, and doctoral students need support while they are trained in doing research. Further, research efforts must be maintained over several years, during which faculty also fulfill demanding teaching schedules.

The successful IS research programs have been quite innovative in growing from a base of zero to their present status. All choose topics and pursue activities that reflect the interests of their faculties and, at times, their funding sources. Most have ebbs and flows of doctoral students, which change their capacities, although most are now involving master's students to expand their student bases. Development of multiple funding sources is key to program growth. For example, Gordon Davis and Gary Dickson at the University of Minnesota have built a strong Minneapolis business-based support group, which funds research in return for involvement in seminars and the school's ongoing work. John Rockart and Michael Scott Morton at MIT have gathered a closed group of large corporate sponsors from across the country who participate in research seminars and act as subjects of research. Henry Lucas and Myron Uretsky at NYU have developed a broad federal, corporate, and foundation portfolio of multiyear funding support.

Choices of research topics respond to several influences. Ephraim McLean noted that a goal at UCLA is to make doctoral research more productive and encourage students' intellectual leadership. Doctoral students' interests often follow the research themes of senior faculty, which in turn are akin to the inclinations of the school. Eugene Webb pointed out that this is consistent with findings in the sociology of innovation--innovation depends on independent actors who reflect the traditions and influence of their institutions. Even the programs of schools pursuing focused research evidence more the interests of senior faculty than a clear choice of program; they may be more successful in controlling dispersion than in encouraging variety.

All research programs are concerned with meeting accepted publication standards so they can disseminate their results. This requires that research be executed to yield publishable outputs.

Another constraint on research is the university promotion process. Senior faculty must assess junior faculties' qualifications for tenure mainly on quality of mind and potential to contribute to knowledge. This judgment is traditionally based on independent efforts documented by publications. A "good" track record is four to five articles in journals that have a qualified academic review process and a book, which must be produced in four to eight years. The time required to find one's way in an institution, formulate a research design, and execute it through publication reduces actual research and writing time to three or four years. Teaching and administrative assignments also exert time pressures. Thus, the research goals of younger, more creative faculty must be creditable and realizable in a short time span. This inhibits much-needed multidisciplinary and longitudinal research in IS.

The heritage of IS further confounds research by biasing its substance. Most IS groups started as subgroups of management science (MS) departments, which were the largest users of IS and therefore the most knowledgeable about it. The MS groups themselves were relative newcomers to business schools--they developed between 1955 and 1960--and therefore were not established power bases. As IS grew, MS began to decline, but MS had already secured a majority of the tenure slots in the department. To gain the few tenured positions available, IS researchers often tended to produce algorithmic studies, irrelevant to IS but publishable. Unfortunately, as William King, editor of MIS Quarterly, noted, this tendency continues.

A final problem in establishing a productive IS research tradition has been the field's evolution. In the 1960s IS teaching tended to focus first on programming and then on systems analysis. It was heavily data processing oriented--how to make problems acceptable to a machine. Textbooks and other teaching materials emphasized descriptions of programming and hardware as they tried to bring light to the computer illiterate. This resulted in an unfortunate image. Because the substance of the field was unintelligible to other faculty, IS was not considered essential to the education of a manager. It was stereotyped as a specialists' domain--like those of accountants or management scientists--which might warrant a few courses, but should be isolated from the main M.B.A. curriculum.

During our evolution from data processing to management information systems to information services, our research at times reinforced this old image, particularly in early implementation studies and work on cognitive style. We labeled individuals as systems knowledgeable (us) or business knowledgeable (them) and documented the communication gulf between the two. Further, in retrospect, it is clear that our attempts to reach top management with visions of total information systems were ill timed and poorly received in the real world.

Subsequently, we tried to document the differences between theory and practice in order to improve both. These efforts often generated field-oriented social science-based research, which drew IS researchers into multidisciplinary teams and in some cases diluted an already vaguely defined area. So by the mid-1970s IS groups were often isolated clusters of specialists still searching for an identity. However, the new multidisciplinary tradition drew on a broader range of specialists, who now represent a variety of disciplines. Lately, as the economics and reliability of systems have changed, IS has made real progress toward becoming a viable business school subject. This is apparent in the research strategy statements included here.

Critique of the Research Agendas

The colloquium discussions' critique of the research agendas in the business schools' strategy statements spent much more time on new opportunities than on analysis of proposed projects. Participants noted that too many resources were being devoted to the fairly narrow area of decision support systems. This research was considered symptomatic of academicians' fascination with the use of technology rather than the management of its use. Management science analyses were also discussed as examples of limited, narrow research versus the broader, action-oriented work that is necessary to solve today's problems.

The topic of relevance wove in and out of several discussions. The group agreed that efforts to solve immediate, pragmatic management problems and attempts to generate organizing concepts that will facilitate improved systems design and management over time are both needed. The question of balance between the two led into a discussion of the differences between research and consulting. Research is more general and should have a broader scope; consulting is shorter in duration and focuses on specific problems. Blurring between the two can develop when institutions work with their funding sponsors to choose research problems. Participants supported this approach if the problems were general and were pursued at multiple research sites. Confusion can also arise when consulting relations grow into research projects because they offer good examples of general problems and are accessible to the researchers. The fuzzy line between research and consulting assignments as appropriate sources for case data reflects the state of the art and the limited number of qualified IS researchers.

Many practitioners voiced concern that the research being done is too computer science oriented and not sufficiently focused on management. In part this was because of its fragmented publication and rigor but also because of the nature of the problems studied. Strong pleas were made for more study of the management rather than the design or use of technology. The knowledge base of the latter is already growing much faster than responsible managers can absorb it. More comparative longitudinal studies of complicated situations were also solicited.

The strategy statements raised the issues of limited funding for faculty support and up-to-date hardware and software in most institutions. This is a particularly troublesome problem because the management issues that business schools study change with new technologies, particularly on-line fourth-generation programming languages and new data structures. One potentially valuable form of university-business cooperation could be joint use of the newer systems or donations of systems by nonhardware suppliers.

There was consensus that funding sources, especially the government, influence the topics under study and at times the methodology used in sponsored research. The large amount of research funding by major computer suppliers aroused particular concern.

The magnitude of research opportunities and the scarcity of qualified individuals to pursue them was another repeated discussion topic. Many researchers are drawn away from the slowly changing university environment into the dramatically growing practitioners' milieu. Business schools might bridge the gap between themselves and the real world by developing new business-university programs to increase managers' participation as researchers and by providing sophisticated working environments that would allow academicians to understand current issues better. Extending the Center for Information Systems Research of MIT or the Management Information Systems Research Center at the University of Minnesota to other institutions and developing nationwide cooperative programs are other possible solutions.

The following list notes the more prominent research opportunities raised in the colloquium discussions.

1. Analysis of the systems and management differences between computer and communications systems

2. Explorations of how the new end user and network systems can be employed to manage IS resources more effectively

3. Comprehensive investigations of the impact of end user computing on individuals, work groups, and organizations

4. A descriptive study to outline the boundaries of systems in business functional terms

5. Research on the quality of work life in all its dimensions
    - More versus less humaneness
    - Freedom versus control
    - Flexibility versus standardization
    - Adaptability versus rigidity

6. Investigations of unplanned or secondary effects of new system implementations

7. Examinations of the broader societal impacts of information technology
    - Unemployment
    - Changing job characteristics
    - Educational opportunities and needs

8. Analysis of the effects of service industry capitalization

9. Definition of the issues involved in managing simultaneous evolution of many innovations

10. Projections of future possibilities in organizational design

11. Development of possible office applications of computer-aided design and manufacturing

12. A multidisciplinary project on human resource management through better use of systems

13. An examination of management of the diffusion of IS technology

14. An epistemological study to define the scope of IS managers' problems

15. Generation of a technological forecasting methodology that encompasses the social system as well as the technology

Current IS Management and Its Implications for Research

A theme that wove in and out of the discussions was the enormity of the change occurring in organizations' use of IS. Richard Nolan called this the "age of discontinuity," in which it is difficult, if not impossible, to extrapolate from past practice into the future. Existing concepts and procedures cannot adequately deal with the explosive growth of end user computing, local area networks, computer-aided design and manufacturing, and similar IS innovations; and new product introduction will be increased by the deregulation of AT&T. New paradigms, methodologies, and means of doing research--in short, a massive shift in focus--are required to address the realities of the day. This issue was raised primarily by managers and consultants, but academicians enthusiastically concurred with them. Suggestions for how research efforts could help managers cope covered a broad range, including use of universities as social-technological laboratories, new approaches to business-university cooperation on longitudinal studies, and a national institute for information systems.

The concept of the university as a comprehensive laboratory came up in a discussion of our need to understand the gestalt of new IS uses' interaction with the social system. Charles Kriebel described the present effort to initiate such a study at Carnegie-Mellon, where all students are being given personal computers. A project team that includes students is designing system use to provide comparative data on social impacts and evolution of the system over the next four years. More experiments of this kind were encouraged.

The need for longitudinal studies generated several suggested approaches to joint university-business research. These included projects in which both parties are active clinicians, studies in which the firm is the laboratory, and more traditional long-term corporate sponsorship of research on particular topics. In-depth examinations of single firms for extended periods and comparative analyses of divisions within a firm, an industry, and a community were among the proposed formats for descriptive studies. Overall goals would be to understand the unforeseen effects of IS technology and to document the fundamental changes as opposed to the superficial impacts, of new tools on the individual and on organizational social systems. A complementary objective would be to investigate the impact of IS on quality of work life to understand better the social-technological influences on the individual at work. This line of research would aim to influence systems design to modulate the harsh effects of technology and build on its positive aspects.

A national institute for information systems was also suggested. Such a body would bring a coalition of universities and practitioners together to raise national policy issues and manage an independent research program. It might also provide needed societal leadership, currently lacking in existing groups such as the Association for Computing Machinery and the Society for Management Information Systems. A national institute, free of the constraints that businesses and universities place on large research projects, could fulfill the demand for multidisciplinary research and address the perceived magnitude of ignorance about IS. The existing Conference on Information Systems planning committee, a loose coalition of most practicing IS researchers, could expand to include interested business partners. Schools that have active joint university-business research programs might organize a research planning effort to generate the basis of a national institute and start the movement. The notion was appealing, but the organizational effort it would require makes short-run implementation unlikely.

The concept of vision, first raised by Thomas Gerrity and later elaborated by Irwin Sitkin, captured a good deal of attention. Events are moving with bewildering speed, yet managers must make decisions that will probably have long-range effects. There is precious little time for planning, let alone careful appraisal of an uncertain future. A description of a likely future information system, including how future managers would function, how firms would operate, and what impact this would have on the social fabric could help IS managers make more effective decisions. Perhaps to provide adequate detail for operational understanding, the system described should be a general model of an industry, such as insurance. This model could be built in several ways: through a series of Delphi-type discussions among a diverse knowledgeable group, through scenarios of development over the next few years for a few companies, or through an ongoing chain-letter effort with occasional review meetings. It seems time for one or more operational versions of Leavitt and Whisler's 1958 article.

The discussion of vision emphasized that the orientation of IS is shifting from management of systems to management of technology transfer. Experience in studying the management of systems implementation was seen as a base for considering the management of change brought by new technology. The recent multitude of new systems forms is expanding the realm of systems technology management, which--in product life cycle terms--includes a mature technology in large-scale data processing, a growing technology in communications, and an innovative technology in end user computing.

The consultants and managers present pointed out that benefits are more likely to come from learning how to transfer the lessons of successful implementations to different environments than from learning how to build and manage systems.

Practitioners know how to do the latter, but they need help with the former. Researchers must build on concepts of systems management to develop an improved scheme for managing the diffusion of IS technology.

The interesting and useful manager-academician dialogue on research generated a better understanding of the role and potential of IS research. Business colleagues gained a broader sense of how they could assist research; in addition to providing funding, they could facilitate studies in their firms, critique research, and suggest relevant topics. The academicians had a few moments of elation over the broad need for their ideas and skills, but these were followed by a sobering reflection on the lack of capacity to meet the demand. However, the recommendations for paradigm development and longitudinal studies stimulated a great deal of interest and discussion. Often these included specific needs with general applicability, such as an insurance executive's desire for a computer-aided design system to perform office design.

Closing Comment

The issue of how to manage a more coherent IS research program was never addressed directly, but the discussions did lead to a better understanding of both its complexities and its opportunities. Foundations for a movement toward more judicious use of resources exist in the Arizona, Harvard, MIT, Minnesota, and NYU programs. Funding will clearly influence the nature of research in the immediate future. Perhaps publication of the papers and business school strategy statements in this volume will stimulate development of more purposeful research strategies that fill market niches of pure ignorance rather than pursuing a few overworked lodes. This colloquium volume is one attempt to encourage more coherence in the field by informing decision makers about what is going on and what could be done.

Most participants and the steering committee were satisfied with the colloquium discussions. Several business representatives encouraged follow-up conferences to continue the dialogue. The academicians benefited from relevant critiques and the number of positive suggestions generated. Candor seemed to dominate. The size of the colloquium and a genuine level of interest facilitated exchange. There is a broad and growing concern about quality research in IS. This gathering focused the effort and perhaps influenced research priorities. It demonstrated to the participants the value of intellectual discussion. The future will prove whether it had a broader impact.

APPENDIX

COLLOQUIUM PARTICIPANTS

Professor Brandt R. Allen
University of Virginia

Professor Robert L. Ashenhurst
University of Chicago

Mr. Vincent P. Barabba
Eastman Kodak Company

Professor Martin L. Bariff
Illinois Institute of Technology

Mr. Gordon Bell
Digital Equipment Corporation

Professor Izak Benbasat
University of British Columbia

Mr. Robert I. Benjamin
Xerox Corporation

Mr. David J. Blackwell
Massachusetts Mutual Life Insurance Company

Mr. Richard G. Canning
Canning Publications, Inc.

Professor J. Daniel Couger
University of Colorado

Mr. Albert B. Crawford, Jr.
Digital Equipment Corporation

Mr. Thomas F. Davenport, Jr.
International Business Machines Corporation

Professor Gordon B. Davis
University of Minnesota

Mr. John di Targiani
Gillette Company

Professor Gary W. Dickson
University of Minnesota

Professor Neil M. Duffy
University of Witwatersrand

Professor James C. Emery
University of Pennsylvania

Dr. Thomas P. Gerrity
Index Systems Inc.

Professor Michael J. Ginzberg
New York University

Professor John C. Henderson
Florida State University

Mr. Alan Holroyde
Wells Fargo Bank

Professor William R. King
University of Pittsburgh

Professor Rob Kling
University of California, Irvine

Professor Benn Konsynski
University of Arizona

Professor Charles H. Kriebel
Carnegie-Mellon University

Professor Edward E. Lawler III
University of Southern California

Professor Henry C. Lucas, Jr.
New York University

Professor F. Warren McFarlan
Harvard Graduate School of Business Administration

Professor James L. McKenney
Harvard Graduate School of Business Administration

Professor Ephraim R. McLean
University of California, Los Angeles

Professor Richard O. Mason
University of Arizona

Professor Alan G. Merten
University of Michigan

Professor Allan M. Mohrman, Jr.
University of Southern California

Dr. Richard L. Nolan
Nolan, Norton & Company

Professor Jay F. Nunamaker
University of Arizona

Professor Margrethe H. Olson
New York University

Mr. James Paisley
Deloitte Haskins & Sells

Dr. Thomas J. Peters
Palo Alto Consulting Center

Mr. Joseph M. Quigley
Continental Group, Inc.

Mr. Carl H. Reynolds
Hughes Aircraft Company

Professor John F. Rockart
Massachusetts Institute of Technology

Professor Everett M. Rogers
Stanford University

Mr. Edward A. Schefer
General Foods Corporation

Mr. James Scott
Procter & Gamble Company

Professor Michael S. Scott Morton
Massachusetts Institute of Technology

Ms. Naomi O. Seligman
Research Board, Inc.

Professor Dennis G. Severance
University of Michigan

Mr. Guerdon Sines
Missouri Pacific Railroad

Mr. Irwin J. Sitkin
Aetna Life & Casualty Company

Professor Ralph H. Sprague, Jr.
University of Hawaii

Professor E. Burton Swanson
University of California, Los Angeles

Mr. William Synnott
First National Bank of Boston

Professor Eugene J. Webb
Stanford University

Professor Karl E. Weick
Cornell University

Professor Andrew B. Whinston
Purdue University

Mr. Frederic G. Withington
Arthur D. Little

Ms. Irma M. Wyman
Honeywell, Inc.

Professor Robert W. Zmud
University of North Carolina, Chapel Hill

NOTES ON CONTRIBUTORS

ROBERT L. ASHENHURST is professor of applied mathematics at the Graduate School of Business of the University of Chicago, where he has been a member of the faculty since 1957. He is chairman of the editorial committee of the Association for Computing Machinery and member at large of the association's council. He was editor in chief of the *Communications of ACM* from 1973 to 1983. He edited the National Science Foundation committee report on graduate professional programs in information systems. His current areas of research are requirement specification methodologies, data and information models, and systems configurations.

IZAK BENBASAT is associate professor of accounting and management information systems at the University of British Columbia Faculty of Commerce and Business Administration, where he has taught since 1974. He is associate editor for theory and research of *MIS Quarterly*. His areas of research include decision theory, the impact of cognitive style and personality on information system design, data base management systems for small businesses, and human-computer interaction.

J. DANIEL COUGER is distinguished professor of computer and management science at the University of Colorado College of Business Administration, where he has taught since 1965. He was previously employed in industry. He is coeditor of the Wiley Series on Business Data Processing, editor of the *Computing Newsletter for Schools of Business*, and a columnist for *Computerworld*. He has been secretary and executive council member of the Society for Management Information Systems, a consultant to universities and major corporations, and a frequent national and international lecturer.

ALBERT B. CRAWFORD, JR., is corporate manager for information services at Digital Equipment Corporation, where he has worked in operations research, communications and information processing systems design and installation, program and general management, and corporate management capacities. He has also been a professional instructor at American University.

GORDON B. DAVIS is Honeywell Professor of Management Information Systems in the School of Management at the University of Minnesota. A pioneer in management information systems, he participated in building Minnesota's MIS program and establishing its Management Information Systems Research Center. The most recent of his 16 books in the field is the second edition, with Margrethe Olson, of *Management Information Systems: Conceptual Foundations, Structure, and Development* (McGraw-Hill, 1984). His research interests are MIS conceptual foundations, MIS planning, information requirements determination, audit and control of information systems, and management of knowledge work.

EDWARD E. LAWLER III is professor of research and director of the Center for Effective Organizations at the University of Southern California Graduate School of Business Administration, where he has taught since 1978. He is also visiting scientist at the Human Affairs Research Centers of the Battelle Memorial Institute and a member of the editorial boards of five journals on organizational behavior and applied psychology. His books include *Managing Creation* (Wiley-Interscience, 1983), *Assessing Organizational Change* (Wiley-Interscience, 1983), *Pay and Organization Development* (Addison-Wesley, 1981), *Organizational Assessment* (Wiley, 1980), and *Managing Organizational Behavior* (Little, Brown, 1979).

F. WARREN McFARLAN is professor of business administration at the Harvard Business School, where he has been a member of the faculty since 1964. His most recent book, with James L. McKenney, is *Corporate Information Systems Management: The Issues Facing Senior Executives* (Irwin, 1983). His current area of research is the use of information systems technology for competitive advantage.

JAMES L. McKENNEY is professor of business administration at the Harvard Business School, where he has been a member of the faculty since 1960. His most recent book, with Warren McFarlan, is *Corporate Information Systems Management: The Issues Facing Senior Executives* (Irwin, 1983). His current areas of research are the management impact of terminal-oriented communications and managing the implementation of distributed systems.

RICHARD O. MASON is professor of management information systems at the University of Arizona College of Business and Public Administration, where he has taught since 1982. He is a member of the editorial board of five journals in management and in information systems and is coeditor of the Jossey-Bass Series on Organization and Management. He is coauthor of the award-winning

The 1980 Census: Policymaking Amid Turbulence (Lexington, 1983), Strategic Management and Business Policy (Addison-Wesley, 1982), Challenging Strategic Planning Assumptions (Wiley, 1981), Creating a Dialectical Social Science (Reidel, 1981), and Measurement for Management Decision (Addison-Wesley, 1981). His current areas of research include strategy and information systems, the history of information systems, and social and ethical implications of information systems.

ALLAN M. MOHRMAN, JR., is research scientist at the Center for Effective Organizations at the University of Southern California Graduate School of Business Administration, with which he has been associated since 1978. He has been a consultant to both public- and private-sector organizations, including the Columbus, Ohio, municipal government; General Electric; and TRW. His research interests are human resource management systems, organization development and design, and social action models for organizations.

RICHARD L. NOLAN is chairman and cofounder of Nolan, Norton & Company, a leading international organization of counselors to management focusing on effective management of computer-based technologies. The author of seven books and more than 100 published articles on computer management, he consults with organizations on the use of computers for competitive advantage. He is originator of the Stages Theory for analyzing computer growth, which he researched and developed while an associate professor at Harvard Business School from 1969 to 1977.

CARL H. REYNOLDS is staff vice president of communications and data processing for Hughes Aircraft Company in Los Angeles. Before joining Hughes in 1971, he held several management positions in the computer and software industry. He is also on the board of directors of Boole and Babbage and the advisory board of Datamation.

JOHN F. ROCKART is director of the Center for Information Systems Research and senior lecturer of management science at the Sloan School of Management of the Massachusetts Institute of Technology, where he has taught and conducted research on management planning and control systems and the use of computer-based information systems since 1966. His most recent research interests are the critical success factors concept, top managerial information use, and the management of end-user computing. He is coauthor, with Michael S. Scott Morton, of Computers and the Learning Process (McGraw-Hill, 1975).

EVERETT M. ROGERS is Janet M. Peck Professor of International Communication at the Institute for Communication Research of Stanford University, where he has taught since 1975. He is author of Diffusion of Innovations (Free Press, 1983) and coauthor, with Judith Larsen, of Silicon Valley Fever: Growth of High-Technology Culture (Basic Books, 1984). He specializes in studying the diffusion of innovations and the social impacts of the new information technologies.

MICHAEL S. SCOTT MORTON is professor of management at the Sloan School of Management of the Massachusetts Institute of Technology, where he has taught since 1966. From 1976 to 1981 he was also associate dean of the school. He is coauthor of Decision Support Systems: An Organizational View (Addison-Wesley, 1978), Management Decision Support Systems (Macmillan, 1978), and Computers and the Learning Process (McGraw-Hill, 1975). He serves on the boards of several corporations and conducts research and consulting on strategic planning, decision support systems, and planning and control systems.

KARL E. WEICK is Nicholas H. Noyes Professor of Organizational Behavior and professor of psychology in the Graduate School of Business and Public Administration at Cornell University, where he has taught since 1972. He is editor of Administrative Science Quarterly, advisory editor of Contemporary Psychology, and a member of the editorial boards of Applied Social Psychology Annual and Journal for the Theory of Social Behavior. He is author of The Social Psychology of Organizing (Addison-Wesley, 1969; revised edition 1979), coauthor of Managerial Behavior, Performance, and Effectiveness (McGraw-Hill, 1970), and author of numerous articles and papers.